1978

A SURVEY OF
APPLIED LINGUISTICS

A Survey of
Applied Linguistics

Edited by
Ronald Wardhaugh
and
H. Douglas Brown

Ann Arbor The University of Michigan Press

Grateful acknowledgment is made to the following publishers for permission to reprint copyrighted material:

The University of Chicago Press for material from "Language Development" by Lois Bloom previously published in the *Review of Child Development Research*, edited by F. Horowitz, E. Hetherington, S. Scarr-Salapatek, and G. Siegel, vol. 4. Copyright © 1975 by The University of Chicago.

Harcourt Brace Jovanovich, Inc. for material from "Burnt Norton" in *Four Quartets* by T. S. Eliot, copyright, 1943, by T. S. Eliot, copyright, 1971, by Esme Valerie Eliot. Reprinted by permission of Harcourt Brace Jovanovich, Inc.

Litton Educational Publishing, Inc. for material from *Let's Write English* by G. E. Wishong and J. M. Burks, copyright 1968, by Litton Educational Publishing, Inc.

Preface

In early 1973 the Editorial Board of *Language Learning: A Journal of Applied Linguistics* met to consider the publication of a special issue of the journal which would summarize the current state of the art in applied linguistics. The board agreed that a need existed for more than a special issue of *Language Learning* consisting merely of articles previously published in the journal. It was clear that what was needed was a comprehensive, timely review of the major domains of applied linguistics with leading scholars contributing original authoritative chapters. Such a volume would serve to isolate a number of distinct areas within the rather vaguely defined field of applied linguistics and to describe current theory and practice in each area.

At the outset the Editorial Board considered a score of potential topics which could well be included as legitimate areas within applied linguistics. It was clear, however, that in order to make the volume of manageable size and appropriate for university courses of study some topics would have to be eliminated. The narrowing process was difficult. Besides the topics now included, some strong contenders were: translation, psycholinguistics, experimental phonetics, animal communication, extralinguistic communication, language planning, and others. The twelve that were finally included in the volume seemed to represent areas which would be of greatest utilitarian value for university students interested in developing some concept of what one can "do" with linguistics. While some of the other topics indeed represent areas of fruitful research, the board considered these twelve to be of major interest to the greatest number of readers.

Each chapter focuses on the major issues and problems in the respective area. The author of the chapter discusses the importance and significance of research findings in as much detail as possible. It should be emphasized, however, that it is difficult to summarize any topic in a matter of a few pages, and the reader should expect to seek the original sources, which are listed in each bibliography, for more detailed information. Some elementary knowledge of general linguistic principles is also necessary if the reader is to gain maximum benefit from the volume. Nevertheless, many of the chapters are at the same time quite understandable to the layman with no formal linguistic training.

The editors wish to thank those who have helped to make the volume a reality. We are grateful to all the authors for their cooperation and acknowledge with appreciation their sincerity and patience during the process of constructing a volume with a minimum of overlap among the chapters and a degree of uniformity of organization and style. We particularly appreciate the advice and assistance of the other three members of the Editorial Board of *Language Learning*: J. C. Catford, Harold V. King, and George E. Luther. The meticulous preparation of the manuscript and other secretarial services provided by Margie Berns, Jan Eichenberger, Debbie Milly, and Louisa Plyler are gratefully acknowledged. And finally, we are indebted to those students who have taken the graduate course in applied linguistics at the University of Michigan. Their comments on the various topics included in the volume together with their keen interest in the field of applied linguistics encouraged us to undertake the present work. We hope that others, in turn, may benefit from *A Survey of Applied Linguistics*.

RONALD WARDHAUGH
H. DOUGLAS BROWN

Contents

I

What Is Applied Linguistics?

H. Douglas Brown

The bounds of linguistic study are difficult to define. It is impossible to engage in the study of language without addressing numerous strictly "linguistic" issues as well as many others involving psychological, sociological, anthropological, and biological matters which may or may not be considered to be properly linguistic in nature. In recent years such interdisciplinary areas as psycholinguistics, sociolinguistics, and ethnolinguistics have developed as linguistic interest has broadened. Linguistics, in all its varieties, is, therefore, a discipline which is relatively new, growing, and still in search of stable philosophical foundations and boundaries.

Perhaps even more difficult to define is the term *applied linguistics*. Applied linguistics has been considered a subarea of linguistics for several decades, and has generally been interpreted to mean the applications of linguistic principles or theories to certain more or less "practical" matters. Second language teaching and the teaching of reading, composition, and language arts in the native language are typical areas of practical application. In the British tradition, applied linguistics is quite often even synonymous with language teaching. However, the applications of linguistics certainly extend well beyond such pedagogical concerns. But the term remains disturbingly vague.

One of the difficulties in understanding the limits and scope of applied linguistics lies in the deliberate distinction between "theoretical" or "pure" linguistics on the one hand, and "applied" linguistics on the other. It is a distinction which every linguist is aware of, and one which has caused considerable controversy and argument. Claims have even been made that there can be no such thing as applied linguistics. But efforts to separate linguistics and applied linguistics have proved to be generally unfruitful and opinionated rather than informed.

One potentially constructive approach to an understanding of what applied linguistics is, or is not, may come from examining the term *linguistics*. If an adequate definition of linguistics can be given, then it may be possible also to define *applied linguistics*. Linguistics is the study of language; it is the "science of language," as some dictionaries state—a scientific discipline the goal of which is the construction of a theory of language or an extended definition of language. One way to gain a grasp of what the issues are in constructing a theory of language is to examine some representative definitions of language. Although such an examination could result in a lexicographer's wild goose chase, it also could lead to a coherent understanding of the limits of applied linguistics. Let us consider the following definitions of *language*:

> Language is a system of arbitrary, vocal symbols which permit all people in a given culture, or other people who have learned the system of that culture, to communicate or to interact (Finocchiaro, 1964, p. 8).

> Language is a system of communication by sound, operating through the organs of speech and hearing, among members of a given community, and using vocal symbols possessing arbitrary conventional meanings (Pei, 1966, p. 141).

> Language is any set or system of linguistic symbols as used in a more or less uniform fashion by a number of people who are thus enabled to communicate intelligibly with one another (Random House, 1966, p. 806).

> Language is a system of arbitrary vocal symbols used for human communication (Wardhaugh, 1972, p. 3).

> [Language is] any means, vocal or other, of expressing or communicating feeling or thought . . . a system of conventionalized signs, especially words, or gestures having fixed meanings (Neilson, 1934, p. 1390).

> [Language is] a systematic means of communicating ideas or feelings by the use of conventionalized signs, sounds, gestures, or marks having understood meanings (Gove, 1961, p. 1270).

Still other common definitions found in introductory textbooks on linguistics include the concepts of (*a*) the generativity or creativity of language, (*b*) the presumed primacy of speech over writing, and (*c*) the universality of language among human beings.

Many of the significant parameters of language are capsulized in these definitions. Some of the controversies about the nature of language are also illustrated through the restrictions present in certain definitions. Finocchiaro, Pei, and Wardhaugh, for example, restrict themselves to the notion of *vocal* symbols while the Neilson and Gove definitions include more than merely vocal symbols as the proper domain of language. Finocchiaro, Random House, and Wardhaugh restrict their definitions to *human* language, thereby implying that animal communication and language are essentially different.

A consolidation of the definitions of language yields the following composite definition:

1. Language is systematic—possibly a generative system.
2. Language is a set of arbitrary symbols.
3. Those symbols are primarily vocal, but may also be visual.
4. The symbols have conventionalized meanings to which they refer.
5. Language is used for communication.
6. Language operates in a speech community or culture.
7. Language is essentially human, although possibly not limited to humans.
8. Language is acquired by all people in much the same way—language and language learning both have universal characteristics.

These eight concepts suggest some specific, albeit overlapping, areas of research. A limited set of examples for each area follows:

1. Explicit and formal accounts of the system of language on several possible levels (most commonly, syntactic, semantic, and phonological.
2. The symbolic nature of language; the relationship between language and reality; the philosophy of language; the history of language.
3. Phonetics; phonology; writing systems; kinesics, proxemics, and other "paralinguistic" features of language.
4. Semantics; language and cognition; psycholinguistics.
5. Communication systems; speaker-hearer interaction; sentence processing.
6. Dialectology; sociolinguistics; language and culture; bilingualism and second language acquisition.

7. Human language and nonhuman communication; the physiology of language.
8. Language universals; first language acquisition.

A very simple definition of language thus suggests many issues and concerns within linguistics, all of which relate directly to the central goal of linguistic study: discovering what language is. However, among the concerns listed are a number which are typically grouped into "applied" rather than "theoretical" linguistics. Is it possible to draw a line of demarcation which separates the applied from the theoretical? The concerns in items 3, 4, 5, 6, 7, and 8 are all treated to some degree in this volume, and yet there is much in all six that is theoretical, that is, which bears on seeking an extended definition, or, a theory, of language. Some might wish to argue that item 1 is surely theoretical; however, the concerns mentioned in items 4 and 5 are involved in considering the nature of the system as it is actually manifested empirically. Perhaps, then, every question about language relates in some way to the formulation of an understanding of what language is—from teaching a foreign language to formulating global rules in Chinook Jargon.

Must we conclude, therefore, that there is really no such thing as applied linguistics? This is indeed too simplistic and too easy a solution. Every discipline has its theoretical and its applied aspects. The theoretical and applied areas simply must not be thought of as necessarily *mutually exclusive*. An area of inquiry may evidence certain applications of theory to practice and at the same time contribute to a better theoretical understanding of the particular phenomenon. Thus items 1 through 8 may all share applied and theoretical aspects. The idea of the mutual inclusiveness, or the complementarity, of applied and theoretical concerns is important, but it does not resolve the issue of where to draw the bounds between the two. Perhaps a look at the comments of some other applied linguists might provide a solution.

Politzer (1972) discusses applied linguistics with particular reference to foreign language teaching. He makes no particular effort to define linguistics, but notes that applied linguistics in foreign language teaching requires the use of linguistics to formulate assumptions about foreign language teaching and learning and also to devise teaching procedures based on these assumptions. "Linguistics is the source of assumptions rather than the source of conclusions . . . . Applied linguistics is thus not a finite body of knowledge that can be acquired . . .[it] is ultimately a habit, a way of using linguistic conceptualization to define and solve pedagogical problems" (p. 5). For Politzer, then, there is a definable area called "linguistics" and "applied linguistics" is simply the process of formulating possible solutions to specific (in this case, pedagogical) problems using linguistic theory. Politzer's conclusion is quite simplistic, in a sense, because he limits his discussion to foreign language teaching. Furthermore, he admits that beyond the language teaching issue, the boundaries between such fields as linguistics, psycholinguistics, and applied linguistics cannot be defined precisely (p. 2).

Pap (1972) discusses the notion of applied linguistics at some length and carries his concern well beyond language teaching. Admitting both an inherent ambiguity in the term as well as its rather vague reference to "practical applications," he concludes that applied linguistics "may in effect be considered a crossroads, an interdisciplinary area, a combination of linguistics with psychology, pedagogy, mathematics, electronics, political science, and so forth" (pp. 111-12). Thus he stresses the interdisciplinary nature of applied linguistics.

Reacting to the common British usage of the term *applied linguistics*, Corder (1973) points out that "whilst applied linguistics and language teaching may be closely associated, they are not one and the same activity" (p. 10). He then offers the following definition of applied linguistics:

> The application of linguistic knowledge to some object—or applied linguistics, as its name implies—is an activity. It is not a theoretical study. It makes use of the findings of theoretical studies. The applied linguist is a consumer, or user, not a producer, of theories (p. 10).

Corder thus proposes a relatively clear formulation of the difference between applied and theoretical linguistics. Corder's view could be misleading, however, if one were to presume that applied and theoretical linguistics are mutually exclusive. Consumers, by virtue of the fact that they are testing and confirming hypotheses generated by theory, provide reinforcement and feedback to theorists. Many important components of a theory have arisen from such "consumer" feedback. In first language acquisition, for example, researchers discovered that the purely syntactic, rational linguistic theories of the 1960s held explanatory power for only a small portion of the actual data. Neither the semantic/cognitive aspect of language nor the social aspect could be accounted for adequately. Partly as a result of the "demands" of first language researchers, and partly through other forces, theoretical linguists quickly began to recognize the semantic component of language, and a new wave of theory, semantics, was born, which brought a renewed interest in psycholinguistic topics in general. Along with this wave has emerged a revived interest in the social aspects of language, formerly considered to be irrelevant to theoretical linguistics. Psycholinguistics and sociolinguistics, once very clearly considered to be "applied" areas, now just as clearly overlap both the applied and theoretical domains.

The purity of so-called pure linguistics is rapidly becoming impossible to maintain, as Lakoff (1976) in her chapter on "Language and Society" in this volume, notes:

> Linguistics is heading in the direction of practicality. There will be in the ensuing years an ever-greater emphasis on application of theoretical discoveries; and application will be considered as valuable in its own right as pure theoretical contributions to knowledge have been. In fact, it will be increasingly recognized that theory severed from application is suspect, that data generated in the rocking chair, tested at the blackboard, and described in learned jargon are probably ridden with errors and inaccuracies (p. 222).

Is there a general conclusion that can be drawn from the various opinions on applied linguistics mentioned above? It would appear that several observations merge to form a coherent conclusion: first, Corder's definition of the applied linguist as a consumer of theories and possibly Politzer's idea of linguistics as a *source* of assumptions and hypotheses tend to concretize to some degree a definition of applied linguistics. Secondly, applied linguistics, by its very name, implies an interdisciplinary relationship, as Pap points out. Third, and perhaps most important, applied and theoretical linguistics are not mutually exclusive; theory and practice are mutually interdependent and complement each other. The strongest theories are those which have been thoroughly tested by applied research; and the best applied activity is that which is carefully and scientifically based on the explanatory power of a theoretical paradigm.

The title of this volume suggests that all twelve topics included are related to applied linguistics in some sense of the term. The three conclusions which have been drawn here substantiate such a claim. But an important aspect of each chapter included here is its potential contribution to the building of a stronger linguistic theory. The reader should look in every chapter for evidence of the empirical "consumption" of linguistic theory and for an account of coherent interdisciplinary application; but the reader should be equally aware of the importance of applied linguistics in meeting the essential goal of all linguistic inquiry: increasing our knowledge about the nature of language.

REFERENCES

Corder, S. P. *Introducing applied linguistics*. Harmondsworth, Middlesex: Penguin Books, 1973.

Finocchiaro, M. *English as a second language: From theory to practice*. New York: Simon and Schuster, 1964.

Gove, P. B. *Webster's third new international dictionary of the English language*. Springfield, Mass.: G. & C. Merriam Co., 1961.

Lakoff, R. Language and society. In R. Wardhaugh and H. D. Brown, eds., *A survey of applied linguistics*. Ann Arbor: University of Michigan Press, 1976.

Neilson, W. A., ed. *Webster's new international dictionary of the English language*. Second Edition. Springfield, Mass.: G. & C. Merriam Co., 1934.

Pap, L. What do we mean by applied linguistics? In R. W. Ewton and J. Ornstein, eds., *Studies in language and linguistics*. El Paso: Texas Western Press, 1972.

Pei, M. *Glossary of linguistic terminology*. New York: Anchor Books, 1966.

Politzer, R.L. *Linguistics and applied linguistics: Aims and methods*. Philadelphia: Center for Curriculum Development, 1972.

Random House dictionary of the English language. New York: Random House, 1966.

Wardhaugh, R. *Introduction to linguistics*. New York: McGraw-Hill, 1972.

II

Language Development

Lois Bloom

The data for studying language development are abundant; virtually all small children are learning to talk. Moreover, it is possible to see in the study of language development a host of relevant issues and ideas that bear on the nature of language in general and, indeed, on the nature of mind and mental development. However, different investigators have observed and described the data differently, and have asked different questions of the data.

A Brief History

Until the 1950s, there were two major thrusts in research in language development: diary studies of individual children and large-scale studies of large numbers of children across age and social class. The diary studies reflected the fascination of a linguist or psychologist parent with a young child's progress in learning to talk. They varied greatly in scope and duration and several have become landmarks in the literature: for example, Ronjat's study of his son's bilingual (French-German) development (1913); the four-volume study by Leopold of his daughter's bilingual (English-German) development (1939-1949); the Sterns's study in German (1907); the studies of French-speaking children by Bloch (1921, 1924), Guillaume (1927), and Gregoire (1937); and the study by Chao of his granddaughter's Chinese development (1951). Renewed interest in these studies is apparent in Bloom (1973), Slobin (1971a), Brown (1973), and Clark (1973).

This chapter is a revised and abridged version of the chapter on language development in F. Horowitz, E. Hetherington, S. Scarr-Salapatek, and G. Siegel (eds.), *Review of Child Development Research*, vol. 4, Chicago: University of Chicago Press, 1975. The preparation of this chapter was supported in part by research grant HD 03828 from the National Institute of Child Health and Development.

However, by far the greatest effort in this same period of time was devoted to normative studies of large numbers of children who varied in age, social class, sex, birth position, etc. These studies were comprehensively reviewed in McCarthy (1954). The study by Templin (1957) was, perhaps, the last and the most important of what have come to be called count or normative studies. It is interesting that the count studies came about in reaction to the diary studies which had begun to appear in the literature at the turn of the century. The swing toward behaviorism and the striving for scientific rigor in psychology in the 1930s and 1940s resulted in a disparagement of information, however detailed and minutely recorded, gathered by a parent-investigator, who, it was presumed, was necessarily biased in what he chose to record in his notes and in what he overlooked. Only objective data that could be counted and described statistically were considered admissible. And, indeed, the major indexes of growth and development have made abundant use of precisely this kind of information.

The studies described certain properties of the *form* of children's speech, for example, the average length, parts of speech, numbers of different words, etc., in a representative number (usually fifty to one hundred) of a child's utterances. The principal result was the specification of developmental milestones that allowed comparison among individual children or groups of children. For example, children produce a variety of babbled sounds in the first year and some time around age twelve months, plus or minus several months, first-born children generally utter their first words. In the last half of the second year, children begin to produce combinations of two and three words; between ages two and three years, children speak in sentences. Developmental milestones such as these have had widespread use in medicine, psychology, speech pathology, and education (see, for example, Lenneberg, 1967).

These milestones provide only a very general and gross index of development, and, more seriously, they ignore the notion of development as continuous *change* over time. Within the single-word utterance period, to take one example, the fourteen-month-old child who is speaking single words, but is not ready to use syntax, is very different from the child of eighteen or nineteen months who is on the verge of using syntax and is still saying only one word at a time. The specific vocabulary and the ways in which the words are used vary markedly within this particular "milestone" (Bloom, 1973). As another example, children's two-word utterances are reductions of their subsequent three- and four-word sentences (Bloom, 1970; Brown, 1973). Thus, important differences in behavior that occur within a particular period of development and the ways in which the different periods are actually interrelated and interdependent were easily overlooked in the developmental studies of the 1930s and 1940s.

The reaction to the objective studies of children's utterances began in the 1950s. Investigators began to seek different kinds of information about children and began asking different kinds of questions in their research on language development. Most important, there was a turn away from descriptions of the form of speech in an effort to discover what children *know* about language at any point in time. Research in the 1950s (for example, Berko, 1958 and Brown, 1957) began to inquire into the knowledge that underlies the ability to speak and understand—the "productive system . . . that [the child] employs in the creation of new forms" (Berko and Brown, 1960).

The new questions required the development of new research techniques for observing children's responses to the manipulation of certain kinds of language and situation variables. Such research generally involved fewer children than was typical of the earlier behaviorist-oriented research, but aimed toward obtaining more basic kinds of information. This era in psycholinguistic research has been very amply summarized and described in a number of reviews (for example, Berko and Brown, 1960; Ervin and Miller, 1963; and Ervin-Tripp, 1966). The studies convincingly demonstrated that children do not learn all of the sounds, words, and possible sentences in a language. Rather, what the child learns is an underlying linguistic system that is, itself, never directly available to the child or the adult. The studies of Brown (1957) and Berko (1958) made this point most explicitly and most elegantly. For example, when children in the Berko study were presented with a nonsense word like *wug* that named a small birdlike animal, they had no difficulty calling two of them *wugs*. Rather than learning singular and plural nouns as separate lexical items, these children had learned one rule (with phonological variants) for making the plural distinction.

The fact that children learned phonological and morphological rule systems had long been suspected by the earlier diarists and other linguists (see, for example, Jakobson, 1968, and Jespersen, 1922). Linguistic field research had generally emphasized discovery procedures in the phonology and morphology of languages. The study of syntax or grammar was quite another matter. It was not at all clear how one could discover the grammar of a language and it was even less clear how much of a grammar existed in early child language. However, with the advent of the theory of generative-transformational grammar (Chomsky, 1957) the search for grammar became the goal of research in language development in the

1960s, evolving in a very natural way from the interest in underlying knowledge that began in the 1950s. In short, attempts to discover what a child knows were pursued in the 1960s as a search for grammar or the description of the rule systems that could account for the use of sentences.

The investigation of child grammar began with the procedures of structural linguistic analysis (Bloomfield, 1933; Gleason, 1961; Hockett, 1958), but the goals of the research derived from developments in linguistic theory (most notably, Chomsky, 1957, 1965; Harris, 1957) with the assumption that underlying knowledge of language is equal to a generative-transformational grammar (Braine, 1963a; Brown and Fraser, 1963; McNeill, 1966; Miller and Ervin, 1964). The children in these studies were a relatively homogeneous sample of first-born children from middle-class university environments. The results were impressive in that they concurred in their essential findings, even though they involved three different and geographically separate populations of children. The children from whom these data were obtained were again fewer than in earlier research: Braine reported on the speech of three children; Brown and his associates described the speech of two children; and Miller and Ervin used a population of five children. However, each child was seen over a long period of time and was visited at home at periodic intervals (for up to several years by Brown and his associates). The important findings of these studies were that early syntax was indeed systematic and words were not juxtaposed at random even in the earliest sentences.

The finding that early sentences were constructed in an orderly and predictable way, and that all of these children, as well as others studied later (for example, Bloom, 1970, and Bowerman, 1973), used many of the same kinds of words (person names, object names, and relational terms like *more*, *all gone*, *this*, *on*, etc.), led to another important shift in child language research at the close of the 1960s. Attention was turned from *description* to an attempt at *explanation* of early sentences. Once the attempt was made to explain why some words occurred more than others and in orderly juxtaposition in early sentences, it became clear that the child's underlying knowledge did not equal a grammar in any simple way. The search began for the cognitive correlates of meaning in language and for the cognitive processes involved in language learning (Bever, 1970a; Bloom, 1970, 1973; Sinclair, 1969, 1970; and Slobin, 1971a). Thus, the emphasis of the 1960s on linguistics and linguistic theory for *describing* language development gave way in the 1970s to an emphasis on cognitive development and cognitive psychology for *explaining* language development.

The Nature of the Code: Describing Language Development

What children learn in the course of their language development is the *substance* of language. This substance will be considered here apart from the *process* of development, to the extent that the two have been considered separately in the literature. The question of how language is acquired will be taken up in the next section. What is learned is a linguistic code—a system of signs and the possible relations among them which, together, allow for the representation of an individual's experience of the world of objects, events, and relations. There is, as yet, no adequate description of the nature of any linguistic code, and linguists have generally not been enthusiastic about the study of language development for just this reason. Nonetheless, linguistic theory and changes in linguistic theory have been major influences on research in language development. The descriptions of child grammar that have appeared in the last decade were derived from methods and theory in linguistics: first of all structural linguistics, then generative-transformational grammar, and most recently, the study of the relation between form and meaning.

To begin with, before describing the syntax of early child sentences, it is worthwhile to consider three alternative views of early multiword utterances. If language develops in the course of trial-and-error learning, there should be an early stage of chaotic nonlanguage when the child misses the mark more often than not. Early sentences would be incoherent, unpredictable, and nonsystematic and one could hope for little more than a catalog of the child's most frequent words and word combinations in any order whatever. Although this is often the layman's view of what goes on in the years from ages two to four, fortunately, it was not the original operating assumption of most research in the 1960s.

Most investigators, influenced by insights in the early diary studies and results of experimental research in the 1950s, assumed that early syntax was indeed systematic but potentially idiosyncratic in either of two possible ways. On the one hand, early syntax could be the result of an idiosyncratic child language in which some system, while different from the adult model, was nonetheless the same for all children. That is, one could speak of child language in much the same way as one spoke of the English language or the French language. This seems to have been the operating assumption in much of the work of Brown and his colleagues at Harvard (Miller and Ervin, 1964 and McNeill, 1966a) and data from different children were sometimes pooled as child language data. On the other hand, child language was seen as potentially systematic but idiosyncratic for individual children. That is, each child could, conceivably, discover and evolve his or her own particular grammar in the course of his or her development. Although there would no doubt be a core of important similarities among all children, there might also be substantive differences as well. Thus, in the studies of Bloom (1970), Braine (1963a), Brown, Cazden, and Bellugi (1969), Cazden (1968), and Miller and Ervin (1964), the speech of individual children was described separately.

The third view is that child speech is a systematic reduction of the adult sentence types, rather than idiosyncratic. It turns out that much of the research that was begun with the different operating assumption, that child language is idiosyncratic, eventually yielded results that supported this third view. That is, although there were important individual differences, children were also alike in many ways. Moreover, child language was more like the adult model than it was different, and the deviations from the model were motivated and coherent rather than errors or mistakes.

Neo-formalism and descriptive child grammars. The goals of research, derived from generative-transformational theory, were to propose generative grammars for samples of child utterances at different times in development. Such grammars would specify the systems that would account for the generation of sentences. Given a large sample of child speech, the goal was to write rules that would account for as many as possible of the utterances that actually occurred or could occur, while not allowing utterances that did not occur and were presumably ungrammatical. The focus was on the earliest syntax, with children who were about two years old.

Although the goals of such grammar writing were derived from generative-transformational theory, there was, unfortunately, no prescribed methodology or discovery procedures for obtaining generative grammars. Moreover, as was pointed out by Chomsky (1964) and Lees (1964), there was no generative-transformational grammar of adult syntax, except for the fragment of a grammar of adult English offered as examples of phrase-structure rules and transformations in Chomsky (1957). Consequently, the search for rules to account for the underlying productivity of child sentences began with methods of distributional analysis. Lists of child utterances were arranged according to frequently occurring words, and the pattern in which these words occurred with other less frequently occurring words was determined. For example, Brown and Fraser (1963) reported utterances with *Mom* and *Dad*, *here* and *there*, and Miller and Ervin (1964) reported all utterances with *off* and *on*, and variants of *this* and *that*.

The major finding on which these studies agreed was that the words that occurred most frequently in the children's speech occurred in ordered relation to other words in sentences. That is, such words as *more* or *it* occurred in either first or second position in two-word utterances, but rarely in both positions (*more juice*, *more read*, *more cookie*, and *fix it*, *have it*, *do it*). Braine (1963a) called this small group of frequently occurring words "pivots"; the remaining words in the child's lexicon, for example, *juice*, *read*, *cookie*, and *airplane*, were grouped together as "x-words." These two classes of words appeared to correspond roughly to the two broad classes of function and content words in the adult model, and, indeed, Brown and his colleagues described them as "functors" and "con-tentives," and Miller and Ervin called them "operators" and "non-operators."

The notion of "pivot grammar" as the child's "first" grammar domi-nated language development research through the mid-1960s. The dis-tributional evidence—the fact that a small group of words occurred with great frequency in fixed order relative to other words in child speech—was indeed impressive. Children were apparently learning different kinds of words and something about word order. However, the difficulties in the "pivot grammar" account were soon apparent. One problem was that the two classes of words did not really have counterparts in the adult grammar. Adult syntax, particularly in a generative account, is considerably more than the juxtaposition of classes of words. There is a hierarchy of structure in the rules of a generative-transformational grammar, and the rules are mutually dependent on one another. Such rules do not just label sentence types. Moreover, the essence of sentence structure is the relationship among constituents, and the function of phrase-structure rules is to specify the grammatical relations among subject-verb-object. Pivot-grammar rules said nothing about the meaning relations among words, and gave little insight into how basic grammatical relations would ultimately evolve in child sentences.

All the accounts of early child syntax that used generative-transformational grammar as a heuristic resulted in a new kind of for-malism. Child utterances were obviously systematic, but the nature of the system was described in terms of the form of linguistic elements and the way in which such elements were arranged relative to one another. The categorization of words as "pivots" or "x-words" was the result of the linguistic description. It had not been demonstrated that the two classes were, in fact, used categorically by the child.

Slobin (1966) found evidence of the same distributional phenomenon in Russian, even though Russian, an inflectional language, depends far less on word order to signal semantic relationships than does English. This finding raised the issue of the extent to which linguistic development was language independent, and inquiry was begun into the possibility of developmental universals as either a corollary, consequence, or cause of the linguistic universals that had long been sought by, for example, Chomsky (1965), Greenberg (1963), and Sapir (1921).

But while the cross-cultural work was begun as a search for pivot grammar, both the goals and the methodology were quickly changed (see Bowerman, 1973, and Kernan, 1970). Parallel developments occurring in the study of language development (Bloom, 1970) and in linguistic theory (see Bach and Harms, 1968) made it apparent that underlying syntax was inextricably bound to the semantics of sentences, and that the essence of language had to do at least as much with underlying meaning as with the surface form of linguistic representation.

The relation between form and meaning.   There were ample grounds for criticizing the pivot-grammar account of child language, and many of these arguments have been presented at length (Bloom, 1968, 1970, 1971; Bowerman, 1973; Brown, 1973). The most compelling arguments against pivot grammar as an account of what children know when they first begin to use sentences are, first, that the distribution which does indeed occur, has to do with what it is that children are learning to talk about. Second, the relationships in which words occur in multiword utterances are only superficially similar. The same order can occur with two very different underlying semantic relations between the words, indicating that children are learning different underlying structures rather than superficial word order. For example, in twenty-nine instances in which *Mommy* occurred in first position in the two-word utterances spoken by a single child described in Bloom (1970), it was possible to identify the following underlying relations being coded by the superficial form "*Mommy* plus x-word": agent-action, agent-object, and possessor-possessed.

Children use certain words far more than others because of what these words mean for them. Certain words happen to code important cognitive distinctions for children between the ages of one and three years. These distinctions have been represented in the speech of just about all of the children whose speech has been intensively studied in the last decade, even though the number of children involved in these longitudinal psycholinguistic investigations is still not many more than twenty. Brown (1973) has looked at both the available contemporary data and the older diary studies and has identified virtually a closed set of such distinctions.

Bloom (1970) and Schlesinger (1971) each reported independent studies that attempted to account for the underlying semantics of early sentences. The basic grammatical relationships between subject-verb-object were represented in early two-word utterances, with subject apparently functioning as agent of an action most often. Although verb-object phrases (or predicates) occurred abundantly, subject-verb and subject-object phrases occurred as well. Thus, all of the basic grammatical relations occurred among the utterances in a corpus, but could not be represented entirely within the bounds of a single utterance, due, apparently, to constraints on linguistic and psychological processing.

There appear to be different strategies for learning syntax as revealed in the study of variation in the extent of lexical representation in early sentences by Bloom, Lightbown, and Hood (1975). In the earliest data from three children (Kathryn, Gia, and Allison), possession was first represented by two substantive words, for example, *Daddy coat*, and both agent and affected object were represented by nominal forms. Possession was subsequently signaled by a possessive marker such as *my* or *your*, and the agent of affected object was represented by the pro-forms *I* and *it*. Location was first represented by two substantives in juxtaposition (for example, *sweater chair*, which was said when Kathryn carried her sweater to the chair) and subsequently by a locative word such as *there*, *up*, *right here*, or *on*. However, in the speech of two other children (Eric and Peter), agent, object, possessor, and location were first signaled by pro-forms (*I*, *it*, *my*, and *there*). This difference among these children represents the two alternative strategies for learning grammar that were suggested in Bloom (1973). One strategy depends upon the child learning to use certain words with constant form and constant meaning (such as the inherently relational terms *more*, *thin*, *no*, and *my*) in two-word utterances, where such words determine the semantic-syntactic relationship. The second strategy involves a linguistic categorization, where different words (such as *Mommy*, *Daddy*, and *Baby*) form a class for the child because they can have the same meaning (for example, agent) relative to other words. In this case, the semantic-syntactic relationship between the words is independent of the lexical meaning of either of the words.

The semantic-syntactic relations between words appeared to develop in two-word utterances as follows. Children used certain words that referred to the existence, nonexistence, disappearance, and recurrence of objects, and the meaning of the relation between the words was derived from the meaning of one of the words, such as *this, more, no,* or *all gone,* in relation to other words, such as *cookie, book, read,* and *fit.* At the same time, there were other relations between words that were not specified by the words themselves, such as the relation between object-located and place of location, possessor and possessed, and agent and object of an action. After the appearance of these relations in two-word utterances, later development consisted of (1) specifying more than one such relation within a longer utterance, for example, *Mommy more juice* or *Drink Mommy juice,* and (2) specifying other relations such as the dative, and other attributive notions such as relative size, color, or state. Thus, in the developmental sequence of syntactic structures, the noun phrase (with "adjectives" other than *more,* etc.) and the morphological markers of plural and possessive /-s, -z, - əz/, or verb tense, etc. were relatively later developments. The explanation for this sequence appears to be largely a psychological one: the order in which children learn syntactic structures apparently reflects the order in which they learn to distinguish and organize aspects of their environment; plurality and relative size and color are apparently not among the earliest distinctions that they make.

There were two important conclusions to be drawn from these results. The first had to do with the fact that the distribution of certain words in children's early sentences could be *explained* as well as *described,* and the explanation had to do with underlying cognitive function. Specifically, the children were using the semantic-syntactic relations between words which coded certain of their mental representations of the world of objects and events. The second conclusion was that the children had learned something about grammatical structure for representing (and distinguishing among) these underlying conceptual representations, a finding which indicated that they knew more about language than simply which word forms could follow one another in speech. Both conclusions influenced subsequent theorizing about language development, and two major issues in language development research at the close of the 1960s had to do with (1) the cognitive prerequisites for language learning and (2) the best linguistic theory and formulation for representing children's linguistic knowledge.

Cognitive prerequisites.   Cognitive development in relation to language learning became the dominant issue in theory and research at the beginning of the 1970s. The relations between language and thought, and the development of each in children, have concerned philosophers and psychologists for centuries. In its contemporary form, the issue has revolved around whether children acquire or somehow know the grammar of a language in the abstract sense proposed by Chomsky (1965) and McNeill (1966a, 1970), or whether they learn language as a representation of their logically prior conceptual learning, as proposed by Piaget (1967).

One of the earliest attempts to deal with this question directly, both experimentally and theoretically, was reported by Sinclair (1969), a close associate of Piaget in Geneva. She distinguished between language as an object of knowing and a means for learning. Her intent in the series of experiments she reported was to determine (1) the linguistic forms used by children who had achieved certain stages in cognitive development, such as the notions of conservation and seriation, and (2) whether or not one might hasten the development of such notions in children who did not yet have them by teaching them the relevant speech forms. That is, would "preoperational" children who could not conserve or seriate be able to do so if they knew the right words and linguistic structures used by "operational" (conservative) children?

Sinclair reported, first, that the language used by the two extreme groups of conservers and nonconservers (there was also an intermediate, transitional group in her study) was different. Preoperational children who did not conserve described the materials presented to them in absolute terms, for example, *This one is big, this one is little*. The children who were able to conserve used coordinate structures, such as *This one is fatter but shorter* or *This one is bigger than the other one*. The two kinds of language were not actually confined to use by only one or the other kind of child. Apparently, some children from both groups used both kinds of language (Kowalski, 1972). However, the major point made by Sinclair was that while it was possible to teach the preoperational children the language used by the operational children (with different materials, of course), they still failed to demonstrate conservation or seriation when retested. Sinclair concluded that knowing the words and structures was not enough and would not lead to the induction of the relevant cognitive operation.

Piaget's contention that language depends upon, as a logical consequence of, the prior development of relevant cognitive structures is strongly supported by the results of research in early language development (Bloom, 1970, 1973). Children learned precisely those words and structures which encoded their conceptual notions about the world of objects, events, and relations. Children learned that things exist, cease to exist, and then can recur; that people do things to objects; that objects can be owned and located in space. In retrospect, it seems quite obvious that these would be the things that children talk about at the end of their second year. The child's awareness of such phenomena has been described by Piaget (1954) as the essence of sensorimotor intelligence as it develops in the course of the child's first two years of life.

The counter argument, that children learn words and structures and then attempt to use these in order to make sense of their environment, can be refuted by several kinds of evidence. It is apparent that children know and can even talk about such phenomena as agency, possession, location, recurrence, disappearance, etc. without knowing the corresponding linguistic forms for their representation. First, as reported in Bloom (1970), the basic grammatical relations were developmentally progressive, that is, children did not characteristically begin talking in sentences with subject-verb-object strings. Although they may have known these grammatical relationships among words and have been limited to only one relation per utterance, they may also first have learned to use one or the other. For example, verb-object predominated in the speech of the three children studied by Bloom (1970); subject-verb predominated in the speech of the three children studied by Bowerman (1973). Moreover, younger children who used only single-word utterances also presented considerable evidence of an awareness of such relationships in experience, although they did not have the structural knowledge for linguistic representation (Bloom, 1973; Greenfield, Smith, and Laufer, forthcoming; Ingram, 1971). Further, in the development of negation reported by Bloom (1970), the children learned to express different semantic categories of negation before they learned different contrasting linguistic structures. When the children began to use syntax to talk about a different concept ("rejection" and then "denial" as categories of negation), they used the primitive structure that they had used earlier to encode syntactically the notions of nonexistence and disappearance.

The search for linguistic universals in child language data in the 1960s was largely motivated by the distributional evidence of word order in the early utterances of English-speaking children. Slobin (1966) had looked for the distribution of pivot and open-class words in Russian literature on language development. Bowerman (1973) studied development in Finnish, and Solberg (1971) studied development in Quechua—both languages depending on inflectional processes rather than on word order—to determine how universal, that is, how independent of specific languages, the systematic word order in early two- and three-word sentences would be. The early results of the search for universals in linguistic development, and the emphasis given to innatist views of the origin of language by Chomsky (1965), McNeill (1966a), and Lenneberg (1967) raised a number of questions concerning the child's cognitive development and the extent of universality of underlying cognitive function as it relates to language development. Slobin (1971a) compared the reports of research in about thirty languages and attempted to specify a set of linguistic-cognitive principles that could account for the cross-linguistic data.

Thus, the beginning of the 1970s marked a major shift in research in language development, away from the description of child language in terms of linguistic theory and toward the explanation of language development in terms of cognitive theory. There was an important change from the early research reports that described such utterances as *Mommy pigtail* and *bear raisin* as "noun + noun" or "x-word + x-word" (Braine, 1963a; Brown and Bellugi, 1964; McNeill, 1966a) to the description of the same utterances as "possessor-possessed" or "agent-object" by Bloom (1970) and Brown (1973). There was also a corresponding shift in the study of linguistics and linguistic theory in the same period of time. The role of semantics in grammar became the major issue in linguistics in the late 1960s as it became increasingly clear that semantics and syntax could not be separated and analyzed apart from one another. Several new semantically based models of linguistic theory began to appear (see Bach and Harms, 1968; Lakoff, 1968). Because of the new interest in meaning and function in child language occurring at the same time, different investigators began looking among these new linguistic models for the "best theory" for representing what children know about language.

The best theory for describing child language.   The grammars proposed in Bloom (1970), following Chomsky (1965), were offered as an account of what children know about syntactic structure. It was explicitly assumed that the syntactic structure of utterances could be described only in terms of the underlying meaning that is encoded in or represented by what the children said. An implicit assumption was that such grammars represent linguistic hypotheses about children's knowledge of sentence structure. Bloom (1970) did not attempt to specify the semantic component of a generative-transformational grammar, which in Chomsky (1965) functioned somehow to interpret syntactic structure. It was assumed that syntax and semantics were mutually dependent and one could not be described or accounted for without the other. The inferred meanings of the children's utterances were the primary data for arriving at the rules of grammar which accounted for the structure of their sentences.

Schlesinger (1971) suggested that children's sentences derived from an underlying semantic basis—specifically, the child's semantic intention—rather than from the syntactic basis specified by the phrase-structure rules of generative-transformational grammar. The form of utterance would be determined by what the speaker intended to talk about, and the syntax of the utterance would depend directly upon its underlying meaning.

The issue of semantics in linguistic theory became a dominant concern in generative grammar after the emphasis on syntax in the original theory revealed that syntax was inseparable from underlying meaning. Innovators in semantic theory proposed that an underlying semantic basis derivationally precedes the operation of rules of syntax (see, for example, Bach and Harms, 1968; Bierwisch, 1970; Chafe, 1971; Lakoff, 1971; Leech, 1970). Because semantics is an account of meaning, and meaning derives from the conceptual representation of experience, the new descriptions of the semantic structure of language began to be used in accounts of early language development.

The one semantic theory that seemed most attractive and most immediately relevant to child-language data was the case grammar proposed by Fillmore (1968). Noun forms characteristically predominate in the speech of children, and many two-word utterances include at least one noun as a constituent. Case grammar accounts for the semantic structure of sentences in terms of the meanings of noun forms, as specified by certain prepositions, in relation to verb forms. The semantics of early child language became the focus of research, and case grammar appeared to be most readily applicable to child-language data (for example, Bowerman, 1973; Greenfield, Smith, and Laufer, forthcoming; Ingram, 1971; Kernan, 1970).

Bowerman (1973) recorded the speech of one English-speaking child, Kendall, and two Finnish-speaking children, Rina and Seppo, in order to compare development in two languages that code meaning differently. English is a language that depends primarily on word order, while Finnish is an inflectional language in which word order is essentially variable. She described semantic structure in terms of case grammar for utterances with mean length less than two morphemes, and compared these case grammars with generative-transformational grammars in order to test the adequacy of the different linguistic theories. The children were found to code essentially the same set of conceptual notions in their speech as Bloom (1970) had reported for English-speaking children. Bowerman concluded that case grammar could account for more of the semantic information that was obtained from the utterances than could transformational grammar. For example, in one child's speech (Seppo), when mean length of utterance was 1.42, *father clock* was specified as dative (person-affected) + objective, and *chick shoe*, where the chick was on the shoe, was specified as locative + objective. The case symbols were unordered in these specifications, and did not necessarily correspond to the order in which the corresponding elements appeared in the children's utterances.

Bowerman proposed that children do not have knowledge of such grammatical structure as subject of sentence, or predicate, or object of verb. Rather, their knowledge is semantic, and they learn such semantic relationships as agent-object, possessor-possessed, person affected-location, etc. However, she found that these relationships were, indeed, marked initially by consistent syntactic word order in both languages. In the Finnish children's speech, there was a preferred word order initially (which matched the preferred word order that she also found in the mother's speech); however, word order became more variable, as in the adult model of Finnish, as mean length of utterance approached two words.

Bowerman's conclusions were similar to those offered by Schlesinger (1971): children first learn semantic relations between words, and these determine the subsequent development of such grammatical notions as subject and predicate. According to Schlesinger and Bowerman, early two- and three-word utterances represent semantic rather than syntactic relationships. However, syntax clearly exists if children discover, as they do virtually from the beginning, that the semantic relations between words can be marked by word order. Moreover, the facts that different words express the same semantic relation, and different relations occur with the same words, such as (in Kathryn's speech) possessor-possessed in *Baby(s) shoe* and *Mommy(s) sock*, agent-object in *Bear raisin* and *Mommy pigtail*, and person-affected-state in *Baby tire (d)* and *Mommy busy*, appear to be evidence of the superordinate categorization of words, as, for example, sentence-subject. Bloom, Lightbown, and Hood (1975) argued that Kathryn, Gia, and Allison expressed the same semantic relation with different words (for example, agent-object: *eat meat, comb hair, read book* and locative action: *sweater chair, sit floor*). However, Eric and Peter used a system in which the same semantic relation was marked by a constant relational term (for example, action-object: *fix it, find it, turn it*; and locative-action: *put there, screw there, sit there*). The fact that the same semantic relations can have two alternative and consistent representations in the speech of different children is evidence that children are learning semantic-syntactic structure, or grammar.

Brown (1973) has reviewed the arguments of Bowerman and Schlesinger and compared each with the analysis reported in Bloom (1970) in an effort to propose the "best theory" for representing children's linguistic knowledge. He concluded that the semantics of children's first sentences could not be as fully represented within the framework of the original theory of generative-transformational grammar as they could be within case grammar. However, generative grammars of child language do account for the syntax of utterances. Generative grammars also represent the semantics of utterances to the extent that the order of elements is semantically determined; the underlying structure of the sentence is the meaning of the sentence. Finally, generative grammars appear to be more powerful than case grammars in accounting for a wider range of structure in the child's continuing and subsequent development and in the adult model.

Unfortunately, as promising as the developments of linguistic theory were for describing the language acquisition data in the beginning of the 1960s, linguistic theory at the start of the 1970s appeared to be of little help. As linguists have begun to look to philosophy and cognitive psychology for the answers to many of their questions about the nature of language, there is no longer a unified theory of generative grammar. Writing grammars for later child speech appears to offer more frustration than ever and no longer seems to be a promising endeavor. There is no available model of what such a grammar might look like nor a consensus on the kinds of information it might account for. Theories of linguistic meaning have come to be thought of as accounting for cognitive meaning and the result has been a blurring of the distinction between *semantics* (meaning as it is coded by natural languages) and *cognition* (the mental structures and processes of thought).

However, one result of the interest in semantics and underlying cognitive function has been attention to the origins of early grammar in the study of children's use of single-word utterances before syntax. Children use different kinds of words and use them differently at different points in time in the period before they use syntax. Certain words make reference to a particular object or person, such as person names or such object names as *bottle*, *blanket*, or a favorite toy, etc. Certain other object-words are used as class names that have been extended to refer to a class of things which share a perceptual likeness, such as cookies, dogs, books, chairs, etc. However, children also use certain words that do not share such perceptually based features in each instance of use. For example, words like *more* and *there* or *this* also occur with great frequency among the early words in the second year. And yet, a child can call a second cookie *more* after he or she has eaten the first cookie and also call a second horse *more* after seeing the first horse go by. The meaning of *more* in the sense of the recurrence of an object depends upon conceptions or organizations of behavior which do not appear to lend themselves to the kind of analysis that is based on perceptual attributes of objects. Such relational terms as these and single object or person names appear to occur before the use of class names, and this sequence depends upon changes in cognitive development in the child's second year (Bloom, 1973).

The period in development between first words (at about twelve months, plus or minus a few months) and the use of two- and three-word utterances at the end of the second year is not a single "developmental milestone." Rather, it is a period of considerable growth and change. The child is learning more than a dictionary of word forms and word meanings. The child at thirteen to fourteen months is not about to use syntax, whereas the child of eighteen to nineteen months is about to use syntax—primarily because of the complex changes in cognitive development in that period of time—even though both are saying only one word at a time.

Semantics and referential function.   In addition to the interest in underlying semantic intention in single-word utterances and early syntax, the recent focus on semantics in the study of child language has stimulated studies of the development of specific lexical items and domains of meaning. In particular, attention has been given to how children learn comparative terms (Clark, 1972; Donaldson and Wales, 1970; Joseph, 1972; Klatzky, Clark, and Macken, 1973; Milligan, 1972; Weiner, 1974); linguistic reference to notions of time (Clark, 1970, 1971; Cromer, 1968, 1971; Harner, 1973); and definite and indefinite reference (Maratsos, 1971).

The acquisition of the comparative terms *more* and *less* and of *same* and *different* are of considerable interest for several reasons. For psychologists these terms are central to the evaluation of cognitive functioning and the measurement of intelligence. For example, Piagetian tasks of conservation depend on the child's use of such terms to describe the outcome of certain transformations of the shape of objects or other matter. Judgments of relative amount ("more" or "less") and identity equivalence ("same" or "different") are central in tests of intellectual achievement, such as the Stanford-Binet. For linguists and psycholinguists, the acquisition of these relational terms provides the opportunity to study how the two terms of an antonymous pair are related to one another.

Studies that have measured young children's comprehension of antonymous pairs of adjectives have reported that positive adjectives are understood earlier than negative adjectives: *more, big, tall, high* were better understood than *less, wee* (small), *short, low* in the studies by Donaldson and Wales (1970); *more* was understood earlier than *less* in the study by Weiner (1974); *big, long,* and *fat* were easier to understand than *small, short,* and *thin* in a study by Milligan (1972). However, there have been conflicting results in studies reporting comprehension tasks with the temporal terms *before* and *after*.

The semantic domain of temporal references has intrigued philosophers and linguists for centuries. Psychologists have long been aware that the conceptual notion of nonpresent time and linguistic reference to past and future events are relatively late developments in the preschool years. For example, among the *wh-* questions that children learn to ask, questions beginning with *when* are usually among the last to occur. It is not clear whether children first learn time-language dealing with past or future. On the one hand two-year-old children typically comment on their intentions, that is, on what they are about to do, more often than on what they have just done (Bloom, Lightbown, and Hood, 1975). However, it is also true that one can have a conception of future events only in relation to events already experienced. The ability to plan for and anticipate events that are yet to be depends in a fairly obvious way on the memory or mental organization of what one has already seen or done.

Studies of how children learn both the concepts and the language of time have not been conclusive. Cromer (1968) reported that the children studied by Brown made reference to future time more often than to past time in the age range from two to five years. Other studies of temporal reference have offered conflicting evidence. In a study of temporal decentering by Cromer (1971), subjects did better in comprehending past tense sentences than future tense sentences, a finding which is in essential agreement with the findings of Clark's (1971) study of comprehension of *before* and *after*.

Clark concluded that the first binary division that children learn in the semantic dimension of time has to do with plus prior and minus prior events. As with the studies of *more* and *less* and *same* and *different*, children apparently learn the semantically positive term, that is, *more, same,* and *before* first, and then learn the semantically negative terms *less, different,* and *after*. Thus far, none of the explanations of this phenomenon appears to be satisfactory. Bever (1970) concluded that four-year-old children understood *before* and *after* clauses when order of mention corresponded to order of occurrence, because the first event in a series was psychologically more salient.

Studies of semantic development have only just begun. In addition to the empirical studies that have appeared, there have also been several attempts to specify a theory of semantic development. One such theory is that children learn a set of hierarchical features of meaning. For example, Clark (1971) proposed that children learn temporal semantic markers in a specific order. Anglin (1970) proposed a "generalization hypothesis" to account for the development of word meanings, with progress from concrete to abstract representation.

Another theory of semantic development, proposed by McNeill (1970), suggests that semantic features enter the child's dictionary of word meanings at large, in two possible ways, and are not restricted to the meanings of individual lexical items. McNeill distinguished between two hypotheses to explain the development of dictionaries: a *horizontal* development which would consist of completing the dictionary entry, that is, adding new features of meaning to those words already acquired, and a *vertical* development in which most or all of the semantic features of a word enter the dictionary at the same time, but such features are unrelated to the features of other words already in the dictionary, and separate from them. Vertical development, then, would consist of collecting such features that are common to separate words "into unified semantic features" that transcend the whole dictionary. The horizontal and vertical development alternatives suggested by McNeill imply that the features of meaning in lexical entries are context free, but it is not at all clear that this is the case. Bierwisch (1970) specified a theory of semantics whereby components of linguistic meaning were related to the mental representation of physical objects and events. Semantic features do not represent "external physical properties, but rather the psychological conditions according to which human beings process the physical and social environment. Thus, they are not symbols for physical properties and relations outside the human organism, but rather for the internal mechanisms by means of which such phenomena are perceived and conceptualized" (p. 181).

It is fairly clear that learning the lexical meanings of words, and the grammatical meaning relationships between words, depends in a rather direct way on (1) how the child perceives and mentally represents objects and events around him, and (2) the ability to process linguistic messages according to the contexts in which they occur.

It would appear then that there is not so much a rigid hierarchy of features of meaning for particular linguistic forms as proposed by Katz and Fodor (1963) and applied to children's development by Clark (1971), as there is a network of features with sensitivity to situational context. Although the grammar of a language may have a fixed number of dictionary items and a finite rule system, its meaning components are probably neither fixed nor finite. A theory of semantic development needs to specify how the child takes into account situational and intrapersonal variability in arriving at the meaning components of linguistic items.

There is much in the child's cognition that is not linguistic; while he does talk about what he knows, he knows about things that he cannot talk about. To be sure, the child necessarily comes to the point where his linguistic capacities can structure his learning—the developmental shift from learning to talk to talking to learn. But the relation between the two and how this transition occurs are not at all clear at the present time.

The later system. The study of the development of grammar, after the emergence of syntax, has been more fragmentary than the study of early sentences and single-word utterances. That is, there have been few attempts to describe the child's later linguistic system as a whole by proposing a grammar. Brown, Cazden, and Bellugi (1969) proposed a tentative grammar to account for the speech of one of their subjects, Adam, after the early stage of syntax in his speech. Gruber (1967) described the utterances of a somewhat older child in terms of topicalization, suggesting that utterances consisted largely of topic plus comment constructions. By and large, however, most accounts of the speech of older preschool children have focused on one or another particular grammatical subsystem.

Studies of questions (Brown, 1968; Brown and Hanlon, 1970; Ervin-Tripp, 1970; Holzman, 1972), negation (Bellugi, 1967; Bloom, 1970; Klima and Bellugi, 1966; McNeill and McNeill, 1968), noun and verb inflections (Brown, 1973; Cazden, 1968), pronouns (Huxley, 1970), have provided data on the language development of two- and three-year old children. The information contained in these studies has not been brought together in a unified account of the development of particular subsystems, but all of the evidence does not appear to be in as yet. The studies of negation, for example, while complementary in several important aspects also present different conclusions about the sequence and stages of development. Other studies have offered only tentative conclusions and hypotheses that remain to be tested.

Brown (1973) compared the findings of an earlier study by Cazden (1968) that had described the noun and verb inflections in the speech of Brown's original three subjects, Adam, Eve, and Sarah, with other reports in the literature on the morphological development of children in the same age range. He reported that the emergence of grammatical morphemes begins when mean length of utterances is between 2.0 and 2.5 morphemes. Although the "modulations" and "tunings" of meaning by grammatical morphemes cannot exist apart from the things and processes that are tuned, it is possible to talk about the things and processes without modulations, which is probably one reason why the nouns and verbs occur first in child utterances. Although rate of development was widely variant, the order of development appeared to be relatively constant among different children, as follows: present progressive, *in, on,* plural, irregular past, possessive, uncontracted copula, articles, regular past, regular third person, irregular third person, uncontracted auxiliary, contracted copula, and contracted auxiliary.

In the study of negation Bellugi proposed that negation in the first sentences consisted of attaching a negative marker (such as *no* or *not*) outside of a simple sentence, for example, *no drop mitten, no the sun shining,* with the negative marker appearing inside of the sentence subsequently. In Bloom (1970), there was an alternative account of the development of negation that considered the syntactic form of negative utterances in relation to their meaning. Three semantic categories of negation appeared in children's sentences in the order nonexistence, rejection, and denial, and there was corresponding sequential development in the form of their syntactic representation. McNeill and McNeill (1968) studied the semantic development of negation in a Japanese child, Izanami, and found a similar sequence of development.

When the meaning relation between the negative marker and the rest of the utterance was taken into account, it turned out that sentences in which the *no* appeared before the sentence subject were not negative sentences at all. Rather, *no* before a sentence was anaphoric in relating back to something else either said or implied, and the sentence itself was actually an affirmative statement.

It was not the case then that the first negative sentence in the children's speech consisted of a negative marker attached to the whole sentence. Rather, when the negative marker occurred in a sentence, the sentence did not include a subject, and negative sentences were generally among the most primitive sentences to occur, usually consisting of either an object noun or a verb. There appeared to be a complexity limit on the children's sentences, so that the operation of negation within a sentence caused a reduction of complexity: for example, sentence subjects did not occur. Subsequently, when sentence subjects did occur in negative sentences, they preceded the negative marker, which appeared within the sentence before the verb. Thus, contrary to Bellugi's (1967) account, negative sentences in the speech of the children described in Bloom (1970), although primitive, were more like the adult model than they were different. Similar results have recently been reported in descriptions of the developmental syntax and semantics of negation in Italian (Volterra, 1971) and French (de Boysson-Bardies, 1972).

In summary, after describing the emergence of syntax in children's two- and three-word utterances, accounts of language development have focused on the acquisition of the linguistic form of particular subsystems of adult grammar. All such studies have reported that individual children were different in their relative rates of development. But, even if some children reach the target language sooner and develop more quickly and, perhaps, more smoothly, all of the children for whom data have been reported appear to converge on the adult model from the beginning.

However, language development in the age range from three to five years has been least adequately described. These were the neglected years in the last decade of research, just as they have often been the neglected years in studies of cognitive development. Children produce increasingly complex sentences and use increasing numbers of different words. But, as the studies of semantic development in this age range have shown, the words used and understood by children do not have precisely the same meanings as the same words in adult speech. Also, at about age three, children begin to use certain aspects of language that appear to be more mature than their underlying cognitive understanding (Bloom, 1970; Bruner, 1966; Inhelder and Piaget, 1964). On the one hand, children learn language in the first two years for coding what they know of the world of objects, events, and relations and they apparently know a great deal more than they are able to talk about. However, there appears to be some sort of linguistic crossover between ages two and three. The syntax of speech, in particular, goes ahead of underlying thought, as in the following example with the adult's speech to the left and child's to the right with the context described in brackets:

Kathryn, at thirty months, three weeks

[During the last session six weeks previously, Mommy had been ironing in the kitchen while Lois and Kathryn played in the living room.]

you came here last night, when my mother was ironing

I came here last night? *yes/*

my mother, my mother ironed/

Oh, your mother ironed last night? *yes/*

What did she iron?	*oh, she ironed some clothes/*
Hm. And what did Kathryn do?	*oh, I played with you/*
Hm. Did you play with me tomorrow?	*yes/*
Yes? Will you play with me yesterday?	*yes/last yesterday/ last night/*

[Mommy had not been ironing the previous night.]

Verb inflection was appropriate in Kathryn's speech in referring to past and future times. However, although temporal adverbs such as *today*, *last night*, and *next Monday* were syntactically correct in the sentences, the reference of these forms was inaccurate or superfluous. Bever (1970a) described a characteristic temporary drop between three and four years in the comprehension performance of two- to five-year-old children who were asked to act out different kinds of sentences. He attributed this apparently developmental dip in performance to a change that takes place at this age in the strategies that children use in perceptually processing sentences, as a result, apparently, of their learning more about language. The study of the changing relation between child language and child thought in the preschool years has only just begun, but it should become increasingly important.

The critical question about development that was stimulated by the theory of generative-transformational grammar remains: How does the child achieve linguistic creativity—the ability to speak and understand infinitely many sentences, never spoken or heard before, that are, moreover, free from eliciting conditions and internal states? There has been, thus far, only a partial answer in terms of the nature of the underlying rule system which the child induces from the samples of speech he hears. This induction of the underlying structure of language occurs, to a large extent, in the preschool years. What may be the more important aspect of the question—how the child subsequently comes to use the linguistic code to talk about events and to process messages about events that are not readily perceivable or imaginable—remains to be explained. This transition from maximum dependence on contextual support to speech which is independent of the states of affairs in which it occurs is the major accomplishment in language development in the early school years. It is not at all clear how empirical or theoretical inquiry can arrive at an adequate account of this transition. But it is clear that until such an account appears or is at least attempted, any theory of language development will be incomplete.

Theories, Processes, and Strategies for Explaining Language Development

An important theoretical conflict dominated attempts at explanation of language development in the early 1960s. On the one hand, the child was seen as the ever-changing product of his own *maturation*. On biological grounds (for example, Lenneberg, 1967) and on linguistic grounds (Chomsky, 1965; Fodor, 1966; McNeill, 1966a, 1970) the child could not escape his fate—barring physical or mental complications, he could not help but learn to talk. Such a view placed heavy emphasis on the child: he learned to talk because he was biologically prepared for it or was linguistically preprogrammed to do so. In contrast, other theorists (most notably, Braine, 1963b, 1971a; Jenkins and Palermo, 1964; Staats, 1971) placed heavy emphasis on the influence of the environment in shaping and controlling the child's *learning*. The child's role in this view was, again, essentially a passive one: his learning was largely determined by the ways in which individuals in his environment responded and reacted to what he said and did. Most recently, attempts at explaining language development have emphasized the active participation of the child, in terms of the *processes* (for example, Brown and Bellugi, 1964; Cazden, 1965; Shipley, Smith, and Gleitman, 1969) or *strategies* (for example, Bever, 1970a; Bloom, 1973; Slobin, 1971a; Watt, 1970) that appear to influence his interactions with linguistic and nonlinguistic aspects of his environment as he learns to talk.

The argument between those who held that language is innate and acquisition is the product of maturation and those who believed that language is learned and shaped by forces in the child's environment began, essentially, with Chomsky's (1959) critique of Skinner (1957). Since that time, a great deal has been written and the argument can be followed in Bellugi and Brown (1964), Dixon and Horton (1968), Jakobovits and Miron (1967), Lyons and Wales (1966), Reed (1971), Slobin (1971b), and Smith and Miller (1966). As the dust has settled, it has become clear that neither explanation could be entirely correct, and there has been a shifting of positions in several directions.

Jenkins and Palermo (1964) put forth one of the most explicit accounts of language learning in terms of mediation and reinforcement theory. Since that time, however, there has been modification of these views and

Palermo (1970) pointed out that explanations of language development in behaviorist terms had been too heavily influenced by learning theory and too little influenced by language theory. Attempts to explain language behavior, after all, must necessarily depend on the nature of language, on what it is that is being learned. Verbal learning studies, in general, had used language to investigate learning; emphasis on learning in order to explain language seemed to have been less fruitful.

There was also reconsideration and shifting of opinion among those to whom the nature of language and linguistic theory were primary. Bever, Fodor, and Weksel (1965) criticized the theory of contextual generalization proposed by Braine (1963b) as being too closely tied to the surface features of speech. Braine had suggested that language learning depended upon the child perceiving the positions of words in sentences. Bever, Fodor, and Weksel (1965) emphasized that most of what was important about language was beneath the surface—that the underlying rule system was not directly perceivable and thus not obtainable from actual utterances. However, in Hayes (1970) there were several papers, for example, Bever (1970a), that pointed out that actual speech was, after all, primary evidence for the child. The child must necessarily process utterances that he hears, and an adequate explanation for language development must include a specification of the strategies he uses in processing speech.

The function of imitation for language development has emerged as an important issue. Throughout the century, the tendency for children to imitate the speech they hear has been repeatedly acknowledged, and has, at least tacitly, been considered as somehow important for learning language. Recently, views of the importance of imitation have been divided. Behaviorists, on the one hand, saw imitation as a necessary precondition for reinforcement and learning (Staats, 1971) or a combination of imitation and reinforcement as relevant to language learning (Sherman, 1971). Generative-transformationalists, on the other hand, have argued that the most important information about a sentence is in its deep structure, so that repeating the surface structure could not be helpful (McNeill, 1966; Slobin, 1968). In support of the claim that imitation cannot be important, Lenneberg (1967) pointed out that it was possible to learn language without being able to speak at all, as in the case of individuals with paralysis of the speech musculature who, nevertheless, understand speech. Ervin-Tripp (1964) compared the spontaneous and imitative utterance in the speech of five children and reported that the same rules of surface word order described both kinds of utterances.

In a study of the spontaneous and imitative speech of six children (Bloom, Hood, and Lightbown, 1974), there were marked differences in the extent to which the different children imitated, and developmental differences between the spontaneous and imitative speech of the individual children. In the speech of two children, Peter and Jane, almost one-third of their utterances repeated something just said to them by someone else. In contrast, in the speech of two other children, Allison and Gia, fewer than ten percent of the utterances that occurred were repetitions of a preceding model. The other two children, Eric and Kathryn, were somewhere between these two extremes. There were important differences between imitative and spontaneous utterances when the two kinds of utterance types were compared for each child. The individual lexical items and the semantic-syntactic structure in multiword utterances that were imitated did not occur spontaneously; the words and structures that were productive in spontaneous speech were not imitated. There was a statistically significant change across the six samples as imitative words became spontaneous, but not vice versa. It appears that imitation is not necessary for language development, but when imitation does occur it is developmentally progressive for both lexical and grammatical learning, and provides evidence of an active processing of utterances relative to the contexts in which they occur.

These results of the analysis of imitative utterances that occur in naturalistic speech are in contrast with the underlying rationale for the use of elicited imitation as a task for evaluating children's knowledge of grammar (Menyuk, 1963a; Rodd and Braine, 1971; Slobin and Welsh, 1973). In elicited imitation, it is presumed that the child processes the presented stimulus sentence through his or her own rule system, and the resulting imitation reflects what the child knows about a particular structure (see Bloom, 1974a, for a critique of this position). In the study of spontaneous imitation by Bloom, Hood, and Lightbown, imitative utterances reflected what the children did not yet know, but were in the process of learning.

Linguistic determinism.   A number of studies have emphasized the nature of language and the linguistic code for explaining the course of language development. The linguistic theory of generative-transformational grammar (Chomsky, 1965) provided a scheme for representing important information about the origin of sentences. A system of integrated rules was proposed for representing how an actual sentence in speech (the form of a spoken sentence) was related to its abstract underlying structure (the specification of the meaning of the sentence). The system of rules in a generative-transformational grammar attempts to specify not only the origin of particular sentences, but also the interrelatedness of all sentences that are possible in the language. Such a system of rules is a linguistic grammar which represents what a speaker-hearer knows about sentences. A *linguistic grammar*, then, attempts to explain sentences in terms of source or derivational history and represents a hypothesis about mental grammar. The *mental grammar* is what a speaker knows about language that makes it possible for him to speak and understand sentences.

The distinction between linguistic grammar and mental grammar has not always been clear and the two have often been confused (see Watt, 1970, for an elaborate discussion of such confusion, and Bloom, 1974b). However, for many people, linguistic grammars and, in particular, generative-transformational grammar, have provided important hypotheses for describing and explaining the data of language development. Brown and Hanlon (1970) provided an account of children's development of truncated and tag-question forms that was strongly tied to the system of rules that linguists have proposed for such forms in adult speech.

Several studies of speech perception by generative-transformational linguists (Garrett, Bever, and Fodor, 1966) attempted to determine the psychological reality of linguistic segments by studying how adult listeners process the linguistic units of sentences. Bever (1970) extended this research to different kinds of studies with small children in an effort to determine the mutual interaction between the child's strategies for speech perception and the actual structure of language itself. Bever proposed a set of processing strategies whereby children were able to retrieve such basic information about sentences as the actor-action-object relations and the interaction between clausal segments. Watt (1970) proposed a somewhat similar processing strategy whereby children analyzed the structure of a sentence by temporally attributing structure to a string of words from left to right. In experiments by Huttenlocher and Strauss (1968) and Huttenlocher, Eisenberg and Strauss (1968), the easiest sentences to understand were those in which the sentence subject was the actor of the action. In each of these proposals and in research reported by Lahey (1974), the primary cue used by children for analyzing sentences to obtain their meaning was word order.

Certain basic capacities and information are already attributed to the child who would be using such processing strategies. For example, in order for the child to know that the string of words he hears contains an agent-action-object sequence, he must already know about such relations in sentences. Such basic linguistic capacities have been largely taken for granted in studies of speech perception and in the linguistically determined theories of language acquisition proposed by McNeill (1970). According to McNeill, the facts of sentences must be available to the child at a very early age, inasmuch as virtually all of his linguistic behavior depends upon it. McNeill has used Chomsky's (1965) notion of "language acquisition device" to explain child language: essentially, such a device would include the formal and substantive features which are common to all languages (linguistic universals) and would provide the child with the set of hypotheses which he would presumably need for determining those aspects of language which are specific to the language in his community. Thus, what the child already knows about language determines what he learns about language. The origin of such prior knowledge about language is not at all clear. Chomsky, McNeill, and others have proposed a strong innate component in acquisition—that children are necessarily born with certain linguistic competencies. Bever, Watt, and others have left the question open, but have allowed the important possibility that the capacities that are "basic" to the processing strategies of two- and three-year-old children are the product of the child's earlier learning in his first two years.

Linguistically determined explanations of language development have attempted to account for children's behavior in terms of what is known or hypothesized about the target language or about language in general. Thus, the linguistic code itself is seen to be the major (if not the only) determining influence on the sequence of development (as, for example, in Brown and Hanlon, 1970) or the mechanism of development (as explained, for example, by McNeill, 1970). Other descriptions of language behavior have implicated more than the linguistic code and offered explanations or described strategies that are cognitively determined.

Cognitive determinism.   Piaget has described development as the result of the child's interaction with his environment. The child comes to know about objects and events through his actions on them. Learning language, in this view, depends upon such interaction. The environment in which the child acts includes speech and his or her interactions must include the speech that is heard in relation to what the child does and the objects and events that he or she sees. Thus, there is complementary interaction among the child's developing perceptual-cognitive capacities and his or her linguistic and nonlinguistic experience. Rather than language being the determining influence on what and how the child learns, what the child learns about language is determined by what the child already knows of the world (see Bloom, 1973; Macnamara, 1972; Sinclair, 1970; Slobin, 1971a).

Slobin (1971a) attempted to bring together the data from developmental studies in a number of languages. He proposed a set of operating principles that would appear to be the child's basis for learning any language. He proposed that, in all languages, semantic learning would depend upon cognitive development, and that children begin to talk about what they know, even though they do not as yet know the adult structure. Thus, the sequence of development would be determined at least initially by semantic complexity rather than by structural or formal complexity. In a bilingual situation in which the child may have the option to use one or the other language, he will presumably choose the language that uses the less complex linguistic form to express a particular notion if the two languages differ in their means of formal representation of the notion.

Bloom (1973) described two alternative inductions which children make about grammar in the form of linguistic strategies for the transition from single words to the use of two- and three-word sentences. Which of the strategies a child uses is presumably determined by his or her cognitive development. Certain conceptions that the child has (for example, notions of the existence, disappearance, recurrence, etc. of objects) can be conveniently coded by words that are inherently relational (*this, away, more*) and that combine in direct and linear relation with other words. The meaning of the relations between such words as these and the words with which they are combined is dependent upon the meaning of one of the relational words. For example, *more cookie* as an expression of recurrence depends upon the meaning of *more*.

Other conceptual categories such as the relationship between object and location, or agent and object, or possessor and possessed can be coded by two words in combination, where the meaning relation between the words is independent of the meaning of either of the words, and it is the structural relation between the words that determines meaning. For example in the utterance *Mommy pigtail*, meaning is independent of either *Mommy* or *pigtail*. The combination of such words is hierarchical in that there are intervening linguistic categories that specify relationships between individual words. However, the same relations can be represented with relational forms such as *there* for location, *it* for object of action, and *my* for possession. The kinds of conceptual distinctions the child has made in his or her experience would appear to influence which of these inductions prevails in early attempts at syntax.

A theory of language development must be able to account for different kinds of data that have emerged in studies of child language. Most important, an explanation of language development depends upon an explanation of the cognitive underpinnings of language: what children know will determine what they learn about the code for both speaking and understanding messages. Even though there has been a strong motivation to discover the universal aspects of language and language development, important individual differences among children have emerged (as exemplified above and earlier in descriptions of two alternative strategies for emerging syntax). Other differences among children have appeared in relation to certain group variables that have been sociologically defined. Both individual and group differences need to be accounted for in explanations of language development.

Conclusion

There have been two main thrusts in attempts to explain how children learn to talk. On the one hand, it was proposed that the course of language development depends directly on the nature of the linguistic system and, more specifically, on the nature of those aspects of language that might be universal and represented in an innate, predetermined program for language learning. On the other hand, evidence began to accrue to support a different hypothesis which emphasized the interaction of the child's perceptual and cognitive development with linguistic and nonlinguistic events in his environment. The issue remains to be resolved, and neither linguistic determinism nor cognitive determinism has yet received unequivocal empirical or theoretical support. However, research in semantic development has led to an increasing awareness of the correlates of language acquisition in the development of perception and cognition.

REFERENCES

Anglin, J. *The growth of word meaning.* Cambridge, Mass.: M.I.T. Press, 1970.
Bach, E., and Harms, R., eds. *Universals in linguistic theory.* New York: Holt, Rinehart, and Winston, 1968.
Bellugi, U. The acquisition of negation. Ph.D. dissertation, Harvard University, 1967.
Berko, J. The child's learning of English morphology. *Word*, 1958, *14*, 50-177.
Berko, J., and Brown, R. Psycholinguistic research methods. In P. Mussen, ed., *Handbook of research methods in child development.* New York: John Wiley and Sons, 1960.

Bever, T. The cognitive basis of linguistic structure. In J. Hayes, ed., *Cognition and the development of language*. New York: John Wiley and Sons, 1970.

Bever, T., Fodor, J., and Weksel, W. On the acquisition of syntax: A critique of "Contextual generalization." *Psychological Review*, 1965, 72, 467-82.

Bierwisch, M. Semantics. In J. Lyons, ed., *New horizons in linguistics*. Harmondsworth, Middlesex: Penguin, 1970.

Bloch, O. Premiers stades du language de l'enfant. *Journal de Psychologie*, 1921, 18, 693-712.

———. Le phrase dans le language de l'enfant. *Journal de Psychologie*, 1924, 21, 18-43.

Bloom, L. Language development: Form and function in emerging grammars. Ph.D. dissertation, Columbia University, 1968.

———. *Language development: Form and function in emerging grammars*. Cambridge, Mass.: M.I.T. Press, 1970.

———. Why not pivot grammar? *Journal of Speech and Hearing Disorders*, 1971, 36, 40-50.

———. *One word at a time: The use of single-word utterances before syntax*. The Hague: Mouton, 1973.

Bloom, L., Hood, L., and Lightbown, P. Imitation in language development: If, when, and why. *Cognitive Psychology*, 1974, 6, 380-420.

Bloom, L., Lightbown, P., and Hood, L. The argument for structure in child language. *Monograph of the Society for Research in Child Development*, 1975.

Bloomfield, L. *Language*. New York: Holt, Rinehart and Winston, 1933.

Bowerman, M. *Learning to talk: A cross-linguistic study of early syntactic development, with special reference to Finnish*. Cambridge, England: Cambridge University Press, 1973.

Braine, M. The ontogeny of English phrase structure: The first phase. *Language*, 1963a, 39, 1-13.

———. On learning the grammatical order of words. *Psychological Review*, 1963b, 70, 323-48.

———. On two types of models of the internalization of grammars. In D. Slobin, ed., *The ontogenesis of grammar*. New York: Academic Press, 1971.

Brown, R. Linguistic determinism and the part of speech. *Journal of Abnormal Social Psychology*, 1957, 55, 1-5.

———. *Social psychology*. New York: Free Press, 1965.

———. The development of wh- questions in child speech. *Journal of Verbal Learning and Verbal Behavior*, 1968, 7, 279-90.

———. *A first language*. Cambridge, Mass.: Harvard University Press, 1973.

Brown, R., and Bellugi, U. Three processes in the child's acquisition of syntax. *Harvard Educational Review*, 1964, 34, 133-51.

Brown, R., Cazden, C., and Bellugi, U. The child's grammar from I to III. In J. P. Hill, ed., *1967 Minnesota Symposia on Child Psychology*. Minneapolis: University of Minnesota Press, 1969.

Brown, R., and Fraser, C. The acquisition of syntax. In C. Cofer and B. Musgrave, eds., *Verbal behavior and learning: Problems and processes*. New York: McGraw-Hill, 1963.

Brown, R., and Hanlon, C. Derivational complexity and order of acquisition in child speech. In J. Hayes, ed., *Cognition and the development of language*. New York: John Wiley and Sons, 1970.

Bruner, J. On cognitive growth: II. In J. Bruner, R. Oliver, and P. Greenfield, eds., *Studies in cognitive growth*. New York: John Wiley and Sons, 1966.

Cazden, C. Environmental assistance to the child's acquisition of grammar. Ph.D. dissertation, Harvard University, 1965.

————. The acquisition of noun and verb inflections. *Child Development*, 1968, *39*, 433-38.

Chafe, W. *Meaning and the structure of language*. Chicago, Ill.: University of Chicago Press, 1971.

Chao, Y. R. The Cantian idiolect: An analysis of the Chinese spoken by a twenty-eight-month-old child. *Semitic Philology*, University of California Publications, 1951, *11*, 27-44.

Chomsky, N. *Syntactic structures*. The Hague: Mouton, 1957.

————. Review of "Verbal behavior," by B. J. Skinner. *Language*, 1959, *35*, 26-58.

————. Formal discussion. In U. Bellugi and R. Brown, eds., The acquisition of language. *Monographs of the Society for Research in Child Development*, 1964, no. 29.

————. *Aspects of the theory of syntax*. Cambridge, Mass.: M.I.T. Press, 1965.

Clark, E. How young children describe events in time. In G. B. Flores d'Arcais and W. J. M. Levelt, eds., *Advances in psycholinguistics*. New York: American Elsevier, 1970.

————. On the acquisition of the meaning of *before* and *after*. *Journal of Verbal Learning and Verbal Behavior*, 1971, *10*, 266-75.

————. What's in a word? On the child's acquisition of semantics in his first language. In T. Moore, ed., *Cognitive development and the acquisition of language*. New York: Academic Press, 1973.

————. On the child's acquisition of antonym pairs in two semantic fields. *Journal of Verbal Learning and Verbal Behavior*, 1972, *11*, 750-58.

Cromer, R. The development of temporal reference during the acquisition of language. Ph.D. dissertation, Harvard University, 1968.

————. The development of the ability to decenter in time. *British Journal of Psychology*, 1971, *62*, 353-65.

de Boysson-Bardies, B. L'étude de la négation: Aspects syntaxiques et lexicaux. Ph.D. dissertation, L'Université de Paris, 1972.

Dixon, T., and Horton, D. *Verbal behavior and general behavior theory*. Englewood Cliffs, N. J.: Prentice Hall, 1968.

Donaldson, M., and Wales, R. On the acquisition of some relational terms. In J. Hayes, ed., *Cognition and the development of language*. New York: John Wiley and Sons, 1970.

Ervin, S., and Miller, W. Language development. In H. Stevenson, ed., *Child psychology*. 62d yearbook of the National Society for the Study of Education, part I. Chicago, Ill: University of Chicago Press, 1963.

Ervin-Tripp, S. Imitation and structural change in children's language. In E. Lenneberg, ed., *New directions in the study of language*. Cambridge, Mass.: M.I.T. Press, 1964.

————. Language development. In L. Hoffman and M. Hoffman, eds., *Review of child development research*. New York: Russell Sage Foundation, 1966.

————. Discourse agreement: How children answer questions. In J. Hayes, ed., *Cognition and the development of language*. New York: John Wiley and Sons, 1970.

Fillmore, C. The case for case. In E. Bach and R. Harms, eds., *Universals in linguistic theory*. New York: Holt, Rinehart and Winston, 1968.

Fodor, J. How to learn to talk, some simple ways. In F. Smith and G. Miller, eds., *The genesis of language*. Cambridge, Mass.: M.I.T. Press, 1966.

Garrett, M., Bever, T., and Fodor, J. The active use of grammar in speech perception. *Perception and Psychophysics*, 1966, *1*, 30-32.

Gleason, H. *An introduction to descriptive linguistics*. New York: Holt, Rinehart, and Winston, 1961.

Greenberg, J. Some universals of grammar with particular reference to meaningful elements. In J. Greenberg, ed., *Universals of language*. Cambridge, Mass.: M.I.T. Press, 1963.

Greenfield, P., Smith, J., and Laufer, B. *Communication and the beginnings of language*. New York: Academic Press, forthcoming.

Gregoire, A. L'apprentissage du language. Vol. 1, *Les deux premières années*. Paris: Droz, 1937.

Gruber, J. Topicalization in child language. *Foundations of Language*, 1967, *3*, 37-65.

Guillaume, P. Les débuts de la phrase dans le language de l'enfant. *Journal de Psychologie*, 1972, *24*, 1-25.

Harner, L. Children's understanding of linguistic reterence to past and future. Ph.D. dissertation, Columbia University, 1973.

Harris, Z. Co-occurrence and transformations in linguistic structure. *Language*, 1957, *33*, 283-340.

Hayes, J., ed. *Cognition and the development of language*. New York: John Wiley and Sons, 1970.

Hockett, C. *A course in modern linguistics*. New York: Macmillan, 1958.

Holzman, M. The use of interrogative forms in the verbal interaction of three mothers and their children. *Journal of Psycholinguistic Research*, 1972, 311-36.

Huttenlocher, J., and Strauss, S. Comprehension and a statement's relation to the situation it describes. *Journal of Verbal Learning and Verbal Behavior*, 1968, 7, 300-304.

Huttenlocher, J., Eisenberg, K., and Strauss, S. Comprehension: Relation between perceived actor and logical subject. *Journal of Verbal Learning and Verbal Behavior*, 1968, 7, 527-30.

Huxley, R. The development of the correct use of subject personal pronouns in two children. In G. B. Flores d-Arcais and W. J. M. Levelt, eds., *Advances in psycholinguistics*. New York: American Elsevier, 1970.

Ingram, D. Transitivity in child language. *Language*, 1971, *47*, 888-910.

Inhelder, B., and Piaget, J. *The early growth of logic in the child*. New York: Harper and Row, 1964.

Jakobovits, L., and Miron, M., eds. *Readings in the psychology of language*. Englewood Cliffs, N. J.: Prentice-Hall, 1967.

Jakobson, R. *Child language, aphasia and phonological universals.* The Hague: Mouton, 1968 (originally published in German, 1941).

Jenkins, J., and Palermo, D. Mediation processes and the acquisition of linguistic structure. In U. Bellugi and R. Brown, eds., The acquisition of language. *Monographs of the Society for Research in Child Development*, 1964, no. 29.

Jespersen, O. *Language: Its nature, development, and origin.* London: Allen and Unwin, 1922.

Joseph, J. The development of understanding of the terms "same" and "different." Ph.D. dissertation, Columbia University, 1972.

Katz, J., and Fodor, J. The structure of semantic theory. *Language*, 1963, *39*, 170-210.

Kernan, K. Semantic relationships and the child's acquisition of language. *Anthropological Linguistics*, 1970, *12*, 171-87.

Klatzky, R., Clark, E., and Macken, M. Asymmetries in the acquisition of polar adjectives: Linguistic or conceptual? *Journal of Experimental Child Psychology*, 1973, *16*, 32-46.

Klima, E., and Bellugi, U. Syntactic regularities in the speech of children. In J. Lyons and R. Wales, eds., *Psycholinguistics papers*. Edinburgh: Edinburgh University Press, 1966.

Kowalski, R. The development of the concept of speed and its associated language. Ph.D. dissertation, Columbia University, 1972.

Lahey, M. Use of prosody and syntactic markers in children's comprehension of spoken sentences. *Journal of Speech and Hearing Research*, 1974, *17*, 656-68.

Lakoff, G. Instrumental adverbs and the concept of deep structure. *Foundations of Language*, 1968, *4*, 4-29.

————. On generative semantics. In D. Steinberg and L. Jakobovits, eds., *Semantics: An interdisciplinary reader in philosophy, linguistics, and psychology*. New York: Cambridge University Press, 1971.

Leech, G. *Towards a semantic description of English*. Bloomington, Indiana: Indiana University Press, 1970.

Lees, R. Formal discussion. In U. Bellugi and R. Brown, eds., The acquisition of language. *Monographs of the Society for Research in Child Development*, 1964, no. 29.

Lenneberg, E. *Biological foundations of language*. New York: John Wiley and Sons, 1967.

Leopold, W. *Speech development of a bilingual child*. Evanston, Illinois: Northwestern University Press, 1939-49. 4 vols.

Lyons, J. and Wales, R. *Psycholinguistic papers*. Edinburgh: Edinburgh University, 1966.

Macnamara, J. Cognitive basis for language learning in infants. *Psychological Review*, 1972, 79, 1-13.

Maratsos, M. The use of definite and indefinite reference in young children. Ph.D. dissertation, Harvard University, 1971.

McCarthy, D. Language development. In L. Carmichael, ed., *Manual of Child Psychology*. New York: John Wiley and Sons, 1954.

McNeill, D. Developmental psycholinguistics. In F. Smith and G. Miller, eds., *The genesis of language*. Cambridge, Mass.: M.I.T. Press, 1966a.

———. A study of word association. *Journal of Verbal Learning and Verbal Behavior*, 1966b, *5*, 548-57.

———. *The acquisition of language: The study of developmental psycholinguistics*. New York: Harper and Row, 1970.

McNeill, D., and McNeill, N. What does a child mean when he says "no"? In E. Zale, ed., *Language and language behavior*. New York: Appleton-Century-Crofts, 1968.

Menyuk, P. A preliminary evaluation of grammatical capacity in children. *Journal of Verbal Learning and Verbal Behavior*, 1963a, *2*, 429-39.

Miller, W., and Ervin, S. The development of grammar in child language. In U. Bellugi and R. Brown, eds., The acquisition of language. *Monograph of the Society for Research in Child Development*, 1964, no. 29.

Milligan, C. Children's understanding of regular and comparative adjectival forms. Paper presented to the Eastern Psychological Association, 1972.

Piaget, J. *The construction of reality in the child*. New York: Basic Books, 1954.

———. *Six psychological studies*. New York: Random House, 1967.

Reed, C., ed. *Language learning*. Champaign. Ill.: National Council of Teachers of English, 1971.

Rodd, L., and Braine, M. Children's imitations of syntactic constructions as a measure of linguistic competence. *Journal of Verbal Learning and Verbal Behavior*, 1971, *10*, 430-43.

Ronjat, J. *Le développement du language observé chez un enfant bilingue*. Paris: Librairie Ancienne *H* Champion, 1913.

Sapir, E. *Language*. New York: Harcourt, Brace and World, 1921.

Schlesinger, I. M. Production of utterances and language acquisition. In D. Slobin, ed., *The ontogenesis of language: Some facts and several theories*. New York: Academic Press, 1971.

Sherman, J. A. Imitation and language development. In H. W. Reese, ed., *Advances in child development and behavior*, vol. 6. New York: Academic Press, 1971.

Shipley, E., Smith, C., and Gleitman, L. A study in the acquisition of language: free responses to commands. *Language*, 1969, *45*, 322-42.

Sinclair-de-Zwart, H. Developmental psycholinguistics. In D. Elkind and J. Favell, eds., *Studies in cognitive development*. New York: Oxford University Press, 1969.

———. The transition from sensory-motor behavior to symbolic activity. *Interchange*, 1970, *1*, 119-26.

Skinner, B. F. *Verbal Behavior*. New York: Appleton-Century-Crofts, 1957.

Slobin, D. I. The acquisition of Russian as a native language. In F. Smith and G. Miller, eds., *The genesis of language*. Cambridge, Mass.: M.I.T. Press, 1966.

———. Imitation and grammatical development in children. In N. Endler, L. Boulter, and H. Osser, eds., *Contemporary issues in developmental psychology*. New York: Holt, Rinehart, and Winston, 1963.

———. Developmental psycholinguistics. In W. D. Dingwall, ed., *A survey of linguistic science*. College Park, Md.: University of Maryland Press, 1971a.

———, ed. *The ontogenesis of grammar*. New York: Academic Press, 1971b.

Slobin, D. I., and Welsh, C. A. Elicited-imitation as a research tool in developmental psycholinguistics. In C. A. Ferguson and D. I. Slobin, eds., *Studies of child language development*. New York: Holt, Rinehart and Winston, 1973.

Smith, F., and Miller, G., eds. *The genesis of language*. Cambridge, Mass.: M.I.T. Press, 1966.

Solberg, M. E. The development of early syntax and sound in a polysynthetic Andean language: The ontogenesis of Quechua. Ph.D. dissertation, Cornell University, 1971.

Staats, A. Linguistic-mentalistic theory versus an explanatory S-R learning theory of language development. In D. Slobin, ed., *The ontogenesis of grammar*. New York: Academic Press, 1971.

Stern, C., and Stern, W. *Die kindersprache*. Leipzig: Barth, 1907.

Templin, M. *Certain language skills in children*. Minneapolis, Minn.: University of Minnesota Press, 1957.

Volterra, V. II "no." Prime fasi di sviluppo della negazione nel linguaggio infantile, 1971.

Watt, W. On two hypotheses concerning developmental psycholinguistics. In J. Hayes, ed., *Cognition and the development of language*. New York: John Wiley and Sons, 1970.

Weiner, S. On the development of more and less. *Journal of Experimental Psychology*, 1974, *17*, 271-87.

III

First Language Teaching

Jean Malmstrom

The applications of linguistics to the teaching of English as a first language are discussed in six areas: usage and dialectology; grammar and rhetoric; linguistics in the curriculum; spelling; textbooks and supplementary materials; and possible conclusions and implications. Most of the attention is focused on the use of linguistics in elementary and secondary schools. Although the discussion is oriented chiefly toward the present state of the art, appropriate historical references are also cited.

Two basic problems permeate the discussion. One is the lag between research and the availability of teaching materials; the second is the gap between available materials and classroom practices. Linguistics, like any field of human knowledge, has its pure scientists, its technologists, and its practitioners. Linguists are the pure scientists. They are usually interested only in advancing linguistic knowledge, and generally give little or no thought as to how that knowledge will be used in any practical way. Curriculum developers, including textbook writers, are the technologists. They can put into their materials only what the linguists have delivered. Their purpose is to demonstrate how linguistic findings can be applied to teaching English. Teachers are the more or less skilled practitioners who use the technology to do the actual classroom teaching.

Success in teaching depends upon a complex of factors: the teachability of the materials; the native intelligence, enthusiasm, and energy of the teacher; the motivation of the students; and respect. Respect is composed of self-respect, mutual respect between teacher and students, and respect for language. The key to the total situation is always the teacher. When English teachers are frightened because they feel threatened, they tend to retreat into the accustomed safety of traditional grammar and traditional attitudes toward language. Preventing such a retreat is a crucial factor in the application of linguistics to the teaching of English in schools.

Usage and Dialectology

The first important impact of linguistics on the teaching of English occurred in the 1930s. In 1932 Leonard's *Current English Usage*, supplemented in 1938 by Marckwardt and Walcott's *Facts about Current English Usage*, advocated a nonprescriptive "linguistic doctrine of usage." Instead of the traditional single standard of arbitrarily "correct English," this linguistic doctrine recognized three "levels of usage." These levels were defined as (1) "formally correct English," (2) "fully acceptable English for informal conversation, correspondence, and all other writings of well-bred ease," and (3) "popular or illiterate speech." The linguistic doctrine soon began to infiltrate professional discussions in journals and on platforms and to appear in textbooks.

These liberal views on usage were supported in 1940 by Fries's *American English Grammar*, the first large-scale quantitative investigation of American English. Fries examined some three thousand letters written by native Americans during World War I to the United States Department of the Interior about serious personal matters. Fries classified the writers into three social groups on the basis of schooling, family circumstances, and certain matters of spelling, capitalization, and punctuation in the letters themselves. Group one writers had a college education and a position of recognized standing in the community. Group two writers had no less than a high school education and no more than one year in college or technical school: they were substantial citizens, neither professionals nor manual workers. Group three writers had no more than an eighth-grade education and had strictly manual and unskilled jobs. Having classified the writers, Fries then analyzed their writing and established three levels of English which he labeled *standard, common,* and *vulgar*. Although Fries paid specific attention to social differences, the full implications of socio-economic factors in American English usage were largely neglected until the sociolinguistic studies of the 1960s.

The National Council of Teachers of English (NCTE) has widely publicized these linguistic attitudes toward usage in American education. The NCTE's official position on usage, stated in 1952 in *The English Language Arts*, was that a rational, modern attitude toward usage was based on the following five principles:

1. Language changes constantly.
2. Change is normal.
3. The spoken language is the language.
4. Correctness rests upon usage.
5. All usage is relative. (pp. 274-77)

The editors of *Webster's Third New International Dictionary of the English Language* (1961) used these five principles as guidelines. However, large segments of the literate population of the United States reacted negatively to their use, thereby attesting to the strength of entrenched conservative attitudes toward "correct usage." Nevertheless, the NCTE has continued to advocate the same liberal principles, even to sponsoring a second edition (1974) of Pooley's *Teaching English Usage* (1946), a classic in the usage tradition.

The introduction of regional dialect study into the schools further extended liberal attitudes toward American English usage. In 1958, McDavid's "The Dialects of American English" appeared as one chapter in Francis's *The Structure of American English*, a college textbook on structural linguistics. McDavid reported regional dialect findings from some of the surveys being conducted for the Linguistic Atlas of the United States and Canada, a set of geographically delimited projects in regional dialectology, which began in the 1930s and are still continuing today. McDavid also related these Atlas findings to literature. Using this chapter as well as findings from other Atlas projects, Malmstrom and Ashley produced *Dialects–U.S.A.* (1963), a textbook for high school students, and the first textbook ever published by the NCTE. Normally, the NCTE publishes for teachers, not for their students. Shuy's *Discovering American Dialects* (1967) updated this regional information and added some data on social dialects. This book, also published as a high school textbook by the NCTE, remains a perennial best seller, widely used in "dialects units" in schools. The immediate and continuing popularity of regional dialect study represents one rare instance where effective teaching materials were produced at the time when teachers were ready and willing to use them. Today, scarcely a language textbook appears without paying some attention to regional dialect study.

Dialect study revealed that an accurate analysis of American English usage required the use of five criteria for evaluation. The first criterion is socioeducational in nature. The spectrum of usage extends from standard to nonstandard English, reflecting the socioeconomic status and education of the users. Probably one of the best definitions of standard English, a troublesome term in professional discussions, is that of *Webster's Third New International Dictionary of the English Language* (1961):

> . . . the English that with respect to spelling, grammar, pronunciation, and vocabulary is substantially uniform, though not devoid of regional differences, that is well-established by usage in the formal and informal speech and writing of the educated, and that is widely recognized as acceptable wherever English is spoken and understood (p. 2223).

Nonstandard English does not exist as an equivalent entity. An individual usage is nonstandard if, in a certain context, it differs from standard English. From time to time in discussions of American English in the past, the term *nonstandard* has been used as a euphemistic synonym for the pejorative label *substandard*. In *Webster's Third New International Dictionary of the English Language*, the two terms *nonstandard* and *substandard* are cross-referenced to emphasize their similarity and to inform the reader that neither by itself is sufficient. In the Explanatory Notes a lexicographical distinction is made between them as usage labels in *Webster's Third New International Dictionary of the English Language*. *Nonstandard* is applied to "a very small number of words that can hardly stand without some status label" but which are "too widely current in reputable context to be labeled substandard." The label *substandard* has much wider application. It "indicates status conforming to a pattern of linguistic usage that exists throughout the American community but differs in choice of word or form from that of the prestige group in that community."

The second criterion is stylistic. It is concerned with the formality or informality of the situation in which the usage occurs. Joos's "The Five Clocks" (1962) suggests five stylistic varieties.

1. Frozen style is the language of poetry locked into its patterns.
2. Formal style is the language of speeches addressed to nonparticipating audiences.
3. Consultative style is the language of interviews and diplomatic negotiations.
4. Casual style is the language of everyday human intercourse.
5. Intimate style is the language of love between lovers.

The third criterion is a methodological one involving the choice between speech and writing. Speech is a native ability of all normal human beings; writing is an artificially acquired skill. We do not speak as we write nor write as we speak; each method of communication has its own signaling system. Speech has intonation; writing has spelling, punctuation, and capitalization.

The fourth criterion is historical. Language extends through time. Children speak differently than their elders; today's citizens speak differently than the pilgrim fathers.

The fifth criterion is geographic. The English language extends through the United States and so becomes the subject matter of regional dialect study.

Although such linguistic ideas on usage have been widely publicized in professional books, journals, and lectures, they still meet constant opposition in actual classroom practice, so strong is entrenched conservative opinion. Indeed since the autumn of 1974, students who take the Scholastic Aptitude Test, prepared by the College Entrance Examination Board, must undergo an objective one-half-hour examination of competence in "standard written English." The new test, rather than concerning itself with varieties of the language, stresses the kind of English used in newspapers, textbooks, and the like. The College Entrance Examination Board has taken the position that students must learn to cope with this kind of English in their education, and the hope of the test writers is that this new test will be used for placement of students in college freshman English courses, rather than for determining their readiness for higher education—the objective of the old examination. The new test seems to be a retreat into conservatism. The NCTE's Conference on College Composition and Communication (1974) has passed a resolution condemning the new objective usage test

> on the grounds that such tests are a measure of copyreading skill rather than a measure of student ability to use language effectively in connected discourse of their composing; such tests place emphasis on mechanical matters of spelling, punctuation, and conventions of usage, rather than on clarity, appropriateness, and coherence of thought; such tests tend to discriminate against minority students whose linguistic experiences often lead them to choose answers different from those expected by the test makers; and the inclusion of such a test may encourage secondary English teachers to teach toward the test at the expense of matters more fundamental to effective writing and sophisticated reading . . . (p. 339).

In the middle 1960s the sociolinguistic study of social dialects was keynoted by the work of Labov, initially in his dissertation (1966). In contrast to Fries and the Atlas dialectologists, Labov used a tested sociological model in studying the speech of more than one hundred randomly selected informants in New York City. Thus, he was able to correlate social class with linguistic variables. His findings were vastly extended by his further studies and the work of other sociolinguists in various cities throughout the United States and later in rural areas also.

These sociolinguistic findings have been crucially important in the education of inner city children and have been published widely. Hess (1972) provides an overview of more than 1,500 current documents related to dialects and dialect learning. She indicates the two major positions that have been taken: (1) standard English should not be taught, and (2) standard English should be taught. Hess cites Cline (1968), Kaplan (1969), Kochman (1969), Lee (1970, 1971), O'Neil (1968), and Sledd (1969, 1972) as holders of the first position. She summarizes their ideas as follows:

> Two major themes pervade the preceding arguments against teaching a standard English. First, most of the individuals contend that bi-dialectalism is morally wrong and should not be taught because it may be psychologically damaging, may alienate nonstandard speakers from their sub-culture, may not result in better jobs or greater social opportunities, and may indeed be a form of racism compelling speakers of nonstandard dialects to conform to a standard which is not consistent with the cultural pluralism the United States presumably values. The second theme states that it is not possible, or at least it is not efficient, to teach students a second dialect. The major points used in support of this view are the following: (a) linguistic descriptions of nonstandard dialects are not complete; (b) there are no available materials with proven effectiveness; (c) the students have little motivation to learn a standard English; (d) because of the limited social interaction of standard and nonstandard speakers, there is little opportunity for the nonstandard speakers to use the standard dialect; and (e) effort directed toward achieving bi-dialectalism could more profitably be spent on developing the child's capacity of using the range of styles afforded by his dialect (p. 39).

The second position—that a standard English should be taught—is much more widely held. This position is generally called bidialectalism. It is that children speaking a nonstandard dialect should be taught a standard English to supplement their native dialect so that they can become fully mobile members of the community. According to Hess's summary, the major points advanced in support of bidialectalism are the following:

1. Standard English is the prestige dialect of the United States.
2. Learning standard English need not be psychologically damaging or alienating.
3. Standard English is an aid to academic achievement.
4. Standard English is helpful to economic advancement.
5. Standard English facilitates communication.
6. Teaching English as standard English is NOT racist.

The social significance of the application of dialect study to the classroom cannot be overvalued. Understanding about dialects can enlighten students and teachers alike on dialect barriers to communication which in the past have caused rejection of cultural diversity. If acceptance of diversity can begin in the classroom, there is hope for the world outside.

Grammar and Rhetoric

Since 1928 the NCTE has advocated that, in order to acquire an accurate conception of the nature of language, college students should become familiar with linguistic knowledge in their courses in the history of English. Nevertheless, the study of grammar remained Latinate until the 1950s. Then the impact of structural linguistics on college English teaching began with publication of *An Outline of English Structure* by Trager and Smith (1951) and *The Structure of English* by Fries (1952). Generative-transformational grammar made its entry with the publication of Chomsky's *Syntactic Structures* in 1957, and Thomas's *Transformational Grammar and the Teacher of English* (1965) applied Chomsky's theory to college courses in methods of teaching English.

These developments were mirrored for elementary and secondary schools in Roberts's books. Beginning with his *Patterns of English* (1956), based on structural linguistics, he moved tentatively toward generative-transformational grammar with *English Sentences* (1962) and followed that book with *English Syntax: A Book of Programed Lessons. An Introduction to Transformational Grammar* (1964). Then in 1966 he produced *The Roberts English Series: A Linguistics Program for Grades 1-8*.

Although Roberts's work has been widely criticized, its initially catalytic influence on the applications of linguistics to the teaching of English grammar is undeniable. Probably more teachers and students learned their linguistics from Roberts's books than from any other single source. His *Patterns of English, Understanding English* (a text for college freshmen published in 1958), and *English Sentences* were written so that teachers could easily learn about linguistics.

Applications of linguistic grammar to the teaching of writing are important, especially in the light of earlier research on the relationship between traditional grammar teaching and the improvement of writing. A review of this earlier research (Braddock, Lloyd-Jones, and Schoer, 1963) reported:

> In view of the widespread agreement of research studies based upon many types of students and teachers, the conclusion can be stated in strong and unqualified terms: the teaching of formal grammar has a negligible or, because it usually displaces some instruction and practice in actual composition, even a harmful effect on the improvement of writing (pp. 37-38).

However, between 1965 and 1973 several studies investigated the relationship between knowledge of linguistic grammar and writing. These studies began with Hunt's *Grammatical Structures Written at Three Grade Levels* (1965) followed by the works of Bateman and Zidonis (1966), O'Donnell, Griffin, and Norris (1967), Christensen (1967), Mellon (1969), Hunt (1970), and O'Hare (1973).

Hunt (1965, 1970) defined a new and practical index for identifying sentences in writing. This new index is the minimal terminable unit, or "T-unit." A T-unit includes one main clause plus whatever other full or reduced clauses are embedded within it. Using the T-unit, Hunt analyzed the increasing complexity of students' writing as they progress through school, and correlated this complexity with levels of syntactic maturity. Hunt's first study was based on structural linguistics, his second on generative-transformational grammar. The work of O'Donnell, Griffin, and Norris (1967) extended and corroborated Hunt's findings with elementary school children of other grade levels also.

Bateman and Zidonis (1966) discovered that some knowledge of generative-transformational grammar apparently reduced students' errors in writing and simultaneously increased the maturity of their sentences. The study did not use Hunt's T-unit and has been criticized on a number of other counts, but nevertheless it stands as a landmark study in the possible affirmative effects of the study of generative-transformational grammar on writing.

Using the T-unit and basing his work on generative-transformational grammar, Mellon (1969) concluded that Hunt's normal rate of growth toward syntactic maturity could be enhanced by formal instruction in generative-transformational grammar and systematic practice in combining sentences transformationally. O'Hare (1971) used Mellon's sentence-combining exercises but omitted any separate study of generative-transformational grammar to prepare students to combine the sentences. Nevertheless, his students showed growth toward syntactic maturity equal to that of Mellon's students. Therefore, O'Hare concluded that the "knowledge of grammar" that underlies skill in sentence combining is the students' innate sense of grammaticality rather than conscious awareness of generative-transformational grammar. Regardless of how the differences between Mellon's and O'Hare's findings are resolved, undoubtedly *teachers* can profit from some knowledge of generative-transformational grammar in order to prepare sentence-combining exercises and to use them intelligently.

The research of Mellon and O'Hare was published by the NCTE, but teachers do not usually read research. However, in this case, classroom materials began to appear with relatively little delay. Strong's *Sentence Combining: A Composing Book* (1973) used ideas from Mellon, O'Hare, and Christensen (1967) in a text for college composition courses, which is adaptable for high school use also. O'Hare himself produced *Sentencecraft: An Elective Course in Writing* (1975), a text for teaching composition in various types of high school curricula. *Language Alive: Linear A and Linear B* (Malmstrom and Bondar, 1975) incorporated sentence-combining insights and techniques into junior high and middle school English language and composition textbooks. Apparently, in this case the rule of lag between research and technology did not hold.

The work of Christensen (1967) suggested some rhetorical applications of transformational sentence combining. He examined a large body of professional writing and discovered certain identifiable characteristics of skilled modern writing. Two characteristics were "free modifiers" and "cumulative sentences." Free modifiers are absolutes and nonrestrictive adjectival or adverbial modifiers. Cumulative sentences are constructed with free modifiers before and/or after their relatively short base clauses. Christensen saw a parallel between cumulative sentences and paragraphs, likening the topic sentence of a paragraph to the base clause of a sentence and the other sentences of the paragraph to the free modifiers in the cumulative sentences.

Although Christensen criticized Mellon's sentence-combining exercises, arguing that they might produce horrendously embedded sentences, nevertheless in *The Christensen Rhetoric Program* (1968) he included "finger exercises" to produce "syntactic dexterity" and to emphasize the use of free modifiers. He believed that such verbal virtuosity and syntactical ingenuity could be made to carry over into expository writing (1967, pp. 14-16). The misunderstanding between Mellon and Christensen seems to be that their purposes, and therefore, their conclusions differed. Mellon's purpose was to enhance the development of syntactic fluency, as defined by Hunt's index of syntactic maturity, the T-unit. Christensen's purpose was to improve students' writing, and he expressed a preference for initial and final free modifiers as indications of skilled writing. Mellon extended sentence combining to include restrictive modifiers in addition to Christensen's free, nonrestrictive modifiers. In view of their different purposes, each achieved satisfactory results.

Christensen's work has been included as six language units in the *Nebraska Curriculum for English, Grades 10-12* (Olson and Rice, 1967) and as a complete high school composition program in *The Christensen Rhetoric Program: The Sentence and the Paragraph* (1968). His work on sentences is the basis of "Phase Two" of Strong's *Sentence Combining: A Composing Book* (1973). Thus Christensen's case was an unusual one where research was quickly implemented by classroom teaching materials.

Spelling

Spelling is the area of the English curriculum that shows the greatest lag between research and classroom applications. Most school programs are still essentially traditional and dictated by their spelling textbooks. The most popular spelling series is *Basic Goals in Spelling* by Kottmeyer and Claus (1974), first published in 1960 and today virtually unchanged. These spelling books contain exercises, spelling rules, and lists of randomly chosen, frequently used words. The rules are often unhelpful or wrong, without any base in linguistic theory, and the word choices are often based on adults' rather than children's needs.

Yet linguists have been publishing theory relevant to the teaching of spelling since Hall's *Sound and Spelling in English* (1961) and Fries's *Linguistics and Reading* (1962). These structural linguists stated that English spelling is predominantly alphabetic. That is, letters (graphemes) usually represent sounds (phonemes) systematically, even though, in this system, one letter does not always represent only one sound (*c* represents /k/ in *cake* but /s/ in *cease*) or is one sound always represented by only one letter (/ŋ/ is represented by *ng* in *sing*, /f/ by *ph* in *phone*, and /ð/ by *th* in *the*). Structuralists characteristically establish their phoneme-grapheme correspondences on the basis of phonetic information alone, rejecting syntactic and semantic cues to spelling.

In 1966, Hanna and his colleagues at Stanford University (Hanna, Hanna, Hodges, and Rudorf, 1966) programmed a computer to use only phonetic cues and determined that in a sample of 17,009 of the most frequently used words, more than one-half of the consonants were consistently spelled 80 percent or more of the time, and that many vowels also matched that level of consistency. Using syntactic and semantic cues, they found that the unpredictability of phoneme-grapheme correspondences could be further reduced. The Stanford Study is fully described in *Spelling: Structure and Strategies* (Hanna, Hodges, and Hanna, 1971), and the study's conclusions are the basis of one spelling textbook series, *Power to Spell* (Hanna, Hanna, Rudorf, Bergquist, and Peterson, 1969) for grades 1-8.

As first explained by Chomsky and Halle in *The Sound Pattern of English* (1968), generative-transformational grammarians believe that, rather than reflecting phoneme-grapheme correspondences, the English spelling system represents morphophonemic contrasts in the language. Since speakers of English "know" their language, they control a vast store of information about its words and how to pronounce them. For example, they know that the plural suffix *-s* on *cats* is pronounced /s/, while the *-s* on *dogs* is pronounced /z/, just as they know that the past tense suffix *-ed* is pronounced /t/ on *walked*, /d/ on *warned*, and /ɪd/ on *wanted*. In other words, the pronunciation is predictable from the phonetic environment. The speaker will automatically make the correct choice; the difference does not need to be reflected in the spelling and is not. However, the spelling should and usually does reflect meaningful, unpredictable /s:z/ and /t:d/ contrasts. Thus, the spellings *sink* and *zink* or *ten* and *den* do show meaningful differences between the members of each pair.

Moreover, spelling often maintains an obvious representation of the underlying root morpheme which may not be obvious in its pronunciation. As C. Chomsky (1970) says, "Good spellers, children and adults alike, recognize that related words are spelled alike even though they are pronounced differently. They seem to rely on an underlying picture of the word that is independent of its varying pronunciations" (p. 303). For example, spelling clearly reveals that *telegraph*, *telegraphic*, and *telegraphy* all have the same root morpheme *telegraph-* even though pronunciation shows surface variations in stress and vowels: /télǝgræf : telǝgræfik :tǝlégrǝfiy/. A phoenetic transcription showing these pronunciation differences conceals their underlying relationships. Awareness of such relationships is an aid to spelling. If *partial* were spelled *parshel*, its relationship to *partition* would be hidden. Spelling *sign* as *sine* would obscure its relationship to *signify* and *signal* in which the g is pronounced. It would also incorrectly suggest a relationship with the homonym, the *sine* of trigonometry. Thus, the spelling system of English, transformationalists state, is a nearly ideal system for representing the underlying relationships among words, especially the Latinate words of the educated adult's vocabulary. The good speller internalizes these relationships. The teacher's task is to foster such spelling awareness in students.

An easily available fuller discussion of these and other generative-transformational insights into the spelling system is O'Neil's article, "The Spelling and Pronunciation of English" in *The American Heritage Dictionary of the English Language* (1964, pp. xxxv-xxxvii). O'Neil also points out how syntax determines pronunciation. For example, it is impossible to know how to pronounce *reject* without determining first whether it is a verb /rijékt/ or a noun /ríyjekt/. Nor can the pronunciation of *read* be known until it is identified as a present or past tense /riyd : red/.

Such facts support the generative-transformational position that English spelling represents an underlying phonological level rather than a surface phonetic level. Therefore, it would seem that both traditional phonics rules and phoneme-grapheme correspondences would be equally useless in teaching spelling.

Unfortunately, such insights have had only incidental impact on the teaching of spelling in the schools. C. Chomsky (1970, pp. 304-7) suggests a number of possible "spelling lessons" to bring out some of the features of the underlying phonological relationships among the various spellings of words. For example, children's attention can be focused on pronunciation shifts among related words by giving them a list of words with a missing reduced vowel and asking them to supply it by thinking of related words that retain that vowel quality, as in the following sets:

pres_dent	preside
comp_rable	compare, comparison
maj_r	majority
imm_grate	migrate

Another exercise on related words could narrow the choice between two or more possible consonants to the one correct letter:

criticize (c, s)	critical
nation (t, sh)	native

righteous (t, ch)   right

racial (c, t, sh)   race

Another exercise could bring to the surface consonants which are silent in some words but pronounced in other related words:

muscle   muscular

bomb   bombard

soften   soft

These and other similarly insightful exercises could be varied in different ways. In other words, textbooks and teaching materials could be developed to use transformational insights in the teaching of spelling. No clearer example of the lag between research knowledge and classroom use exists in the English curriculum.

Linguistics in the Curriculum

In the 1960s Project English gave impetus to the curricular application of many aspects of linguistics—phonology, morphology, grammar, history, lexicography, for example. This federally funded project was launched by the United States Department of Health, Education, and Welfare in 1961. It was to provide for extensive research in English teaching, to develop demonstration centers throughout the country, and to hold national conferences on important teaching problems. It was, according to Shugrue (1968), "an isolated high-water mark in the history of the relationship between the federal government and the scholarly community" (p. 37).

When Carlsen and Crow (1967) reviewed the material produced by the Project English Curriculum centers, they summarized the "central prevailing tendencies" of language study, showing the new importance of linguistics in the English curriculum.

> That language is a human institution having a history, a geography, a sociology, a psychology, a structure, and a theory is an established point of view of the Curriculum Centers. Language as an institution is a subject matter content to be studied as a part of general education by all young people. The University of Minnesota Center, devoted exclusively to this concept, has developed the most detailed and the greatest number of units to be used in Grades 7 through 12.

The most commonly appearing language units are dialects, lexicography, and semantics. Florida indicates that the most successful unit in eliciting student interest is dialects. Morphology and syntax seem to be continuing concerns taught year after year in much the same way that "school grammar" has held sway in the past. One has the feeling that kernel sentence patterns are about to take the place of the eight parts of speech in being taught from pre-school through the senior year in high school (p. 988).

From 1965 through 1968, summer institutes in the teaching of English were supported federally under the National Defense Education Act. These institutes were for retraining experienced elementary and secondary teachers of English. Each participant had available free the curricular materials produced by the Curriculum Development centers, and many of the teachers became devoted converts to some kind of linguistics as a result of their institute experiences. However, only about 18 percent of the English teachers were enrolled in institutes and, moreover, Project English ended when the war in Vietnam severely limited funds for educational research. Nevertheless Project English did introduce linguistics massively into English teaching. *The Nebraska Curriculum, Grades 1-12* (Olson and Rice, 1967) and *The Oregon Curriculum, Grades 7-12* (Kitzhaber, 1968), both containing linguistically based units, were commercially published and thus received national distribution.

However, once again the lag between available materials and their classroom use became evident. Squire and Applebee (1968) reported that "recent developments in scholarly discussion of language and grammar have led to confusion and a virtual end of language teaching in the high school today" (p. 255). They went on to describe the situation further:

Teachers not only need to become familiar with new developments in the study of grammar and usage, but also need help in the more practical problems of relating such studies to the other areas of the language arts. Few teachers recognize the natural bridge which the language of literature can provide to linguistic studies; fewer still effect a successful and continuing integration (p. 257).

The state of linguistics in the curriculum was even more pessimistically reflected in Hillocks's study (1972). This report concerned the increasingly widespread curricular practice of offering high and middle school students several optional English courses each semester, each quarter, or for even shorter periods of time. Hillocks had reports from seventy-six schools in thirty-seven states, questionnaire responses from eighty-four department chairpersons and supervisors in charge of elective programs, and various other published and unpublished materials. In all, well over one-hundred programs provided the data for his study. Hillocks gives a table of courses (p. 25) offered by twenty-one or more of the programs he examined. No type of language course appears in this table. In another table (p. 33), Hillocks summarizes the language courses offered. These total sixty-five courses, about 3.2 percent of the total number of courses. Eleven specifically "linguistics" courses are offered, or 0.6 percent of the total number of courses. Further analyzing the group of sixty-five language-oriented courses, Hillocks divides them (pp. 70-72) into three main groups:

1. general language
2. modern grammar
3. traditional school grammar and mechanics of writing.

Of the twenty-four "general language" courses, ten focus totally or in part on the history of the English language. Several of these courses also examine American dialects; one deals exclusively with American dialects. Except for one course in general semantics, the other general language courses focus on broader aspects of language: its nature, social function, psychological effects, and so forth. There are only eleven courses in the "modern grammar" group, devoted to structural or transformational grammar. Some also include some emphasis on dialects and the history of English, and others deal only briefly with modern grammar. Hillocks comments that "it is interesting to note that with all the emphasis on linguistics in professional meetings and publications over the last ten or twelve years, there are so few courses devoted to 'modern' grammar and nearly three times as many to traditional school grammar and usage" (p. 72). Thirty courses compose this last group, and they are often prerequisites for composition courses or are required courses preceding entry into an elective program. Hillocks concludes sadly that "linguists should ponder what they have wrought" (p. 73).

Textbooks and Supplementary Materials

In the 1970s all major publishers include some linguistically oriented offerings in their lists. The formats of these texts reflect the various curricular patterns popular in the schools. Publishers know that the success or failure of a curriculum depends upon the teacher who puts it into classroom action. They also know the corollary of this fact: for all but the most inspired, energetic, and intelligent teachers, the most important single factor controlling instruction is the textbook. Therefore, textbooks are usually the most powerful factor in the application of linguistics to the teaching of English.

As mentioned above, Roberts was the trailblazer in linguistically oriented textbook writing between 1956 and his death in 1967. After his death, the *Roberts English Series* went immediately into a second edition, apparently to bring it more into line with teachers' convictions about elementary education. Later, the series was extended to grades nine and ten, synthesized into the *Complete Course* (1967) suitable for grades eleven and twelve, and abridged for college use in *Modern Grammar* (1967).

The *Roberts English Series* is a prototype of one kind of linguistically oriented textbook. Each book in the series has three "strands": literature, language, and composition. The language strand deals with phonology, morphology, and syntax—presented quite formally and abstractly—with some attention to general semantics and much less to usage and the history of English. Each strand is relatively independent of the others. Indeed, it was this fact that accounted for the college text *Modern Grammar*. It contains only the language strand of the series.

The strand approach is still popular in basal series published in the 1970s. For example, *The Arts and Skills of English* (1972) for grades 1-6, by Thomas and Stroh, has the same three strands as the *Roberts English Series*. The language strand presents what Thomas and Stroh call "a strictly pedagogical grammar," which incorporates insights from traditional and structural as well as from transformational grammar. The language strand also deals with dialects, dictionaries, the history of English, and usage. This series, like the *Roberts English Series*, perhaps uses more grammatical apparatus than is necessary for elementary school children.

Another basal series, for grades K through 9, *The Laidlaw Language Experiences Program* (1973), by Harsh et al., divides the language strand into four substrands: "Nature of Language," "Speech Sounds," "Word Formation," and "Sentence Structure." Both structural and transformational linguistics are drawn upon, with a progression of complexity through the series. The substrands are developed "inductively" for "ungraded programs." The words *inductive* and *ungraded* are popular in education in the 1970s. Textbooks which are called "ungraded," however, are always marked systematically so that the teacher can use them selectively and sequentially with students in open classrooms.

Finally, *Concepts in Communication* (1974), a hardcover series for grades 7-12, edited by Kitzhaber, presents the perennial Oregon Curriculum in somewhat updated, more informal fashion. In addition, the language strand has also been published separately as six paperbound books suitable for elective programs. This dual publication reflects the fluidity of curricular patterns and publishers' problems in predicting future trends. The language strand includes discussion of transformational grammar, lexicography, the nature of language, the history and nature of writing, the history of English, usage, the history of grammar, and relations of language to style.

Other publishers offer sets of individual paperback volumes suitable for elective programs. One example is *The Random House English Series* (1973) by Judy et al., for grades 7-9. It consists of eleven separate textbooks and a handbook. Its two "linguistic strands" deal with grammar and "nonsyntactic language," as defined below. The three books in the grammar strand use transformational grammar to lead students inductively to make linguistically valid generalizations on the basis of transformational insights. The four books in the nonsyntactic language strand deal with dialects, general semantics, kinesics, and the nature of language. Another set of separate paperbacks is *Domains in Language and Composition* (1972). It consists of twenty-five volumes, each written by a different author, for elective programs in middle and high schools. Of the books, seven deal with aspects of linguistics: the history of English, the nature of language, American English dialects and their history, lexicography, semantics, etymology, and syntax. The paperbacks in these sets vary greatly in quality, interest, and teachability. Publishers report that this variety is reflected in the sales of the different books in the sets.

Several linguistically oriented basal series for elementary students focus on the child as language learner and user rather than on linguistic theory and terminology as such. One example is *Communicating: The Heath English Series* (1973), for levels 1-6, by Botel and Dawkins. As stated in the Teacher's Edition, the series is based on the learning theory derived from the work of Piaget (1955) and Vygotsky (1962), and popularized by Bruner (1961)—a learning theory independently supported by the psycholinguistic studies stimulated by Chomsky's linguistic theories. Thus the series is concerned with the learner's stages of concept development and with structures of knowledge in literature, language, and composition. The approach is exploratory and open-ended, and the content is linguistically sound and varied. To emphasize the primacy of children's experiences with oral language, the textbooks are supplemented by records of the literary selections in each book.

One program is so idiosyncratic that it is only tangentially "linguistic." *Interaction: A Student-Centered Language Arts and Reading Program, K-12* (1973) is Moffett's implementation of the theories explained in his *Teaching the Universe of Discourse* (1968b) and detailed in *A Student-Centered Language Arts Curriculum, Grades K-13: A Handbook for Teachers* (1968a). Moffett believes that all language arts should be studied together, reinforcing each other. Language is seen not as a subject but as a growth process through which the students expand their ability to communicate. These ideas have been put into action in a massive set of classroom materials: booklets, activity cards, cassettes, consumable booklets, games, films for students, teachers' guides, and diagnostic materials for teachers. The teacher becomes chiefly a guide to and through materials. It will be interesting to watch the progress of this expensive experiment.

Some other materials for applying linguistics in the teaching of English may be mentioned. *Leaflets on Historical Linguistics* (n.d.), compiled by the NCTE Committee on Historical Linguistics, consists of six leaflets, one each on *Beowulf*, the *Peterborough Chronicle*, Chaucer, Caxton, Shakespeare, and Pope. Each leaflet has a photo facsimile of a page from the original manuscript, a passage of the text with transcription when necessary, a discussion of the work, and exercises for study. These leaflets combine scholarly depth and accuracy with practical teaching suggestions.

Zero-In: New Perspectives through Linguistics (1971) by Hughes is a multimedia in-service kit for elementary and secondary teachers. It consists of two parts: a tape or cassette containing thirty-five humorous skits dramatizing language situations, divided into four workshops to be used sequentially with the workbook; and a workbook, divided into four programmed workshops, each with a different focus, and a Leader's Manual. This kit focuses on the continuing problem of convincing teachers that a single standard of "correct" usage is unrealistic and uninformed. The kit approaches the problem of appropriateness in usage in a light-hearted, but convincing, way. Moreover, the material is so clearly presented that anyone can handle it as leader. It requires no expensive "linguistics expert" to present it, and it is quite inexpensive to purchase.

Two recordings are especially useful in teaching English linguistically. One is *Our Changing Language* (n.d.) by Gott and McDavid. Side one of this recording traces changes in the English language with readings in Old English, Middle English, and Early Modern English; then it contrasts British and American English. Side two gives dialect readings from twelve regions of the United States accompanied by a key word list. The second recording is *The Dialect of the Black American* (1970), which briefly presents some of the characteristics of Afro-American English and suggests that this dialect is a systematic and viable means of communication. This recording can be expected to evoke a variety of reactions in following discussion.

Dialects and Dialect Learning (1973), by Hess, Long, and Maxwell, is another useful, but expensive, linguistic aid in the teaching of dialectology. This is an in-service kit for individual or group use at all levels of instruction. It is intended to produce the skills needed for teaching a regionally standard dialect acceptable in the larger society without criticizing the child's own dialect. Obviously, the kit supports the bidialectal position.

In addition, the NCTE is now publishing cassettes of speeches presented at their national conferences. Many of these cassettes deal with linguistic subjects and are useful for teachers of English. The quality of the cassettes varies, and the teacher must select intelligently; however, the recording venture is to be commended.

In the middle 1970s, the application of linguistics to the teaching of English is more evident in curricular materials than in classrooms. A 1973 curriculum planning manual for the English Language Arts K-12 published by the NCTE shows a combination of wishful thinking and a covert attempt to convert reluctant teachers to linguistics. Such statements as the following are typical of new curricula. They show that more teaching materials have been generated than teachers are yet using.

> Although Miss Fidditch may object, today's language scene is one of inquiry and exploration rather than one of workbook drills. Part of the inquiry should probably center on the rich subject matters of linguistics—semantics, lexicography, and dialectology, among others—but part of it should also relate to the language of now—politics, religion, popular music, advertising, and so on. With language continuously shaping the institutions that surround us—not to mention the quality of our daily lives—it seems only reasonable to balance work in grammar and usage with anthropological explorations into the meaning-making dimensions, with students taking very active rather than passive roles. These explorations of language "in the present tense" can provide a context for questions about language structure and etiquette (O'Donnell, 1973, p. 31).

Linguistically based textbooks do present linguistic inquiry and exploration in organized fashion, and a hopeful tendency is the appearance of a new kind of elementary and secondary textbook writer. These authors are curriculum developers rather than linguists. They are characteristically trained in English and education as well as in linguistics, and therefore they are well informed about both linguistic theory and educational practice. Such authors dissociate themselves from the Roberts's rule-oriented approach to generative-transformational grammar because it merely substitutes another set of "correct answers" for the old traditional ones. These authors are aware that traditional school grammar and language attitudes are wrong and psychologically damaging. Consequently, they are willing to devote time and energy to translating linguistic theory into classroom practice. An important part of their task is to foster certain linguistic attitudes in students. These include: (1) a knowledge that language is a structured system not a chaotic mystery; (2) a love of linguistic exploration rather than a fear of linguistic error; (3) a discovery that a question may have several appropriate answers rather than a single correct one; and (4) a belief that studying language is not only useful but also interesting.

Some Conclusions and Implications

The preceding analysis of applications of linguistics to first language teaching suggests certain conclusions and implications, which may be organized in terms of the two basic problems initially cited. The first problem is the lag between research and its implementation in teaching materials. The second basic problem is the gap between available teaching materials and classroom practice.

In the long view, the lag between research and its implementation in teaching materials has been at least partly overcome. Linguistically oriented textbooks and supplementary materials of varying degrees of excellence exist for every relevant curricular area, with the possible exception of spelling. These books and materials have been produced by the NCTE and every major publisher, and they embody eclectic presentations of linguistic information and insights. They also reflect the many different curricular patterns currently popular.

To be properly defined as linguistically oriented, textbooks and materials build upon students' native knowledge of English, and they encourage descriptive, not prescriptive, attitudes toward language. In addition, linguistically oriented classroom materials reveal relationships between language and life outside the classroom. In other words, such materials are psycholinguistically and sociolinguistically sound. On the other hand, to be also pedagogically realistic they minimize linguistic terminology and emphasize linguistic ideas and insights, integrating these consistently into the teaching of literature, language, and composing, as explained in Malmstrom and Lee (1971).

However, the second basic problem still persists. Actual classroom practice continues to reveal teachers' failure to understand and use available materials. The comments of Squire and Applebee (1968) and of Hillocks (1972) are echoed by Edmund Farrell, assistant executive secretary of the NCTE (1973). As he argues for the crucial importance of language in contemporary society, Farrell criticizes teachers for slighting the teaching of language and for subordinating it to the teaching of literature. If teachers are unable or unwilling to use linguistically oriented books and materials, the reasons probably lie equally in the nature of their education and in the exigencies of their employment.

Ideally, in the process of their education, English teachers take college courses in both linguistics and in methods of teaching English. However, according to the Center for Applied Linguistics (Grognet, 1972) only about eleven percent of the colleges and universities in the United States offer courses in linguistics. Usually linguistics is considered a luxury rather than a necessity. Therefore, it may be impossible for the prospective teacher to take a course in linguistics. Moreover, even if a course in linguistics is available and required, teachers may receive no information from it about how to apply theoretical linguistic concepts to the teaching of English in elementary or secondary schools. On the other hand, college courses in methods of teaching English tend to emphasize the teaching of literature and composition rather than of language. Unless the methods professor is well informed about linguistics and convinced about its relevance to the teaching of English, the course may fail to persuade prospective teachers of the importance of linguistics in their future teaching. Therefore, it is not surprising if they are unable or unwilling to use linguistics in their classrooms.

A second possible reason for the gap between the availability of linguistically oriented books and materials and actual classroom teaching probably lies in the conditions of English teachers' employment. Maloney (1973) explains the complexity of the high school English teachers' situation. Their workload is decided by custom rather than reason. Usually no careful consideration is given to the characteristics of the students, the community values and expectations, the physical plant, and the financial and supportive resources available. The teachers' complex responsibilities include multiple class preparations, curriculum development, innovation, evaluation, and research, professional growth and involvement, and many nonteaching duties—school committees, chaperoning, and money collecting. Therefore, it is clear why self-education is often practically impossible for high school teachers, even though they are officially encouraged or required to take courses and become involved in professional organizations. The situation of elementary teachers makes self-education even less likely, since they are required to teach many subjects other than language, even though they normally devote about sixty percent of their time to "the language arts," including reading. Therefore, it seems that the responsibility for adequate education of teachers lies primarily with the colleges and universities. Broader education by professors in English teaching methods courses may eventually narrow the gap between available teaching materials and their intelligent use in elementary and secondary classrooms.

REFERENCES

The American heritage dictionary of the English language. Boston and New York: American Heritage and Houghton Mifflin, 1969.

Bateman, D. R., and Zidonis, F. J. *The effect of a study of transformational grammar on the writing of ninth and tenth graders*. Urbana, Ill.: National Council of Teachers of English, 1966.

Botel, M., and Dawkins, J. *Communicating: The Heath English series*. Lexington, Mass.: D. C. Heath, 1973.

Braddock, R., Lloyd-Jones, R., and Schoer, L. *Research in written composition*. Urbana, Ill.: National Council of Teachers of English, 1963.

Bruner, J. S. *The process of education*. Cambridge, Mass.: Harvard University Press, 1961.

Carlsen, G. R., and Crow, J. Project English curriculum centers. *English Journal*, 1967, *56*, 986-93.

Chomsky, C. Reading, writing, and phonology. *Harvard Educational Review*, 1970, *40*, 287-309.

Chomsky, N. *Syntactic structures*. The Hague: Mouton, 1957.

Chomsky, N., and Halle, M. *The sound pattern of English*. New York: Harper and Row, 1968.

Christensen, F. *Notes toward a new rhetoric: Six essays for teachers*. New York: Harper and Row, 1967.

———. *The Christensen rhetoric program: The sentence and the paragraph*. New York: Harper and Row, 1968.

Cline, V. B. Person perception from the standpoint of an empiricist. Paper presented at the American Psychological Association Convention, San Francisco, September, 1968.

Conference on College Composition and Communication. Resolutions presented at the CCCC annual business meeting, no. 6. *College Composition and Communication*, 1974, *25*, 339.

The dialect of the black American. New York: Western Electric Co., 1970.

Domains in language and composition. New York: Harcourt Brace Jovanovich, 1972.

Farrell, E. Where's the good word? *English Journal*, 1973, *62*, 977-83.

Francis, N. *The structure of American English*. New York: Ronald Press, 1958.

Fries, C. C. *American English grammar*. New York: Appleton-Century-Crofts, 1940.

————. *The structure of English*. New York: Harcourt Brace Jovanovich, 1952.

———— .*Linguistics and reading*. New York: Holt, Rinehart and Winston, 1962.

Gott, E., and McDavid, R. I., Jr. *Our changing language*. St. Louis: Webster Division, McGraw-Hill, n.d.

Grognet, A. G., ed. *University resources in the United States and Canada for the study of linguistics, 1971-1972*. Arlington, Va.: Center for Applied Linguistics and the Secretariat of the Linguistic Society of America, 1972.

Hall, R. A., Jr. *Sound and spelling in English*. Philadelphia: Chilton, 1961.

Hanna, P. R., Hanna, J. S., Hodges, R. E., and Rudorf, E. H., Jr. *Phoneme-grapheme correspondences as cues to spelling improvement*. Washington, D. C.: Office of Education, Department of Health, Education, and Welfare, 1966.

Hanna, P. R., Hanna, J. S., Hodges, R. E., Rudorf, E. H., Jr., Bergquist, S. R., and Peterson, D. J. *Power to spell, grades 1-8*. Boston: Houghton Mifflin, 1969.

Hanna, P. R., Hodges, R. E., and Hanna, J. S. *Spelling: Structure and strategies*. Boston: Houghton Mifflin, 1971.

Harsh, W., Head, J. S., Ney, J. W., Folta, B., Steet, M. L., Rus, L. C., and Rausch, R. W. *The Laidlaw language experiences program*. River Forest, Ill.: Laidlaw, 1973.

Hess, K. M. Is learning a standard English important? An overview. *Florida FL Reporter*, 1972, *10* (1 and 2), 39-42, 54.

Hess, K. M., Long B., and Maxwell, J. C. *Dialects and dialect learning*. Urbana, Ill.: National Council of Teachers of English, 1973.

Hillocks, G., Jr. *Alternatives in English: A critical appraisal of elective programs*. Urbana, Ill.: ERIC Clearinghouse on Reading and Communication Skills, National Council of Teachers of English, 1972.

Hughes, T. *Zero-in: New perspectives through linguistics*. Detroit, Mich.: Michigan Council of Teachers of English, 1971.

Hunt, K. W. *Grammatical structures written at three grade levels*. Urbana, Ill.: National Council of Teachers of English, 1965.

————. Syntactic maturity in school children and adults. *Monograph of the Society for Research in Child Development*, 1970, 35 (1).

Joos, M. The five clocks. *International Journal of American Linguistics*, 1962, 28 (2).

Judy, S. N., Summerfield, G., Peck, R., Reynolds, W., Lester, M., and McDavid, V. *The Random House English series 7-9*. New York: Random House, 1973.

Kaplan, R. B. On a note of protest (in a minor key): Bidialectism vs. bidialecticism. *College English*, 1969, *30*, 386-89.

Kitzhaber, A. R., ed. *The Oregon curriculum: A sequential program in English, grades 7-12*. New York: Holt, Rinehart and Winston, 1968-70.

Kitzhaber, A. R., ed. *Concepts in communication, grades 7-12*. New York: Holt, Rinehart and Winston, 1974.

Kochman, T. Social factors in the consideration of teaching standard English, *Florida FL Reporter*, 1969, 7 (1), 87-88, 157.

Kottmeyer, W. A., and Claus, A. *Basic goals in spelling*, 4th ed. St. Louis: Webster Division, McGraw-Hill, 1972.

Labov, W. *The social stratification of English in New York City*. Arlington, Va.: Center for Applied Linguistics, 1966.

Lee, R. R. Preliminaries to language intervention. *Quarterly Journal of Speech*, 1970, *56*, 270-76.

————. The social evaluation of speech: Implications from the laboratory to the classroom. Unpublished paper, 1971, Florida State University.

Leonard, S. A. *Current English usage*. Urbana, Ill.: National Council of Teachers of English, 1932.

Malmstrom, J., and Ashley, A. *Dialects–U.S.A*. Urbana, Ill.: National Council of Teachers of English, 1963.

Malmstrom, J., and Bondar, B. *Language alive: Linear A*. New York: Harper and Row, 1975.

————. *Language alive: Linear B*. New York: Harper and Row, 1975.

Malmstrom, J., and Lee, J. *Teaching English linguistically: Principles and practices for high school*. New York: Appleton-Century-Crofts, 1971.

Maloney, H., ed. *Workload for English teachers: Policy and procedure*. Urbana, Ill.: National Council of Teachers of English, 1973.

Marckwardt, A. H., and Walcott, F. *Facts about current English usage*. New York: Appleton-Century-Crofts, 1938.

Mellon, J. *Transformational sentence-combining: A method for enhancing the development of syntactic fluency in English composition*. Urbana, Ill.: National Council of Teachers of English, 1969.

Moffett, J. *A student-centered language arts curriculum, grades K-13: A handbook for teachers*. Boston: Houghton Mifflin, 1968a.

————. *Teaching the universe of discourse*. Boston: Houghton Mifflin, 1968b.

————. *Interaction: A student-centered language arts and reading program*. Boston: Houghton Mifflin, 1973.

National Council of Teachers of English Commission on the English Curriculum. *The English language arts*. Urbana, Ill.: National Council of Teachers of English, 1952.

National Council of Teachers of English Committee on Historical Linguistics. *Leaflets on historical linguistics*. Urbana, Ill.: National Council of Teachers of English, n.d.

O'Donnell, B., ed. *Aids to curriculum planning, English language arts K-12*. Urbana, Ill.: ERIC Clearinghouse on Reading and Communication Skills, National Council of Teachers of English, 1973.

O'Donnell, R. C., Griffin, W. J., and Norris, R. C. *Syntax of kindergarten and elementary school children: A transformational approach*. Urbana, Ill.: National Council of Teachers of English, 1967.

O'Hare, F. *Sentence combining: Improving student writing without formal grammar instruction*. Urbana, Ill.: National Council of Teachers of English, 1973.

————. *Sentencecraft: An elective course in writing*. Lexington, Mass.: Ginn (Xerox), 1975.

Olson, P. A., and Rice, F. M. *The Nebraska curriculum for English, grades 1-12*. Lincoln: University of Nebraska Press, 1967.

O'Neil, W. Paul Roberts rules of order: The misuses of linguistics in the classroom. *Urban Review*, 1968, *2*, (7), 12-17

Piaget, J. *The language and thought of the child*. Cleveland, Ohio: World, 1955.

Pooley, R. C. *Teaching English usage*. New York: Appleton-Century-Crofts, 1946.

———. *The teaching of English usage*. Urbana, Ill.: National Council of Teachers of English, 1974.

Roberts, P. *Patterns of English*. New York: Harcourt Brace Jovanovich, 1956.

———. *Understanding English*. New York: Harper and Row, 1958.

———. *English sentences*. New York: Harcourt Brace Jovanovich, 1962.

———. *English syntax: A book of programmed lessons. An introduction to transformational grammar*. New York: Harcourt Brace Jovanovich, 1964.

———. *The Roberts English series: A linguistics program*. New York: Harcourt Brace Jovanovich, 1966.

———. *Modern grammar*. New York: Harcourt Brace Jovanovich, 1967.

Shugrue, M. F. *English in a decade of change*. New York: Pegasus, 1968.

Shuy, R. W. *Discovering American dialects*. Urbana, Ill.: National Council of Teachers of English, 1967.

Sledd, J. Bi-dialectalism: The linguistics of white supremacy, *English Journal*, 1969, *58*, 1307-15, 1329.

———. Doublespeak: Dialectology in the service of big brother. *College English*, 1972, *33*, 439-56.

Squire, J., and Applebee, R. K. *High school English instruction today*. New York: Appleton-Century-Crofts, 1968.

Strong, W. *Sentence combining: A composing book*. New York: Random House, 1973.

Thomas, O. *Transformational grammar and the teacher of English*. New York: Holt, Rinehart and Winston, 1965.

Thomas, O., and Stroh, N. *The arts and skills of English, grades 1-6*. New York: Holt, Rinehart and Winston, 1972.

Trager, G. L., and Smith, H. L., Jr. An outline of English structure. *Studies in Linguistics: Occasional Papers*, 1951, no. 3.

Vygotsky, L. S. *Thought and language*. Cambridge, Mass.: M.I.T. Press, 1962.

Webster's third new international dictionary of the English language, 3rd ed., unabridged. Springfield, Mass.: G. and C. Merriam, 1961.

IV

Orthography

Richard L. Venezky

The study of writing systems and especially of orthographies was proscribed for many years from the proper activities of linguists, yet few
twentieth-century American linguists have failed to include writing or
orthography in the range of their studies. Even Bloomfield and Hockett,
both of whom advocated most emphatically the separation of writing from
language, published studies or opinions about orthography and its role in
the acquisition of literacy (Bloomfield, 1942; Hockett, 1963). Whatever
position one now wishes to assign to writing in formal linguistic studies, it is
undeniable that the study of writing is important to applied linguistics. For
more than a century philologists and linguists have been engaged in the
design of writing systems for preliterate cultures (Lepsius, 1855; Meinhof,
1928; Pike, 1947); more recently linguists have engaged in the development of pedagogy for teaching reading (Bloomfield and Barnhart, 1961;
Fries, 1962; H. L. Smith, 1956). Properties of orthography, the discovery
of which is left generally by default to applied linguistics, are also invoked
in spelling reform debates (Wijk, 1959; Zachrisson, 1930, 1931), in diachronic studies (McIntosh, 1956; Wrenn, 1943), and now also in psychological models for word recognition (Gough, 1972; Rubenstein, Lewis, and
Rubenstein, 1971; Smith and Spoehr, 1974).

This chapter treats three major problems which concern applied
linguists in dealing with orthographies: (1) the basic structure of English
orthography; (2) the design of new orthographies; and (3) the role of
orthography in reading. For a discussion of the study of written language as
an end in itself, the reader is directed to the pioneering work of Vachek
(1959, 1973). McIntosh (1956) and Wrenn (1943) discuss the problems of
using spelling as evidence for diachronic studies; Daunt (1939), Hockett
(1959), and Stockwell and Barrett (1961), provide an adequate introduction

to the controversies involved in the interpretation of Old English scribal practices. Spelling reform, which is not treated here, is discussed most rationally in Vachek (1973).

Writing Systems and Orthographies

The study of writing systems encompasses not only orthography—that is, the inventory of contrastive visual forms (graphemics), their conventional patterning (graphotactics), and their relationship to speech—but also the shapes of the visual forms (graphics), and the norms or conventions which control the use of writing within a language community. This latter topic has received surprisingly little attention except from graphologists and spelling reformers. Evidence for societal norms on handwriting and spelling, for example, can be found in the changing roles assigned to these topics in public school curricula in the twentieth century, as well as in the attention given to them in trade schools and in employment requirements. The Palmer Handwriting Method and the spelling bee, while still extant, receive nowhere near the attention they did in the 1920s and 1930s, nor does "proper" punctuation, which in the height of the prescriptive era was taught with catechismic vigor.

In countries which have active language academies, such as Italy, France, and Israel, the pressures and processes which lead to changes in a writing system are generally well documented. In the United States, on the other hand, where the notion of a language academy has never received substantial support from either lettered or common sources, attempts to influence the writing system, such as those made by Noah Webster, Theodore Roosevelt, and the *Chicago Tribune* are poorly documented. The best source on language academies, and in particular the British attitude toward them, is still Baugh (1957). No major work has yet appeared on the changing attitudes in American society toward writing and writing conventions.

The Structure of English Orthography

For reasons which are beyond the scope of this paper (see Venezky, 1965), English has the most complex relationship between spelling and sound of any major modern language. This relationship, however, is neither the primeval chaos portrayed by spelling reformers nor the ideal underlying structure for phonological representation claimed by Chomsky and Halle (1968). Careful examination shows English orthography to contain a native base, mixed with prominent streaks of borrowed elements, scribal tinkering, and the orthographic debris of 1300 years of conditional and sometimes erratic sound changes. To understand the patterning of English orthography, one must attend to the graphemic units of the system, their combinations and alternations, and their mappings into phonological elements. These matters comprise the subject matter of the following section, which is adapted from Venezky (1967). For more extensive treatments of English, see Wijk (1966) and Venezky (1970); for a comparison of different approaches to English orthography, see Wardhaugh (1968). In the discussion which follows, graphemic forms will be given in italics, morphophonemic forms between doubled slants, for example, //n//, and phonemic forms between single slants, for example, /n/. Vowel phonemes are classed following Kurath (1964, pp. 17-20) as *free* or *checked*.

Approaches to Spelling-Sound Relationships

The traditional approach to describing English orthography is based upon direct mappings from spelling into sound. By this approach, *n* in *sign* corresponds directly to /n/, *n* in *think* to /ŋ/, and *n* in *autumn* to /∅/. Although appropriate for most applications, direct mappings from spelling to sound fail to reveal a major portion of the patterning of the orthography, and more importantly, fail to show clearly the separate roles of graphemic, morphemic, and phonological influences. In the mappings for *n* presented above, for example, both graphemic and phonological conditioning are present, but cannot be extracted from the direct mappings. The *n* in *sign*, *think*, and *autumn* can be viewed as representing, at an abstract level between spelling and sound, a single unit, //n//. In *sign* and most other words this unit is mapped into the phoneme /n/; before velar stops as in *think*, //n// is mapped into /ŋ/, while in final //mn// clusters as in *autumn*, //n// is mapped into /∅/. However, note that before suffixes which begin with a vowel, as in *autumnal, hymnal*, and *damnation*, //n// is mapped into /n/. Positing an abstract level between spelling and sound allows for a separation of mapping rules based strictly upon graphemic considerations from those which are based upon morphology and phonology. The former rules are unique to English spelling while the latter are, for the most part, present in the oral language habits of English speakers (or represent language patterns which are no longer active).

In this chapter spellings will be mapped first onto an intermediate level, called the morphophonemic level, and then onto a phonemic level. The morphophonemic level is a device for explicating certain patterns of

English orthography which from the direct spelling-to-sound approach often appear as irregularities. It is a linguistic construct and is not assumed to correspond to any psychological reality nor to be appropriate for teaching children how to relate spellings to sounds.

For mapping spellings into sound through the morphophonemic level, letters are first grouped into two types of functional units: *relational units* and *markers*.

A relational unit (see table 1) is a string of one or more graphemes which has a morphophonemic correspondent which cannot be predicted from the behavior of the unit's smaller graphemic components.

A marker is a string of one or more graphemes whose primary function is either to indicate the mappings of relational units into morphophonemes or to preserve a graphotactical or morphological pattern. It has no morphophonemic correspondence of its own, that is, it corresponds to zero.

The division of graphemes into functional units depends partially upon the environments in which they occur. Thus, *gn* in *cognac* and *poignant* is a single relational unit which corresponds to the morphophonemic cluster //nj//. However, *gn* in *sign* and *malign* is not a relational unit, but a combination of two relational units which separately correspond to the morphophonemes //g// and //n//. Morphophonemic alternation rules map //g// into either //ø// or //g//, depending upon allomorphic considerations (compare *sign: signal*; *malign: malignant*).

The selection of relational units is based upon function and composition. Any string of graphemes that corresponds to a morphophoneme is a potential relational unit. However, only those strings whose morphophonemic correspondences cannot be predicted by general rules based upon smaller units contained in the strings are classed as relational units. *Ch* in *chair*, for example, is a relational unit since the morphophoneme //č// cannot be predicted from general rules based upon *c* and *h* separately. However, geminate consonant clusters are not single relational units since their morphophonemic forms can be obtained from rules based upon their separate constituents. (The leveling of clusters like //ff// to //f// can be accounted for by a general phonotactical rule, as long as morpheme boundaries are marked.)

Relational units are classed as consonants or vowels depending upon the class of the morphophonemes into which they are mapped (glides are classed as consonants). Some relational units are classed as both consonant and vowel, for example, *u* in *language* (consonant) and *during* (vowel). Within these classes major and minor patterns are distinguished on the basis of frequency of occurrence. Thus, *ch* is classed as a major consonant

TABLE 1
Major Relational Units

Consonants					Compound	Primary		Secondary	
Simple									
b	gh	n	s	w	ck	a	ai/ay	ie	ue
c	h	p	sh	y	dg	e	au/aw	oa	ui
ch	j	ph	t	z	tch	i	ea	oe	
d	k	q	th		wh	o	ee	oi/oy	
f	l	r	u		x	u	ei/ey	oo	
g	m	rh	v			y	eu/ew	ou/ow	

u is a consonant unit when it corresponds to //w//, as in *quack, language*, and *assuage*. It may also be a vowel unit, or part of a vowel unit (*ou*), or a marker (*guest, plague*).

w is a consonant unit when it corresponds to //w//, as in *warm* and *beware*. It also appears as part of a vowel unit (*ow, aw*) but never as a vowel unit in itself.

y is a consonant unit when it corresponds to //j//, as in *yes* and *beyond*. It also appears as a vowel unit and as part of a vowel unit, as in *cycle* and *boy*.

ck is a consonant unit in words like *rack* and *tack*. In words like *picnicking*, however, the *k* is a marker. That *ck* in *picnicking* is identical to the relational unit *ck* is immaterial, since the base form *picnic* ends in *c*, not *ck*.

wh is classed as a relational unit solely because the order of the sounds it represents is reversed from the order of the letters. This curiosity is due to Anglo-Norman scribes who reversed the letters in the Old English cluster *hw* (*hwat* 'what'; *hwa* 'who') in an attempt to improve the visual discrimination of short letters.

The minor relational units include *kh* (*khaki, khan*), *sch* (*schist, schwa*), *gn* (*cognac, poignant*), *ae* (*aesthetic, algae*), *eau* (*bureau, beautiful*), *eo* (*jeopardy, leopard*), and *uy* (*buy, guy*).

---

unit, but *kh* (*khaki*) is classed as a minor unit. Although the major-minor classification may appear arbitrary, it distinguishes frequently occurring, productive patterns from infrequent patterns which generally occur only in a small number of borrowings.

Consonant relational units are classed as functionally simple or functionally compound, a distinction needed for an accurate statement of a general correspondence rule. In the sequence *single-letter vowel + con-*

sonant + *final e, vowel* is generally mapped into its free alternate if *consonant* is a functionally simple unit (or this type of unit plus *l* or *r*), and into its checked alternate if *consonant* is a functionally compound unit, or a cluster (see table 2). Vowel units are classed as primary (*a, e, i, y, o, u*) or secondary (all others).

TABLE 2

Pronunciations of Primary Vowels before Simple and
Compound Consonant Units

Free Alternate	Checked Alternate
bake	axe
ache	badge
concede	edge
lichen	kitchen
clothe	hodge
crude	luxury

Markers are used in many writing systems to indicate particular pronunciations when more than one could occur for a letter. In Spanish, for example, a *u* is inserted after *g* to show a /g/ pronunciation where otherwise it would indicate an /x/ (for example, *guiar*: /gyar/). If the *u* marker is pronounced, then another marker, the diaresis, is placed over it (for example, *güipil*: /guipil/). In Hebrew, a midpoint (*dagesh*) is placed within the letters *bet, kaf,* and *pe* to mark a stop pronunciation (/b, k, p/) rather than a fricative (/v, x, f/). English uses markers in this way, but also employs them for morphological and graphotactical functions.

Only graphemes mapped into zero can be classed as markers. However, graphemes with non-zero morphophonemic correspondences, though properly classed as relational units, can also perform marking functions. For example, the *i* in *city*, besides corresponding to //ɪ//, marks the correspondence *c*→//s//. A geminate consonant cluster also performs a marking function since it regularly indicates the correspondence of the preceding vowel.

The strongest evidence for a separate class of markers in English orthography is found in orthographic alternation patterns. For example, final *e* as a marker for the pronunciation of a preceding *c* or *g* is dropped before a suffix which begins with a letter that will perform the same function as *e*. Therefore, *notice* drops the final *e* before *ing* (*noticing*) since *i* also marks the correspondence *c*→//s//, but retains the *e* before *able* since *noticable* would have *c*→//k//. Similarly, the *e* added to an otherwise terminal *u* is dropped before any suffix since the only function of the *e* is to avoid having word-final *u*, for example, *argue* and *arguing*.

The more important markers in English orthography are summarized below; marginal uses, such as in the graphemic distinction of homophones (*aid*: *aide*; *bell*: *belle*), are not included.

Markers of vowel or consonant correspondences

1. Final *e* marks the free pronunciation of a vowel in the pattern *VCe* or *VCle* (*mat*: *mate*; *cut*: *cute*).
2. Final *e* marks the //s// pronunciation of *c* or the //ǰ// pronunciation of *g* (*trace*, *rage*).
3. Final *e* marks syllabic *l* or *r* (*able*, *acre*).
4. *u* marks the correspondence *g*→//g// or *c*→//k// (*guest*, *guide*, *catalogue*; *circuit*).
5. *k* marks the correspondence *c*→//k// before a suffix which begins with *i*, *e*, or *y* (*picnic*: *picnicking*; *panic*: *panicky*).
6. A doubled (geminated) consonant after a stressed, primary vowel indicates the checked pronunciation of the vowel.
7. Final *e* marks a voiced interdental spirant (*breath*: *breathe*; *bath*: *bathe*).

Markers of graphotactical patterns

1. A final *e* is added after *v* or *u* to avoid having either of these in final position. (Note, however, such exceptions for *u* as *thou* and *you*.)
2. A final *e* is used after many two letter nouns and verbs to limit the stock of two letter strings to common function words (*doe*, *foe*, *hoe*, *toe*).
3. *al* is inserted between a final adjectival *ic* and the adverbial *ly* if an adjective in *ical* does not exist (*basically*).

Markers of morphophemic patterns

Final *e* is generally added after nonmorphemic *s* to avoid the appearance of a morphemic *s* (*moose*, *nurse*, *hearse*, *else*, *noise*).

(However, if the *e* would also indicate a free pronunciation of a vowel, as it would if added to *us*, *his*, and *tennis*, it is not added.)

Correspondence patterns can be classed according to their predictability and complexity. Predictable correspondences can be further divided as either invariant or variant. The letter *f*, for example, is invariant since it corresponds regularly to //f//. Several other consonant spelling units like *ck*, *m*, *v*, and *z* are also invariant, or nearly so. The vowel spellings are rarely invariant, though not irregular in most cases.

Variant correspondences are those correspondences that are still predictable, but that relate the same spelling to two or more morphophonemes depending upon regular graphemic, phonological, or grammatical features. The letter *c*, as an example, corresponds to //s// when it occurs before *e*, *i*, *y*, plus a consonant or juncture; in most other positions, it corresponds to //k//. (The correspondences for *c*→//s//, as in *social*, are also predictable, but a full explanation of this phenomenon is beyond the scope of this chapter.) The spelling *k* corresponds to zero in initial position before *n*, for example, *knee*, *know*, and *knife*; in all other positions *k* corresponds to //k//. However, this pattern is explained most adequately by a phonotactical rule: when prohibited consonant clusters would otherwise occur in morpheme-initial position, the first consonant is dropped, as in *knee*, *gnat*, *ptarmigan*, *pneumonia*, and *psychology*.

Position alone may determine the correspondence of a spelling unit. For example, initial *gh* always corresponds to //g//: *ghost*, *gherkin*, and *ghoul* but never to //f// as assumed in the spelling reform creation *ghoti*; however, medial and final *gh* have pronunciations besides //g//. Stress may also be a conditioning factor for predictable, variant correspondences. The correspondences for intervocalic *x*, for example, depend upon the position of the main word stress. If the main stress is on the vowel preceding *x*, the pronunciation is //ks//, as in *exit*; otherwise, it is //gz//, as in *examine* and *exist*. Although this rule is similar to Verner's Law for the voicing of the Germanic voiceless spirants, it is not a case of pure phonological conditioning. Words like *accede* and *accept* have the identical phonetic environments for //gz//, yet have //ks//.

Another situation in which stress is important is in determining when certain spellings correspond to //s, z, t, d// and when they correspond to the palatalized forms //š, ž, č, ǰ //. This form of palatalization generally occurs when the spellings concerned are followed by an unstressed vowel, as in *social*, *treasure*, *bastion*, and *cordial*. In all cases, however, the spellings are mapped into unpalatalized morphophonemes. Then, the same palatalization rules which account for the //ž// in //réžjəl// (*I'll raise you*) and the //č// in //géčə//(*I'll get you*) are applied. The retention or deletion of medial /h/ in most cases also depends upon the position of the main word stress. Compare *prohibit*: *prohibition*; *vehicular*: *vehicle*. In each pair the first member, which has the stress on the vowel following *h*, has an //h//, while the second member, with an unstressed vowel after *h*, has no //h//. This rule also holds for *vehement, shepherd, philharmonic, annihilate, rehabilitate*, and *nihilism*, all of which generally have no //h//. (Some forms like these may have //h// occasionally preserved by over-correct pronunciations.)

Stress also plays a major role in the pronunciation of vowels; the patterns, however, are highly complex and beyond the scope of this chapter. (For more on this topic, see Chomsky and Halle, 1968, and Oswalt, 1973).

Irregular spelling-to-sound correspondences also show important differences. *Arcing* and *cello*, for example, both have irregular correspondences for *c*, yet there is an important distinction between these two irregularities. *Arc*, from which *arcing* is derived, has the correct correspondence for *c*. When suffixes beginning with *e*, *i*, or *y* are added to words ending in *c*, a *k* is normally inserted after the *c*, as in *picnicking* (*picnic*) and *trafficked* (*traffic*). The irregularity in *arcing*, therefore, is in the irregular formation of the derivative. *Cello*, on the other hand, contains an aberrant correspondence for *c*, paralled only in a few other Italian borrowings.

Descriptive Model for Relating Spelling to Sound

Any system of rules chosen to relate spelling-to-sound not only must be as accurate and as simple as possible, but also must allow a differentiation of the more important levels of patterning in the orthographic system. To present the *x* patterns, which depend upon a graphemic distinction and stress placement, as parallel to the *c* patterns discussed previously would be to provide an unsatisfactory account of the current orthography. It should also be noted that a descriptive model for spelling-to-sound correspondences is not something that should necessarily be implemented on a machine or be applied in any way to the teaching of reading. Rather, it is a technique for organizing and testing the various rules which are posited for predicting sounds from spellings.

In the model presented here, graphemic words are divided into their graphemic allomorphs and then an ordered set of rules relates morphophonemic units. Other rules then alter the morphophonemic units and finally map them into phonemic forms. All rules which are based upon nongraphemic features are applied in an ordered sequence at the morphophonemic level, yielding various sublevels of intermediate forms for each word. The final morphophonemic form is then mapped automatically onto the phonemic level. As stated earlier, the function of the intermediate level is to separate graphemically dependent rules from morphologically and phonologically dependent ones. To demonstrate how this model organizes spelling-to-sound rules, the mappings for *social* and *signing* are as follows:

> *social* would be mapped into //sosɪæl// by the grapheme-to-morphophoneme rules for the separate units *s, o, c, i, a, l*. On the first morphophonemic level, the main word stress would be placed on the first syllable, resulting in //sósɪæl//. Then, through vowel reduction, //ɪæl// would become //jəl// and the resulting //sj// would be palatalized to //š//. The form //sóšəl// would then be mapped onto the phonemic level, giving /sóšəl/.

> *signing* would first be broken into *sign* and *ing* and then each of these graphemic allomorphs would be mapped onto the morphophonemic level, yielding //sɪgn// and //ɪng//. Upon combination of the two forms and the application of stress and certain phonotactical rules, the form //sɪgnɪng// would result. By the rules for leveling consonant clusters, final //ng// would become //ŋ// and //gn// would become //n// with compensatory alternation of //ɪ// to //aɪ//. These operations yield //sáɪnɪŋ//, which is automatically mapped into /sáɪnɪŋ/.

The Design of Writing Systems

Basic principles.   The design of new writing systems is being undertaken today either to promote literacy or to reform and replace an existing writing system. While these goals are different, both are concerned with the more general problem of developing an orthography that is (1) mechanically suited for the language it is to reflect; (2) compatible with, or, at a minimum, not alien to its social-cultural setting; and (3) psychologically and pedagogically appropriate for its speakers. In the last twenty years the linguistic, political, and social-cultural aspects of writing systems have been discussed widely, especially by Burns (1953), Gudschinsky (1959), Pike (1947), and Sjoberg (1966). Only recently, however, have the psychological problems been considered seriously. Although conflicts between the linguist's phonological classifications and the native speaker's perceptions have been noted in the past, no attempt has yet been made to explore these systematically; consequently, the design of new orthographies is still derived primarily from the linguist's systemization, based upon the highly suspicious principle that "in an ideal orthography there is a one to one correspondence between the symbols and the phonemes of the language" (Gudschinsky, 1959, p. 68).

The first set of principles for orthographic design which were based on modern linguistic interpretations were set forth by the International African Institute (1930). The basis of this system was a phonemic representation of speech, using single letters, digraphs, and a minimal number of diacritics. Psychological and pedagogical factors, drawn primarily from Huey (1908), were also considered in the design. One innovation was the suggested deviation from pure phonemic representation for some instances of tones, a suggestion which had been anticipated by Westermann (1929).

Current attitudes in the United States of America toward orthographic design were developed primarily by workers of the Summer Institute of Linguistics, particularly Gudschinsky (1953), Nida (1954), and Pike (1947). They began with the concept of using one symbol for each phoneme; however, this concept has been modified as experience has demonstrated its nondesirability in particular situations. Exceptions to the one-letter, one-sound approach to practical orthographies have been expressed by DeFrancis (1950), Hockett (1951), and Jones (1950), in particular for distinguishing homophones, showing popular alternative spellings, and avoiding cumbrous spellings, especially when little graphemic ambiguity results.

A careful consideration of the uses of orthographies shows three considerations to be important in the design of a practical system: (1) the permanency of the orthography; (2) the process of acquiring literacy; and (3) the structure of the language which the system is to reflect.

Even though the basic function of an orthography is to promote literacy, a separation must be made between transitional orthographies and permanent orthographies, that is, between those systems which are meant only for the initial acquisition of literacy, usually in a "native language," after which the learner transfers to reading in some other language (generally called the *target language*), and those systems which will become the primary and permanent systems for written expression. A transitional orthography should be designed in relation to the target orthography, although transfer of reading ability from one system to the other does not appear to be a major problem. More importantly, a transitional orthography is concerned primarily with the initial stages of reading, while a permanent orthography must be concerned with both initial and advanced stages.

In the initial stages of acquiring literacy, the reader is perfecting the mechanics of oral reading, with emphasis on relating writing to speech. In the advanced stages, on the other hand, the reader is rarely engaged in oral reading, but is doing rapid, silent reading in which whole words, or groups of words rather than individual letters are processed as single units. For the beginner, the orthography is needed as an indicator for the sounds of words through which meanings are obtained as in listening, but for the advanced reader, a more direct access to meaning is needed. This conflict between the needs of beginning and advanced readers forces certain compromises upon the design of a practical writing system.

Considerations of the language which an orthography is to reflect must be directed toward the entire language structure, and not just toward its phonology, although in most instances the phonology will be given priority. Morpheme and word identity, for example, are important for rapid reading as is the graphemic distinction of homophones and foreign words. To serve these needs, deviations from a one-letter, one-sound system are required. The most crucial decisions, however, are those concerning which phonemic distinctions to differentiate graphemically. Although an alphabetic system should give unique representations to all major segmental units, there is little justification for retaining contrasts which carry low functional load, especially if the contrasts are those that tend to be recorded with superscripts (that is, suprasegmental contrasts). To do so is to burden the graphemic repertoire with forms that increase the difficulty of word recognition and spelling. Justification for the retention of all phonemic contrasts is usually based upon the argument that children learn to read much more quickly with a regular (that is, phonemic) writing system, than they do with a system which deviates in any way from this ideal. There is no evidence to support this claim; in fact, experiments with the Initial Teaching Alphabet (i.t.a.) have produced, at best, equivocal results (Bond and Dykstra, 1967).

Dialect differences.   Dialect differences appear to pose a greater problem in theory to the design of new orthographies than they do in practice. In English, for example, there is no evidence that dialect differences themselves are a barrier to learning to read. In theory, systematic phonological differences between dialects should have no effect upon orthographic design, assuming that each orthography is to be based upon a single dialect. If all occurrences of phone A in one dialect correspond to phone B in another, then the correspondence rules for the two dialects are isomorphic. If, however, phone A has two reflexes in the second dialect, depending upon environment (or some other feature which native speakers can observe), then the correspondence rules are no longer isomorphic, but are still predictable for both dialects. This is the situation in English for r. In postvocalic positions before consonants and juncture it corresponds to /Ø/ in some dialects; in all other positions it is /r/ uniformly.

Where we might predict reading problems are those cases in which a phone in the dialect on which an orthography is based has two or more reflexes in another dialect and this distribution is not totally predictable. This situation occurs for Upper Midwestern /æ/ which corresponds unpredictably to either /a/ or /æ/ in Eastern New England (compare *mass* and *grass*). But no reading problem has ever been attributed to this misalignment. Dialects, by nature, are characterized by systematic phonological differences. Where major differences do occur, the designer can resort to either a common core representation (which is probably undesirable) or to a different system for each dialect. The actual decision, however, probably will depend more upon political and economic considerations than it will upon linguistic and psychological ones. (On proposals for teaching reading to speakers of black English using a modified orthography, see DeStefano, 1973.)

Experimental design.   Experimental approaches to the formation of new orthographies are difficult to design, due to the nature of the reading task. People who read an orthography well can continue to read that orthography even when it is full of distortions and deletions. English, for example, can be read by competent readers even when all the vowels are deleted or when the bottom halves of the letters are covered over (see Anderson and Dearborn, 1952). The illiterate, on the other hand, if he is truly an unbiased subject, is not only unfamiliar with letter forms, but does not know yet that he can relate them to sounds and words which he already produces. It is both laborious and expensive to obtain his preferences, or to test his learning rate for alternate writing systems. The few attempts to study orthographic design experimentally have concentrated on the preferences or performances of adult literates. Walker (1969) cites an experiment in which speakers of Zuni indicated their spelling preferences on a multiple choice test for Zuni words which an experimenter dictated. Although there were systematic preferences for some nonphonemic spellings, all subjects were literate in English and therefore English spelling conventions could have biased the results. Furthermore, even if these results could be shown to be valid for spelling preferences, they could not automatically be assumed to represent reading preferences, especially since they were derived from words in isolation. Rabin (1968) reports a comparison of alternate forms for spelling Hebrew, using reading rates and comprehension of seventh grade pupils as dependent measures. As would be expected from an inspection of the two writing systems, no significant differences were found between them for either measure.

It is doubtful that much of pedagogical importance could be gained from such limited studies except in the extreme situation in which a particular orthography is so cumbersome as to inhibit its use—and this fact could be learned from inspection alone. The utility of a new orthography will generally depend upon the way it is used, that is, upon the extent to which it is incorporated into sound instructional methodology, the prestige rendered it within (and from without) its cultural setting, the extent to which it is used in newspapers, literature, and official documents, and the interest which members of the culture display in learning it. Its composition will have considerably less influence.

The role of orthography in reading.   After almost one hundred years of experimental work on the reading process, most major problems related to reading remain unsolved, including the roles of orthography in literacy acquisition and in competent reading. In learning to read with alphabetic writing systems, beginners form letter-sound generalizations regardless of the mode of initial instruction (Calfee, Venezky, and Chapman, 1969; Johnson, 1970; Venezky, 1973). Furthermore, recent studies have shown that by the end of the second or third grade American children have already acquired a sense of the patterning of English spelling, as evidenced by their differential responses to synthetic words which do or do not follow English spelling rules (Rosinski and Wheeler, 1972). However, letter-sound correspondences have at best a marginal value for the accomplished reader, being called upon only when unfamiliar words are encountered—and often not even then. Nevertheless, several different word recognition models have been postulated recently in which letter-sound generalizations are applied internally to facilitate recognition (Gough, 1972; Rubenstein, Lewis, and Rubenstein, 1971; Smith and Spoehr, 1973). Support for these models is inferred from studies of the recognition of isolated words, but in no case has any serious attention been given to the number and types of rules which are required for such a process to be possible. More extensive criticisms of these models are given in Massaro (1975). For oral reading, it is highly unlikely that natural fluency could ever be achieved through letter-by-letter reading. Instead, it appears that words (or short phrases) in context are perceived as whole units, and that pronunciations are generated from stored patterns, as in speaking. For some languages, smooth letter-by-letter reading is conceivable, but still highly unlikely. For English, due to the relatively high unpredictability of vowel pronunciations and stress placement, it is probably impossible.

What function, then, do letter-sound correspondences serve in learning to read or in reading? The simplest answer, although still speculative, appears to be that they are essential reinforcers for acquiring word-recognition abilities. The child who cannot "sound out" a word must depend for evaluation of his oral reading upon contextual fit, which is not always reliable, or upon other readers, who are not always available. But the child who can apply letter-sound correspondences has an independent test of his recognition ability. Besides using context, he can check what he thinks a word is from visual recognition against the pronunciation he generates from its spelling. For beginning readers, word recognition and letter-sound encoding probably are applied together, proceeding in parallel until a positive identification is made. The net result of using letter-sound correspondences is not just an increase in correct feedback, but also an increase in motivation.

It is assumed here that the beginning reader can apply three different strategies in reading words within sentences: whole word recognition; prediction from context; and generation of pronunciation from spelling. Reports on reading errors of first grade children (Biemiller, 1970; Weber, 1970) show that at least the first two of these strategies are operative; whether letter-sound generalizations are being used or not at this level is difficult to determine from reading error reports, since a distinction between word recognition errors and letter-sound generalization errors is often difficult to make. If, for example, *want* is given in response to *went*, we would not know if *went* as a unitary item was misperceived as *want*, or if, in letter-by-letter pronunciation, an inappropriate pronunciation was given to *a*. Other studies show that substitution errors in reading connected discourse most often approximate the visual form of the stimuli through age seven, but by age nine are more often appropriate for the meaning of the sentences than they are visually similar to the stimuli. Weber (1970) found that approximately 90 percent of the misreadings of both good and poor readers were appropriate for the preceding grammatical context. Weber also found an inverse relationship between the use of graphic cues and the use of syntactic cues by beginning readers. Biemiller (1970) found that syntactic/semantic cues are used earlier than visual cues. (But see Barr, 1972, for an alternate interpretation of Biemiller's data.)

The interrelationship among the three identification strategies depends upon the abilities of the reader, the reading task (for example, oral reading vs. silent reading for general meaning), and the difficulty of the material. Word identification and letter-sound generation appear to be more closely related to each other than either is to prediction by context. The latter skill may be used as a prompter and a check on the results of applying the other two strategies.

A second use of letter-sound generalization is in generating the pronunciation of a word not encountered before in print, but which may be in the reader's listening vocabulary. For either this function or the one just mentioned, perfectly predictable correspondences are not necessary because in both situations the reader has other cues to work with; the pronunciation of the printed form need only approximate the actual pronunciation for the appropriate match to be made. For example, in the sentence *The cowboy ran the horse into the street*, the word *ran* may, if not recognized correctly by sight or context, be pronounced /ren/ initially; however, if the reader is aware of the preceding context (and speaks a standard brand of English), he will probably recognize that this is not the correct form and try another pronunciation. Observations of children in oral reading show exactly this process at work. Without the ability to approximate sound from spelling, the child would be dependent upon other readers for substantiating his word identifications, and consequently, would develop this ability quite slowly.

The reliance on letter-sound generalizations in word recognition slowly decreases as word identification ability increases. The competent reader probably makes little use of such generalizations in normal reading. Nevertheless, the ability to apply letter-sound generalizations continues to develop at least through the eighth grade. Whether this development is due to a continual reliance upon sounding out words or results from increasingly more efficient use of memory is not known. But since the use of letter-sound generalizations appears to depend heavily upon examples stored in memory, organization and retrieval probably account for a significant part of the development.

Acquisition of Specific Letter-Sound Patterns

The acquisition of specific letter-sound patterns has been studied recently by means of pronunciations which subjects give to synthetic (nonsense) words which are constructed on the basis of specific spelling patterns. Calfee, Venezky, and Chapman (1969) compared responses to synthetic words of second, fourth, sixth, and eighth graders, high school juniors, and college undergraduates. Major differences were noted between the long-short vowel patterns and the *c* patterns, in that the long and short patterns were well learned by sixth grade but *c* patterns showed a strong bias for the /k/ pronunciation well into high school. Good readers and poor readers differed both in their overall response accuracy and in the relative percentages of wild (that is, nonoccurring) responses. Johnson (1970) compared first, second, and third graders' responses to digraph vowels, using synthetic words as stimulus items. By the end of the first grade most children in this study were capable of generating plausible responses to synthetic words from their spellings. For digraph vowel spellings in which the type counts predicted different pronunciation rankings from the token counts, the responses tended to agree with the type count predictions.

Venezky, Chapman, and Calfee (1972) extended the earlier Calfee, Venezky, and Chapman (1969) study to a larger subject population and to a more extensive testing of each pattern. The results of this study form the basis of the summary which follows.

The different pronunciations for the letter *c* are among the most predictable in English orthography; yet in spite of this predictability correct generalization of the *c* pattern develops slowly through the elementary grades and seldom approaches the theoretical level of predictability. The correct responses for *c* in initial and medial position before *a, o, u,* and in final position are well learned by sixth grade (92 percent, 86 percent, and 82 percent, respectively), but the responses to initial and medial *c* before *e, i,* and *y* are correct in only 50 percent and 64 percent respectively of their occurrences at this same grade level. Initial *c* before *a, o,* and *u* shows the highest percentage of correct responses, progressing from about 82 percent in second grade to almost 92 percent by sixth grade. Initial *c* before *i, e,* and *y,* on the other hand, shows the lowest percentage of correct responses, advancing from about 22 percent in second grade to 59 percent in sixth grade.

Equally revealing about responses strategies are the errors which are made in pronouncing the letter *c,* particularly for initial *c* before *e, i,* and *y* where the correct (/s/) plus plausible (/k/) pronunciations account for almost 88 percent of the responses in the second grade and progress to about 96 percent of the responses by sixth grade. That these percentages are quite high, and are nearly identical for *a, o, u,* and *e, i, y* even in the second grade where there is a significant difference between correct responses for the two patterns, indicates that the range of plausible responses for *c* is learned early, but that the /k/ pronunciation is so dominant that it persists for *c* before *e, i,* and *y* past the fourth grade. If the subjects were attempting to apply the appropriate rule, we would expect a greater similarity between the correct response totals for the two patterns. Instead, it appears that a single response, /k/, is available for all occurrences of initial *c*, and only slowly gives way to /s/ for *c* before *e*, *i*, or *y*. A possible reason for this response bias is that words with initial *c* before *e*, *i*, and *y* are rarely introduced in reading lessons until after the time when emphasis is given to letters and sounds. In part, this results from the distribution of *c* pronunciations in the English vocabulary; among the more common words, few have initial *c* before *e*, *i*, or *y* and most of these, by tradition, are proscribed from readers before the fourth grade.

The *g* patterns are theoretically similar to the *c* patterns in that both behave differently before high- and mid-front vowels than they do in any other environment. However, in initial position the exceptions to the *g* pattern among common words (for example, *get*, *gift*, *give*) outnumber the examples. For medial position, the exceptions are restricted to *-ger* forms (*anger*, *finger*, *tiger*, etc.) plus a few miscellaneous items (for example, *begin*, *target*, *bogey*). In responses to synthetic words, /ǰ/ pronunciations before *i* and *e*, even at college level, are relatively infrequent in initial position and exceed 50 percent for medial position only at the college level. The percentages correct when /g/ is the correct response are nearly identical to the corresponding *c* responses when /k/ is correct. The low number of correct responses through college for *g* before *e* and *i*, particularly in initial position, suggests that examples are more influential than verbalization of rules for *g* pronunciations. If a generalization for *g* before *e* or *i* is to be taught, then a suitable pool of examples will be required, but these examples cannot be introduced under present attitudes toward grade-level vocabulary until the higher primary grades, and at these levels letter-sound generalizations are rarely stressed. Even under ideal circumstances, it is not evident that this generalization merits any attention. From the child's standpoint, it may be easier to learn that *g* is pronounced /g/, except for words in a certain list (for example, *gem*, *general*, *genius*, *giant*) than to have a more complex rule with an equally long list of exceptions.

Free and checked vowel patterns show the steepest improvements between second and fourth grades, but continue to improve through the sixth grade where both receive over 85 percent correct responses. The lack of an appreciable difference between correct responses for free and checked vowels is surprising in that the checked vowels are usually introduced first in the reading program. Of special interest is the contrast between the development of these patterns and the *c* patterns. Both involve two major pronunciations which can be predicted on the basis of the following graphemes. Furthermore, in both one pronunciation is usually introduced first in the teaching of reading and learned to a high criterion level before the second pronunciation is exposed. Yet there are major differences in what is actually learned. For c, there is a strong bias toward the pronunciation introduced first (/k/), yielding a high percentage of correct responses in second grade for c before a, o, and u, but a low percentage of correct responses at the same level when e, i, or y follows. The most significant improvement in the c pronunciations involves a gain in /s/ at the expense of /k/, the percentage of correct-plus-plausible responses showing little gain.

For the checked and free vowels, on the other hand, there are gains in both correct responses and in combined correct-plus-plausible responses for the two different categories. Over this period not just the appropriate responses are learned for each pattern, but so is the range of plausible responses. There is no tendency at the second grade level to assign one pronunciation to both the checked and free environments of each letter. Furthermore, at all grade levels there are more correct responses to the free/checked patterns than there are to c before e, i, and y.

One of the most important distinctions between good and poor readers at the second and fourth grade levels is their responses to invariant consonant spellings (for example, m, n, b). For initial position the lowest quartile is only slightly lower than the highest quartile in percentage of correct responses, but for medial and final positions the differences in performance are large, with the lowest group showing a marked degeneration. That the responses for the lowest quartile for initial position are consistently in the 90 percent range shows that the letter-sound correspondences have been learned. What appears to be lacking is a concern for word details beyond the beginning of the word, a phenomenon also reported by Marchbanks and Levin (1965) for word recognition by kindergarten and first grade children and by Bennett (1942) for oral reading errors of poor readers in the third, fourth, and fifth grades. Whatever the source of the problem—lack of appreciation of detail, low criterion level for identification, or impulsivity—instructional procedures for overcoming it are needed before certain letter-sound relationships can be learned.

Teaching Letter-Sound Patterns

The teaching of letter-sound patterns involves many issues which are beyond the range of applied linguistics. Nevertheless, it would be irresponsible to conclude a paper on orthography and reading without at least mentioning the controversies in which an applied linguist might find himself ensnared if he works on reading.

Almost all modern methods for teaching reading include letter-sound learning somewhere in the teaching sequence, although the amount and exact placement of this training accounts for the central disagreement among methods. Phonics or linguistic programs tend to initiate the teaching procedure with emphasis on letters and sounds, while global or synthetic-analytic methods tend to begin with whole words or phrases, which only at a later stage are analyzed into syllables and unit sounds.

The basic tenet of the phonics school is that since letter-sound relationships are needed in reading, they should be taught from the beginning of reading instruction. The counter argument is not that letter-sound correspondences are unnecessary, but that the beginning reader has difficulty in dealing with such abstractions, and that more efficient learning is achieved by beginning with whole words. (For a different view, see F. Smith, 1971.) Nonsystematic procedures such as those that Bloomfield inveighed against in the 1940s are no longer in the majority. Hence the differences between methods have become more and more reduced to differences in the sequencing of learning as opposed to differences in goals or basic philosophy.

Chall (1967) discusses the various labeled approaches to initial reading instruction, as does Austin (1973). Foremost among those who attribute reading failure to the irregularities of English orthography are the advocates of the Initial Teaching Alphabet (Downing, 1967; Pitman, 1964). Although it is undeniable that some learning difficulties result from the capriciousness of English spelling, neither the errors which poor readers commonly make nor the techniques which tend to succeed in remedial instruction, nor the results of studies with reformed orthographies support the notion that English spelling is a *major* barrier to the acquisition of literacy. Reading errors do not occur more frequently on irregularly spelled words than they do on regularly spelled ones, and children who have difficulties in reading tend to display a wide variety of symptoms, many of which are unrelated to the specifics of letters and sounds. Furthermore, studies in the United States, Israel, and Finland show that the ability to translate letters into sounds does not guarantee good reading comprehension (Venezky, 1976).

If the applied linguist wishes to help in the development of improved reading instruction, he must attend not only to the structure of English orthography (and the English language) as more recently described, but also to such quasi-linguistic factors as frequency of occurrence and utility—factors which only recently have been admitted into linguistic studies. Some interesting work in this direction has been done by Cronnell (1969) in developing letter-sound sequences for teaching reading and by Greenbaum (1974) in discussing the role of frequency in linguistic analysis.

REFERENCES

Anderson, I. H., and Dearborn, W. F. *The psychology of teaching reading.* New York: The Ronald Press, 1952.
Austin, M. United States. In J. Downing, ed., *Comparative reading.* New York: The Macmillan Co., 1973.
Barr, R. C. The influence of instructional conditions on word recognition errors. *Reading Research Quarterly,* 1972, *7,* 509-29.
Baugh, A. C. *A history of the English language,* 2nd ed. New York: Appleton-Century-Crofts, 1957.
Bennett, A. An analysis of errors in word recognition made by retarded readers. *Journal of Educational Psychology,* 1942, *33,* 25-38.
Biemiller, A. The development of the use of graphic and contextual information as children learn to read. *Reading Research Quarterly,* 1970, *6,* 75-96.
Bloomfield, L. Linguistics and reading. *Elementary English Review,* 1942, *19,* 125-30, 183-86.
Bloomfield, L., and Barnhart, C. L. *Let's read.* Detroit: Wayne State Press, 1961.
Bond, G. L., and Dykstra, R. The cooperative research program in first grade reading instruction. *Reading Research Quarterly,* 1967, *2,* 5-142.
Burns, D. Social and political implications of the choice of an orthography. *Fundamental and Adult Education,* 1953, *5,* 80-85.
Calfee, R., Venezky, R., and Chapman, R. Pronunciation of synthetic words with predictable and unpredictable letter-sound correspondences. *Technical Report No. 71,* Madison, Wisconsin: Wisconsin Research and Development Center for Cognitive Learning, 1969.
Chall, J. *Learning to read: The great debate.* New York: McGraw-Hill, 1967.
Chomsky, N., and Morris, H. *The sound pattern of English.* New York: Harper and Row, 1968.
Cronnell, B. Annotated spelling-to-sound correspondence rules. *Research Memorandum,* Southwest Regional Laboratory, 1969.
Daunt, M. Old English sound-changes reconsidered in relation to scribal tradition and practice. *Trans. Philological Society,* 1939, 108-37.
DeFrancis, J. *Nationalism and language reform in China.* Princeton: Princeton University Press, 1950.
DeStefano, J. S. *Language, society, and education.* Worthington, Ohio: Charles A. Jones Publishing Co., 1973.
Downing, J. A. *Evaluating the initial teaching alphabet.* London: Cassell, 1967.
Fries, C. C. *Linguistics and reading.* New York: Holt, Rinehart and Winston, 1962.
Gough, P. B. One second of reading. In J. F. Kavanagh and I. G. Mattingly, eds., *Language by ear and by eye.* Cambridge, Massachusetts: M.I.T. Press, 1972.

Greenbaum, S. Frequency and acceptability. Unpublished manuscript, Department of English, University of Wisconsin, Milwaukee, 1974.

Gudschinsky, S. *Handbook of literacy*. Norman, Oklahoma: Summer Institute of Linguistics, 1953.

———. Recent trends in primer instruction. *Fundamental and Adult Education*, 1959, *6*, 67-96.

Hockett, C. Review of John DeFrancis's, *Nationalism and language reform in China*. *Language*, 1951, *27*, 439-45.

———. The stressed syllabics of Old English. *Language*, 1959, *35*, 575-97.

———. Analysis of English spelling. In H. Levin, et al., eds., *A basic research program on reading*. Ithaca, N. Y.: Cornell University, 1963.

Huey, E. B. *The psychology and pedagogy of reading*. New York: The Macmillan Co., 1908. (Reprinted, with an introduction by Paul A. Kolers, Cambridge: M.I.T. Press, 1968.)

International African Institute. *Practical orthography of African languages*. Memorandum I. London: Oxford University Press, 1930.

Johnson, D. Factors related to the pronunciation of vowel clusters. *Technical Report No. 149*, Madison, Wisconsin: Wisconsin Research and Development Center for Cognitive Learning, 1970.

Jones, D. *The phoneme*. Cambridge, England: W. Heffer and Sons, Ltd., 1950.

Kurath, H. *A phonology and prosody of Modern English*. Ann Arbor: University of Michigan Press, 1964.

Lepsius, C. R. *Standard orthography for reducing unwritten languages and foreign graphic systems to a uniform orthography in European letters*, 2nd ed. London and Berlin, 1855.

McIntosh, A. The analysis of written Middle English. *Transactions of the Philological Society*, 1956, 26-55.

Marchbanks, G., and Levin, H. Cues by which children recognize words. *Journal of Educational Psychology*, 1965, *56*, 57-61.

Massaro, D., ed. *Understanding language*. New York: Academic Press, 1975.

Meinhof, C. Principles of practical orthography for African languages. *Africa*, 1928, *1*, 228-39.

Nida, E. Practical limitations to a phonemic alphabet. *The Bible Translator*, 1954, *15*, 35-39, 58-62.

Oswalt, R. L. English orthography as a morphophonemic system: Stressed vowels. *Linguistics*, 1973, 102 ff.

Pike, K. L. *Phonemics: A technique for reducing language to writing*. Ann Arbor: University of Michigan Press, 1947.

Pitman, Sir J. The future of the teaching of reading. In A. E. Traxler, ed., *Keeping abreast of the revolution in education*. Washington, D. C.: American Council on Education, 1964.

Rabin, C. *The influence of different systems of Hebrew orthography on reading efficiency*. Jerusalem: The Israel Institute of Applied Social Research, 1968.

Rosinski, R. R., and Wheeler, K. E. Children's use of orthographic structure in word discriminations. *Psychonomic Science*, 1972, *26*, 97-98.

Rubenstein, H., Lewis, S. S., and Rubenstein, M. A. Evidence for phonemic recoding in visual word recognition. *Journal of Verbal Learning and Verbal Behavior*, 1971, *10*, 645-57.

Sjoberg, A. F. The development of writing systems for preliterate peoples. In W. Bright, ed., *Sociolinguistics: Proceedings of the UCLA Sociolinguistics Conference*, 1964. The Hague: Mouton, 1966.

Smith, E. E., and Spoehr, K. T. The perception of printed English: A theoretical perspective. In B. H. Kantowitz, ed., *Human information processing: Tutorials in performance and cognition*. Potomac: Erlbaum Press, 1974.

Smith, F. *Understanding reading*. New York: Holt, Rinehart and Winston, 1971.

Smith, H. L. *Linguistic science and the teaching of reading*. Cambridge, Mass.: Harvard University Press, 1956.

Stockwell, R., and Barrett, C. W. Scribal practice: Some assumptions. *Language*, 1961, *37*, 75-82.

Vachek, J. Two chapters on written English. In *Brno Studies in English*, 1959, *1*, 7-34. Praha: Atatni Pedagogicke Nakladatelstvi.

———. *Written language*. The Hague: Mouton, 1973.

Venezky, R. L. A study of English spelling-to-sound correspondences on historical principles. Ph.D. dissertation, Stanford University, 1965.

———. English orthography: Its graphical structure and its relation to sound. *Reading Research Quarterly*, 1967, *2*, 75-106.

———. *The structure of English orthography*. The Hague: Mouton, 1970.

———. Letter-sound generalizations of first-, second-, and third-grade Finnish children. *Journal of Educational Psychology*, 1973, *64*, 288-92.

———. Language and cognition in reading. In B. Spolsky, ed., *Current trends in educational linguistics*. The Hague: Mouton, 1976.

Venezky, R. L., Chapman, R. S., and Calfee, R. C. The development of letter-sound generalizations from second through sixth grade. *Technical Report No. 231*, Madison, Wisconsin: Wisconsin Research and Development Center for Cognitive Learning, 1972.

Walker, W. Notes on native writing systems and the design of native literacy programs. *Anthropological Linguistics*, 1969, *11*, 148-66.

Wardhaugh, R. Linguistic insights into the reading process. *Language Learning*, 1968, *18*, 235-52.

Weber, R-M. First graders' use of grammatical context in reading. In H. Levin and J. Williams, eds., *Basic studies in reading*. New York: Harper and Row, 1970.

Westerman, D. The linguistic situation and vernacular literature in British West Africa. *Africa*, 1929, *2*, 337-51.

Wijk, A. *Rules of pronunciation for the English language*. London: Oxford University Press, 1966.

Wrenn, C. L. The value of spelling as evidence. *Trans. Philological Society*, 1943, 14 ff.

Zachrisson, R. *Anglic, a new agreed simplified English spelling*. Uppsala: Anglic Fund, 1930.

———. Four hundred years of English spelling reform. *Studia Neophilologica*, 1931, *4*, 1-69.

V

Reading

Rose-Marie Weber

The serious study of language is as relevant to how people grasp messages from print as it is to how they grasp them out of thin air. The differences that follow from their using the eyes instead of the ears are made small by the common factor that people bring into play as they read or listen—their knowledge of how language is organized to express meaning. Too often descriptions of reading have reflected a shallow notion of what a competent reader must do in order to reconstruct the message of the writer. They tend to suggest that reading is no more than identifying words one by one and fail to take into account the knowledge of linguistic structure that readers must surely bring to bear in making sense of even the simplest sentences. The basic contribution of linguistics to the understanding of reading has been to make evident that it is the complex of abstract linguistic categories and relations shared by writers and readers that constitutes the communicative power behind print.

Beyond this fundamental contribution, contemporary language study has lent a substantial dimension to current thinking about what reading is and how reading skills are learned (Smith, 1973; Wardhaugh, 1969; Weber, 1973). Many psychologists and educators have incorporated findings from linguistics into their studies of the abilities of skilled readers and the strategies of beginners. To be more specific, the detailed description of written language, particularly the spelling system of English, has provided the basis for characterizing what must be mastered by a person learning to read, especially at age six or so when formal reading instruction usually begins. An understanding of the principles that guide sentence formation and place limitations on acceptable strings of words and letters has led to informed hypotheses on the use to which readers put their knowledge of their language in reading the words, sentences, and texts that they encounter. A comparison of speech and writing has raised questions about how hearing and skilled reading might be similar yet different in other than obvious ways. The study of language acquisition, revealing the construction of rule systems by young children, has invited comparison with reading acquisition. Today, this range of interest has come to be called the psycholinguistics of reading; it is an area of spirited discussion and exploration.

Linguistics has also contributed to thinking about how reading should be taught, an area of more stubborn conviction. Some educators and linguists have not only drawn implications from linguistic study for introducing children to reading, but they have gone on to design and implement specific programs of instruction with these implications in mind. Their persistence in finding regularities between the language and the writing system and their insistence that these regularities should be made accessible through direct teaching have been strongly felt in reading education. In another vein, linguists' appreciation of multilingualism, dialects, and style have moved them to examine reading difficulties with respect to linguistic variation and to propose methods of reading instruction which take such variation into account. Perhaps most important to the climate of reading instruction today, however, is the basic notion that children, even though illiterate, already know a great deal about getting meaning from print by virtue of knowing how to make sense of speech.

This chapter will touch on these subjects as it examines how the results of language study have been incorporated into efforts to understand reading and to improve reading instruction. It will not, however, deal with several other related topics that nevertheless deserve passing mention. First of all, it will not discuss reading in languages other than English. The questions raised invite comparisons with conditions presented by other writing systems and traditions, alphabetic and nonalphabetic, but they have not been systematically pursued. It seems safe to assume, though, that once reading is well under control, the nature of the writing system has little influence on how it is done. Secondly, this chapter will deal almost exclusively with the reading of children at the beginning stages of learning and that of highly skilled adults. This limitation reflects the state of thinking about reading as influenced by linguistics. At this point, relatively little consideration has been paid to the development of reading during the elementary school years. Sometimes reading acquisition is referred to as though there were a sharp dividing line between not knowing how to read at all and knowing all there is to know. It should be kept in mind that even the most apt children take a long time to develop reading ease and speed congruent with their intellectual growth and linguistic maturity. Psycholinguistics has also neglected the capacities that adults learning to read or wanting to refine their skills bring to bear on the task, although there is a great need to complement the practical experience that teachers of adult education have accumulated here and abroad. Finally, this chapter will refrain from reporting on the principles that have guided linguists as they have worked on the creation and standardization of writing systems, the establishment of written traditions, and the fostering of literacy education in communities around the world.

The Distinctiveness of Written Language

Linguists apply their energies to describing the workings of a language in order to specify what speakers must control in order to understand and speak. Their goal is to capture the basic principles that speakers follow in constructing and comprehending sentences and passages of text that are considered correctly formed, that make sense, and that are appropriate to the social settings in which they are uttered. In examining written language, they have found, of course, that the principles which guide its use diverge somewhat from those of spoken language. In the history of languages, as in the history of individuals, acquisition of the spoken variety precedes acquisition of the written. Any similarities between the written and spoken varieties arise from the fact that one is derived from the other. Many of the differences which must be mastered by the person aspiring to literacy follow from the special qualities of writing itself.

The essential quality of the written language, of course, is its semipermanence, which makes the expression of sentiments, reports, instructions, and the like accessible to potential readers (including writers themselves) through long periods of time and over wide distances. Unlike speech, which normally requires some sort of social engagement among participants on the spot, the reading of a message does not ordinarily take place in the same social context as its writing.

By and large, writing is expected to conform to rather specific standards of spelling, neatness, and composition, and to show no signs of editing. Removed from social engagement with readers, writers can reflect on their intentions, hesitate, and revise their texts to meet these standards. Texts are expected to be more or less complete and coherent since they do not depend on features in the setting or on the feedback of their audience for their development, as many speech acts do. Rather specific means for drawing together strands of meaning explicitly and compactly through a discourse are important to maintaining coherence. For instance, referents to terms like *it* and *this* must occur within the text unambiguously, and hierarchies of general and supportive remarks demand more deliberate marking by conjunctive phrases such as *to be more specific* and *for example* than they do in speech. Because they encompass their own world of time and space, texts often include devices to establish context, such as introductions and the headings of letters. Although the syntax of writing conforms closely to that of the spoken language, some forms have developed that are peculiar to written language, such as labels and instructions on objects (*Keep out of reach of children*), dictionary entries, and application forms. Another aspect of written language worth noting is that its varieties tend to be a notch higher on a scale of formality than spoken varieties in the choice of vocabulary and the construction of sentences; compare a letter of complaint to a telephone call with the same purpose. It is conventions such as these which must be mastered if readers are to take full advantage of the written means for expressing meaning.

Learning to read also entails, of course, getting to know the principles by which the language is represented in letters rather than in the acoustic smear of speech. Although the English writing system has more or less direct correspondences to the phonological system, it too leads an existence somewhat independent of the spoken variety, especially after a history of more than a thousand years. Basically a letter in writing corresponds to a sound segment in the spoken language; however, features of letters, such as ascenders, correspond only mildly to sound features. It is easy to demonstrate necessary qualifications to the sound-letter principle by pointing to discrepancies between the number of sound segments and the number of letters in the representation of a word and to collate examples of sounds that are represented in spelling in more than one way. Such an analysis would certainly show incontrovertible irregularities and arbitrariness. However, an analysis of the writing system which takes into account the identity of morphemes and their phonological representations more abstract than phonetic segments reveals broader patterns of relationships than letter to sound. It shows that an important principle at work in the system is that a morpheme is generally represented by the same string of letters, although there may be significant variation in the phonetic representation of the morpheme. The variation may arise by virtue of a morpheme's occurrence in different words, such as *politic-* in *politic(s)*, *political*, and *politicize*, where the qualities of stress, vowel, and the final consonant differ; in syntactic structures, such as *He can really play* in contrast to *He sure can*, where the stress and vowels of *can* differ; and in various styles and dialects which may, for instance, differ in the pronunciation of postvocalic *r* in words like *far*. The writing system thus bypasses some phonological detail and represents meanings in a more direct way. Within the framework of generative phonology, it has been proposed that the spelling system relates most closely to the underlying phonological representation to which phonological rules are subsequently applied (Chomsky, 1970). Another principle at work in the writing system, although not as consistent, is that morphemes that sound alike are kept apart in writing by differences in spelling, for example, *pair*, *pare*, and *pear* or *sole*, *soul*, *Seoul*, and sometimes *sold*.

Still further analysis of the writing system shows a set of principles with respect to letters that have no counterparts in the sound system yet are almost certainly significant in reading. An important one in English is the doubling of consonant letters under certain circumstances after lax vowels so that *hopped/hoped* and *shinny/shiny* are distinguished. Another is the set of distributional constraints on certain letters and letter clusters. Although these constraints tend to be congruent with constraints in the phonology, there are many independent ones. For instance, *-dge* corresponding to /ǰ/ is restricted to morpheme final position, while *j* corresponding to the same sound never occurs finally in morphemes.

A comparison of spoken and written varieties of a language leads to the conclusion that when language is set down on paper it takes on a rather separate identity, follows different principles for the organization of texts, and serves different functions from its spoken counterpart. Reading requires knowledge of special conventions to exploit the meaning behind print. Learning to read entails extending one's linguistic competence to assimilate messages in slightly different form from the way that they arrive in speech.

Fluent Reading

Psychologists undertake the study of reading with the principal aim of specifying the intricacies of the operations that readers carry out in deriving meaning from print (Gibson and Levin, 1975; Kavanagh and Mattingly, 1972; Levin and Williams, 1970; Smith, 1971). Since reading involves vision, memory, the identification of language, and the integration of linguistic and general knowledge, it presents a significant challenge to a discipline concerned with the exploration and appreciation of human mental capacities. On the other hand, since the teaching of reading is a responsibility assumed by our formal education system, study is also motivated by the desire to provide the best possible foundations for educational practice.

Investigators find it useful to think of reading as a way of processing information. Accordingly, some of them construct models of the process, often displayed as flow diagrams intended to specify in a comprehensive way the multiplicity of perceptual and cognitive operations that readers must carry out. The tentative nature of these attempts must be emphasized: they call on differing experimental evidence and interpretations for support; they are pure invention in places; and they are deficient in various respects, for example, in failing to take into account the different strategies that readers might apply over a wide range of reading tasks, from checking a grocery list to reading philosophy in a foreign language. Nevertheless, they provide a valuable frame of reference for analyzing and raising questions about the various processes that come into play in reading (for examples, see Geyer, 1972; Gough, 1972; Smith, 1971).

The information-processing models differ in details, yet all seek to take into account and relate three main aspects of reading: scanning, word identification, and comprehension. During fluent reading, the eyes sweep quickly across a page from one point to another, fixating at each point for about one-quarter of a second. The visual information that is extracted at each fixation is stored for at least another one-quarter of a second and is subjected to very rapid analysis while the eyes move on. Such analysis consists in classifying and relating the visual information to background knowledge of the written representation of words so as to derive lexical meaning from what is seen, either directly or through the intermediate step of assigning it a phonological representation. For comprehension to take place, the meaning of the individual words must be remembered and integrated into the grammatical and semantic organization of the text (a process so mysterious that it has been dubbed "Merlin"), and the results related to general knowledge about the world and specific knowledge about the subject at hand. Some models propose the continuous prediction of subsequent information on the basis of preceding analysis and include a step for checking on the validity of the prediction by comparing it with a sampling of new information—a process called analysis-by-synthesis. If the task is oral reading, a further step of converting the derived information into speech is necessary. All of these activities demand exquisite coordination, since new material is being scanned while old material is at various stages of being stored, identified, and comprehended.

These models—and criticisms of them (Gibson and Levin, 1975)—are proposed on the basis of answers to questions that investigators have explored in laboratory settings, interpreted in the light of current linguistic and psychological theory, and qualified by serious introspection. The questions are very specific ones: how long do readers take to do this task and how accurate are they? But they are posed carefully to provide evidence one way or another for a characterization of the processes that reading subsumes. In the laboratory readers are presented with carefully controlled materials, for example, nonsense words in contrast to real words or sentences with identical surface structures but different deep structures. The material to be read is often presented in special ways, for example, exposed for only a fraction of a second or transformed so that the letters are perversely upside down or backwards. The point, of course, is to manipulate the situation in such a way that readers' strategies for dealing with print are laid bare. The general assumption is that the experiments capture the activities that readers use in ordinary situations. But psychologists are acutely aware that skilled readers adjust their strategies as they peruse newspapers, figure out bills, study technical manuals, and even participate in reading experiments.

An important type of inquiry in the study of reading, complementing the work on visual processes, memory, and word identification, has been the examination of how readers use their knowledge of linguistic structure to derive meaning from print. The focus of much of this work has been on syntax as one aspect of the meaning of sentences. There is substantial evidence that readers expect the sentences that they encounter will make sense and that they will be grammatical. An analysis of readers' errors is particularly instructive (Kolers, 1970). Subjects presented with texts whose letters and lines have been reversed and otherwise transformed make many substitutions for the words on the page. These errors consistently conform to the grammatical structure of the preceding part of the sentence in which they occur. For example, the sentence *He said to throw it away* might produce errors that fit the sentence such as *He said to throttle. . .* or *think* or even *them*, but not *He said to though* or *threw*. These kinds of responses reveal that readers use their knowledge of syntax to narrow down the identity of subsequent items in a sentence.

This knowledge also impinges on readers' visual strategies. The more contextual information that they can apply, the less visual information they need to pick up from a page. This is shown most clearly by the finding that it takes readers less time—measured in fractions of a second—to identify a word in the context of a sentence than standing alone (Tulving and Gold, 1963). Furthermore, they give less visual attention to grammatical structures that are more highly constrained or expected by virtue of syntactic rules and common usage. Speakers report that they expect to find relative clauses modifying object noun phrases (*The librarian liked the kid that*

Stan brought) more frequently than such clauses modifying subject-noun phrases (*The kid that Stan brought hated the librarian*) and that passive sentences with agents introduced by *by* (*The wood was dragged by the horse*) are more "natural" than the same surface structures without agents (*The wood was dragged by the house*). These expectations are reflected in the findings that as subjects read, they move through the more expected structures faster, as shown by studies of oral reading and of eye fixations (Levin and Kaplan, 1970; Wanat, 1971). It is not unreasonable to suppose that fluent readers have a highly developed skill for picking up the minimum visual information needed to serve their purposes.

Readers' application of their knowledge of the language is also brought into play in the identification of individual words. They do not examine them letter by letter unless that is their purpose, as in proofreading. The relevant evidence includes the findings that readers can identify words under conditions in which they cannot identify the component letters, they have difficulty identifying words if the letters are presented one at a time, they can identify whole words about as quickly as single letters, and, in general, they move through passages too quickly to identify each detail (Smith, 1973). The much-disputed question of how words are identified is not at issue here. Rather, the point is that in order for readers to avoid identifying every letter, they must certainly use their knowledge of the constraints on letter strings (perhaps more accurately, feature strings) and their frequencies as they read. They take advantage of the fact that not all letters have the same probability of occurrence after one another. They know, for example, that *th-*, *ta-*, *tr-* and *ty-* are possible in English but occur with different frequencies; however, *-tp-*, *-tm-*, *-td-* and *-tl-* occur only across morpheme boundaries. Some of these possible strings, of course, are peculiar to the written language, but they closely reflect the constraints in the spoken language. Readers also know that not all possible English strings of letters constitute real words; consequently, they can exploit the redundancy in the representation of words and disregard some graphic detail with impunity.

Among the recurrent questions that remain unsettled in the study of reading is the extent to which reading and listening are identical. Because spoken and written language conform to the same basic principles of organization, it is reasonable to suppose that reading involves the same linguistic processes as listening. In fact, it is easy to suppose that reading is a matter of transposing writing to speech—perhaps silent speech—and letting the language capacities for getting meaning from speech take over. The evidence to support this position includes the reports of skilled readers that it is the "voice in the head" that allows them to pick up special sound effects in texts, such as puns, rhymes, or awkward prose. Related experiments as well as studies of movements of the speech musculature during reading—which can be suppressed—provide further support that readers construct an inner sound representation while reading silently (Mattingly, 1972). A modified position here is that readers do take advantage of the phonological system, but bypass the phonetic level and directly represent the sentences in an abstract phonological form (Gough, 1972). A counter position holds that although readers can mediate word identification by sound, they do not have to. The main argument here is that at the rate that they move through extended texts—500 words a minute with excellent comprehension—they simply do not have time to "say" words to themselves. Rather, words must be identified directly by virtue of their letter or feature patterns as linguistic entities without relation to their sound. If they are "said" internally, it is only after they have been identified and understood (Smith, 1971). The relatively abstract spelling of English lends itself to such direct identification. The findings here are inconclusive, yet the issue is central to determining the degree to which reading is an ability independent of the ability to understand speech.

The detailed study of reading has led to a conception of fluent reading which recognizes readers' application of their linguistic abilities in the strategies they employ to derive meaning from print. It has helped to shape the view that they bring to bear not only knowledge of the world and of the subject and a particular purpose, but also expectations of the way texts are organized and specific principles for interpreting the linguistic structure that they meet. Along with these they bring their knowledge of the redundancy in the language so that they look at the letters and apply a minimum of effort. Therefore, it is clear that only a small part of the information necessary for reading with understanding comes from the printed page.

Children and Learning to Read

Developmental and educational psychologists approach the study of learning to read from two directions. On the one hand, they examine the process in and of itself and they also look at it for what it reveals about psychological growth. In this respect, the acquisition of reading skill exemplifies how children can exploit and extend their abilities to marshall attention, abstract sames from differing events, filter out irrelevancies, construct rule systems, and apply linguistic knowledge (Gibson and Levin, 1975). On the other hand, psychologists study the process in relation to questions of instruction, specifically the planning and testing of given teaching programs for their assumptions, content, sequencing, and effectiveness (Ruddell, 1974). A particular concern is the search for ways to prevent and deal with the failure of many children to learn to read with ease.

It is important to note that it is quite reasonable to examine the emergence of reading abilities in children apart from the instruction that they might have received. For one thing, many children—and not necessarily gifted ones—learn to read on their own with only casual clues from their elders. Furthermore, it is clear that much of the learning involved is not addressed at all in teaching, or is touched on in only a perfunctory way. For example, since what is really significant to the identification of words remains elusive, it is impossible to teach children a precise strategy for rapid word identification. On the other hand, much in current instruction intended to facilitate learning to read may engage children in empty exercise. It may be possible, as some believe, that the time taken to present explicitly the detailed correspondence between sounds and letters is time taken from giving children the opportunities to construct their own strategies for identifying words.

At around age six, when reading instruction usually begins, children are very much in control of the language spoken in their community, with the exception of some refinements. In general, their sentences conform to adults' norms of grammaticality and seem adequate to express their intentions, but they do not include certain complex and infrequent types, as exemplified by *She didn't drive, nor did she care to*; *Swinging on the vine, he lost his grip*. The vocabulary of six-year olds extends well into the thousands of words and continues to grow rapidly. However, they may not control all of the grammatical characteristics of the words they do know. For example, even though they understand the meaning of *promise* and a sentence like *Stan promised to write*, they may pass over the intricacies of the complement construction in a sentence like *Stan promised Mary to write*, identifying Mary as the one who will do the writing (Chomsky, 1969). With respect to phonology, children by the age of six control not only the refinements of consonant and vowel articulation, but sentence stress, intonation, timing, and some stylistic variation as well. But they still lack, in large part, the sets of derived multisyllabic words that reflect abstract phonological relations, such as *biography/biographical*; *democratic/democracy*; *televize/television*. It is reasonable to suppose that children's growth in vocabulary, syntax, and phonological complexity comes about in part as a result of their experience with written language. Nevertheless, six-year olds have a strong foundation on which to begin learning how to read. In fact, an extensive study of the syntax of the spoken language of elementary school children and of the syntax of the written language in their reading texts showed that the children's own sentences were more complex than those in their books (Strickland, 1962).

Research on the acquisition and refinement of reading skills from the perspective of current psycholinguistics is growing. An important issue is whether beginning readers use their knowledge of the language to narrow down the identity of words in sentences. Although some experimental work has been done with children, the principal method employed by investigators has been to observe children reading aloud from familiar materials just as they might routinely do in class. Their errors—sometimes called miscues—are noted and analyzed for what is *right* about them, that is, for how closely they approximate the correct reading, especially with respect to letters, and for how their errors fit into the syntactic and semantic contexts. An error such as *He cold . . .* in a sentence like *He could play* is taken to indicate that a reader is using graphic information, but disregarding the preceding context, since it results in an ungrammatical string. An error such as *wants* for *could* in the sentence is taken to indicate that a reader is using preceding contextual information rather than the graphic display to identify the word. An error such as *came* for *could* is taken to indicate that a reader is using either or both kinds of information. On the basis of large samples of errors, investigators infer the sources of information that readers use in making the errors and therefore in making correct responses.

Results of error studies show that from the time that children begin to read, they make errors that are syntactically appropriate to preceding context and that demonstrate their sensitivity to constraints within the language (Goodman and Burke, 1970; Weber, 1970). In fact, there is evidence that at the very beginning of reading, when children do not have the skills for discriminating large numbers of words on the basis of their letters, they show an inordinate dependence on context, substituting words that hardly match the written word but do conform to context. After a while, they may balk at many words, as though they realize that they cannot depend on context but do not know how to identify the words positively. Then they show that they are learning to take better advantage of the graphic information, for they balk less often and their errors match the letters of the written words more closely (Biemiller, 1970). Some children who later on do not read fluently or with good comprehension show that they have difficulty integrating their use of context with their analysis of written words, especially through the grammatical inappropriateness of their errors. It is as though in struggling to identify words in terms of their letters they lose grip of their expectations that sentences should be grammatical as well as meaningful.

It is widely but not universally assumed that in order to learn to read an alphabetic writing system, children must learn to segment speech into sounds, learn the correspondences of letters to sounds, and be able to integrate the segments of a word that they might "sound out" into recognizable speech. Some children find the analysis of the sound system especially difficult, particularly segmenting and categorizing the speech stream. It demands that they dissociate meaning from speech and concentrate on its form—an unnatural task. Examples of the difficulty are common enough, as when a teacher asks for words beginning with the sound [f] and one child suggests *face*, another *finger*, but a third suggests *glove*. Segmenting and categorizing the speech stream also demands that children acquire a consciousness of units that are variously represented phonetically, such as the *t*'s in *top*, *stop*, *spotty*, and *spot*. Furthermore, children may be at odds with their teachers about what constitutes the same sound, since there is evidence that they categorize sounds with more sensitivity to phonetic detail than adults, for example, taking note of the aspiration of stops or the similarity of tongue height of such lax and tense vowels as [I] and [i] in *bit* and *beet* (for example, Read, 1971). In experiments (Zhurova, 1973) children as young as four have shown themselves to be capable of tasks requiring segmentation and categorizing. In less formal circumstances they show their ability to separate sounds from meaning by their use of rhyme and alliteration. However, some children in the primary grades find the task of isolating sounds so difficult that they fail to master sound-letter rules.

Although it has been suggested that children progress in reading from stage to stage constructing strategies for unlocking written language in ways that resemble first language learning, there is little supportive evidence for such a suggestion. Moreover, significant differences between the two types of learning must be kept in mind. It is obvious that learning to read is not as brilliant, inevitable, or essential to human definition as acquiring a first language. Growth in reading abilities seems particularly dependent on learners' motivation to make sense of written language and on their progress in coordinating and expanding their cognitive and linguistic abilities to that end. If children's interests lie elsewhere, if they get no satisfaction for their efforts, they can resist engaging themselves to their fullest. Perhaps the more appropriate analog to learning to read is second language learning, which builds on past linguistic experience, progresses as a result of learners' construction and revision of rule systems, depends as much on exposure as instruction, and yet is subject to fluctuations in interest, to anxiety, and to social evaluation.

Reading Instruction

Methods for teaching reading, especially at the beginning stages, have varied especially with respect to the unit that receives most attention in teaching. Most reading programs emphasize either the whole word or the individual letter-sound correspondences (phonics) or some combination of these. Many reading programs introduce words primarily on the basis of their frequency in the language and interest to children; others take these into account but present the words in groups according to the similarity in spelling patterns, for example, *can/man; cane/mane*. Another approach builds on children's abilities to use sentences and talk about events of interest to them by having them write and then read their own materials, using their own words without concern for letter-sound correspondences. Today many programs are deliberately eclectic in that they try to give children practice in recognizing words on sight, to provide the key to assigning at least approximate pronunciations to any words that they might encounter by some sort of correspondence rules, and to use any means, rigorous or not, that will engage children's interests and capacities toward becoming independent readers.

Research and insights into reading from linguistics and psychology have not immediately led to conclusions on how reading instruction might best be carried out. The study of fluent reading has not made obvious how fluency is learned or suggested how it should be taught. Nevertheless, linguists and educators have attempted to draw implications from the study of written language, variation in spoken language, and differences across languages for instructional policy. In fact, they have suggested specific instructional approaches that anticipate the difficulties that children might face in learning to read. Although these proposals rest to some extent on untested assumptions about how children learn and how they bring language into play while reading, their influence has been strong in current reading instruction. The issues raised in some of the more serious and widely implemented proposals are discussed below.

The linguistic method.   The method for teaching reading that has come to be called the linguistic method grew out of proposals made to improve reading instruction over thirty years ago, yet was extensively adopted and evaluated only in the 1960s. Because they were dissatisfied with the content of reading instruction, as well as the assumptions on which it was based, several structural linguists, including Bloomfield (1942) and later Fries (1962) described what they saw as the implications of linguistics for initial reading instruction. Partly in response to the widespread notion that written language is somehow more legitimate and fundamental than spoken language, they insisted that writing is essentially speech written down. They emphasized that the central task which confronts children learning to read is mastery of the correspondences between sounds and spelling since they already know the syntax and vocabulary of the written language by virtue of knowing the spoken language. In order for learners to understand texts they must first pronounce the words they find on the printed page, although they cut this process short after extended practice in the skill.

Bloomfield and Fries, like many others before and after, objected to instruction by whole words which were chosen without concern for spelling because such a procedure obscured the many systematic correspondences between writing and speech. At the same time, they objected to the usual phonics instruction because it led to segmenting speech and distorting the sounds. Furthermore, since phonics dealt with individual letters, it obscured much of the systematic correspondence between strings of letters and strings of sounds, as in *fight/might/sight*. The linguists therefore proposed to teach the regularities between the systems of sound and writing by presenting groups of words such as these and pointing out that just where the words are alike in sound they are also alike in spelling and that where the words differ in sound they differ in spelling. Learners were to be made aware of how sounds relate to letters, but only in the context of whole words; consequently, constraints on the position of letters, markers such as the silent -*e* and other aspects of the organization within the writing system were to be implicitly yet systematically presented.

The instructional materials which the linguists prepared for beginners and which were developed into full-fledged reading programs for the elementary grades are notable for a rather thorough presentation of sound-spelling patterns along with stories created from vocabulary exemplifying the patterns. Clearly, this method for teaching reading goes beyond linguists' observations of the English writing system to assumptions of how children best learn to deal with it. Since other approaches to teaching the same observations are possible, many linguists object to the term linguistic method to describe this one. Nevertheless, it has turned out to be at least as effective as any other method for teaching children to read

(Bond and Dykstra, 1967) and has been influential in heightening the concern to teach children the means for identifying words that they have never seen before.

The Initial Teaching Alphabet.   A persistent explanation in the minds of many people for the sluggishness and frustration that children suffer in learning to read is the irregular correspondence between letters and sounds in English, particularly in the most frequent and indispensable words. The proposal, therefore, has often been made to revise the spelling system to make it correspond more closely to the sound system, not necessarily for general use but for the particular purpose of introducing beginners to reading.

The most widely adopted and studied of these special pedagogical orthographies is the Initial Teaching Alphabet, or i.t.a. (Downing, 1967), created and refined in England and adapted for American use. The alphabet is made up of forty-four characters, most of them familiar Roman lower case letters, many of them a linked combination of two, all of them chosen to deviate minimally in shape and sound correspondence from traditional orthography. The general principle behind the alphabet is that each sound segment in a carefully spoken word should have one character to represent it. There are, however, two other principles that supplement and to some extent conflict with the one-sound/one-letter principle. The first is that each word has only one standard representation in i.t.a., despite stylistic, social, and regional variations in pronunciation. For instance, *r*'s are to be written in words, even in *r*-less dialects. In this respect it is similar to traditional orthography, sacrificing phonetic closeness for consistency in the representation of meaningful units. The second, and very significant, principle is that some of the conventions of the traditional orthography are maintained in i.t.a. in order to facilitate the learner's transfer to traditional orthography. For example, double consonant letters in words like *happy* and *better* are written in i.t.a., although the consonant in speech is neither long nor double. In other words, i.t.a. was created not only to present children with regular correspondences between sounds and letters, but also to anticipate some of the abstractness and patterning in traditional orthography.

It is worth noting that i.t.a. was intended as an alphabet only, not as a teaching method. Adopting i.t.a. does not necessarily entail a commitment to sound-letter analysis, to whole word presentation, or to any other type of instruction. In fact, many reading books and exercise books printed in i.t.a. have identical editions in traditional orthography.

The results of comparative studies—all subject to difficult methodological problems—show that children who learn to read through i.t.a. show a small advantage over those who learn the traditional orthography directly (Bond and Dykstra, 1967; Warburton and Southgate, 1969). Some studies report that children who learn to read through i.t.a. move ahead in reading earlier, at a faster rate, and with apparently greater ease. If they do not exceed the performance of other children, at least they do not fall behind. When they transfer to traditional orthography, usually before the end of the second grade, they show signs of some slippage on standard tests. Few children fail to regain their proficiency quickly. But it is clear that whatever advantage they had in their early years fades in relation to other children after the third grade.

Nonstandard dialects. The pressure for improved education for poor children in recent years, especially black children who live in urban centers, has commanded serious attention from linguists (Baratz and Shuy, 1969). It is incontestable that those groups of children whose reading performance falls short of national norms tend to speak varieties of English different from those which are accepted as standard.

Detailed analyses of the range of nonstandard varieties spoken by young blacks have shown a host of subtle and interrelated differences in form and usage from standard English. Relative to the standard, for instance, they show absence of [l]'s and [r]'s, as in *tool* or *sore*, in certain contexts and the simplification of consonant clusters, so that *shaft* and *laugh* rhyme. The general tendency is for the spoken word to have fewer sounds than the written word has letters. As a consequence, some educators and linguists have suggested that the mismatch between sounds and letters is so much greater for these children than for those who speak the standard that it contributes significantly to their reading failure. The differences in the sound system have been found to reinforce differences in inflectional morphology as well. Where standard English has *walked* or *walks*, nonstandard black English often has *walk*; where standard has *stones* or *Mr. Brown's*, nonstandard sometimes has *stone* or *Mr. Brown.* Again, some have thought that the differences in syntax—verbs and negatives in particular—create even further problems for children learning to read. In order to become literate, such children need to invest supplementary energy in learning the relationship between the standard variety of the language and their own, or they have to learn to use the standard variety itself.

Furthermore, some investigators have pointed out that an extralinguistic factor may contribute to the reading problems of children, that is, the failure of teachers to distinguish linguistic differences from reading difficulties. A teacher might count as incorrect reading *Mr. Brown talk too much* for *Mr. Brown talked too much* and suppose that the reader is being careless about reading details rather than being true to the dialect.

The possible interference created by the distance between spoken nonstandard varieties and written varieties has been questioned in the light of reflection on the extent of variation in English, its significance to comprehension, and how it is acquired. For one thing, speakers of nonstandard black English show a good deal of variation in their use of both standard and nonstandard forms from one occasion to another. Even from the time that they first enter school, urban children show that they include a range of pronunciation and forms within their repertoire and that they find it perfectly appropriate to use a standard, somewhat formal pronunciation when they read aloud. There is no reason to suppose that they would do otherwise, considering the widely known abilities of children at ages six or seven to pick up new varieties of speech from their environment—if they care to do so. Finally, even if no learning of the standard variety takes place, the question of how the differences might affect comprehension is difficult to assess, especially given the superficiality of the differences, the redundancy within the language, and the contribution of extralinguistic context to the interpretation of meaning. In American discussions on dialect, it is noticeable that the experience of children who learn a significantly distinct variety, such as those who speak Swiss German dialects and yet learn to read High German, or children of India who speak colloquial varieties of their languages and yet learn to read literary varieties, has hardly been mentioned, to say nothing of English-speaking children around the globe who in spite of the differences in their speech encounter an almost uniform variety in their books.

With the conviction that children speaking nonstandard English receive the best pedagogical efforts to help them close the breach between what they say and what they read, linguists and educators have made and implemented several suggestions (Wolfram, 1970). One proposal has been to prepare special materials in which the spelling would hardly differ from the standard, but the sentence structure, vocabulary, and ways of speaking would approach the children's own. The difficulty here has been in testing the effectiveness of such materials, in part because parents and teachers have resisted accepting nonstandard written English in the classroom, even as a pedagogical tool. Another proposal has been to prepare materials for all and any English-speaking children that would be free of dialect differences, including only those constructions common to all. The difficulty here is that the differences between standard English and nonstandard English show up in most ordinary sentences. Avoiding them would result in rather unnatural distortions of the language. Another proposal to bridge the gap has been to give beginning readers intensive instruction in the standard variety of the spoken language. Experience in this effort has led to no positive effects and even to some negative effects; one group of children given training in the standard, for example, did not learn to read quite as well as their counterparts who received no such training (Rystrom, 1970). The most widely supported proposal has been neither to adjust the materials nor drill the children in speech, but to allow them to read the usual standard materials in their own speech, even though it may include nonstandard forms. This solution calls for special understanding on the part of the teacher, who must interpret the children's oral reading performance for evidence of comprehension rather than for pronunciation or syntactic deviations from the page. Finally, another proposal is to have children prepare their own materials, without concern for standard locutions at the early stages, but with a good deal of concern for giving children a feeling for the purpose and meaningfulness of the written language.

On the whole, the evidence is not clear that dialect differences in English significantly increase the difficulty experienced in learning to read. Many teachers and investigators remain unconvinced that the mismatch interferes with children's attempts to grasp meaning. They see the correlation between nonstandard speech and low reading performance as the combined effect of social conditions in and out of the classroom rather than the effect of linguistic differences.

Bilingualism. If reading is a skill that entails knowledge of the language to be read, it seems counterproductive to try to teach children to read a language that they cannot speak. Yet this has been in the practice in many parts of the world as nation states have taken on the responsibility for schooling. The various states have each adopted an official language—in some cases more than one—which is taken to be the medium for conducting their affairs, including instruction in the schools. Often, however, considerable numbers of children do not speak the language when they enter school. In the Americas, for example, three groups have faced this situation: indigenous peoples from Alaska to Argentina speaking a multiplicity of languages; immigrants who arrived without knowledge of the official language in the country where they settled; and Africans who lost their own languages but who developed new creoles in the Caribbean area distinct from the official languages there. Every country has a different history, of course, but until recently few made allowance for the children who had to learn the official language as they learned to read it (Rubin, 1968). Many children have succeeded, but it is not clear what cognitive strategies they mustered along the way. At the same time, many have failed to be at ease using the second language and have not derived much value from schooling.

During the past ten years schools in the United States have increased their concern for children who do not speak English. They have used various approaches toward the goal of teaching such children to read. One has been to give the children time to acquire English, for instance, letting the first grade go by before starting reading instruction. Another has been to teach the children the second language orally in a rather systematic way and have the children read precisely what they have been taught to say. Still another has been to teach children to read in their mother tongue and only then introduce them to reading in English. This, in fact, is the strategy that has been adopted in current "bilingual" programs intended to provide young Americans who speak Spanish, French, Cherokee, or Navajo among others, an early education in their dominant if not only language. There is some evidence that this approach, by taking advantage of children's abilities to use their knowledge of their language in reading, brings greater success, not only in learning how to read, but also in reading the second language (Modiano, 1968).

Conclusion

Linguistics has brought to educational research and practice a recognition of the abstract linguistic abilities that children can apply in expressing and interpreting ideas through language. It has attempted to specify in part the knowledge that children bring to the task of learning to read as well as the knowledge of language that they must acquire in order to be literate. It has given considerable depth to the understanding of the psychological processes of reading by making explicit at least some aspects of linguistic organization, particularly syntactic and graphophonological, that mediate between the intention of the writer and the comprehension of the reader. It has, however, fallen short of providing the foundations for a fully elaborate theory of reading. To be specific, how sentences are organized and interpreted in texts has received relatively little attention. Furthermore, and more fundamentally, what it means to know the meaning of a word, sentence, or text has yet to be characterized in an adequate way. However, these are areas of increasing interest in linguistics (Grimes, 1975). Linguists feel not only the imperative need for exploring these difficult topics at this stage of their discipline, but they also recognize the necessity to respond to persistent questions raised in the psychology and teaching of reading.

REFERENCES

Baratz, J. C., and Shuy, R. W., eds. *Teaching black children to read*. Washington, D.C.: Center for Applied Linguistics, 1969.

Biemiller, A. The development of the use of graphic and contextual information as children learn to read. *Reading Research Quarterly*, 1970, 6, 75-96.

Bloomfield, L. Linguistics and reading. *Elementary English Review*, 1942, 19, 125-30, 183-86.

Bond, G. L., and Dykstra, R. The Cooperative Research Program in first-grade reading instruction. *Reading Research Quarterly*, 1967, 2, 5-141.

Chomsky, C. *The acquisition of syntax in children from 5 to 10*. Cambridge, Mass.: M.I.T. Press, 1969.

————. Reading, writing, and phonology. *Harvard Educational Review*, 1970, 40, 287-309.

Downing, J. *Evaluating the Initial Teaching Alphabet*. London: Cassell, 1967.

Fries, C. C. *Linguistics and reading*. New York: Holt, Rinehart, and Winston, 1962.

Geyer, J. J. Comprehensive and partial models related to the reading process. *Reading Research Quarterly*, 1972, 6, 541-87.

Gibson, E. J., and Levin, H. *The psychology of reading*. Cambridge, Mass.: M.I.T. Press, 1975.

Goodman, K. S., and Burke, C. When a child reads: A psycholinguistic analysis. *Elementary English*, 1970, 47, 121-29.

Gough, P. B. One second of reading. In J. F. Kavanagh and I. G. Mattingly, eds., *Language by ear and by eye*. Cambridge, Mass.: M.I.T. Press, 1972.

Grimes, J. *The thread of discourse*. The Hague: Mouton, 1975.

Kavanagh, J. F., and Mattingly, I. G., eds. *Language by ear and by eye*. Cambridge, Mass.: M.I.T. Press, 1972.

Kolers, P. A. Three stages of reading. In H. Levin and J. Williams, eds., *Basic studies on reading*. New York: Basic Books, 1970.

Levin, H., and Kaplan, E. L. Grammatical structure and reading. In H. Levin and J. Williams, eds., *Basic studies on reading*. New York: Basic Books, 1970.

Levin, H., and Williams, J. P., eds. *Basic studies on reading*. New York: Basic Books, 1970.

Mattingly, I. G. Reading, the linguistic process, and linguistic awareness. In J. F. Kavanagh and I. G. Mattingly, eds., *Language by ear and by eye*. Cambridge, Mass.: M.I.T. Press, 1972.

Modiano, N. National or mother tongue in beginning reading. *Research in the Teaching of English*, 1968, 2, 32-43.

Read, C. Preschool children's knowledge of English phonology. *Harvard Educational Review*, 1971, *41*, 1-34.

Rubin, J. Language and education in Paraguay. In J. Fishman, C. A. Ferguson, and J. Das Gupta, eds., *Language problems of developing nations*. New York: John Wiley, 1968.

Ruddell, R. B. *Reading-language instruction: Innovative practices*. Englewood Cliffs, N.J.: Prentice-Hall, 1974.

Rystrom, R. Dialect training and reading: A further look. *Reading Research Quarterly*, 1970, 5, 581-99.

Smith, F. *Psycholinguistics and reading*. New York: Holt, Rinehart, and Winston, 1973.

————. *Understanding reading*. New York: Holt, Rinehart, and Winston, 1971.

Strickland, R. The language of elementary school children: Its relationship to the language of reading textbooks and the quality of reading of selected school children. *Indiana University Bulletin of the School of Education*, 38.

Tulving, E., and Gold, C. Stimulus information and contextual determinants of tachistoscopic recognition of words. *Journal of Experimental Psychology*, 1963, *66*, 319-29.

Warburton, F. W., and Southgate, V. I.t.a.: An independent evaluation. London: John Murray and W. and R. Chambers, 1969.

Wardhaugh, R. *Reading: A linguistic perspective*. New York: Harcourt Brace, 1969.

Wanat, S. *Linguistic attention and visual attention in reading*. Newark, Del.: International Reading Association, 1971.

Weber, R-M. A linguistic analysis of first-grade reading errors. *Reading Research Quarterly*, 1970, 5, 427-51.

————. Linguistics and reading. In E. E. Ekwall, ed., *Psychological factors in the teaching of reading*. Columbus, Ohio: Charles E. Merrill, 1973.

Wolfram, W. Sociolinguistic alternatives in teaching reading to nonstandard speakers. *Reading Research Quarterly*, 1970, *6*, 75-96.

Zhurova, L. Y. The development of analysis of words into their sounds by preschool children. In C. A. Ferguson and D. I. Slobin, eds., *Studies of child language development*. New York: Holt, Rinehart, and Winston, 1973.

VI

Second Language Learning

Jack C. Richards

The learning of a second language would appear to be a relatively straightforward task. Millions of people succeed at it without giving it very much thought, and bilingualism is the norm in a great number of communities around the world. Some might find it surprising that interest in second language learning is as strong as it is, generating a respectable number of books and professional articles, and consuming considerable amounts of money in some countries as aspects of second language learning are investigated at the individual, community, and national level. However, the apparent simplicity of second language learning turns out to be deceptive on closer examination; instead there is a complex spectrum of unanswered questions and competing hypotheses.

The difficulties in adequately conceptualizing the nature of second language learning are related to our limited understanding of the nature of language itself. While the phenomenon of language is now studied within an increasing number of disciplines, including linguistics, psychology, anthropology, and biology, conclusive insights into the nature of language itself are not available. Although recent linguistic theories go some way toward explaining certain aspects of language, such as, how speakers are able to produce and understand sentences they have never heard before, none of these disciplines has produced a detailed and convincing specification of how we actually construct, code, transmit, monitor, receive, and store meaning through language. Until central questions concerning a model of first language structure and learning are answered, questions relating specifically to the learning of other languages can be answered only tentatively. Therefore, what follows is an attempt to formulate relevant questions and points of approach, rather than to provide definitive answers.

Specifying the Learning Task

Any attempt to define precisely what has to be learned when we study a second language will depend on which aspects of language we wish to stress. Language can be viewed in a number of different ways. It involves the individual in relation to himself; hence the psychology of mind and thought are one dimension. It is the primary means by which the individual interacts with others; hence the sciences of social behavior are implicated. In addition, language can be examined independently of its individual and social functions; such has been the approach of traditional linguistics. In the case of second language learning we may be interested in the manner in which the acquired language influences the patterns of thought of the learner, or in what characteristics of individuals appear to correlate highly with success in acquiring a second language (Bever, 1972; Gardner and Lambert, 1972). Alternatively, our primary interest may be in how the social role and functional applications of the new language affect the learner's understanding, use, and attitude toward it (Huxley and Ingram, 1971). We may be interested in the coding system involved, in which case we would need to consider the type of coding system language is, and how such a system is typically acquired by human learners (Crothers and Suppes, 1967). Or our interest may be in the way the new system of codification is related to existing coding systems in both language storage and production, in which case models of the bilingual's actual behavior will be relevant (Kessler, 1971; Swain, 1971; Weinreich, 1967). Each of these perspectives, as well as others which might be adopted, offers different views of the tasks confronting the second language learner. This chapter will consider the problem of second language learning from a broad perspective which encompasses some of the relevant questions raised by the variety of approaches to second language learning.

Linguistic Aspects of Second Language Learning

A first approximation to specifying what has to be acquired in linguistic terms might identify the major problem as a question of grammar learning. This view would certainly seem to be confirmed by the experience of many students of second languages. On closer analysis, however, it raises a variety of questions, since grammar is clearly inseparable from other dimensions of the task. All linguistic theories view language as a phenomenon which can be analyzed at several different levels. There is the traditional division between grammar and vocabulary for example, and a further distinction between levels of sounds, grammar, and meaning. But it is meaning rather than grammar which can be thought of as determining the basic structure of the sentence. A model of sentence production must begin with meaning (Schlesinger, 1971). Prior to the production of a sentence, the speaker presumably forms an abstract structure which in some way represents the meaning he wishes to communicate (see level 2, figure 1, p. 118). This abstract structure or set of features is then given grammatical and phonological expression in the form of a sentence. Current views of semantics suggest we are dealing with a peculiarly human use of cognitive structures and procedures that code experience into basic semantic and conceptual units, which are used as the basis of sentence production and reception. The nature of these minimal semantic units is as yet far from clear (Chafe, 1970; Leech, 1974), but their role is seen in a consideration of the following sentences:

1. John *leaves* tomorrow at five.
2. John *is leaving* tomorrow at five.
3. John *is going to leave* tomorrow at five.

Each sentence contains a different view of the event of leaving. That different semantic units underly the choice of verb form is seen more clearly if other verbs are substituted. We can say *It is going to rain tomorrow* but not *It rains tomorrow* or *It is raining tomorrow*. The drowning man shouts *Help, I'm drowning* and not *Help I drown*. Likewise, *I am enjoying my holiday at the moment* is possible but not *I enjoy my holiday at the moment* or *I am going to enjoy my holiday at the moment* (Close, 1962; Hirtle, 1967; Leech, 1971). The conceptualization of the event in (1) is that of a "postdated completed event." The simple verb form as in *John leaves* used for planned future events conceptualizes them as scheduled and certain (in this sense, complete). Nothing more is required for their realization than the passing of time. The progressive form in (2) *is leaving* sees the process as already begun but as not yet completed. It is the fact that the planning has already begun, the event thus being "in motion" but incomplete, that calls for the progressive form, which is typically used for events that are in some way viewed as incomplete. The verb in (3) *is going to leave* might be described as "future fulfilment of a present intention." An analysis of the different meanings illustrates aspects of the semantic structure of English verbs. The system involves, for certain events, a choice between conceptualization of the event as complete or incomplete, and this choice in turn governs the selection of tenses with a consequent wide range of effects at the level of the sentence. This choice is a cognitive one made at some deep level of structure in the sentence. A quite different problem exists at the level of expression: we are obliged to say *John leaves tomorrow* if we intend the meaning of (1), and not *John leave tomorrow, John to leaves tomorrow, John leaving tomorrow*, or *Leaves John tomorrow*, etc. The choice of the simple or progressive form for realizing an event as complete or incomplete must be matched by the appropriate rules of expression, that is, with correct rules of word order, syntax, morphology, and phonology.

In trying to delimit the area of what is to be learned in acquiring a foreign or second language, we have to consider at what point we are dealing with systems of such an abstract and fundamental type that they are part of the cognitive machinery of all language users (that is, are universals), and at what point we are dealing with elements that are peculiar to the language being learned and which do form part of the learning problem. Is second language learning simply a question of learning a new set of production rules? In other words, is the progressive form simply a rule-learning problem for the foreign language learner, or does it involve the acquisition of a cognitive system that is not present in the learner's own system?

A number of scholars have tried to demonstrate the universality of particular semantic and syntactic relationships. A convincing demonstration of the existence of semantic and syntactic universals, whether in Greenberg's implicational or substantive sense (1966), in McNeill's (1966) or Chomsky's (1965) formal sense, in Ayer's (1952) logical sense, or in the empirical sense of the writers of *A Field Manual for Cross Cultural Study of the Acquisition of Communicative Competence* (Slobin et al., 1967) would be of fundamental importance to those who study the question of the acquisition of semantics and syntax in a second language.

The case theory of language accounts for the basic underlying level of language knowledge in terms of a set of relationships between the nominal and verbal elements of the underlying sentence—the abstract structure which is the basis for sentence generation. These relationships between noun and verb may be manifestations of a closed class of case categories, such as agentive, experiencer, instrumental, object, source, goal, locative, time, comitative, and benefactive (Di Pietro, 1971; Fillmore, 1968; Kessler, 1971). Such underlying universal categories are realized in particular languages through the syntactic and phonological rules of that language.

This theory of language has wide applications for second language learning. If this abstract set of relationships and cases is common to all languages (and all speakers of languages), it is available to the language learner no matter what his age. Second language learning would then consist of the acquisition of a new set of syntactic, transformational, and phonological rules for the realization of these language-independent deep structures. Presumably, the set of basic cases and relationships between nominal and verbal elements at the deepest level can incorporate or generate a much wider range of semantic distinctions than any language will actually make use of. Second language learning thus would appear to involve primarily the acquisition of a new set of realization rules by which the new language expresses underlying relationships of a universal type. The system which realizes these relationships at the grammatical level appears to have much in common with what linguists characterize by a generative-transformational grammar. For the second language learner, there is a central language-independent coding system, rather than a separate coding for each language, though of course at some stage during the encoding/decoding processes involved in listening and speaking, the speaker's languages are handled separately. Processes which are more fundamentally "cognitive" or "conceptual" need not be regarded as the product of particular linguistic systems; particular linguistic systems are manifestations of the same universal set of conceptual cases. These different levels of cognitive and linguistic structure are illustrated in figure 1.

There is hence no need to propose different "world views" or "patterns of thought" in moving from one language to another. As Bever (1972) comments:

> . . .it does not appear to be impossible to translate basic concepts from one language to another—there is only an occasional difference in the perceived completeness and directness of expression. But if language does *not* affect thought, why do bilingual speakers feel that the true translation of concepts is impossible? A possible resolution of this puzzle lies in the distinction between two kinds of information contained within each concept shared by members of a culture, *semantic meaning* and *linguistic idea*. The linguistic structures of a particular language could determine certain features of the *linguistic ideas* embedded in concepts, without these features themselves being critical components of the semantic meanings of those concepts (p. 101).

The Concept of Difficulty

A consideration of the "depth" of language differences raises a host of questions. One issue which has received considerable attention in the

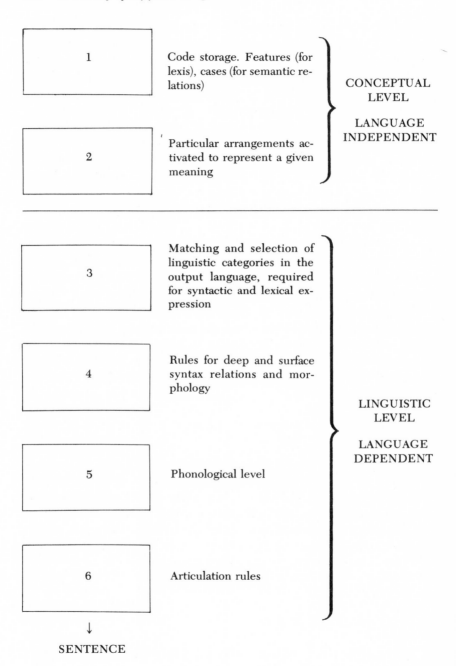

Fig. 1. Levels involved in sentence production.

literature is the concept of difficulty in language learning. Subjective observation of second language learning suggests that the linguistic units themselves which make up the expression system of language (phonemes, morphemes, syntactic devices) are not all of equal difficulty or simplicity for the learner. Some items may be inherently difficult to learn no matter what the background of the learner. For example, it is well known that the English pairs /v/ and /ð/ and /f/ and /θ/ are very hard to distinguish, not only for nonnative speakers but also for native speakers (Delattre et al., 1962). The study of linguistic difficulty, as Rodgers (1971) points out, can be approached either from the concept of inherent linguistic difficulty, which implies "focus on physiological, maturational, and temporal factors which suggest that certain linguistic units and unit sequences are universally more difficult to articulate, audit or process than other units and unit sequences" or from the approach of contrastive linguistic difficulty, which begins from the assumption that "linguistic habit renders certain non-native utterance types differentially more difficulty to articulate, audit, or process than more practised native utterance types" (p. 109).

The concept of difficulty may be assumed to affect the learner's organization of what he perceives (for which the term *learning strategy* may be useful) and the organization of what he produces (for which the term *communication strategy* may be used), difficulty being but one of several relevant variables. Focusing on learning strategies directs attention to the cues which the learner uses to make identification of elements in the new language easier. Where cognates, derivatives, and loan words exist for example, these may assist in the identification of certain elements in the new language; likewise, where the target language structures parallel structures in the native language. Prediction of difficulty in terms of interlingual difference (the motivation for contrastive analysis, Haugen, 1973) presumes, however, that it is feasible to compare categories across languages, a comparison which in practice may not be possible. What is syntax in one language may be vocabulary in another. Torrey (1971) comments:

> . . .many aspects of language learning are very difficult to analyze into specific responses, and even where it is possible the responses are various and at different levels (one item may belong to two levels in one language and four in another). . . .degrees of learning would have to be examined in terms of specific instances rather than with the general category of responses (p. 236).

The "area of commonality," of course, varies between different combinations of first and second languages, so that for speakers of a given language different second languages constitute learning problems of different degrees of difficulty. In Rodgers's terms, there is a general aspect of the problem and a specific contrastive aspect for any language pair. In addition, even if we accept the position that minimal semantic units are the same across languages, the realizations of certain basic concepts are *obligatory* in some languages (that is, they are part of the language system of that language) and *optional* in others (expressed by a lexical item or a paraphrase). The second language learner has to learn to readjust his optional and obligatory categories in the language he is learning. Tense, for instance, is obligatorily realized in English, but optional in Malay; conversely Malay has an obligatory purposive-nonpurposive distinction in the verb system which is optional in English.

What the learner finds difficult will also depend on what he has acquired of the second language. His knowledge of the target language will form part of the data by which he infers the meaning of new elements. Carton (1971) suggests that "cues such as specific pluralizing markers applicable only to nouns, tense markers applicable only to verbs and word order constraints of a given language will fall into this category" (p. 50). Tucker et al. (1969) found that native speakers of French are able to determine the gender of nouns with either real or invented examples, without awareness of the processes they used, from their knowledge of the distinctive characteristics of the endings of French words. English speakers, however, exposed randomly to French have great difficulty with gender and require special training to recognize such features. Their errors indicate their search for regularities in the French gender system. Crothers and Suppes (1967) have investigated learning strategies used in identifying the morphology and syntax of Russian in a detailed experimental study.

Difficulty in language learning has been defined by psycholinguists in terms of such factors as sentence length, processing time required, derivational complexity, types of embedding, number of transformations, and semantic complexity. Experimental evidence has not, however, confirmed a direct relationship between the ease of comprehension of an utterance by an adult listener and the number of rules used by the linguist to describe the utterance. Ease of comprehension seems to be more adequately defined by the type of rule involved (Fodor and Garrett, 1966). Russian work on the factors affecting the order of development of grammatical categories suggests that the difficulty of the concepts expressed by the category rather than formal grammatical complexity influences order of acquisition. Categories of more concrete reference develop before those expressing more abstract or relational ideas. The conditional in Russian develops relatively late, although its structure is quite simple (Braine, 1971).

The learner's comprehension and efforts at comprehension can be compared with his production. His output may likewise be organized in terms of what he finds easiest to say, which is not necessarily identifiable with what he knows. Learners often avoid a word or structure they find difficult to say. The result may be choice of a wrong tense: *Je vais vous téléphoner ce soir* instead of *Je vous téléphonerai ce soir*. Facility and economy of effort could explain why first learned words and structures tend to be overused and to resist replacement by later taught items. This is often the case with such a contrast as the simple present and the present continuous. Once the present continuous is introduced (or the simple present) it is often used more frequently than necessary. Likewise, an early learned question form may preempt all other question forms in the learner's speech, despite constant exposure to other types of questions. Words with broad semantic extension may become overused in preference to more specific vocabulary learned later. Nickel (1971) refers to this as the factor of chronology:

> We all know that patterns learned first have priority over patterns learned at a later date because of the convenient simplicity of these basic structures. This kind of intrastructural interference will take place even against an interstructural contrastive background. Thus Norwegian learners of German will very often use word order of the main clause type in subordinate clauses even though conditions in their mother tongue are similar to those in the German target language, because the main clause word order has been deeply engrained in the brains of the learners (p. 191).

Having delimited the area of learning to the acquisition of the particular syntactic, transformational, and phonological rules by which underlying grammatical and semantic categories are realized, we may now consider how the learner actually goes about this task at the level of phonology and syntax. One problem with some traditional approaches to second language learning has been to regard a single theory as appropriate for explaining all the dimensions of what is involved. But it is obvious that second language learning involves many different types of learning problems, and a theory which works well at the level of vocabulary learning may be unsuited to explaining syntax learning, just as a technique for learning vocabulary, such as memorization of word lists, does not seem to have any generalization to syntax learning. Not only does the second language learner approach different aspects of the task differently (for some sounds, imitation of lip movements may be helpful; for others, the perception and production of new acoustic patterns is required), but the researcher also needs to develop appropriate theories for the different areas of the task. Contrastive analysis, for example, appears to have higher predictive power at the level of phonology than of syntax. This fact confirms that syntax learning has different dimensions from phonology learning and requires a different explanatory model (Sampson, 1971).

Learning the Sounds of a Second Language

Let us consider briefly the problem of learning the sound system of a new language. Traditional studies of second language learning, employing the concept of phoneme and comparing categories and distributions across languages, have been moderately successful in documenting the resistance to innovation of existing phonological systems, the learner tending to replace new elements with elements from existing categories, the patterns of replacement giving a substantial basis to the learner's foreign accent. The difficulties of learning the phonological system of a new language would appear to be twofold. There is the problem of perceiving sound contrasts which are not distinctive in the learner's own language, and then there is the articulatory problem of producing unfamiliar sounds, or of using familiar sounds in unfamiliar positions, such as the difficulty an English speaker finds in placing an unaspirated [p] at the beginning of a word. But the actual difficulties of second language learners cannot be entirely predicted simply from a cross-language comparison of the relevant linguistic and articulatory features, as a number of empirical studies have shown (Brière, 1968; Nababan, 1971). A variety of substitutions are often made by learners with the same mother tongue, including substitutions of some sounds which are not used in the mother tongue. So other factors are involved.

There are significant individual variations. Some people have less trouble with pronunciation than others, the result of differential aptitude (an individual's capacity for learning the relevant distinction) or motivation (the desire to make the necessary effort). An ethnocentric attitude, for example, has been found to play a negative role in learning the phonology of a second language, influencing one's willingness to give up the security of personal speech patterns (Gardner and Lambert, 1972). In some parts of South America English pronunciation is for some reason considered effeminate; hence male students face a psychological conflict with their Latin "machismo." Apart from questions of individual psychology, there is also the factor of age, since the range and nature of substitutions made by young learners is not necessarily the same as that made by adult learners.

Considering just the linguistic variables, Brière (1968) stresses the importance of the syllable as a basis for analyzing learners' errors in pronunciation. Tarone (1972) likewise emphasizes the primacy of the syllable as a universal articulatory unit used as the basis for phonological encoding and decoding of the speech signal. She sees in learners' errors a reversion to a basic consonant-vowel syllable as the basis for the learners' attempts to construct new phonological systems. Looking at the problem in terms of distinctive features, Carter (quoted by Ervin-Tripp, 1973) proposes that although the same features may be present in both languages, the feature hierarchy may differ across languages. Differences in the hierarchical order of phonological oppositions is discussed by Sampson (1971), who uses a modification of Carter's theory to account for many of the problems which Cantonese encounter in learning English phonology.

Summarizing the various approaches to the learning of phonology, Ervin-Tripp (1973) observes:

> . . . in sum, it appears that the most permeable processes are the learning of new discriminations, and the development, in limited articulation, at least, of new phonetic locations. Second in difficulty is the development of new phonological rules. The hardest aspect of the acquisition of a new sound system is the articulation of new feature combinations, with considerable over-generalization occurring in the process (p. 107).

She emphasizes that "any learning model which predicts language learning on the basis of input without regard to the selective processing by the learner, will not work, except for trivial problems" (p. 93). The difficulty becomes even more apparent when we consider syntax learning in a second language.

The Learning of Syntax

We have defined the target of learning for the second language learner, at least from the linguistic point of view, as the translation of the abstract and underlying categories and relationships which define the deep structure of the communication into the appropriate syntactic, morphological, and phonological rules of sentences in the new language. The task of the learner involves those processes outlined in stages three to six in figure 1. The linguist might describe this task as the construction of a linguistic system that will enable the learner to produce and understand all the possible sentences of the new language. Generative-transformational theory proposes a model for this ability: it posits the existence of a basic set of rules for generating the underlying components of a sentence, which are related through transformational rules to the external form of the sentence as it occurs in an actual discourse. Transformational relations between sentence elements and devices such as subordination and coordination are used in all languages to create a variety of sentence types from a finite stock of syntactic elements. However, the linguistic means used to express these relations show considerable diversity across languages. The most immediate task for the second language learner is to discover the grammatically crucial elements of the syntactic system of the new language, such as how to recognize the noun phrase and the verb phrase and their structures of modification in the new language, and how the major syntactic categories are realized.

Different areas of syntax in a second language typically pose different types of learning problems for the second language learner. Within syntax there are areas which are relatively similar across languages, and others which are very different. Subject-verb-object word order is found in various languages for example, while the representation of tense, aspect, and number differ substantially from one language to another. Ervin-Tripp (1973) observes that the rate at which new syntactic rules are acquired varies considerably:

> Sequences which affect basic grammatical relations; modifier-head, subject-predicate, verb-object, are learned very fast and learners rapidly acquire coordinate rules (that is, rules for the new language) for representing these relations. Thus French bilinguals almost always maintained a difference in noun-adjective sequence for English and French, and Japanese newcomers to English, keep S-V-O in English and S-O-V in Japanese. On the other hand, they have great difficulty in maintaining separate rules for adverb placement. . . . Transformations reflecting basic grammatical relations may be learned faster and may be more resistant to change than those reflecting secondary relations or categories (p. 87).

The progress of syntactic development in first and second language learning is now receiving closer attention, and some common characteristics of the learning process seem to be emerging from longitudinal studies. Learners typically begin with general rules of wide application and with lexical items that seem essential to communication. In the acquisition of English as a second language, the effects of this process are seen in the overuse of the present tense in place of the past tense and in the overuse of the uninflected verb in place of the third person inflected form (*He go* instead of *He goes*). Learners form tentative hypotheses which they modify as they add new rules. There is a general tendency to simplify the grammar of the target language. One grammar appears to give way to another in the sense that the learner follows predictable stages as one set of rules is replaced by another. As Nemser (1971) has observed:

> The speech of a learner . . . is structurally organized, manifesting the order and cohesiveness of a system, although one frequently changing with atypical rapidity and subject to radical reorganization through the massive intrusion of new elements (p. 116).

The second language learner's syntax may be characterized as an attempt to work out the rules needed to mold what has been acquired of the language into an efficient system of communication. Mother tongue interference, overgeneralization of previously learned rules to inapplicable contexts, idiosyncractic rules that he may have developed through partial understanding of a feature in the target language, are recurring features of his speech (Richards, 1974). These deviant linguistic systems can of course operate quite adequately for many functions of language that do not involve either an aesthetic dimension or great precision; consequently, any motivation for further learning may cease.

Studies of the acquisition of English as a second language by younger learners with a variety of mother tongues (Dulay and Burt, 1972) report that young learners' errors are largely developmental, that is, they exhibit a similar order of acquisition in the second language as they do in the first language. In addition, idiosyncratic errors and mother-tongue interference also appear. Spanish subjects, when acquiring English grammar, thus produced sentences reflecting Spanish syntax like *I know to do all that* instead of *I know how to*, and sentences characterized by normal developmental overgeneralizations of the sort made by children acquiring English as a first language, sentences like *I didn't weared any hat* and *He took her teeths off*. They also produced sentences like *She name is Maria* and *Now we will talking about that* which are neither Spanish nor English but probably derive from confusion within the learner's handling of the target language. A similar range of errors was evidenced in an analysis of errors made by speakers with a wide variety of different mother tongues in a study of their common errors (Richards, 1971).

Learning to Perform

The second language learner does not merely have to learn the rules of the linguistic system itself. He also has to learn how to perform in the new language, whether it is writing English in a particular style or register which is his goal, or speaking English in the style required of a particular communicative role. Learners learn foreign languages to satisfy any one of a multitude of goals. Formal language teaching, particularly at the intermediate and advanced levels, is concerned with turning competence into performance: with translating a general capacity for second language reception and production into the particular set of performance capabilities required of, for example, a bilingual secretary or a tourist in a foreign country. Language teaching is thus concerned in the initial stages with creating conditions from which the learner can construct the "realization rules" of the new language, and then with teaching how the rules are typically applied in a preselected set of contexts. In the initial stages of learning, performance is secondary to competence; the learner's deviant syntax and his telegraphic speech, or *interlanguage* (Corder, 1967; Richards, 1972; Selinker, 1972), are accepted as normal signs of a complex rule system in a state of development. At a later stage attention shifts to performance itself and the significance of appropriate (that is, grammatically and stylistically acceptable) performance.

Performance can also be used to describe the processes of sentence production and reception. Performance in this sense is clearly highly complex from a psychological perspective, much more complex than figure 1 suggests, and any account of the actual psycholinguistic and neurolinguistic processes involved in language production and reception remains highly speculative. Within a normal stretch of discourse, the speaker is simultaneously involved in a number of different tasks. Some of these might be listed as follows: planning; monitoring; anticipating; utilizing knowledge of probabilities and collocation; employing pragmatic knowledge of the real world; applying linguistic rules of transformation, deletion, and anaphoric cross reference; and choosing appropriate levels or styles of vocabulary and syntax. For example, once we begin a sentence, we must coordinate the tense of what has been said with what is being said, and at the same time we must plan ahead for what is going to be said. As we speak, we monitor what we say so that what is said is compared with what was intended, and if necessary, corrected or restated. As we listen, we make use of probabilistic information regarding lexical and syntactic items, which is both linguistic and pragmatic in nature. Certain words and situations lead us to predict what will come next. If, when we enter a friend's room, he gestures toward a chair and says *Would you like to . . . .* we can safely predict that he is going to invite us to sit down, and so act accordingly. Miller (1964) quotes a striking illustration of how expectations influence language perception:

> The English psychologist David Bruce recorded a set of ordinary sentences and played them in the presence of noise so intense that the voice was just audible, but not intelligible. He told his listeners that these were sentences on some general topic—sports, say, and asked them to repeat what they heard. He then told them they would hear more sentences on a different topic, which they were also asked to repeat. This was done several times. Each time the listeners repeated sentences appropriate to the topic announced in advance. When at the end of the experiment Bruce told them they had heard the same recording every time—all he had changed was the topic they were given—most listeners were unable to believe it (p. 22).

A second language learner's linguistic behavior, even at the inter- mediate levels of language mastery, may be hindered in a number of crucial ways which affect his performance. His ability to store sentences in the new language in short-term memory long enough to process them and extract their deep structure or meaning may be limited because of the unfamiliar- ity of the words or structures. The native speaker is able to make use of his knowledge of what is likely in his language. Our knowledge of expectancies for certain word and structure sequences enables us to understand a complete message from an impartially analyzed or communicated seg- ment. Hence, in our mother tongue we can follow a telephone conversation even though the full range of acoustic data is not transmitted; we can understand a conversation in a noisy room or readily understand a telegram or newspaper headline written in truncated language.

Second language learners, however, lack the ability to predict what should be there on the basis of a knowledge of probabilities. They find it difficult to make a telephone conversation, or to read a text from which one-half the words have been omitted. They take more time to process sentences since they must make a fuller analysis of language than the native speaker. Our normal reaction when we speak to foreigners reflects this fact. We attempt to speak more slowly and clearly, providing additional ges- tures. The cloze procedure as a testing device makes use of the learner's ability to predict as a measure of his knowledge of the second language. The ability to supply a missing word in a sentence is thought to depend on one's overall knowledge of syntax and word distribution, both of which contri- bute significantly to knowledge of a language.

Spolsky (1973) has demonstrated how our knowledge of language probabilities affects comprehension. He compared

> the performance of native speakers of English and non-natives (including some with very high competence) in writing down English sentences that were read to them on a tape to which varying amounts of noise had been added. We were not surprised to find that the more noise we added, the more mistakes were made; nor were we surprised to find that some non-natives did as well or better than natives when there was no added noise; but what was important was the clear distinction that one found between natives and non-natives as soon as any noise was added. This is to be explained by the non-native's inability to function with reduced redundancy, evidence that he cannot supply from his knowledge of the language the experience on which to base his guesses as to what is missing. In other words, the key thing missing is the richness of knowledge of probabilities on all levels—phonological, grammatical, lexical, and semantic—in the language (p. 169).

Children and Adult Learners

A commonly asked question about second language learning is whether an adult can acquire a foreign language as well as a child learns a new language. Teenagers and adults often do not attain high standards of achievement in foreign language classes, and the hypothesis that children have special language learning capacities that are unavailable to adults has been advanced to explain the differences in achievement (Lenneberg, 1967). On the other hand, the degree of success which *is* possible in adult language learning is sufficient to cast doubts on any theory of first language learning which advocates cognitive and processing strategies being uniquely available to child learners. It is not difficult to find cases of adults achieving mastery of a foreign or second language. Braine (1971) for example, refers to statistics on language use among immigrants to Israel to show that under favorable conditions adults can learn a new language relatively quickly (as the evidence of special language classes for carefully selected and motivated military personnel has frequently demonstrated). Braine comments:

> . . . from the 1961 census figures for immigrants between 1948 and 1954, it is worth noting that among the 87,000 males in the 30-40 age group (that is, who were young adults aged 17-34 at the time of immigration) 73 percent were using Hebrew as their main or only

language in 1961, 21 percent used Hebrew as a secondary language, and Hebrew was not in daily use in only 6 percent (p. 71).

Adults clearly have the capacity to learn a second language. The real issue is whether they acquire a language in the same way as children, and in unsuccessful instances, what factors hinder second language development in adults.

One significant difference between child and adult learners is, of course, the factor of maturation. The child begins learning his mother tongue at a time when cognitive and other aspects of mental development are not complete. If we assume that the development of the child's linguistic system is intimately connected with the development of cognitive and conceptual processes and categories, we would expect linguistic development to follow the progress of cognitive maturation. It is indeed the regular order in which items appear in child language development which suggests that development is not simply a reflection of language input. Bellugi-Klima presents the following data on the development of language items in two subjects:

Inflection	Age of appearance (in months)		Combined rank order in mother's speech
	Adam	Eve	
Present progressive, -ing	28	19½	2
Plural on nouns, -s	33	24	1
Past on regular verbs, -ed	39	24½	4
Possessive on nouns, -s	39½	25½	5
Third person on verbs, -s	41	26	3

(Bellugi-Klima, in McNeill, 1970, p. 83.)

The order of development of the items was the same in both children, a fact which cannot entirely be explained by the frequency of occurrence of the items in the parents' speech. What seems to govern the development of rules in children's speech is the generality of application of the rule in question, its transformational complexity, and its semantic complexity. The first two factors would also be expected to influence the order of development of rules in the syntax of adult learners, but not necessarily the third. There is no reason why an adult should experience the same problem as a child with conditionals, comparatives, and other semantically complex items, and there are doubtlessly many areas of syntax in which we would not expect an item to develop in a parallel way in the first and second language. However, where the learning of a rule is governed by general rule-learning strategies, such as overgeneralization and learning the most general before the most particular, first and second language development appear to follow similar lines. Negation rules seem to be a case in point.

Other differences reflect different learning modalities between adults and children. Adults are often literate and perhaps as a consequence appear to be very conscious of vocabulary and slower at learning syntax than children. Much of adult language development in the first language is lexical. Rapid acquisition of syntax, so characteristic of child language learners, is difficult for adults. Halle has suggested that grammar learning in adulthood is difficult "because the adult has lost the ability to make sweeping revisions in his internalized network of rules" (in Crothers and Suppes, 1967, p. 265). Lenneberg (1967) sees the period between age two and puberty as a biologically critical period for language learning. He attributes difficulties in adult language learning to lack of "cerebral plasticity," a consequence of the development of cerebral dominance. Krashen (1972), however, has recently offered an alternative interpretation of Lenneberg's data which does not support the theory of a biologically critical period for language learning. To the extent that child language learning *is* generally more successful than adult language learning, a number of other hypotheses could be offered. These might concern degrees of inhibition in children and adults, the presence or absence of egocentric speech in children and adults, and functional differences between child and adult speech (Kennedy, 1973; Macnamara, 1973).

Another major difference between child and adult language learning which makes meaningful comparison difficult arises from the very different social functions of language which distinguish child and adult learning. For the child learning his mother tongue, language is a vital social tool. Failure to acquire language would be fatal psychologically, whereas success initiates the child into social bonds with family and peers which provide emotional and social support. Adult language learning rarely has the same degree of urgency. Where it does so, however, it is successful to the degree that the learner is able to make the language a key to real social links. The motivation to make sufficient effort to sustain the lengthy learning process can come only from a perception of the value of the language in realizing deeply felt personal goals. No amount of skill in language teaching can compensate for the absence of such motives on the part of the learner, and for this reason much school language teaching is unsuccessful. In "real life," language is generally used to realize goals which are nonlinguistic. Mastery of language "for its own sake" is unlikely to provide genuine and lasting motivation. Language teaching is rarely able to avoid this dilemma.

Motivation

Although we have spent some time discussing the nature of the rules with which language is constructed and those which operate in its actual use, and briefly considered how the language learner goes about learning such rules, we have suggested that in instances of successful language learning the learning of rules is secondary to the learner's primary purpose, which is to make use of the language for what may be termed "extra-linguistic" functions. Psychologists have distinguished two major attitudinal factors which play an important role in determining how willing the learner is to persevere with the task (Gardner and Lambert, 1972). On the one hand, there are foreign language learners who view the language as a key to social and cultural enrichment through the opportunities it provides for association with members of a different culture. This type of *integrative motivation* is characteristic of many successful language learners. Really wanting to be able to learn the foreign language as a means for close communication and acceptance by people who speak it provides the will power necessary to persevere with the task. Good motivation leads not only to perseverance but to a heightened concentration or intensity of attention that produces more rapid learning. On the other hand, the learner may simply be studying the language for an immediate short-term goal which does not involve his wanting to be accepted by and integrated into a target culture group. Simply learning a language to acquire course credits, or to carry out a limited range of tasks that do not involve the learner in close face-to-face interaction as an equal (for example, a taxi driver learning enough English to collect tourists at an airport) does not generally lead to a high degree of accomplishment in learning. Foreign language or second language learning in such cases is typically poor, characterized by acquisition of only the rudiments of grammar and by tolerance of a relatively low standard of achievement.

The colonies of expatriates in cities around the world conveniently illustrate this attitudinal dichotomy and its consequent effect on levels of achievement. In cities like Tokyo and Jakarta one finds either foreigners who state that they do not have the time to learn the local language and who feel they can get by without it or those who see their lives as expatriates enriched by the access to local life and thought that knowledge of the local language gives, and who consequently apply themselves energetically to acquiring it.

This type of attitudinal contribution to second language learning is not of course under the control of the teacher, though he may be able to encourage and influence an integrative motivation toward the target language group. But there are also the day-to-day activities of classroom language learning and it is in those that the teacher's contribution to the motivational dimension can be important. The classroom teacher is faced with the problem of trying to guide the learning process so that at every step the learner is motivated through the satisfaction of achievement, but at the same time perceives the need for further progress. The actual experience of learning a foreign language, however, is often a disillusioning one because of the unrealistic assumptions about language learning which learners hold when they begin. The student who expects to be able to converse with ease after three months of study may be bitterly disillusioned to find that the acquisition of conversational skills is more likely to take thirty months of intensive practice. The student who wants only a reading knowledge of the foreign language will find that the effort to build up a basic recognition vocabulary of 5,000 to 7,000 words is considerable, and even then in reading he may encounter six to ten words per page that he does not know.

Many conventional language teaching techniques likewise are not likely to sustain any but the most devoted student in the arduous learning task. Some language teaching textbooks continue to be teacher-oriented, planned in terms of "items" and "teaching points." Often the long-term aims of the textbook writer, based on his syllabus of structural and lexical items, ignore the short-term realities which face the learner in the day to day classroom routine. A half century ago, Palmer (1921), one of the founders of British language teaching theory, noted that the tendency among educators of the day was toward "methods involving the intelligent use of the intelligence, methods which develop the reasoning capacities, methods which form judgment. Geography is no longer a process of learning lists of place-names by heart, history is no longer represented as a catalogue of dates, arithmetic is taught by playing with cubes" (p. 89). Palmer rejected this movement as irrelevant to language teaching, because he did not see such methods leading toward automatism and habit formation. The view of language as a *habit* rather than a *process* has tended to have an inhibiting effect on the development of language teaching materials and has led to a proliferation of techniques and methods based on memorization and repetition. More recent views on language have led to the investigation of teaching techniques which more directly involve the learner in communicative tasks, problem solving, and information seeking. These techniques require the learner to utilize language creatively as an instrument of learning (Dykstra and Nunes, 1970). The additional motivation generated by such procedures is said to make learning more meaningful and effective.

The Social Role of the Second Language

We have seen that the target of study, the second language, may represent different values for different learners. Our starting point in studying second language learning could be from a consideration of the different types of relationships that may exist between the language learner and the social group represented by the target language. There are at least two quite distinct situations that lead to fundamentally different language learning settings. The first is the case of learning a language which is not one of the languages of the country. The language is learned as a *foreign language*, as is German in American schools or French in British schools. The learners have the freedom to establish their own goals, since the language has no major social functions in their own country. Success or failure does not have immediate social consequences for the learner. It may give added prestige to an Englishman to be able to speak French, but his prestige is not dependent upon it. The second is the case of language learning in a multilingual country in which the target language already has a fixed role within the nation, and where a prescribed set of functions and values exists for it. The term *second language* is used for such situations: English among segments of the population in India, Nigeria, Malaysia, and Singapore; Malay for non-Malays in Malaysia; Bahasa Indonesia in Indonesia; or Spanish in Paraguay. In multilingual settings in which a second language is required for social functions rather than just simply to fill a slot in the school syllabus, the second language generally operates in functions complementary to those of the first language. Some languages in the community have high prestige, that is, they function in certain prescribed and high status settings such as in government and administration, urban city life, business, and education, and they take on some of the values of modernity and nation building (Richards, 1972). Such is the case of French and English in former French and English colonies, and of Indonesian in Indonesia. Other languages might be limited to lower prestige functions, since they operate perhaps only in the home setting, or in the market place, or within a particular ethnic group or social class.

Learners in multilingual settings may come from a variety of social and economic positions and will consequently have different perceptions of the second language. The motivation for learning may be partly functional (the language is needed for a specific set of economic functions within the society) and partly identificational (the language of an admired group). The learner either consciously or unconsciously adopts attitudes toward elements of society for whom knowledge of the more prestigious forms of a language (or of the more prestigious language) has taken on social meaning. The same situation exists for certain North American Indian and immigrant groups, for whom standard English encountered in the school may represent a totally different set of values from the variety of English which the community itself has developed and preserved as a product of their particular pattern of contact with Anglo civilization (Richards, 1972).

Conclusion

Foreign and second language learning has not received its share of attention within the disciplines which traditionally study language. The central role contemporary linguistic theory attributes to the "ideal speaker-listener in a completely homogeneous speech community" (Chomsky, 1965, p. 23) has led many scholars to ignore questions concerning language and its use and status in heterogeneous communities. If a knowledge of more than one language is considered the norm, however, a realistic account of language will have to explain how speakers produce and receive messages in a variety of codes or registers. Central questions will concern how language-independent semantic systems are constructed, and how these are related to the syntax and lexis of particular codes (languages A, B, C, etc. or language varieties Aa, Ab, Ac, etc.). This emphasis places second language learning much more within the present sphere of interest of sociolinguistics than within the current sphere of interest of general linguistics.

Until quite recently accounts of second language learning were dominated by ideas originating in learning and linguistic theory. However, the field of second language learning is now becoming more autonomous, and a wide variety of issues are considered worthy of serious enquiry. This review has suggested some of the questions that arise from a consideration of the nature of second language acquisition. While we lack an adequate theoretical framework with which to analyze the complexity of behavior subsumed under "second language learning," the empirical observation and experimental work of the last few years has made a significant contribution toward establishing second language learning as both a testing ground for linguistic, psycholinguistic, and sociolinguistic theory, and as a field which requires its own theoretical models and approaches. In addition, and more importantly, educators look to the field of second language learning for clarification of issues in areas such as foreign language teaching, language planning, language education of minority groups, and bilingual education. As further insight is gained into the linguistic, psychological, social, and cultural nature of second language learning, so too our understanding and control of important educational and social problems will be enhanced.

REFERENCES

Ayer, A. J. *Language, truth, and logic.* New York: Dover Publications, 1936. (Republished, 1952.)

Bever, T. G. Perceptions, thought, and language. In J. B. Carroll and R. O. Freedle, eds., *Language comprehension and the acquisition of knowledge.* New York: Wiley, 1972.

Braine, M. D. S. The acquisition of language in infant and child. In C. E. Reed, ed., *The learning of language.* New York: Appleton-Century-Crofts, 1971.

Briere, E. J. *A psycholinguistic study of phonological interference.* The Hague: Mouton, 1968.

Carton, A. S. Inferencing: A process in using and learning language. In P. Pimsleur and T. Quinn, eds., *The psychology of second language learning.* London: Cambridge University Press, 1971.

Chafe, W. *Meaning and the structure of language.* Chicago: University of Chicago Press, 1970.

Chomsky, N. *Aspects of the theory of syntax.* Cambridge, Mass.: M.I.T. Press, 1965.

Close, R. A. *English as a foreign language.* London: George Allen and Unwin, 1962.

Corder, S. P. The significance of learners' errors. *International Review of Applied Linguistics (IRAL),* 1967, 5, 161-70.

Crothers, E., and Suppes, P. *Experiments in second language learning.* New York: Academic Press, 1967.

Delattre, P. C., Liberman, A. M., and Cooper, F. S. Formant transitions and loci as acoustic correlates of place of articulation in American fricatives. *Studia Linguistica,* 1962, 16, 104-21.

Di Pietro, R. J. *Language structures in contrast.* Rowley, Mass.: Newbury House, 1971.

Dulay, H. C., and Burt, M. K. Goofing: An indicator of children's second language learning strategies. *Language Learning,* 1972, 22, 235-52.

Dykstra, G., and Nunes, S. S. The Language Skills Program of the English Project. *Educational Perspectives,* 1970, 9, 31-36.

Ervin-Tripp, S. Structure and process in language acquisition. In A. S. Dil, ed., *Language acquisition and communicative choice*. Stanford: Stanford University Press, 1973.

Fillmore, C. The case for case. In E. Bach and R. Harms, eds., *Universals in linguistic theory*. New York: Holt, Rinehart and Winston, 1968.

Fodor, J., and Garrett, M. Some reflections on competence and performance. In J. Lyons and R. J. Wales, eds., *Psycholinguistic papers*. Chicago: Aldine Prey, 1966.

Gardner, R. C., and Lambert, W. E. *Attitudes and motivation in second language learning*. Rowley, Mass.: Newbury House, 1972.

Greenberg, J. H. Language universals. In T. A. Sebeok, ed., *Current trends in linguistics*, 3. The Hague: Mouton, 1966, 61-112.

Haugen, E. Bilingualism, language contact, and immigrant languages in the United States: A research report 1956-1970. In T. Sebeok, ed., *Current trends in linguistics*, 10. The Hague: Mouton, 1973, 505-91.

Hirtle, W. H. *The simple and progressive forms: An analytical approach*. Quebec: Laval University Press, 1967.

Huxley, R., and Ingram, E., eds. *Language acquisition: Models and methods*. London: Academic Press, 1971.

Kennedy, G. Conditions for language learning. In J. W. Oller Jr. and J. C. Richards, eds., *Focus on the learner*. Rowley, Mass.: Newbury House, 1973.

Kessler, C. *The acquisition of syntax in bilingual children*. Washington, D. C.: Georgetown University Press, 1971.

Krashen, S. D. Lateralization, language learning and the critical period: Some new evidence. *Language Learning*, 1973, 23, 63-74.

Leech, G. N. *Meaning and the English verb*. London: Longmans, 1971.

————. *Semantics*. Middlesex: Penguin, 1974.

Lenneberg, E. H. *Biological foundations of language*. New York: John Wiley, 1967.

Macnamara, J. The cognitive strategies of language learning. In J. W. Oller, Jr. and J. C. Richards, eds., *Focus on the learner*. Rowley, Mass.: Newbury House, 1973.

McNeill, D. Developmental psycholinguistics. In F. Smith and G. A. Miller, eds., *The genesis of language*. Cambridge, Mass.: M.I.T. Press, 1966.

————. *The acquisition of language*. New York: Harper and Row, 1970.

Miller, G. The psycholinguists. In M. Lester, ed., *Readings in applied transformational grammar*. New York: Holt, Rinehart and Winston, 1970.

Nababan, P. W. J. A note on transfer and interference in foreign language learning. University of Hawaii, *Working Papers in Linguistics*, 1971, 3 (4), 17-23.

Nemser, W. Approximative system of foreign language learners. *IRAL*, 1971, 9, 115-23.

Nickel, G. Variables in a hierarchy of difficulty. University of Hawaii, *Working Papers in Linguistics*, 1971, 3 (4), 185-94.

Palmer, H. E. *The principles of language study*. London: Oxford University Press, 1921. (Republished, 1965.)

Richards, J. C. A non-contrastive approach to error analysis. *English Language Teaching*, 1971, 25, 204-19.

———. Social factors, interlanguage and language learning. *Language Learning*, 1972, 22, 159-88.

———, ed. *Error analysis: Perspectives on second language acquisition*. London: Longmans, 1974.

Rodgers, T. The concept of linguistic difficulty. University of Hawaii, *Working Papers in Linguistics*, 1971, 3 (4), 109-20.

Sampson, G. P. The strategies of Cantonese speakers learning English. In R. Darnell, ed., *Linguistic diversity in Canadian society*. Edmonton: Linguistic Research, Inc., 1971.

Schlesinger, I. M. Production of utterances and language acquisition. In D. Slobin, ed., *The ontogenesis of grammar*. New York: Academic Press, 1971, 63-102.

Selinker, L. Interlanguage. *IRAL*, 1972, 10, 209-31.

Slobin, D. et al. *A field manual for cross-cultural study of the acquisition of communicative competence*. Berkeley: University of California, 1967.

Spolsky, B. What does it mean to know a language; or how do you get someone to perform his competence? In J. W. Oller Jr. and J. C. Richards, eds., *Focus on the learner*. Rowley, Mass.: Newbury House, 1973.

Swain, M. Bilingualism, monolingualism and code acquisition. Paper presented at the Child Language Conference, Chicago, November 22-24, 1971.

Tarone, E. A suggested unit for interlingual identification in pronunciation. *TESOL Quarterly*, 1972, 6, 325-31.

Torrey, J. W. Second language learning. In C. Reed, ed., *The learning of language*. New York: Appleton-Century-Crofts, 1971.

Tucker, G. R., Lambert, W. E., and Rigault, A. Students' acquisition of French gender distinctions: A pilot investigation. *IRAL*, 1969, 7, 51-55.

Weinrich, U. *Languages in contact*. The Hague: Mouton, 1967.

VII

Second Language Teaching

William E. Rutherford

For most areas of modern life the past fifteen or twenty years has been a period of considerable unrest and upheaval. It has been a time of great turbulence not only in political affairs, science, religion, and the arts, but also in education. In pedagogy, as elsewhere, fundamental beliefs are being reexamined, cherished assumptions questioned, "expert" authorities challenged, and dogmatic positions assaulted. This kind of ferment can be observed in the language arts curricula as well as in education in general.

Contesting forces in the field of second language teaching have been identified by turns as rationalist/empiricist, transformational/nontransformational, cognitive code/audio-lingual, and even sectarian/eclectic. Despite the conflict of competing rationales, however, it is still possible to discern at least one area of philosophical agreement: the content of nearly all available second language teaching materials of whatever doctrinal persuasion suggests that teaching a language means among other things teaching the grammar of that language. It means, in the broadest sense, bringing certain matters of the target language system to the grammatical consciousness of the learner.

The usefulness for second language learning of the skills associated with grammatical consciousness has upon occasion been challenged (Newmark, 1970; Newmark and Reibel, 1970), and there are a few materials on the market which make no appeal to such consciousness whatever. There is considerable evidence (Carroll, 1965), however, that ability to verbalize grammatical relations in sentences is closely connected to degree of success in language learning. Jakobovits (1970) characterizes the ability in this way:

The successful foreign language learner is apparently capable of the following task: given a word italicized in one sentence (e.g., "The man went into the *house.*") he can identify that word in another sentence which has the same grammatical function (e.g., picking one of the italicized words of the following sentence: "The *church* next to the *bowling alley* will be built in a new *location* next *year.*"). We know of course that the individual is capable of recognizing the grammatical relations in the second sentence (otherwise he could not give it a semantic interpretation), so the ability must be one of explicit verbalization of implicitly known rules and relations (p. 19).

Even Newmark (1970), who makes much of the alleged nonnecessity and insufficiency of teaching the grammatical form of utterances rather than their "use," admits to "the student's *craving* for explicit formulization of generalizations" (p. 82, italics added). Ausubel (1968) says that "providing guidance to the learner in the form of verbal explanation of the underlying principles almost invariably facilitates learning and retention and some-times transfer as well" (p. 504). Other arguments in support of paying classroom attention to the matter of how the language to be learned is put together can be found in many of the articles in Jankowsky (1973).

This chapter will explore some of the many ways in which such consciousness can be and has been activated, will examine the different forms of what is generally deemed worth bringing to the awareness of the language learner, will assess the degree of usefulness of such forms for pedagogy, and will suggest some kinds of language research which have potential pedagogical relevance. These issues will be discussed in three sections, focusing on (1) linguistic *implications* of a general nature, (2) linguistic *applications* of a more specific nature, and (3) important facets of language that have thus far resisted attempts at linguistic formalization. The principal point of reference throughout these discussions will be the notion of "linguistic relationship."

General Linguistic Implications

Agnation.   It is an axiom in educational psychology that learning takes place more quickly, and that what is learned is retained for a longer period of time (*a*) when that which is to be learned relates directly to something which is already a part of the learner's knowledge or experience, and (*b*) when the learner perceives the nature of this relationship. A corollary to these principles is that relationships should hold also among the things being taught. Mackey (1965) writes that "the relations among components of a pattern must be known before its individual members can be understood" (p. 6). Jakobovits (1970) states that "it is clear that knowledge of language at all levels consists of knowing patterns of relations rather than constituent elements [and that] the usefulness of efforts to teach the latter is in doubt" (p. 197). A more precise term *agnation* is the choice of Stevick (1971), following Gleason (1965), in discussing the interlocking components of language viewed as a unified whole.

Agnation as an organizational device is not new to second language teaching. Long before the advent of generative-transformational grammar, language teachers had already perceived and incorporated into their lessons correspondences like those of active-passive, declarative-interrogative, affirmative-negative, etc. Such surface structure correspondences, in fact, were all that was involved in the early attempts to put language teaching materials into a "transformational" framework. But "transformation" as a pedagogical device cannot be much more than this; the linguistic concept of "transformation" as a process wherein certain formal operations are performed to convert strings of underlying phrase markers to surface phrase markers could never really have found its way into pedagogy, although there have been some attempts in this direction (see Rutherford, 1973b).

The relationship represented by two surface structures with the same meaning—mutually convertible surface structures—turns out to be one of two frequently found "applications" of transformational grammar to language teaching. The other prime application is that of sentence combining, accompanied by instructions to put, for example, one sentence into another in some particular way. Completion of such exercises usually requires that the constituent sentence be "transformed" before insertion into the matrix sentence (Frank, 1972; Rand, 1969; Rutherford, 1968). Sentence-embedding exercises of this kind, however, have implications beyond the limited use to which they have been put in the materials cited. These implications have to do with assumptions about the ways in which language is organized.

The linguistic cycle.   Teaching materials produced during the heyday of American structuralism were a reflection of the theoretical assumptions of American structuralism. Among the typical sentence-producing devices in pedagogical materials of the period is the one where columns of surface structure elements with identical co-occurrence possibilities are placed side by side in such a way that the student, by selecting a word from each column, can trace a path through the pattern and produce a possible sentence in the language.

(Thirty-six sentences are possible.)

			Mary was born.
This is	the house		the murder took place.
I have seen	the village	where	your grandmother lives.
Have you ever been to	the place		the poet stayed.

(Wishon and Burks, 1968.)

Writing after all does move from left to right; therefore, why not employ the kind of schema shown above for sentence creation? (Witness the superficial similarity to a Markov process "finite state grammar," discussed in Chomsky, 1957, pp. 18 ff.) Although it is possible that sentence producing devices such as these are at times useful for language learning, they at best indicate no more of language organization than the taxonomy of grammatical elements, and in the above arrangement some of the elements are not even constituents. It is possible, however, to devise other pedagogical schemata that more closely approximate the ways in which we suspect language is organized. Such organization would depend in part upon the linguistic "reality" of rules, for example, cyclical rules.

What are some of the pedagogical consequences of choosing a representation of language that relies to some degree upon selective application of the principle of the linguistic cycle? Perhaps the most obvious consequence is the opportunity afforded the student to have tightly controlled practice in writing sentences of great complexity, in which he brings to bear all at once a number of interacting rules of syntax. A sentence like *The defendant chose to ignore his lawyer's preference for the defendant to turn over the remaining documents that have been subpoenaed* could then result from successive embeddings as follows:

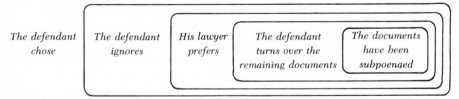

The documents have been subpoenaed becomes a relative clause contained in the sentence *The defendant turns over the remaining documents that have been subpoenaed*, which in turn becomes a *for-to* nominalization contained in another sentence *His lawyer prefers for the defendant to turn over the remaining documents that have been subpoenaed*. This sentence becomes a factive nominal contained in still another sentence *The defend-*

ant ignores his lawyer's preference for the defendant to turn over the remaining documents that have been subpoenaed, and finally a *for-to* nominalization contained in the matrix sentence *The defendant chose for the defendant to ignore his lawyer's preference for the defendant to turn over the remaining documents that have been subpoenaed.* All that remains to be done is to delete *for the defendant* in the last embedding in order to reach the original surface sentence. We can imagine, furthermore, that the individual constituent sentences might have been the student's own creations before the teacher gave him any directions for combining. Even the matter of the learner's choosing the correct complementizers in sentences like the above need not depend entirely upon his remembering some otherwise arbitrary strict subcategorization restrictions on long lists of verbs, nouns, and adjectives, since, as Kiparsky and Kiparsky (1968) have shown, these restrictions can to some extent be predicted from the meanings of the lexical items themselves (Rutherford, 1970).

Awareness of cyclical rules can also afford students the opportunity to locate the source of some of their own writing errors. In teaching the formation and use of relative clauses, for example, teachers can reduce student errors significantly through appeals to the sentence from which they have been derived. Thus, the impossibility of a head noun + relative clause like *a world which many people don't have enough to eat* (produced by a foreign student and typical of many such attempts) is a direct consequence of the impossibility of *Many people don't have enough to eat the world,* the sentence that would have to underlie it. This procedure presupposes of course that the student knows a relative clause when he sees one, or that he can at least distinguish a relative clause (whatever he may call it) from other types of clauses.

Ungrammaticality.   Many language teachers assume that it is harmful to expose students to ungrammatical samples of the language they are trying to learn. Lee (1965, 1972), for example, asks "why present the pupils needlessly with incorrect patterns?" Brooks (1964) states that "the principle method of *avoiding* error in language learning is to observe and practice the right model a sufficient number of times." The belief in linguistic contamination by exposure is one of the natural consequences of subscription to an audio-lingual habit theory of second language acquisition and it is perhaps no surprise that such beliefs are less frequently articulated as the audio-lingual theory continues to lose favor. Now that cognitive-code approaches to language teaching have begun to find new respectability we find increasing discussion of the pedagogical usefulness of sentences displaying varying degrees of grammaticality. Of course, convincing evidence has never been offered that occasional exposure to anything less than totally acceptable language affects competence adversely. And how could it, if the classroom semisentences constitute a mere fraction of the degenerate language data that typify much of everyday speech? Jakobovits (1970) discusses the matter of semigrammaticality in light of the question of whether or not it is desirable to attempt to replicate in the classroom the supposed stages of development of the learner's competence by exposing him "to utterances which are grammatically progressive at each stage but which fall short of having the full complexity of well-formed sentences" (p. 23). Although Jakobovits leaves the issue unresolved, one could still question the wisdom of tampering in this way with the student's learning strategies when we have as yet so little understanding of what those strategies actually are.

A somewhat different approach to the question of the use of semi-grammaticality is offered by Lakoff (1969), whose suggestions follow logically from a belief in the rationalist theory of language learning. She writes that:

> the teacher must give the learner a boost to making his own generalizations, to learning how the native speaker understands and intuitively uses . . . sentences. This necessarily implies that it is essential to give the learner ungrammatical sentences, so that he can study these along with the grammatical ones to decide for himself what the difference is, so that when he is on his own and has to make a decision for himself, he can rely on his own new generalizing ability in this sphere to make the right generalizations (pp. 125-26).

As for the materials:

> the text will be rationalistically oriented—it will encourage students to ask themselves why sentences are good and bad—and in this sense will be truly "transformational" in accordance with the beliefs held by transformational grammarians about the nature and acquisition of language (p. 117).

What is left undiscussed, however, by both Jakobovits and Lakoff and by anyone else who suggests the pedagogical utility of sentences that are less than grammatical is the question of which semisentences to use and how to use them. In other words, selection of such samples for classroom use must surely be no less principled than selection of what *is* grammatical. We may choose semisentences that are somehow specifically designed to benefit the student's learning strategy in the sense of Jakobovits; or we may feed him semisentences that are more reminiscent of the starred examples typically selected by linguists to highlight generalizations and lead to the formulation of rules, which is what Lakoff seems to be suggesting. These are choices, however, whose validity still needs empirical justification (see also Echeverria, 1974).

Some nonapplications of linguistics.   Central to the concept of agnation for pedagogy is the language user's unquestioned need to be able to express a given idea or feeling in more than one way. This need can be filled only by an organizational arrangement of teaching materials which may be largely incompatible with the view, widely held by empiricists until relatively recently, that such materials should be determined almost exclusively by linguistic criteria. Linguistically, of course, it is fallacious automatically to assume that semantically equivalent surface structures necessarily share some common underlying form, but the useful pairing of such structures for learning purposes in no way depends even upon prior formal proof of a shared source.

It likewise remains to be proven that a teachable relationship exists between two contrasting strings which independently undergo transformations with identical structure indices. It may be true, for example, that verb-particle movement and indirect-object movement can be learned more effectively together than separately, but this fact in no way follows necessarily from the linguistic fact that a single formal rule can account for the following word-order changes:

*look - up - the word   look - the word - up   *look - up - it*
*give - Ed - the book   give - the book - to Ed   *give - Ed - it*

The horizontal arrangement reveals relationships that are at least products of a rule of the language; the vertical arrangement is a direct consequence of no more than the artifact (namely, a structure index) that we happen to have chosen to represent the structures in question.

Although the possible rearrangement of surface structure constituents provides the language user with alternative modes of expression, this fact in itself is of marginal relevance for pedagogy without reasons for choosing one mode over another. The speaker must not only know what his options are but also have some basis for exercising a given one at a given time. It is not enough to know that *John wrote a letter to the official* is a word-order variant of *John wrote the official a letter*; but also necessary to know that when a fair-sized relative clause is to be added to either the direct object or the indirect object, the speaker must choose the variant which lets the relativized noun phrase come last, that is, *John wrote the official a letter that he had been talking about writing for a couple of days / *John wrote a letter that he had been talking about writing for a couple of days to the official*.

What enables the linguist to avoid generating the above starred example is probably a constraint something like the Complex Noun Phrase Shift Rule (Ross, 1967). This rule requires that an internal noun phrase dominating a sentence permute with an adjacent constituent. One may well call this (or an updated version of it) a rule of the language, possibly many languages, and as such, the rule is part of the knowledge that any speaker has about English. Yet, if the rule is at all worth bringing to student consciousness, it would certainly not be appropriate to state it in terms of the permutation of internal sentence-dominated noun phrases. Furthermore, Lawler (1973) has pointed out that discussion of syntactic constraints of the kind formulated by Ross (1967) perhaps need not take up language learning time at all since these constraints are presumed to operate in all languages. On the few occasions when errors (by native speakers as well as second language learners) are attributable to violation of universal constraints, "the speaker had backed himself into a syntactic corner from which he could extricate himself only by a violation without starting over" (Lawler, 1973, p. 50).

In perhaps the most quoted article in applied linguistics, Chomsky (1966) discusses "certain tendencies and developments within linguistics and psychology that may have potential impact on the teaching of languages" (p. 45). Two of the developments that Chomsky cites are "the abstractness of linguistic representation" and "the universality of underlying linguistic structure." These are concepts that we ultimately touch upon in any investigation of the usefulness for language pedagogy of the linguistic cycle, semigrammaticality, structure indices, and universal constraints. We turn now to pedagogical consideration of linguistic features of a more specific kind.

Specific Linguistic Applications

If the concept of agnation is at all valid for the construction of materials and the teaching of second languages, that validity is probably demonstrated not so much in the teaching of "transformationally" related surface forms (that is, those which are judged, in formal linguistics, to share an underlying structure at some stage of generation) but rather more in the teaching of relationships between elements within the sentence itself.

Relative clauses and bracketing.   English relative clauses present varying degrees of difficulty to non-English speakers, the incidence of error being somewhat predictable according to native language (Schachter, 1974). Faulty relative clause constructions produced by foreign students—where the fault lies in the relativization process itself and not in the other mechanics of the clause—fall roughly into three general categories. The first is represented by sentences like *The question that it gave me the most trouble was number four*; the second by *The question it gave me the most trouble was number four*; and the third by *The question gave me the most trouble was number four*. In the first example the shared noun phrase in the constituent sentence has been both relativized and pronominalized, leaving two references where there had been only one. In the second example pronominalization of the shared noun phrase has occurred rather than relativization, leaving a full sentence inside a full sentence. In the third example there is no trace at all of the original shared noun phrase in the constituent sentence. Recent research has shown that errors of this kind may be reduced through a method of classroom explanation and verification based upon constant recognition of (*a*) the relative clause as an embedded sentence and (*b*) the relationship between head noun and relative marker. The above example then, in its acceptable form *The question that gave me the most trouble was number four* would be explainable as follows:

> *The question* [*The question* gave me the most trouble] was number four.

The student learns that a relative marker replaces the inside shared noun phrase. For the example in question nothing further remains now but to erase the brackets in order to reach the usable sentence. Where the embedded shared noun phrase functions as something other than the subject of its sentence, however, one additional rule must be invoked: the relative marker moves to the front of its clause. Thus, from the simple representation:

> *The question* [I found *the question* most troublesome] was number four.

we produce by relative marker substitution:

The question [I found *which* most troublesome] was number four.

and then by fronting the marker and erasing the brackets:

The question which I found most troublesome was number four.

Once the student has grasped these basic principles it would be appropriate to bring in additional rules that delete the marker, or marker + *be*, under specific conditions. Exercises to practice the formation of restrictive relative clauses can take the shape of lists of forms like the above first two examples with brackets, or a list having thematic unity, or a thematically unified sequence of forms the rewriting of which produces a complete paragraph. Since student paragraph writing, especially that of speakers of the Indo-European languages of modern India, tends toward a succession of short sentences, it is often useful to begin with a paragraph made up of grammatically correct but simple sentences (1. *Rice is one of the world's most important foods.* 2. *Rice grows in Asia and the Middle East.* 3. *etc.*) accompanied by instructions to combine them two at a time. The student thus produces relative clauses not by means of bracket representation but by following instructions such as "Put sentences 1 and 2 together as *Rice, which is . . . ."*

What a student must do in order to convert an underlying representation to its usable surface form can be clearly specified for the most part by form, by positioning, or by some pedagogical signaling devices that we can add. The distinction between restrictive and nonrestrictive relative clauses, for example, can, for pedagogical purposes, be represented structurally in a way that still preserves brackets for both but adds a conjunction for the nonrestrictive. The restrictive and nonrestrictive interpretations of *I talked to John's wife who commutes from Pasadena* are thus:

RESTRICTIVE
I talked to *John's wife* [*John's wife* commutes from Pasadena]

NONRESTRICTIVE
I talked to *John's wife* [AND *John's wife* commutes from Pasadena] or [*John's wife* commutes from Pasadena AND] I talked to *her*.

For teaching purposes, the difference between the potentially confusing bracketed relative clauses and bracketed noun complements could simply be that for complementation there will be no (italicized) shared noun phrase:

He has *an idea* [*I don't like him*]   NOUN COMPLEMENT

(He has an idea that I don't like him.)

He has *an idea* [I don't like *the idea*]   RELATIVE CLAUSE

(He has an idea that I don't like.)

However, the whole notion of pedagogical bracketing is vulnerable to attack. It can be argued that bracketing reflects only the theoretical linguistic allegiance we happen to hold at this time, and that therefore it does not necessarily have any relevance to language learning. (See Engels, 1973, for a defense of abstract symbolization in foreign language learning.) If bracketed representation of underlying structure has any kind of "psychological reality" for the language learner, this fact still remains to be demonstrated. In the meantime, we have enough evidence to suggest that investigations of the pedagogical usefulness of rudimentary linguistic abstractions like the above would be a potentially profitable undertaking.

Case grammar.   Until relatively recently most applied linguistic research having to do with grammar was confined to reexamination of formal relations among the various constituents of a sentence. Now, under the influence of increasing formal linguistic studies in semantics, we find applied linguists also paying more attention to the semantic aspects of grammatical relations.

Some implications for language learning of a cognitive approach that is semantically based are to be found in Brown (1972). Brown hints at possible utilization of notions and categories like "potentiality, capability, futurity, agent, locomotion, locative, time," etc., the likes of which presumably can be employed to reveal the semantic relationships which syntax obscures among the possible alternative ways (for example, passive, compounding, sentence conjunction, etc.) of restating a sentence like *I saw a boy who had red hair*. This idea of borrowing bits of the case grammar model is fascinating, but again the real consequences for practical classroom implementation need to be spelled out. It is certianly true that the notions of "subject" and "object" can be very misleading to foreign students trying to learn English, since, as Brown correctly points out, *the city, the rush hour*, and *the motor* can all be subjects of the verb phrase *is noisy*. But then he writes that "to describe 'the city,' 'the rush hour,' and 'the motor' all as subject noun phrases is probably farther from reality than to differentiate the three by describing them, respectively, as a 'locative,' a 'temporal,' and an 'instrumental'" (p. 266). Nilsen (1971) would employ similar differentiation in teaching classes of verbs having similar case frames. Even though the case frames and their associated terminology may be more real in some sense, it is not easy to see what would be accomplished by actually bringing all of it into the classroom. Again, it is a matter of making use of what insights theoretical linguistics has to offer while at the same time managing somehow to leave behind the formal apparatus that goes with it.

The linguistic relationships that case grammar captures so neatly can probably be put to some pedagogical use without the concomitant terminology and its inevitable complications (Rutherford, 1970, 1973a). It is not necessary, for example, to know that *window* is "objective" in order to appreciate the fact that the relationship between *window* and *break* remains constant throughout the following sentences, despite the fact that four different nouns occur in subject position:

> The child broke the window with a hammer.
> The hammer broke the window with its impact.
> The impact broke the window.
> The window broke.

Some current research includes experimentation with the use of unmarked case frames for sentence-producing exercises in an attempt to prevent errors of the type *The accident was happened yesterday*. Such exercises consist quite simply of sequences of a verb plus some associated noun phrases, for example,

> include - the West - the Rocky Mountains

with instructions to move something into subject position (an obligatory rule in English). The relationships which the semantic content of the words themselves suggest are also a help in choosing the correct case-marking prepositions for the full sentence. The obligatoriness of subject-position occupancy coupled with the impossibility of a final copula with only one associated case (except for an occasional rarity like *God is*), for example,

> be - several different geographic sections

focuses graphically upon the need for a dummy subject, in this case *there*. For tightly controlled extended writing requiring sentence connectors, transitional phrases, etc., one can devise exercises like the following in which brackets again enclose embedded sentences and capital letters signal the beginning of a new sentence:

include - the West - the Rocky Mountains

However,

be - several different geographic sections

For purposes of study

be easier - [We divide the area into smaller sections]

In this way

remember more easily - we - *the states* [*The states* make up each section]

and

learn - we - something of the geography of each section

The student is required to do essentially four things in each separate sentence: move an appropriate noun phrase into subject position; choose an appropriate verb tense; bring all embedded sentences to their required surface form; and mark with prepositions the case forms of those noun phrases that require such marking. Additionally, of course, copula + adjective (*be easier*) can be shown as adjective only, forcing the student to determine as well when to supply the copula, that is, to distinguish verbs from adjectives. Dependency upon technical terminology is at a minimum, however, and the evidence to date suggests that further experimentation to determine the possible "psychological reality" of such representations might prove to be worthwhile.

The syntactic relationships discussed so far are of several kinds: (*a*) those holding between constituents of a sentence, as, for example, between a relative clause and its head noun, or a verb and its complement; (*b*) those holding between two semantically equivalent surface forms of the same grammatical status, whether or not they would be treated transformationally, as, for example, in most passive-active pairings, or simple "equivalents" like *John beat Bill in chess* ~ *Bill lost to John in chess*; and (*c*) those holding between two surface forms which are mere rearrangements of each other, for example, in numerous instances of preposing, postposing, optional permutation of constituents, etc. We turn now to relationships of still another kind.

Morphosyntax.   One of the most productive areas of linguistic relationships for learning purposes is that in which identical syntactic functions are captured by different morphologically related lexical items. It is extremely important, for instance, for a student of English to learn that a phrase like

Germany's invasion of Poland is somehow a morphosyntactic "copy" of the sentence *Germany invaded Poland*, with the semantic units in identical order, as they are also in the variant copies of *Poland was invaded by Germany*, *Poland's invasion by Germany*. Furthermore, the student needs to know that if the adverb *suddenly* occurs in one of the sentence versions (*Germany suddenly invaded Poland*), then the adjective *sudden* must appear in the corresponding phrase version (*Germany's sudden invasion of Poland*). The choice between sentence or phrase will be determined by other syntactic choices that the student will have made. If the larger sentence that he is saying or writing begins *Europe was in turmoil* . . . and then finishes with a reason adverbial, he could choose to express the reason with either *because* or *because of*. The selection of *because* will force the full embedded sentence *Germany suddenly invaded Poland*, whereas the selection of *because of* requires the phrase version *Germany's sudden invasion of Poland*. To those who might argue that it would not be necessary to know both forms, since either will convey the meaning quite well, it is only necessary to point out that often there is no choice. If the student wanted to say that the turmoil was also caused by the economic crisis, he would need to do so by letting the two developments appear as conjuncts within the reason adverbial. Notice, however, that the two conjuncts have to occur in phrase form (*Europe was in turmoil because of the economic crisis and Germany's invasion of Poland*), because if they were full embedded sentences other elements of the syntax would force a change in the meaning such that the word *and* is interpreted as *and so*. Consequently, contrary to the intent of the writer, the economic crisis sounds like the cause of the invasion (*Europe was in turmoil because there was an economic crisis and Germany invaded Poland*). The best way for the learner to be equipped to exercise options like these is for the curriculum to focus upon the linguistic relationships that make the options possible. The kind of exercise material perhaps best suited to engender such competence would include restatements of the kind we have just seen:

1. Everyone was unhappy because the bus arrived late and departed early.

    Everyone was unhappy because of the bus's *late arrival* and . . . .

2. The United Nations was intended to be an agency which could relieve economic and social misery and settle international disputes peacefully.

    The United Nations was intended to be an agency for *the relief of economic and social misery* and . . . .

3. Etc.

If awareness of morphosyntactic relationships plays an important role in language learning, then it would seem sensible to let the need for such awareness be part of the rationale for organizing the student's classroom exposure to the language. This principle does not seem to have been considered in most of the texts currently on the market. Some, typified by *New Concept English* (Alexander, 1967), make no attempt to call attention to anything structural or make meaningful generalizations. *Modern American English* (Dixon, 1971) includes statements about English but pays no attention whatever to morphosyntax. The *Lado English Series* (Lado, 1972) goes the familiar route of "vocabulary expansion" via affixation (*prevent + ion = prevention*) but stops short of an explanation or exercises concerning the function of the derived forms in the syntax. In *Let's Learn English* (Wright, Van Syoc, and Van Syoc, 1973) there are fill-in-the-blank exercises but very little on the syntactic match between sentence and phrase. The occasional glimpses of morphosyntax in action to be found in *Using English* (Danielson and Hayden, 1973) are fortuitous by-products of focus upon other matters.

Morphophonemics.   That the teaching of the syntactic settings of paired lexical derivatives should be virtually ignored in current materials is all the more puzzling in that such pairings could be a useful repository as well for many of the important facts of English morphophonemics and a remedy for the kind of student spelling errors that stem from morphophonemic misconception. These errors fall into two very broad categories: (*a*) those arising from mistaken attempts to assign vowel quality to English weak-stressed (reduced) vowels, and (*b*) those arising from attempts to assign quality (vowel or consonant) independently of an operating alternation. An example of the former would be spelling the word *atom* with an *e* instead of an *o*; an example of the latter would be spelling the word *medicine* with an *s* instead of a *c*. It is fairly obvious that where the orthography is an accurate guide to the spelling of a vowel in only one of two related words (that is, the vowel has been reduced in the other) they should be taught as a pair. The second syllable vowels in the words *industry*, *artistry*, and *ancestry* are all pronounced with the weak-stress "schwa," though the orthography shows these vowels to be *u*, *i*, and *e*, respectively. Someone hearing those words pronounced for the first time could not be expected to know how to spell the reduced vowels until he compared the pronunciation of the three words with that of their corresponding adjectives (*industrial*, *artistic*, *ancestral*), in which a stress shift now gives the three vowels the phonetic quality indicated by their orthographic representations. Similarly, someone hearing the words *discretion* and *confession* pronounced for the first time could not be expected to know that their palatal sibilants are spelled differently until he heard the corresponding words *discreet* and *confess*. Taking these factors into consideration, we can thus assign students the following kind of task:

> Each of the following words will be pronounced for you along with another, closely corresponding word. By comparing the two, see if you can determine the spelling of the missing weak-stressed vowel /ə/.
>
> | | | | |
> |-----|---------|-----|----------|
> | 1. | gramm__r | 6. | minist__r |
> | 2. | sup__r | 7. | regul__r |
> | 3. | min__r | 8. | superi__r |
> | 4. | popul__r | 9. | equat__r |
> | 5. | edit__r | 10. | simil__r |

(The corresponding "clue" words for comparison, which the student would hear but not see, are 1. *grammatical*, 2. *superior*, 3. *minority*, 4. *popularity*, 5. *editorial*, 6. *ministerial*, 7. *regularity*, 8. *superiority*, 9. *equatorial*, 10. *similarity*.)

Ideas for similar kinds of exercises can be drawn from the research of Brengelman (1970), C. Chomsky (1970), Cronnell (1972), and Schane (1970).

Expectation and redundancy. Another parameter in the concept of linguistic relationships has a direct bearing on the nature of the reading process. Eskey (1973) has shown that although we do not yet really know what mental faculties are brought to bear in reading, much less what actually happens in the act of comprehending a written text, still we *are* able to isolate at least some of the skills that the typical reader employs. A clue to one of these skills, Eskey writes, "is the relatively high redundancy level typical of natural human languages. Because of it every successful reader quickly learns to respond to a limited number of critical signals at increasingly higher levels of abstraction; he soon learns, that is, to get by without reading, first every letter, then every word, and eventually even larger chunks of the text" (p. 172). Contributing greatly to linguistic redundancy are sets of structural devices that signal relationships, such that when the first item is brought into play the general character of what follows is somewhat predictable. This is true not just of the well-known correlative conjunctions like *not only . . . but also, both . . . and, (n)either . . . (n)or,* etc., but also of the less common signals like *in other words, to change the subject, similarly, finally,* and a hundred more, some of which will be discussed in a different context in the third section of this chapter. Thus, if the writer starts his paragraph with the words *to begin with,* followed by whatever point follows, the reader can reasonably expect to encounter at least another point matching the content of the first and also possibly a signaling device like *next* or *second.* If the writer begins with an *although* clause, the reader can always anticipate a main clause of contrasting force to balance the concession. If the *although* clause is a long one, an additional structural device (viz. *still*) can serve to signal the beginning of what the reader has anticipated. This is precisely what occurred in the second sentence of this paragraph. The principle of structural redundancy can be utilized to devise an exercise technique wherein the students read a succession of incomplete passages. After each partial passage the student has to guess the *general* content of what follows by relying on the meaning of what he has just read. The kinds of predictions the student is asked to make are whether the remainder of the passage will offer a contrast, a reinforcement, a disclaimer, a cancelation, and so on. These same aspects of the implied meaning of the passage can also be questioned for comprehension tests, as shown by Yorio and Perkins (1974).

Composition correction.   Recognition of the importance of intralanguage relationships leads, as we have seen, to some clear pedagogical implications, not the least important of which is the need to avoid treating language elements—be they sentences, clauses, phrases, words, or even segmented sounds—as self-contained, hermetically sealed entities. The error, for example, in choosing the present perfect over the simple past in a sentence like **I have gone there yesterday* is tied to the presence of the "point-of-time" adverbial *yesterday.* The error of the missing determiner in a sentence like **I bought new car* has its explanation in the fact that singular count nouns like *car* cannot stand alone. The nonexistent comma at one end of a sentence-internal nonrestrictive relative clause turns out sometimes to be an error only because the writer did elect to put a comma at the other end. The error in a clause like **while we arrived* resides exclusively in neither the subordinator nor the verb but rather in the incompatibility of *while* and "achievement" verbs like *arrive* that are not in the continuous. What is wrong with a sentence like **To smuggle and kidnapping are illegal* is not the choice of either the infinitive or the gerundive but rather the conjunction of the two. It would seem then that the way to deal with such violations when they appear in student compositions is not merely to identify a particular item that may be the wrong choice, may have the wrong form, or perhaps should not be there at all, but rather to call attention to a violated relationship—an impossible juxtaposition, a reference without an antecedent, lexical incompatibility, etc. One way in which to focus such attention is simply to connect the mismatched elements with a line in order to lead the student himself to discover the source of the violation and to choose the form of correction that coincides with his original intent.

The kinds of linguistic relationship that play a part in composition correction, stimulus-response exercises, and other controlled classroom activity can be defined reasonably well in linguistic terms. It is such activity that many applied linguists (Paulston, 1970; Prator, 1965; Rutherford, 1968) have assumed will lead ultimately to the student's ability to use the language for communication, although such assumptions have been seriously questioned (Newmark, 1970; Oller, 1972). Whether or not one subscribes to the concept of language learning through a continuum of decreasingly controlled exercises, it will still be necessary for the student's attention to be drawn to ways in which he can *use* the syntax of his new language. He will need to know that *(Won't you) have more coffee* is an offer, whereas *(Would you) have more patience* is a request; he will need to learn that *Why don't you try harder?* is not necessarily a question; he will need to understand that *How long have you been in the United States?* can be uttered only in the United States. These are aspects of language whose explanation lies beyond syntax, and it is to this area of applied linguistics that we next turn our attention.

Some Remaining Problems

It is obvious that there are parameters of any language that have so far resisted formalization. Indeed, some of these parameters have to do with the very function of language itself as a medium of communication. That language as communication should have been ignored in so much of the linguistically based classroom materials published since World War II is not surprising when one considers that such materials depended for substance and rationale exclusively upon linguistics, whether structural or transformational, and that the heaviest (structural) influences upon pedagogy were above all those in which the role of communication was far from primary. The degree of dependency of language teaching upon linguistics during that period is graphically illustrated by the fact that some of the

theoreticians (Fries, Hall, Twadell, etc.) were their own classroom practitioners. It is interesting that as late as 1968 DeCamp called attention to
this fact in a paper titled "The Current Discrepancy Between Theoretical
and Applied Linguistics" (DeCamp, 1968). He noted that "during the
1940s and early 1950s nearly every major linguist authored at least one
language textbook," and cited a whole list of examples. Then he followed
with the lamentation, "but where are the language textbooks written by
Chomsky, Halle, Postal, Klima, Fillmore, Ross, or even textbooks which
seem to be very much influenced by them?" (p. 3). That this question can
now, such a short time later, be faintly amusing is an indication of how
pedagogical thinking has shifted. DeCamp's thesis in 1968 was that a
"discrepancy" (whatever that term means in this context) between linguistic
theory and classroom practice was necessarily undesirable. Nowadays the
existence of such discrepancies seems to be no longer a major issue.

Linguistics in perspective.   A glance at the tables of contents of some of the
language materials currently being published is revealing. It seems that the
generalizations that are being laid out for the student—indisputably one of
the purposes of a text—are being organized more and more according to
semantic, psychological, pragmatic, and pedagogical criteria as well as
syntactic criteria. For example, instead of treating all the subjunctive forms
together as language texts so often do, one recent book (Danielson and
Hayden, 1973) breaks up the subjunctive into its different uses, letting the
"suggestion" use appear with other ways of making suggestions, letting the
"unreal situation" use appear with other ways of talking about unreal
situations, and letting the "necessity and urgency" use appear with other
ways of conveying necessity and urgency. Another text (Rutherford,
1975) at one point gathers together various syntactic items traditionally
treated separately as passive, cleft sentence, pseudo-cleft, emphatic stress,
and word-order change and puts them under the heading of "topicalization." In short, linguistic considerations for the *arrangement* of language
forms within a pedagogical text are not the only considerations; they may
even prove to be not the most important ones. Where linguistics does play
a crucial role is in the breadth of generalizations about language that it
allows us to make and, even more important, in the fundamental attitudes
about language that we ultimately hold.

    We are realizing more and more that no single academic discipline can
claim exclusive relevance in language teaching research. What is important
for successful teaching and successful learning has to be gleaned from a
large number of contributory disciplines, including linguistics, to be sure,

but also sociology, educational psychology, ethnomethodology, and perhaps even communication theory. But practical common sense and one's own everyday awareness of what communication is really like are also important ingredients. Slager (1973) emphasizes the importance of the language teacher in the communicative aspects of language learning and suggests that the teacher be a so-called collector of context. Slager writes that:

> a textbook . . . is properly regarded as a series of lessons each one of which may be more or less successful in blending grammar and context. Rightfully used, it should be no more than a kind of outline. If this view is accepted, it implies an important creative role for the classroom teacher; for it is the teacher who is ultimately responsible for adapting each lesson to meet the specific needs and interests of his students. The teacher, as well as the textbook writer, must be a contextualizer (p. 49).

Extra-sententials. It might be useful, however, to point out that the teacher can be a collector not only of contexts but also sometimes of what goes into those contexts. There are numerous bits of commonly used language, for example, that are seldom if ever touched upon in textbooks. One whole such area is that of the so-called extra-sententials, that vast collection of syntactic forms of many varieties which, in linguistic terms, never form a constituent with the sentences to which they are attached, yet are indispensable for communicative precision and for the natural-sounding give-and-take of discourse. These include adverbs like *confidentially, frankly, personally*; prepositional phrases like *in all seriousness, in short, in my opinion*, and maybe a hundred more; participial phrases like *roughly speaking, using the word loosely; if* clauses like *if you know what I mean, if I may interrupt, if I remember correctly*; and other subordinate clauses such as *while we're on the subject, as I was saying, unless I'm mistaken, in case you're wondering, since you ask,* and *before you begin.*

These expressions are by no means isolated linguistic oddities. They recur in discourse with great frequency, and there are many more of them than this sampling would suggest. Syntactically, they are distinctly different from their counterparts within the sentence proper, as evidenced by pairs such as *In plain view the thieves made off with the crown jewels/In plain English, the thieves made off with the crown jewels;* or *Marvin has given up teaching to write short stories/Marvin has given up teaching, to make a long story short;* or *Mary doesn't know if you ask her/Mary doesn't know, if you ask me;* or *As I was talking there was this loud crash/As I was saying, there was this loud crash.*

What all of these expressions, which represent a variety of syntactic forms, have in common is their reference to some aspect of one of the various kinds of speech acts. These expressions have no grammatical connection with the sentences to which they are attached, but refer instead in some way to the locutionary event of uttering sentences themselves. It is unimportant, pedagogically speaking, that linguists have, for the most part, not yet dealt with the matter of how to generate these locutionary expressions, whether to attach them to the abstractly represented speech act, or, in some roundabout way to the actually spoken sentence. One need not wait for linguistics to resolve the dilemma, for in language pedagogy there need not be a dilemma. What is important is that communication will be severely impeded if the speaker cannot economically say that he is continuing where he previously left off, or that he is changing the subject, making a long story short, or talking confidentially.

Context and communication.   Locutionary expressions, then, are basic tools for communication. By themselves, they carry very little, if any propositional content; rather, they are often the means by which the speaker inflects the tone of his utterance, gains or keeps the attention of his hearer, relinquishes the floor, signals the sentence type to follow, or interrupts a previous speaker. The importance of teaching foreign students when, where, and how to interrupt without being rude—in other words, to gain the floor—has been demonstrated by Dubin (1973), who attacks "the problem of devising strategies for teaching interactional rules in English" by suggesting classroom exercises in which students try to break into ongoing conversation using various techniques, or they replay scenes where they change one feature of the role relationships, the setting, the degree of intimacy, or the occupation of the participants. Significantly, Dubin's bibliography includes a roster of contemporary sociologists, with not one linguist cited. The sociolinguistic contributions of researchers such as Goffman (1971), Sacks (1974), Schegloff (1972), and Hymes (1974) will very likely play an increasingly important role in the construction of classroom materials that will be appearing in the years to come. Grimshaw (1973) even writes of his interest in "the possibilities of a universal syntax of social interaction," because "the varieties of behavior described by scholars who have studied questioning, or teaching, or learning in different societies may obscure . . . the probable existence of a set of underlying principles and relations which hold for all such behavior—however different surface manifestations may be" (p. 107).

Current research in linguistics is making us aware of the need to take into consideration factors of situational context in order to provide satisfactory explanations for data that we previously believed could be accounted for syntactically (Lakoff, 1970, 1972). It is interesting, however, that those of us previously caught in the transformational spell tend to forget that many linguists of other doctrinal persuasions never doubted the importance of contextual matters. Lakoff (1972) has expressed this point very well:

> As should be apparent to anyone familiar with other than purely transformational linguistic tradition, the notion that contextual factors, social and otherwise, must be taken into account in determining the acceptability and interpretation of sentences is scarcely new. It has been anticipated by a veritable *Who's who* of linguistics and anthropology: Jespersen, Sapir, Malinowski, Firth, Nida, Pike, Hymes, Friedrich, Tyler, and many others. But the idea has not merely been forgotten by transformational grammar; rather, it has been explicitly rejected (p. 926).

Even an educational psychologist, Carroll (1971), has pointed out that "it is impossible to write, in the usual linguistic manner, rules about the proper use of the definite and indefinite articles in English. *One must make an appeal to the communicative situation—to the perceptions and intentions of speaker and hearer*" (p. 106, italics added). It is very curious that one of our contemporaries has to remind us of the importance for all our research of keeping in mind the fact that language is after all communication. Carroll's statement is very reminiscent of another one made half a century ago by the great Danish linguist, Otto Jespersen, in his book *The Philosophy of Grammar*. These words of Jespersen are even today as useful a reminder for the pedagogical grammarian, the textbook writer or the language teacher as they are for the theoretician:

> The essence of language is human activity—activity on the part of one individual to make himself understood by another, and activity on the part of that other to understand what was in the mind of the first. These two individuals, the producer and the recipient of language, or as we may more conveniently call them, the speaker and the hearer, and their relations to one another, should never be lost sight of if we want to understand the nature of language and of that part of language which is dealt with in grammar (1968, p. 17).

Conclusion

Modern linguistics has for some time been the major influence on research in second language teaching. Linguistics will most likely continue to be an influence as long as we find it desirable to formulate generalizations about language for the benefit of students who wish to learn a new language. Applied linguistics and second language teaching are not synonymous, however. We have left an era in which many believed that linguistics alone could, and should, provide the substance for language teaching. We have now entered a period in which a new found awareness of the immense complexity of human language is matched by the realization that successful teaching of that complexity should draw support from the research of other disciplines as well. Yet, the contributions to language teaching that linguistics itself can make are as important as ever.

Linguistics will continue to broaden its scope of inquiry and to probe ever more deeply into the workings of the human mind, as these workings are revealed through language. What we continue to learn thereby about the structures of languages and the structure of language will unquestionably be of pedagogical value (although that value can never be assumed on purely linguistic grounds). We can also look forward to a steady supply of invaluable insights into such heretofore unknown or neglected language areas as the relationships between utterances and their various contexts—social, physical, and linguistic. And we will undoubtedly learn more about language in relation to the various purposes for which it is used. Second language teaching will continue to be an exciting, challenging area of study in the foreseeable future.

REFERENCES

Alexander, L. G. *New concept English*. London: Longman, 1967.
Ausubel, D. P. *Educational psychology: A cognitive view*. New York: Holt, Rinehart and Winston, 1968.
Brengelman, F. Generative phonology and the teaching of spelling. *English Journal*, 1970, 59, 1113-18.
Brooks, N. *Language and language learning*. New York: Harcourt, Brace and World, 1964.
Brown, H. The psychological reality of "grammar" in the ESL classroom. *TESOL Quarterly*, 1972, 6, 263-69.
Carroll, J. B. The prediction of success in intensive foreign language training. In R. Glazer, ed., *Training research and education*. New York: Wiley, 1965.

————. Current issues in psycholinguistics and second language teaching. *TESOL Quarterly*, 1971, *5*, 101-14.

Chomsky, C. Reading, writing, and phonology. *Harvard Educational Review*, 1970, *40*, 287-309.

Chomsky, N. *Syntactic structures*. The Hague: Mouton, 1957.

————. Linguistic theory. In J. R. C. Mead, Jr., ed., *Northeast Conference on the Teaching of Foreign Languages, Reports of the Working Committees*. New York: Northeast Conference, 1966, pp. 43-49.

Cronnell, B. Spelling-sound relationships in ESL instruction. *Language Learning*, 1972, *22*, 17-28.

Danielson, D., and Hayden, R. *Using English*. Englewood Cliffs: Prentice-Hall, 1973.

DeCamp, D. The current discrepancy between theoretical and applied linguistics. *TESOL Quarterly*, 1968, *2*, 3-11.

Dixon, R. J. *Modern American English*. New York: Regents, 1971.

Dubin, F. The problem "who speaks next?" considered cross-culturally. Paper presented at the 1973 TESOL Conference, San Juan, 1973.

Echeverria, M. S. On needed research in second language learning in the light of contemporary developments in linguistic theory. *International Review of Applied Linguistics*, 1974, *12*, 69-77.

Engels, L. K. Linguistic versus psycholinguistic models in teaching foreign languages to university level students. In K. R. Jankowsky, ed., *Georgetown University Round Table on Language and Linguistics*, 1973, pp. 1-9.

Eskey, D. A model program for teaching advanced reading to students of English as a second language. *Language Learning*, 1973, *23*, 169-84.

Frank, M. *Modern English*. Englewood Cliffs: Prentice-Hall, 1972.

Gleason, H. A. *Linguistics and English grammar*. New York: Holt, Rinehart and Winston, 1965.

Goffman, E. *Relations in public*. New York: Harper Colophon Books, 1971.

Grimshaw, A. D. Rules, social interaction, and language behavior. *TESOL Quarterly*, 1973, *7*, 99-115.

Hymes, D. *Foundations in sociolinguistics*. Philadelphia: University of Pennsylvania Press, 1974.

Jakobovits, L. A. *Foreign language learning*. Rowley, Mass.: Newbury House, 1970.

Jankowsky, K. R., ed. *Georgetown University Round Table on Languages and Linguistics 1973*. Washington, D. C.: Georgetown University Press, 1973.

Jesperson, O. *The philosophy of grammar*. London: George Allen and Unwin, 1968.

Kiparsky, P., and Kiparsky, C. Fact. In Bierwisch and Heidolph, eds., *Recent advances in linguistics*, The Hague: Mouton and Co., 1968.

Lado, R. *The Lado English series*. New York: Regents, 1972.

Lakoff, R. Transformational grammar and language teaching. *Language Learning*, 1969, *19*, 117-40.

————. Tense and its relation to participants. *Language*, 1970, *46*, 838-49.

————. Language in context. *Language*, 1972, *48*, 907-27.

Lawler, J. M. The eclectic company; or, explanatory power to the people. In K. R.

Jankowsky, ed., *Georgetown University Round Table on Languages and Linguistics 1973*, pp. 39-53.

Lee, W. R. *Language teaching games and contests*. London: Oxford University Press, 1965, 1972.

Lester, M., ed. *Readings in applied transformational grammar*. New York: Holt, Rinehart and Winston, 1970, 1973.

Mackey, W. *Language teaching analysis*. Bloomington: Indiana University Press, 1965.

Newmark, L. How not to interfere with language learning. In M. Lester, ed., *Readings in applied transformational grammar*. New York: Holt, Rinehart and Winston, 1973, pp. 211-19.

Newmark, L., and Reibel, D. A. Necessity and sufficiency in language learning. In M. Lester, ed., *Readings in applied transformational grammar*. New York: Holt, Rinehart and Winston, 1973, pp. 220-44.

Nilsen, D. L. F. The use of case grammar in TEFL. *TESOL Quarterly*, 1971, *5*, 293-99.

Oller, J. W. Controversies in linguistics and language teaching. *UCLA Workpapers in English as a Second Language*, 1972, *6*, pp. 39-50.

Paulston, C. B. Structural pattern drills: A classification. *Foreign Language Annals*, 1970, *4*, 187-93.

————. Teaching writing in the ESOL classroom: Techniques of controlled composition. *TESOL Quarterly*, 1972, *6*, 33-59.

Prator, C. H. Development of a manipulation-communication scale. NAFSA Studies and Papers. *English Language Series*, 1965, *10*, 57-62.

Rand, E. *Constructing sentences*. New York: Holt, Rinehart and Winston, 1969.

Ross, J. R. Constraints on variables in syntax. Ph.D. dissertation, M.I.T., 1967.

Rutherford, W. E. *Modern English*. New York: Harcourt, Brace and World, 1968.

————. From linguistics to pedagogy: some tentative applications. In R. C. Lugton, ed., *Preparing the EFL teacher: A projection for the 70's*. Philadelphia: The Center for Curriculum Development, 1970, pp. 29-44.

————. *Sentence sense*. New York: Harcourt Brace Jovanovich, 1973a.

————. Review of M. Lester, ed., *Readings in applied transformational grammar*. *Language*, 1973b, *49*, 474-79.

————. *Modern English*. 2d edition. New York: Harcourt Brace Jovanovich, 1975.

Sacks, H. *Social aspects of language: The organization of sequencing in conversation*. Englewood Cliffs: Prentice-Hall, 1974.

Schachter, J. Contrastive analysis and error analysis. Paper presented at the 1974 NAFSA Conference, Albuquerque, 1974.

Schane, S. Linguistics, spelling, and pronunciation. *TESOL Quarterly*, 1970, *4*, 137-41.

Schegloff, E. A. Sequencing in conversational openings. In Gumperz and Hymes, eds., *Directions in sociolinguistics: The ethnography of communication*. New York: Holt, Rinehart and Winston, 1972.

Slager, W. R. Creating contexts for language practice. *TESOL Quarterly*, 1973, *7*, 35-50.

Stevick, E. *Adapting and writing language lessons*. Washington, D.C.: Foreign Service Institute, 1971.

Yorio, C., and Perkins, K. Grammatical complexity and the teaching of reading in an ESL course. Paper presented at the 1974 TESOL Conference, Denver, 1974.

Wishon, G. E., and Burks, J. M. *Let's write English*. New York: American Book Company, 1968.

Wright, A. L., Van Syoc, W. B., and Van Syoc, F. S. *Let's learn English*. New York: American Book Company, 1973.

VIII

Bilingualism

Bernard Spolsky

While bilingualism is a phenomenon that affects people throughout the world, it has, as Mackey (1967) points out, generally been considered a marginal problem, never central to any of the disciplines involved in its study. In Dingwall (1971), for instance, the only important reference to bilingualism is in a chapter by Slobin on developmental psycholinguistics in which studies of bilingual children are used for evidence as to the nature of language development. The early (and in some cases continuing) parochialism of many United States educators' approaches to bilingualism and bilingual education is illustrated by Pacheco (1971), who in a review stated that "bilingual education is still in its infancy" in the United States (p. 116), whereas it is slowly being recognized now in other parts of the world. Useful correctives to this view are Lewis (1965, and forthcoming [a]) on the antiquity of bilingual education and Fishman (unpublished) on how widespread it is.

In an early paper, Haugen (1950) mentioned that there were few linguists who made bilingualism their primary concern. The field called for much more study, and few countries were more ideally suited for such work than the United States. Haugen's own study of the Norwegian language in America (1953) is a classic study of bilingualism. He describes in detail the nature of a bilingual community and shows how the speaker's knowledge and use of each language are affected by changing sociological and linguistic contexts. Appearing in the same year, Weinreich's *Languages in Contact* (1953) is still the basic text for students of bilingualism, summarizing ably the work done until then and proposing areas for future study that will keep scholars busy for years to come. His bibliography and the more specialized one prepared by Haugen (1956) are fundamental.

The international conferences that have been devoted to the topic reflect the growth of interest in the field. As early as 1928, there was an important conference on bilingualism and education in Luxembourg. But the real flurry of interest has come in the last fifteen years. In 1960, an international seminar on bilingualism in education took place at Aberystwyth; two years later, a symposium on multilingualism was held in Brazzaville; in 1967, an international seminar in Moncton was devoted to the description and measurement of bilingualism (Kelly, 1967). Bilingualism and other language problems formed the theme of the international African seminar in Dar es Salaam (Whitely, 1968); bilingualism and language contact were the topics of the Georgetown Round Table in 1970 (Alatis, 1970); the learning of two or more languages or dialects by young children was central to the Chicago Conference on Child Language (Anderson, 1971); and the pace of international conferences and seminars devoted to bilingualism continues to grow.

This chapter seeks to summarize the main trends of recent work. The following sections will deal with (1) definition, description, and measurement; (2) bilingualism, diglossia, and bidialectalism; (3) cognitive advantages or disadvantages of being bilingual; (4) bilingualism as a problem; (5) producing bilinguals—elite bilingualism; (6) the legal aspects of bilingualism; and (7) bilingualism and biculturalism.

Definition, Description, and Measurement

A bilingual person is popularly believed to be someone who can function with equal skill in two or more languages; in the same way, people think that a bilingual society is one in which two or more languages are used with equal regularity and effect. In actual fact, as Mackey (1962) has suggested, bilingualism is not usefully considered something that does or does not exist in an individual. It is rather "a relative trait" that needs to be described and measured in some detail. The fact that a person can use two languages does not mean that he can use them equally well or that he uses them equally often; as Bruce Gaarder (1969) observed, "balanced bilingualism is a theoretical construct."

Some of the complexity of the description and measurement of bilingualism is apparent in the report of the Moncton seminar (Kelly, 1969). A group of international scholars spent a week discussing such basic questions as how bilinguals develop, how their bilingualism can be measured, how their behavior can be described, how interlingual effects can be measured, and how the roles of each language can be characterized.

One of the more elaborate models has been proposed by Mackey (1968). Mackey believes that "bilingualism is the property of the individual." It arises when a person must function in two distinct language communities. He sees little justification for such definitions as Bloomfield's (1933, p. 56) "the native-like control of two languages," preferring to define bilingualism as "the alternate use of two or more languages by the same individual." A more precise definition requires measuring a number of dimensions. The first of these is degree. For each of the languages used by a bilingual, it is necessary to test mastery of the four skills of listening, reading, speaking, and writing on each of the appropriate linguistic levels (phonological or graphic, grammatical, lexical, semantic, and stylistic). The second is function: What use does the bilingual make of each language and under what conditions? Mackey distinguishes external functions from internal. For the former, he proposes a matrix with one dimension listing contacts (people in the home, community contacts, school, mass media, correspondence) and the other noting duration and frequency of the contact (how often this person speaks to his grandfather, etc.), and the pressures that apply in each area of contact: economic, administrative, political, etc. Internal functions include counting, praying, cursing, dreaming, and note taking. The third dimension for description is alternation. How readily and how often does the bilingual switch languages? Under what conditions does he switch? How much of the time does he speak each of his languages? Finally, there is interference. How much does the bilingual fuse his languages: do words, grammatical patterns, or sounds from the one language influence his use of the other? Is his speech in either language markedly different from that of a monolingual? With all of these dimensions described, Mackey believes that one can start to give a clear picture of an individual's bilingualism.

Some scholars choose to focus on the bilingual or multilingual community rather than the individual bilingual. In a description of multilingualism in the Soviet Union, Lewis (1972) characterizes a number of different levels of bilingualism. On the first level, there are stable bilingual communities, where over centuries two linguistic communities have been in contact without any tendency toward role differentiation or assimilation. At a second level is dynamic bilingualism. Here, as a result of social mobility and role differentiation, there is a beginning of social and linguistic assimilation. The third level involves overlapping functions: thus, in many parts of the Soviet Union, laws are published in both Russian and the national language. There is a tendency at this level for increasing penetration by the central or civic language, leading ultimately to its exclusive use.

The fourth level is almost complete assimilation, with only vestigial and symbolic bilingualism.

Lewis goes on to propose a number of types of bilingualism. One of the most important of these concerns the oral/literate dimension. There are cases where bilingual speakers are literate in neither language and others where speakers are literate in either or both. A common situation is literacy in only the civic, national, or formal language. Another important distinction, he suggests, is between vehicular bilingualism, where one language is used for limited or personal uses, and comprehensive or cultural bilingualism, where the language is used as a means of entry in the full culture.

Much of the work on bilingualism in the last few years is modeled on, and all is influenced by, the description of a bilingual Puerto Rican community in Jersey City by Fishman, Cooper, Ma, and others (1971). This two-year study, involving "hundreds of subjects, several disciplines, and an extremely complex cluster of problems" is a rich mine of facts, theories, and methodology. It shows how a bilingual community can be studied and how its societal bilingualism can be measured and described. Of fundamental importance is the careful analysis of the relationships between sociological and linguistic factors. There are also valuable studies of psychological and linguistic variables. Fishman himself summarizes (chapter 18) the four main contributions of the studies: the validity of measures of self-report; the usefulness of domain analysis; the value of factor analysis in establishing varieties and networks; and the feasibility of a parsimonious set of instruments for sociolinguistic description of large communities.

Bilingualism, Diglossia, and Bidialectalism

In the previous section, a distinction was made between individual and societal bilingualism. One kind of societal bilingualism is called *diglossia*. The term is used to refer to a society where two distinct varieties of language each have a distinct set of functions. The phenomenon of diglossia has its classic manifestation in a society which uses one variety of language for public, important, cultural activities and the second variety for intimate, personal, home-related uses. One of the most commonly quoted examples, following Ferguson (1962), is a distinction between Classical Arabic which is used as a written language (and in a modified form, as a formal spoken language) throughout the Arabic-speaking world, and is considered the standard language to which every educated person should aspire, and the various national or local dialects used freely in informal activities but much less likely to be used in public. Altoma (1970) describes the educational consequences of the situation:

Language education in Arab countries is complicated by the fact
that Classical Arabic, around which the program revolves, differs
considerably from the colloquial Arabic spoken daily by school children. . . . This implies that the pupils have to unlearn or suppress
most of their linguistic habits while trying to acquire new ones based
on Classical Arabic as the language program requires. The burden of
internalizing or reinforcing these acquired habits is compounded by
conflicting practices: on the one hand the program deliberately ne-
glects the actual speech of the pupils, and on the other Classical Arabic
in practice does not encompass all classes, since teachers themselves
(especially of other subjects) tend to use the colloquial for one reason
or another. In the absence of pertinent studies, it is not possible to
determine accurately the "kind" of Classical Arabic employed in the
class situation or the extent of its use, but there are indications which
suggest that even teachers of Arabic at high school level tend to use
other than Classical Arabic in their instruction or in conversation with
their students outside the class (pp. 690-91).

Another classic case of diglossia exists in Switzerland. In the German
speaking cantons described by Weinreich (1953), both Schwyzertutsch and
standard German are used. The functions of familiar dialogue, as contrasted with formal monologue (public addresses, lectures, sermons, etc.),
are served by Schwyzertutsch. Also, ordinary subject matter, as contrasted
with technical matter, is dealt with in this language (p. 81).

Note that in both of these cases the two varieties concerned are closely
related: from a historical point of view, they derive from the same source. A
similar kind of analysis is often tried in various cases of what is sometimes
labeled *bidialectalism.* The key point of distinction between diglossia and
bidialectalism is whether or not the two varieties are mutually intelligible.
Haiti is usually cited as a case where the creole is sufficiently different in
phonology and grammar from standard French to make the two languages
mutually unintelligible. But Valdman (1969) suggests that there is evidence
now of the development in some urban areas of an intermediate form which
might lead ultimately to a bidialectal situation. Such a process has taken
place in the English-speaking parts of the West Indies, where there has
developed what DeCamp (1971) calls a post-creole community:

For some time now I have been calling a speech continuum like that of
Jamaica a *post-creole* speech community in order to distinguish it from
the diglossia of creole areas like Haiti. Not every creole has a post-
creole stage in its life cycle. I suggest that both of the following
conditions must be present: first, the dominant official language of the

community must be the standard language corresponding to the creole. . . . Second, the formerly rigid social stratification must be *partially* (not completely) broken down. That is, there must be sufficient social mobility to motivate large numbers of creole speakers to modify their speech in the direction of the standard, and there must be a sufficient program of education and other acculturative activities to exert effective pressures from the standard language on the creole (p. 351).

In such cases, then, one has what Craig (forthcoming) now calls a bidialectal educational situation:

> The natural language of children differs from the standard language aimed at by schools, but is at the same time sufficiently related to the standard language for there to be some overlap at the level of vocabulary and grammar.

Bidialectalism of the kind described in the West Indies is not uncommon, but there is often some reluctance to admit that it exists. The difficulty involved is well illustrated by the controversy concerning the speech of American blacks, variously labeled *black English, nonstandard Negro English, Negro nonstandard dialect,* etc. A first issue is whether the variety of English spoken by blacks differs in essential ways not just from the standard language, but also from other nonstandard dialects of English (Dillard, 1972). The second issue is what to do about it: arguments over bidialectal education rage in learned journals (Sledd, 1972) and at conferences (for example, Stewart, 1970). (For more on this topic, see the chapter by Shuy on dialectology.)

The term *diglossia* has also been extended to situations where the two varieties concerned are clearly different languages. Fishman applies it to Paraguay, where Spanish and Guarani are used by members of the speech community for clearly compartmentalized roles. Accepting this widening of the term, we find many more cases of diglossia:

> These observations must lead us to the conclusion that many speech communities that are normally thought of as monolingual are rather marked by both diglossia and bilingualism, if their several registers are viewed as separate varieties or languages in the same sense as the examples listed above. Wherever speech communities exist whose speakers engage in a considerable range of roles (and this is coming to be the case for all but the extremely upper and lower levels of complex societies), wherever the access to several roles is encour-

aged or facilitated by powerful social institutions and processes, and finally, wherever the roles are clearly differentiated (in terms of when, where, and with whom they are felt to be appropriate), both diglossia and bilingualism may be said to exist (Fishman, 1972, p. 97).

Cognitive Advantages or Disadvantages of Being Bilingual

Does it make any difference to your cognitive development whether you grow up speaking one language or more? The linguistic relativity question, that is, the notion that thought is in some way dependent on language, and consequently that people who speak different languages perceive reality and think differently is a widespread one, most influentially stated by the American linguist, Benjamin Whorf. In a number of papers, many of them published after his death in 1941, he stated the principle that an observer's perception of the world around him is controlled in some fundamental way by the language that he speaks. Whorf compared an Indian language, Hopi, with what he called Standard Average European to see how each handled such concepts as time, space, substance, and matter. Standard Average European languages use their verbs to place an action in time; there is a distinction between past, present, and future, a linear notion that fits in easily with ideas of progress. Hopi, on the other hand, does not have verb tenses, but makes statements about a speaker's knowledge of the validity of what he is asserting, distinguishing between reports, expectation, and general truths. Whorf suggested that there are areas in which language might constrain thoughts.

Another semantic area that has been carefully studied is that of color names in various languages. Many cases have been quoted. Navajo, for instance, has a single word for gray and blue. Hebrew does not have one word for blue, but must distinguish between sky blue and sea blue. Shona has the same word for orange, red, and purple. Color seems a useful domain to work with because it can be described objectively. Any color can be specified by reference to the three criteria of brightness, hue, and saturation. Given this way of controlling or describing physical reality, one should be able to examine how different languages use words to organize it. By asking speakers of different languages to name all the colors, one should be able to investigate differences in semantic structure and perception. However, as Lenneberg (1967) says:

> The empirical research . . . indicates that the cognitive process-
> es studied so far are largely independent from peculiarities of any

natural language and, in fact, that cognition can develop to a certain extent even in the absence of knowledge of any language (p. 364).

Basically, although there are clear surface distinctions in the ways languages map physical reality and although there are some signs that these distinctions make memory and description more easy, there is no evidence that the differences are fundamental, or that they prevent formulation of concepts. It is true that the Eskimo has many different words for snow, but the English-speaking skier is able to express all the distinction he needs. No evidence has so far been produced to show that it will in any way harm a child's cognitive development if he speaks one language rather than another; no evidence shows that any language is a straightjacket preventing thought outside its constriction (see Fishman and Spolsky, in press).

As Hymes (1973) points out, all languages are in some way unsatisfactory to their speakers: every language is an instrument shaped by its history and patterns of use, such that for a given speaker and setting it can do some things well, some clumsily, and others not intelligently at all. The real limitation, he agrees with Sapir, is a monolingual's "naive acceptance of fixed habits of speech as guides to an objective understanding of the nature of an experience" (p. 74). Sapir praises linguistic study as a method of liberating one from this "dogged acceptance of absolutes."

Lambert and Tucker (1972) argue for a similar intellectual advantage for the bilingual or for the child who learns a second language. Lambert suggests that the bilingual, because he understands that words are only labels (he has at least two labels for most objects) does not risk confusing the word with the thing and so is capable of abstract thought more easily then the monolingual. Whatever the truth of this hypothesis, there are likely to be a great number of social and cultural advantages in having access to two cultures, two societies, two ways of thinking and feeling about things.

Bilingualism as a Problem

Folk bilingualism which might be defined as the case where the general population rather than some elite group of it is bilingual, is very common, for there are a great number of societies in which people need to speak more than one language. "Polyglottism," remarks Glyn Lewis (forthcoming), "is the earliest linguistic characteristic of human societies, and monolingualism a cultural limitation." Even in the smallest social units, it is common for there to be more than one variety, each with its significant place and use. Whatever distinctions exist within a society, they will be reflected in some aspects of the society's linguistic repertoire. Thus, languages come to reflect distinctions (and discrimination) between males and females, between elites and the masses, between rulers and ruled, and between rich and poor. For instance, an increasing number of recent studies deal with the differences between male and female speech, showing not just that there are perceived and actual differences, but that these differences are interpreted and interpretable in terms of the status assigned to women (see Barron, 1971; Edelsky, 1974; Haas, 1964; Lakoff, 1973). Studies such as those by Labov (1972) in New York City and by Trudgill (1974) in the United Kingdom have shown that social variables (socioeconomic status, sex, and age of speaker) account for variation in language on phonological and syntactic levels. And a study by Blanc (1964) has shown how nonregional dialects in Baghdad correspond with membership of the three major religious groups.

Given this general coincidence of language difference with social difference, it is not surprising to find that there is often advantage or disadvantage in speaking or not speaking a specific language. In many contemporary societies, there are in fact great advantages—social, economic, political, and cultural—in being a member of the group speaking the standard language or dialect as a mother tongue. This group itself is often monolingual; bilingualism then comes to be synonymous with membership of the disadvantaged part of society. In such societies, the term *bilingual* is often used for members of a disadvantaged group, and the bilingual is seen as having special educational needs. If one looks at the Bilingual Education Act or at court decisions such as *Lau versus Nichols*, the focus is clear. While the goal is stated to be bilingual education, the emphasis is on educating bilinguals rather than producing a society of bilinguals. The bilingual's first need, his or her constitutional right, is to be helped to learn English, the standard language. Part of this instruction may need to be given in the native language, resulting in the use of more than one language as media of instruction in school, but the fundamental notion is that bilingualism is a problem to be dealt with, and that bilinguals are people who need to be helped rather than produced.

In much of the world, one of the first tasks of an educational system is to take people who do not speak the standard language, whether it be Spanish, Russian, English, French, or Arabic, and teach it to them as quickly and effectively as possible. Sometimes, the school is willing for them to remain bilingual; very rarely, the program encourages them to maintain their second language in certain spheres. But in the majority of cases, the school is either hostile or at the most neutral, to the existence of the second language. Its aim then is to move people from one kind of monolingualism to another.

This view often coincides with the assumption that it is a disadvantage to be bilingual. It is connected with what has been called the balance theory, which holds that an individual has only a certain amount of language learning capacity. If this must be divided between two languages, the individual's knowledge of each language will be weaker than if he or she had learned only one. It is impossible to find empirical data to settle the truth or falsity of this hypothesis, for our language testing instruments are insufficiently precise. A good number of studies do, however, tend to support the thesis, to the extent that bilinguals have usually been shown to be weaker than monolinguals in their common language. There is usually no clear evidence, however, on the level of proficiency attained by bilinguals in their other language. One study, for instance (Keston and Jimenez, 1954), reports that fifty bilingual children did better on the English version than on the Spanish version of a test. There are a number of factors which account for this result, different from the general view; there is no evidence of the relative difficulty of the two tests or the degree to which the test measured linguistic attainment. Confounding the various studies is variation in the definition of bilingual. In one study, a bilingual may be a member of the lower socioeconomic group learning the standard language; in another he might be a member of the elite learning a second world language.

Support for the existence of a balance effect is provided by Macnamara (1966), who argues that there is clear disadvantage "where the time devoted to the second language is so extensive that the time available for the mother tongue is reduced" (p. 136). Macnamara found that native speakers of English who spent nearly one-half their time learning Irish fell behind others who were not taught Irish in English and arithmetic, and did not reach the level of Irish speakers in Irish. On the other hand, the Montreal English-speaking children studied by Lambert and Tucker (1972) are reported to show no disadvantage in English or other subjects as a result of their French immersion programs.

The issue is relevant and vital to decisions about the language of instruction to be used in school, but the evidence is contradictory. In a study in Chiapas, Modiano (1973) showed that Mexican-Indian children who were taught to read in their own language first and in Spanish second turned out to read better in Spanish three years later than children who received all the education in this language. Similar results were reported in the first Iloilo experiment in the Philippines (Davis, 1967). But there is a contradictory case from the Philippines; in the Rizal experiment, children taught all in English seemed to have done better than children taught bilingually. There have been a number of such studies, but the results remain confusing and inconclusive. In a recent paper written for the Ford Foundation, Engle reviewed twenty studies and reported that none had answered the question of the relationship of the choice of the medium of instruction to consequent achievement in language skill for other subject matter.

The existence of these seeming contradictions suggests they have been using a limited evaluation, assuming that bilingual education is related only to what happens in the classroom and is to be measured only by that kind of effect. The issue will probably not be resolved until more complex evaluation models are used (Spolsky, Read, and Green, in press).

Producing Bilinguals—Elite Bilingualism

The goal of many educational systems is to produce students who can function in more than one language; foreign language education is directed to this end. There are countries (for example, Canada and the Union of South Africa) that have aimed from time to time at producing a bilingual society. Based on the assumption that there is some intellectual or political good in individual or societal bilingualism, such an approach aims to produce as many bilinguals as possible. But given the difficulty of developing functional bilinguals when school is the only instrument (Fishman, forthcoming), it is often the case that this approach of "let's all be bilinguals" comes to be applied only to, or is successful only with, an elite. Its target group then are members of the middle or upper socioeconomic class who choose to have their children able to function in another language as well as their own.

Academic or elite bilingualism is produced by formal education in school. As a general rule, the children are taught a second standard language or world language. Their program concentrates on developing control of that language for formal use in the public domain. This is typical foreign language education; usually it assumes its greatest importance in the high schools or colleges, marking its particular relevance to the children of the elite who go on to secondary or tertiary education. The tentative moves toward the teaching of foreign languages in primary schools may thus be seen as signs of democratization:

> Learning another language is no longer regarded as a privilege and a luxury available only for selected groups of children who go to

school beyond the period of compulsory education. Instead, it is widely held today that foreign language learning should be part of the education of every child, even if he receives only the minimum of compulsory education (Stern, 1967, p. vii).

The languages chosen to be taught are limited in number—English, French, Russian, Spanish, and German are the main ones taught throughout the world—and the students concerned generally already speak another of these languages. In a sense, this kind of second language teaching replaces the earlier European tradition of education in Latin: an educated person is expected to know something of a language other than his own. He is expected to know especially how to read it: oral control has much lower priority. As a result of this emphasis, the languages taught are inevitably ones with well-established literary traditions and a clear relationship to modern technology. An illustration is foreign language teaching in the United States. Emphasis tended in the past to be on languages chosen for their cultural value. Thus, French, for a long time had more popularity than Spanish, even though the latter was clearly of more potential relevance for Americans. When Spanish was taught, it was the classical literary variety, and certainly not the "poor" local version spoken by Mexican Americans or Puerto Ricans living in the vicinity or attending the school.

Recognizing the need for access to technological material written in various foreign languages, the Soviet Union has in the last fifteen years established a number of special schools to combine technological and language instruction (Bartley, 1971). By 1964, about two-hundred general secondary polytechnical schools were designated as specialized in foreign languages: one-half were devoted to English, 20 percent each to French and German, and the remainder to other foreign languages. After five years of teaching a foreign language, instruction is given in it in geography, literature, sciences, and technical translation for the next five years.

There are many programs that aim specifically at the creation of bilinguals. For details of those at the secondary level, see Fishman (unpublished). Among the better known and certainly the best researched of these are the growing number of programs among English-Canadians aimed at giving their children some degree of mastery of French. After years of assuming that it was up to French-Canadians to become bilingual if they wished to take part in Canadian life, there has now been a switch in emphasis. In several parts of Canada, extensive programs are being developed to teach French to English children. The technique that has been followed generally is referred to as immersion. In the early immersion program, children are taught in the first two or three grades in French by French speakers; in the intermediate program, English-speaking children are grouped together at the seventh grade level in schools where only French may be spoken; and there are immersion programs at the eleventh grade level. In Montreal now, over 70 percent of the children in the English-speaking minority schools (French speakers make up 80 percent of the population of the city) take part in a French immersion program of some kind. Both the early programs (Lambert and Tucker, 1972) and the seventh grade programs (Tucker, in press) have all instruction given in French. In Ontario, too, there have been several immersion programs (Swain and Barik, forthcoming).

Careful evaluation of these programs shows that the children gain good mastery of French, with little evidence of loss in English skills and in their general school subjects. But certain features of the programs mark their academic bias. First, they are definitely school related, with the French immersion a result of teacher-controlled activity. The schools remain part of the English-speaking establishment; the pupils are all English speaking; there is no mixture with French speakers. Second, the kind of French taught is standard rather than local. A large proportion of the teachers come from outside Canada (France, North Africa, the French Caribbean) and almost all consider Continental French rather than Canadian French as a model for instruction. It is unwise to make predictions without more careful study, but there are signs of a tendency to develop, through these programs, an English-speaking elite with control of standard French, but with limited ability for social interaction with French Canadians. The political and social consequences of such a development alarm some observers.

Less clear is the effect of such immersion techniques on children of lower socioeconomic groups. Something similar, without any of its more attractive features, has been imposed on American Indian children and on Spanish American children for many years; the results have sometimes involved the learning of English, in some cases have led to the extinction of American Indian languages, and seldom have produced the kind of successful bilingual that the French program seemed to expect to get. But new studies in Montreal suggest that the immersion programs can perhaps be expected to work with lower-class children too. It seems evident then that one is dealing also with some basic attitudinal and socioeconomic factors that go far beyond the effect simply of the language policy.

Legal Aspects of Bilingualism

Among the many possible approaches to the study of bilingualism, the legal questions are of comparatively recent but increasing interest. A recent study by Falch (1973) analyzes European laws affecting language and linguistic communities. In twenty-one out of thirty European countries studied, he found some kind of legal protection or assigned position for minority languages. Ten provided for some kind of equal bilingualism or pluri-lingualism (Belgium, Czechoslovakia, Cyprus, Finland, Ireland, Luxembourg, Malta, Norway, Switzerland, Yugoslavia); the other ten provide some special recognition for minority languages.

Legal aspects of bilingualism in the United States have been described by Leibowitz (1969), who traces the history of state and federal laws discriminating against non-English-speaking Americans, and shows how various laws continue to be used to reduce their rights:

> The thesis of this article is that, in general, English literacy tests and other statutory sanctions applied in favor of English were originally formulated as an indirect but effective means of achieving discrimination on the basis of race, creed, and color (p. 7).

Recent legislation supporting bilingual education is thus a major change in direction.

Bilingualism and Biculturalism

Cardenas (1972) attempts to classify the interplay of compound and coordinate bilingualism with compound biculturalism. By adding the extra domain of culture, he is able to describe the problems of many second- or third-generation Mexican-Americans who speak two languages but seem to use each to refer to a single culture.

The cultural dimension is extremely important. Accompanying and reflecting the rapid development of technology and the increasing urbanization of modern life, there is now an overall increase in biculturalism. One culture, labeled civic culture by Lewis (1972), is associated with cities, bureaucracy, internationalism, and technology. It is expressed generally through the standard form of a world language such as English, Russian, French, or Spanish. The other culture, which Lewis calls group, associated with family, local, or ethnic loyalties, is likely to be expressed in a nonstandard variety. There are few societies that are not developing this special kind of biculturalism and consequent diglossia, and it is generally the case that a good segment of the population is bilingual in the two varieties as well as bicultural. Fishman (unpublished) labels the distinction *particularism* versus *globalism*. He argues that, with the exception of a few scholars, scientists, musicians, and artists, there is no global community in a societal sense and that for most people who associate with it, it is rarely the primary or sole society to which they belong. He argues thus for the basic value of bilingualism as parallel to biculturalism. Similarly, Christian and Sharp (1972) give a reasoned, cautious, but ultimately optimistic account of the argument for bilingual education in the United States. They see in bilingual education not just a way of dealing with the problems of minority groups, but also "a cultural alternative to a system noted throughout western society for its emphasis on manipulation, standardization, dehumaniza-tion" (p. 371). These views are clearly echoed by Haugen. Bilingualism, Haugen (1973) argues, is not so much a problem as it is a solution. Bilin-guals have problems; they are suspected of divided loyalties; they are some-times labeled as mentally handicapped; they find it hard often to keep their languages apart. But bilingualism is the "only human and only hopeful way" (Haugen, 1973, p. 56) to deal with the situation created by the natural diversification of languages.

REFERENCES

Alatis, J. E., ed. Report of the twenty-first annual round table meeting on linguis-tics and language studies. Washington, D.C.: Georgetown University Press, 1971.

Altoma, S. J. Language education in Arab countries and the role of the academies. In T. A. Sebeok et al., eds., *Current trends in linguistics*, vol. 5. The Hague: Mouton, 1970.

Anderson, T., ed. *Preprints of the Conference on Child Language*. Quebec: Laval University Press, 1971.

Barron, N. Sex-typed language: The production of grammatical cases. *Acta Sociologica*, 1971, *14*, 24-42.

Bartley, D. E. *Soviet approaches to bilingual education*. Philadelphia: The Center for Curriculum Development, Inc., 1971.

Blanc, H. Communal dialects in Baghdad. *Harvard Middle Eastern Monographs*, 1964, *10*.

Bloomfield, L. *Language*. New York: Holt, 1933.

Cardenas, D. N. Compound and coordinate bilingualism/biculturalism in the Southwest. In R. W. Ewton and J. Ornstein, eds., *Studies in languages and linguistics*, 1972-73. El Paso: Texas Western Press, 1972.

Carroll, J. B. Foreign language proficiency levels attained by language majors near graduation from college. *Foreign Language Annals*, 1967, *1*, 131-51.

Christian, C. C., and Sharp, J. M. Bilingualism in a pluralistic society. In D. L. Lange and C. J. James, eds., *Foreign language education: A reappraisal*. Skokie, Illinois: National Textbook Company, 1972.

Craig, D. R. Bidialectal education: Creole and standard in the West Indies. *International Journal of the Sociology of Language*, in press.

Davis, F. B. *Philippine language teaching experiments*. Quezon City, Philippines: Alemar-Phoenix Publishing House, 1967.

DeCamp, D. Towards a generative analysis of a post-creole continuum. In D. Hymes, ed., *Pidginization and creolization of languages*. New York: Cambridge University Press, 1971.

Dillard, J. L. *Black English: Its history and usage in the United States*. New York: Random House, 1972.

Dingwall, W. O., ed. *A survey of linguistic science*. Linguistics program, University of Maryland, 1971.

Edelsky, G. Evidence for the existence and acquisition of an aspect of communicative competence: Recognition of sex of speaker from linguistic cones—or knowing how to talk like a lady. Ph.D. dissertation, University of New Mexico, 1974.

Falch, J. *Soviet approaches to bilingual education*. Philadelphia: The Center for Curriculum Development, Inc., 1973.

Ferguson, C. A. Diglossia. *Word*, 1959, *15*, 325-40.

Fishman, J., ed.*Language loyalty in the United States*. The Hague: Mouton, 1966.

———. Domains and the relationship between macro- and microsociolinguistics. In J. J. Gumperz and D. Hymes, eds., *Directions in sociolinguistics*. New York: Holt, Rinehart, and Winston, 1972a.

———. *The sociology of language*. Rowley, Mass.: Newbury House, 1972b.

———. The sociology of bilingual education. In B. Spolsky and R. L. Cooper, eds., *Frontiers of Bilingual Education*. Rowley, Mass.: Newbury House, in press.

———. A sociology of bilingual education. Final report of research conducted under contract OECO-73-0588 for the U. S. Office of Education.

Fishman, J., Cooper, R. L., Ma, R. et al. *Bilingualism in the barrio*. Bloomington: Indiana University Research Center, 1971.

Fishman, J., and Spolsky, B. The Whorfian hypothesis in 1975: A sociolinguistic re-evaluation. In H. Fisher and R. Diaz-Guerrero, eds., *Language and logic in personality and society*. New York: Academic Press, forthcoming.

Gaarder, B. Bilingualism. In D. Walsh, ed., *A handbook for teachers of Spanish and Portuguese*. Boston: D. C. Heath, 1969.

———. *Bilingual education and the survival of Spanish in the United States*. Rowley, Mass.: Newbury House, in press.

Greenfield, L., and Fishman, J. A. Situational measures of normative language views of person, place and topic among Puerto Rican bilinguals. In J. A. Fishman, R. L. Cooper, R. Ma, et al., eds., *Bilingualism in the barrio*. Bloomington: Indiana University Research Center, 1971.

Haas, M. Men's and women's speech in Loasati. In D. Hymes, ed., *Language in culture and society*. New York: Harper and Row, 1964.

Haugen, E. *The Norwegian language in America: A study of bilingual behavior.* Philadelphia: University of Pennsylvania Press, 1953.

———. *Bilingualism in the Americas: A bibliography and research guide.* University, Alabama: University of Alabama Press, 1956. Publication of the American Dialect Society (no. 26).

———. The curse of Babel. *Daedalus*, 1973, *102*, 47-57.

Hymes, D. Speech and language: On the origins and foundations of inequality among speakers. *Daedalus*, 1973, *102*, 59-85.

Joos, M. *The five clocks.* Bloomington, Indiana: Publications of the Research Center in Anthropology, Folklore, and Linguistics, 1962.

Kelly, L. G., ed. *Description and measurement of bilingualism: An international seminar, University of Moncton, June 6-14, 1967.* Toronto: University of Toronto Press, 1969.

Labov, W. *The social stratification of English in New York City.* Washington, D.C.: The Center for Applied Linguistics, 1966.

———. *Sociolinguistic patterns.* Philadelphia: University of Pennsylvania Press, 1972.

Lakoff, R. Language and woman's place. *Language in Society*, 1973, 2, 45-80.

Lambert, W. E., Frankel, H., and Tucker, G. R. Judging personality through speech: A French-Canadian example. *The Journal of Communication*, 1966, *16*, 305-21.

———. A social psychology of bilingualism. In W. H. Whitely, ed., *Language use and social change.* London: Oxford University Press, 1971.

Lambert, W. E., and Tucker, G. R. *Bilingual education of children: The St. Lambert experiment.* Rowley, Mass.: Newbury House 1972.

Leibowitz, A. H. English literacy: Legal sanction for discrimination. *Notre Dame Lawyer*, 1969, *45*, 7-67.

Lenneberg, Eric H. *Biological foundations of language.* New York: John Wiley and Sons, 1967.

Lewis, E. G. Bilingualism: Some aspects of its history. In *Report on an international seminar on bilingualism in education.* London: Her Majesty's Stationery Office, 1965.

———. *Multilingualism in the Soviet Union: Language policy and its implementation.* The Hague: Mouton, 1972.

———. Bilingualism and bilingual education in the ancient world. In B. Spolsky and R. L. Cooper, eds., *Case studies in bilingual education.* Rowley, Mass.: Newbury House, in press (a).

———. Bilingualism in education in Wales. In B. Spolsky and R. L. Cooper, eds., *Current trends in bilingual education.* The Hague: Mouton, in press (b).

———. Factors influencing bilingualism in Wales and the USSR: A comparative study, in press (c).

Mackey, W. F. *Bilingualism as a world problem.* Montreal: Harvest House, 1967.

———. The description of bilingualism. In J. Fishman, ed., *Readings in the sociology of language.* The Hague: Mouton, 1968.

———. *Bilingual education in a binational school: A study of equal language maintenance through free alternation.* Rowley, Mass.: Newbury House, 1972.

Macnamara, J. *Bilingualism and primary education: A study of Irish experience.* Edinburgh: Edinburgh University Press, 1966.

Modiano, N. *Indian education in the Chiapas Highlands.* New York: Holt, Rinehart, and Winston, 1973.

Pacheco, M. T. Approaches to bilingualism: Recognition of a multilingual society. In D. L. Lange, ed., *Britannica review of foreign language education.* Encyclopaedia Britannica, Inc., 1970, vol. 3, 97-124.

Report on an international seminar on bilingualism in education. London: Her Majesty's Stationery Office, 1965.

Rubin, J. *National bilingualism in Paraguay.* The Hague: Mouton, 1968.

Schmidt-Rohr, G. *Die Sprache als Bildnerin der Völker.* Jena, 1932.

Sledd, J. Doublespeak: Dialectology in the service of Big Brother. *College English,* 1972, *33,* 439-56.

Spolsky, B. The Navajo Reading Study: An illustration of the scope and nature of educational linguistics. In J. Quistgaard, H. Schwarz, and H. Spang-Hanssen, eds., *Proceedings of the Third International Congress of Applied Linguistics, Copenhagen,* 1972. Heidelberg: Julius Groos Verlag, 1974.

Spolsky, B., Read, J., Green, J., A model for the description, analysis and perhaps, evaluation of bilingual education. In R. Kjolseth and A. Verdoodt, eds., *Language in Society,* in press.

Stern, H. H. *Foreign languages in primary education.* London: Oxford University Press, 1967.

Stewart, W. A. Sociological issues in the linguistic treatment of Negro dialect. *Report of the Twentieth Round Table.* Washington, D.C.: Georgetown University Press, 1970.

Swain, M., and Barik, H. C. Bilingual education in Canada: French and English. In B. Spolsky and R. L. Cooper, eds., *Case studies in bilingual education.* Rowley, Mass.: Newbury House, in press.

Symposium on multilingualism. Publication 87, CCTA/CSA, 1962.

Trudgill, P. *The social differentiation of English in Norwich.* London: Cambridge University Press, 1974.

Tucker, G. R. Methods of second-language teaching. *Canadian Modern Language Review,* in press.

Valdman, A. The language situation in Haiti. In R. Schaedel, ed., *Research and resources in Haiti.* New York: Research Institute for the Study of Man, 1969.

Weinreich, U. *Languages in contact: Findings and problems.* The Hague: Mouton, 1963.

Whitely, W. H., ed. *Language use and social change.* London: Oxford University Press, 1971.

IX

Dialectology

Roger W. Shuy

Like many other terms, *dialectology* has meant different things at different times in its history, and the current definition tends to reflect the most recent biases, interests, and methodologies. However, there is also an additional complication. Some scholars whose work clearly involves some of the premises, concerns, and even strategies of what has been called dialectology in the past are now using different terms to refer to that work. For them dialectology refers only to the study of regional variation whereas for others it refers more broadly to the examination of observable variation in language for whatever purpose and from whatever perspective.

Until the mid 1960s in the United States, dialectology clearly referred to the study of regional variation. Such study was sometimes called *linguistic geography* or *dialect geography*, both terms more specific than *dialectology* but certainly characterizing the work accurately. Dialectologists also dealt with social differences in a rather vague and general fashion but relatively little was made of the social differences that existed among informants. The great age of regional dialectology in America was the period between the 1930s and the 1950s, during which time the Linguistic Atlas of the United States and Canada was proposed, researched, and, to a limited extent, published. Major atlas studies were done in the East under the direction of Kurath (1949), in the Upper Midwest under the direction of Allen (1973), in the South and Mid-Atlantic States under the direction of McDavid, in the Great Lakes States under the direction of Albert H. Marckwardt (1957), in the West under the codirection of David Reed (1954) and Carroll Reed (1961), and in the Southwest largely under the influence of Atwood (1962). Today, most of the thousands of interviews conducted by atlas fieldworkers reside in the file cabinets of the directors or their successors. In most cases, the projects fell victim to one of the classic problems of linguistics, that of being data-bound. The dialectologists who collected all of these field records from all of the many communities surveyed then faced the difficulty of making their data available for ultimate analysis and interpretation. The pattern set by the atlas work in the eastern United States was soon seen to be far too bulky and expensive to be duplicated elsewhere. Consequently, Allen (1973) devised an ingenious alternative model for representing the data of the Upper Midwest. Various derivative studies based on atlas files have made much of the data more easily accessible, but, on the whole, the work of atlas dialectologists has remained unseen.

Additional problems have handicapped the continuous progress of atlas-style dialectology. One difficulty grew out of the sudden growth of interest in social concerns related to minorities in the early 1960s. With this development, the study of regional variation was assumed to be less relevant than social differences. The consequence was a further problem, that of attracting a sufficient number of students to continue the work. Another problem grew out of an unfortunate schism concerning methodology. The relative unsophistication of linguists in matters concerning research design, sampling, interviewing, and statistical analysis has been long-standing. Most of the linguistics of the 1940s and 1950s ignored these matters entirely. Whole grammars were based on the speech of one informant, a fact which, though perhaps justifiable under current conditions and pressures, did little to impress other social scientists of the generalizability of linguistic data and claims. Ironically enough, dialectologists, the only group of linguists paying any attention at all to multiple informants, were the ones who came most seriously under attack (Pickford, 1956).

The methodology issue became particularly critical as the focus of attention moved from older informants in a rural setting to younger informants in an urban setting. Both the traditional sampling methods used by linguists and the accepted pattern of nonquantitative analysis were scrutinized carefully by Labov (1966), as he turned his attention to New York City, and by Shuy, Wolfram, and Riley (1967), in Detroit. Different attempts were made to utilize extant samples, to devise new ones, to focus on younger informants, to make use of cross-sectional designs, and to work with a number of complex social variables. Such studies as these signaled a major change in the study of dialects in the United States. Unfortunately, there are very few linguistic-geography projects currently underway at this time, a fact which has less to do with the merits of such work than it does with the problems noted above. And, although much of the current interest of scholars working with social dialects seems somewhat removed from atlas procedures and data, a great debt is owed to the concern of linguistic geographers for variation, for realistic data, and for providing a necessary stage in the current research strategies of sociolinguists, whose work clearly dominates the study of dialectology at this time.

The study of dialectology in the United States today might be viewed in terms of its various missions: to linguistics, to education, and to other fields. Like all missions, those of social dialect study began with a set of purposes which have been, to date, only partially accomplished.

The Mission to Linguistics

Perhaps it is characteristic of all academic disciplines that their beginnings are found in the real conflicts of life, but that their development involves the processes of abstraction and of theory creation. For linguistics, at least, Chomsky and his followers heavily emphasized the abstract, the universal, and the theoretical. And linguistics certainly needed the academic respectability of theory in order to maintain itself as an academic field. In fact, today it is clearly evident that such a focus may have saved linguistics as an academic field. But such changes almost always bring about overreactions and polarizations. For example, in the concentrated effort to find universals, linguists tended to ignore particulars. In the attempt to find underlying rules, they tended to overlook interesting patterns on the surface. In the efforts to develop a sound theory, they tended to imply that everything else was trivial.

In linguistics, the one-sidedness of such an approach began to change when it became clear that the more we learned about the universals of language, the less likely it was that a grammar could ever be written. Speculative arguments over the best ways of deriving surface features from deep structures began to take on the appearance of academic game playing. Nothing was verifiable (except through rationality) and variability was swept under the rug and called uninteresting. Annual meetings of The Linguistic Society of America gradually turned from their formerly broad concern for language in its psychological, historical, social, educational, geographical, physiological, and theoretical states to an almost exclusive focus on language as grammatical theory. Anthropological linguists, psycholinguists, applied linguists, and even historical linguists began to give their papers at more congenial and specialized meetings.

At least three things began to bring about a change in this state of affairs. The first was the general broadening of linguistic interests in the 1960s which led to new kinds of interdisciplinary studies. The second was the previously mentioned development of interest in problems faced by minority peoples, especially in the schools. The third was related to the general discomfort of separating the study of formal grammar from the study of the semantic aspects of language. Linguists also began to take an interest in urban language and to understand that past research and analytical methodologies were no longer viable. New data-gathering techniques and new modes of analysis were needed. Meanwhile, linguists who had been interested in language variation as it is found in the creolization and pidginization of languages also began to apply their knowledge to urban, northern black English speakers. Their work provided important historical backgrounds for language change and offered new analytical insights. The general focus, of course, was on variability, not on abstract uniformity, and the variability within vernacular black English provided the critical measurement point. Vernacular black English deserved educational attention. It was also thought to be an interesting source of study by psychologists— behavioral psychologists thought the language embodied attitudes and cognitive psychologists thought it inferred them. Everything seemed ripe for this focus on vernacular black English except for one thing—nobody in the academic world seemed to know very much about it.

As is so often the case, a problem faced in the classroom took several years to find a solution from the disciplines which could best provide insights: psychology, anthropology, linguistics, and sociology. Rumors developed that the vernacular-speaking child was nonverbal, that he had no communicative exchanges with his parents, that he had a miniscule vocabulary, and that he was crushed by noise in the home, a multitude of siblings, and some sort of inordinate squalor. His language was considered unsystematic and haphazard and he was thought to reflect cognitive deficits in the failure of his oral language to match that of his middle-class teachers. If ever there was a field in need of research, it was this one.

Yet the research that was attempted was met with criticism almost on every side. Educators got to the problem first and offered suggestions for altering the speech of black children to match classroom expectations (Golden, 1965). Later this kind of work was to be attacked as merely wiping out the children's culture. Equally serious was the criticism by linguists that the teachers had not analyzed the language accurately (or at all) and had stressed the teaching of insignificant features rather than crucial ones. Gradually, various analyses of vernacular black English emerged. Seminal studies were done in New York (Labov, Cohen, Robbins, and Lewis, 1965), in Detroit (Shuy, Wolfram, and Riley, 1967), in Washington (Fasold, 1972), and in Los Angeles (Legum, 1971). Generalizations about the findings of these studies have been made by Fasold and Wolfram (1970) in relatively nontechnical language. These studies have also been attacked, frequently by black scholars who can see error in the analysis or who have determined that whites can never understand how black English actually functions, that this is just another case of whites trying to belittle or hold back blacks by calling attention to weaknesses rather than strengths, that not all blacks talk that way, or that the white analysts have improper or self-serving motives for studying (even exploiting) blacks. Conservative school people have attacked such studies as permissive and generally contributing to the "anything goes" philosophy which presumably characterizes linguists anyway. Lastly, linguists have attacked each other's analyses for various reasons (quite predictably in a field which encourages and fosters such behavior).

In terms of actual analytical approaches, the current study of social dialects by linguists is represented by three major viewpoints. The first advocates the identification of social groups as the primary, independent variable, with language differences as dependent variables. The second view argues for the essential quality of social and linguistic variables, letting the predominating differentiation rise to the top via statistical measures. The third view advocates that linguistic variation should be primary, with social grouping growing out of it as a dependent variable.

The social group as primary.   Several important characteristics contrast these recent approaches of Labov, Shuy, Wolfram, Fasold, and others with the study of variation carried out by dialect geographers. In addition to using a more sophisticated sampling technique, the new social dialect study attempted to provide a less structured and more natural body of data from each informant. The need for large amounts of continuous free conversation was stressed and the single-item response formats of the atlas questionaires were down-played. Deliberate efforts were made to obtain speech samples in different styles (narrative, reading, casual, formal, etc.) and considerable effort was put into solving the problem of the precise identification of the informant's socioeconomic status by employing strategies usually borrowed from sociology, including those of Warner (1962) and Hollinshead (1958). Dialectologists who were unfamiliar with these methodologies were initially distressed by what appeared to be such a subservience to sociologists with the emphasis on statistics, sampling, and so on, and by an initial confusion about what such strategies implied. For example, the new descriptions of vernacular black English included features which dialectologists knew to be characteristic of whites as well. It was observed, in fact, that in certain aspects there really was no difference between the speech of blacks and whites in, for example, the South. If one used a methodology which ignored the frequency of occurrence of given linguistic features, such an observation would be natural. But the newer research in social dialects indicated that in communities in which a given feature, a stigmatized feature, was used by more than one socioeconomic status (SES), by more than one race, or by more than one group of any social category, a clearly discernible stratification was frequently evident. Figure 1 clearly demonstrates such stratification.

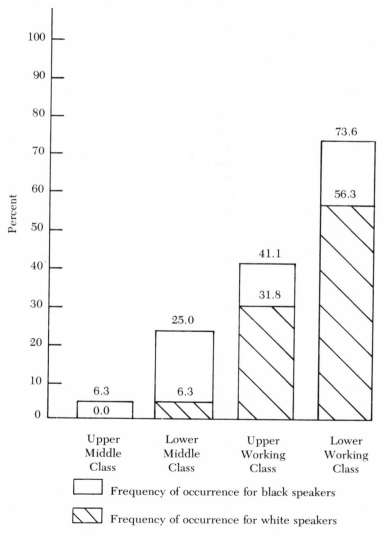

Fig. 1. Multiple Negation: Frequency of occurrence in Detroit, by SES group (Shuy, Wolfram, and Riley, 1967, p. 88).

Note that the frequency of occurrence of the use of multiple negation across the four SES groups in Detroit is maintained regardless of the race of the speakers, but that blacks use multiple negatives more frequently than do whites. Further information reveals that men use them more frequently than women. Such data cannot tell us that blacks use multiple negatives and that whites do not, nor that men use them and women do not. But they do offer rich information about the tendencies toward higher or lower variability usage than we could ever obtain from a methodology which offered only a single instance of such usage as evidence of use or non-use. The figures represent a number of informants in each of the four SES groups and a large quantity of occurrences of the feature for each informant represented in the group. In the case of multiple negatives, it was also necessary to see them in relationship to all negative possibilities. Thus, all the single and multiple negatives in each speaker's speech sample were added together to form a universe of potential multiple negatives. Figure 1 displays the ratio of the occurrence of multiple negatives to all potential multiple negatives.

It is reasonably safe to assume that the extent of language variation is much broader than typical atlas research methodologies ever revealed. If an informant is asked, for example, what he calls the stuff in the London air, he may respond only once /fag/. If he should happen to use the /a/ vowel before a voiced velar stop only one-half of the time during all the occasions in which he refers to this concept during a ten-year period, this variability will be totally lost in this single representation in the interview. If he talks continuously for thirty minutes or so, he might use this pronunciation a dozen or more times, giving an increasingly more probable representation of his actual usage. Of course, such data gathering techniques work better for pronunciations in which the inventory of possible occurrences is very high than they do for lexicon. On the other hand, research in social dialects indicates that phonology and grammar are more crucial indicators than lexicon, a factor which certainly justifies highlighting them for research.

A second, rather serious misunderstanding of recent social dialect research by dialect geographers relates to the different focus of spatial investigation. In the study of Detroit speech, for example, little effort was made to relate the results to the situations that exist in Memphis or Boston. It was a synchronic study of one urban area. No effort was made to obtain only native speakers, since a native-only population does not represent Detroit speech any more than does a nonnative population. The question was not, How do native Detroiters talk? (however interesting such a question might be). Rather, the focus was on Detroit speech at a given point in time. Perhaps more controversial were some of the generalizations made as a result of similar studies of vernacular black English in Detroit, Washington, D. C., and New York. These studies revealed an amazing similarity in the language behavior of black speakers in these three different kinds of cities. However, the generalizations about urban, northern black vernacular English were mistakenly taken to mean that they represented all vernacular black English speakers in the country. We should observe that recent research seems to indicate a decreasing frequency of occurrence of certain features of vernacular black English as one moves spatially away from the deep South (Wolfram, 1972).

In short, then, the newer focus on social dialects tended to build on the previous work of dialect geographers, adding the dimensions of a finer sampling procedure (random or stratified, rather than convenience sampling), and an emphasis on grammar and phonology (as opposed to lexicon). It also focused on quantitative data (in contrast to single occurrence representation), an examination of urban rather than rural informants, and a sense of the primacy of the social group (rather than the regional area) as the unit for correlation with linguistic variation.

This approach to language variation is the view originally taken by Labov (1966) in his classic study *The Social Stratification of English in New York City*. Labov's aim was to work with units that were socially determined in advance. Thus, the approach advocated gathering data from a large number of people who were each characterized as belonging to specific social classes, ages, sexes, and races, or whatever other variable was relevant. This approach was also followed by Shuy, Wolfram, and Riley (1967) in the Detroit Dialect Study, which used a modified Hollinshead scale to quantify the SES of all 720 informants in the stratified sample.

The need to use such social groupings becomes obvious if one examines the further developments of variation theory in the study of social dialects. Taking advantage of the known SES indicators, Labov began looking to them for explanations of the language behavior of his informants. Such information was then incorporated into the actual formal linguistic rules which described this speech. These rules were called variable rules. They contrasted with the more traditional optional rules in grammars in that they improved the explanatory power of such rules by taking advantage of the impressively regular constraints on variability noted in the above studies.

One major goal of variable rule analysis, then, was the attempt to incorporate such variability into the main body of linguistic theory. Labov wanted to learn just exactly how variation works in language, but he was also interested in discovering the limits of grammatical competence. He believed that there is no end to the writing of grammars since the form that the grammar takes is a set of quantitative, variable relations (Labov, 1972). A rule which accounts for contraction in vernacular black English, for example, is shown as follows (Labov, 1969, p. 748):

$$
\begin{bmatrix} +\text{voc} \\ -\text{str} \\ +\text{cen} \end{bmatrix} \longrightarrow (\emptyset) / \begin{bmatrix} *\text{Pro} \\ \alpha V \end{bmatrix} \#\# \begin{bmatrix} \overline{\quad +\text{T}} \end{bmatrix} \ C^{\frac{1}{0}}_{[*\text{nas}]} \begin{bmatrix} \alpha V b \\ \beta g n \\ \gamma \text{-NP} \end{bmatrix}
$$

This rule deals with the removal of a schwa $(+\text{voc}, -\text{str}, +\text{cen} \rightarrow \emptyset)$ which occurs initially before a single consonant $(C^{\frac{1}{0}})$ in a word with a tense marker $(+\text{T})$ incorporated. When a pronoun precedes (Pro) or a nasal consonant follows (nas), the rule is categorical (*). Variable rule analysis not only mentions the various alternative possibilities (structural grammar did as much, but swept some variations under the rug while calling them free variation), but also ranks how they constrain the rule. In this case, the alpha (α), or greatest constraint, does not show a high degree of ordering in that a preceding vowel (αV) and a following verb $(\alpha V b)$ have approximately equal effect on the application of the rule. The effect of a *gonna* (gn) following is less than either of these, however, and is therefore given the beta (β) constraint. The gamma (γ) constraint, the presence or absence of a noun phrase, is even less powerful.

Not satisfied with the sort of analysis which mapped linguistic features onto populations, a group of ethnographers proposed a somewhat different approach to the study of social dialects. Although anthropologists had been doing ethnographies for decades, only recently have they begun working on the notion that the place of language in society is cross-culturally variable (Hymes, 1966). The perspective of such scholars (Abrahams, Bauman, Gumperz, Hymes, Sherzer, and others) is that the language forms studied by social dialectologists cannot be understood properly unless all the pertinent social facts surrounding those forms are first known. They appreciate some of the usefulness of the more conventional sociolinguistics in which linguistic data and sociological data are discovered in separate operations but they feel that ethnographic investigation is "logically prior to it, as a means of determining what the culturally relevant variables are in the first place" (Bauman, 1973, p. 158). Such an investigation begins with a definition of the speech community to be studied (intuitive, speculative, and subject to later modification), then determines the elements of speaking behavior within the community. Such components typically include the linguistic varieties in use (styles, dialects, and languages), the linguistic units of description (speech acts, events, situations, and genres in use). They also include the rules governing what is talked about, the tones or manners that may be conducted (serious, mocking, etc.), the locally defined contexts for speaking, the participants, the goals, norms of interaction (interrupting, voice raising, etc.), and the norms of interpretation (what to take seriously, etc.).

The social group and linguistic variety as equal.   Labov's variable rules are written for specially well-defined and previously determined social groups and are based on the frequency of occurrence of the feature under specific conditions. Cedergren and Sankoff (1974) adopt basically the same approach but bring a more sophisticated mathematical theory to the task of describing such variation. Specifically, they make use of probabilities associated with rules rather than frequencies. They feel that a person's performance is a statistical reflection of his competence. The frequencies observed in individual performance are used to determine the probabilities that each constraint, whether linguistic or social, contributes to the application of a particular rule. Naturally, it is not believed that such precise numbers exist in the heads of the speakers; rather that statistical tendencies are what is reflected. In such a manner, rules are written for the speech community and such rules specify the linguistic constraints on their applications. They are accompanied by tables which provide the probabilities determined for each of the linguistic constraints and the probabilities for any relevant social parameters.

In an effort to test the appropriateness of this approach, Cedergren and Sankoff performed an experiment on r-spirantization. Once the probabilities associated with linguistic and social constraints were determined for the speech community, the researchers tested to see how well the results applied to actual individuals. In this case, the significant social constraint turned out to be social class. The researchers set the input probability at the probability level associated with each speaker's social class and checked the match between the predictions made by the rule and the observed data. The predictions turned out to be fairly close, confirming the hypothesis to their satisfaction. This equal use of social parameters and linguistic constraints to account for language variation, then, operates somewhere between the extremes of social constraints as primary and linguistic constraints as the independent variable.

Linguistic constraints as primary.   In order to discuss the primacy of the linguistic constraint in the study of language variation, it is first necessary to describe a linguistic method known as implicational analysis. Although implicational scales have been used in other disciplines (especially in sociology, where they bear the name of Guttman scales), they are relatively new to linguistic analysis. DeCamp (1971) began to experiment with such scales as he worked with Jamaican creole and the approach has also been used by linguists on various social dialects in the Americas (Bickerton, 1972; Wolfram, 1974).

Bailey (1974) is a prominent advocate of the "linguistic constraint as independent variable" philosophy of language variation. His goal is to write panlectal rules which cover the entire language system. Each individual has a subset of the rules and more general forms of the rules than the panlectal rules which account for them. A speech community, in this case, is a group of people who evaluate linguistic variables in the same way (as favored or as stigmatized) and who have the same algorithms.

Implicational scales are used in rule writing in such a way that a pattern of outputs is implied in the rule itself. Bailey maintains that the time factor accounts for all other kinds of differentiation, whether geographical, social, stylistic, or whatever. Thus, his rules include the notions of marking (based on further developments of the phonological marking of Jakobson, 1968, and Chomsky and Halle, 1971) and implicational coefficients in such a way that each rule generates an implicational pattern of outputs which also take into consideration the environments in which the outputs occur. This series of outputs makes up a series of temporally differentiated lects which are minimally different from those which follow (called *isolects*). According to Bailey, this temporal differentiation reflects the social parameters of language. The relevant social parameters are probably best identified by trial and error, as Fasold, Wolfram, Labov, and others have done with the variables of social class, race, sex, style, and age. Among the dynamic aspects of language, age factors seem to be the most obvious differentiations, but this need not always be true.

If a given rule has four environments, in such a way that environment 1 is heavier-weighted than environment 2, which is heavier than 3, which is heavier than 4, the implicational output will generate the application of the rule first in 1 and last in 4. Since 4 is the lightest-weighted environment, its presence implies the presence of all heavier environments. In vernacular black English, for example, the rule for *t, d* deletion in the environment of word boundary and following vowel may be described in a multidimensional sociolinguistic matrix at one particular time as follows:

	Most Informal	Rather Informal	Rather Formal	Most Formal
Upper Middle Class	2	1	–	–
Lower Middle Class	3	2	1	–
Upper Working Class	4	3	2	1
Lower Working Class	+	4	3	3

\+ = categorical rule application
\– = *no* rule application

The change here is seen to have begun in the lowest class in informal speech. The wavelike characteristic of the outputs is clearly indicated. Sociolinguistic algorithms can be used to determine what temporal isolect is used by a person with certain social characteristics when the isolect associated with one set of characteristics is known. An algorithm might state, for example, for change involving disfavoring, that one isolect is less advanced for each more monitored style. In this way the linguistic aspects are treated as central, and a rule can be written to generate temporal differentiation which will then fit the social differentiation (keeping in mind that, in this model, various types of social differentiation are embraced as temporal differentiation in language change). Bailey feels that the reason linguists have paid so little attention to variation in language is because it is really a part of language change, a topic less favored for linguistic study for many years.

At the present time, therefore, at least three approaches to the linguistic analysis of social dialects are visible. Within each approach, various modifications and variations are under constant development. The result has been a healthy ferment in the field of linguistics, leading to a new theoretical posture which goes under several labels, including *variation theory*. Thus, out of an initial concern for social dialects a mission to the field of linguistics itself has developed, a mission which has opened the doors of inquiry considerably wider than they had been during the time when the only legitimate concerns of linguistics were for abstract universals. This newer focus has clearly demonstrated that the concern for variability is not a concern for mere surface level triviality and that human society must be considered along with the human mind as we examine the fantastic complexity we call language.

The Mission to Education

Until very recently, the mission of applied linguistics in America has been carried out almost exclusively in the fields of education and, within it, very heavily in the area of teaching English as a second language. It seems quite obvious that linguistics can be applied, as well, to problems of native language learners, but it took the "discovery" of the social dialects of minorities in American education to begin to bring this change about (Shuy, 1973). The attitude that "other people have problems, not us" is still with us, however, even as we extend the definition of applied linguistics from foreigners to native American minorities. The curious thing is that many of the same principles which have been used to describe the problems of minorities are equally applicable to white, suburban school systems. All people must come to grips with variation, receptively and productively, in speaking, writing, listening, and reading. Of course, when one weighs the cruciality of the problems of the minority with those of the majority, one must admit that the need of minorities to survive is more critical than the need of majorities to improve their effectiveness. Thus, the focus on the minority child is probably justifiable. Such a focus has begun to have effects on the teaching of oral language, on the teaching of reading, on the teaching of composition, on the development of teacher training programs and on procedures of evaluation. Again, it began with the study of vernacular black English. Expansion into other areas, though slow, is finally beginning.

The teaching of oral language. Before the intensive study of social dialects began, language variation was scarcely considered as a possible topic in the teaching of oral language in the American classroom. Characteristically, a preschool language program followed a deficit model. One descriptive brochure reads as follows:

> In order for children to achieve in school, they must learn the language used in school. . . . The role of the teacher of young children in fostering the development of good language skills is especially impor-

tant. He must realize that language competence is a necessary first step in intellectual development. As a child learns more about language, he progresses in his ability to think symbolically and abstractly. Without sufficient language development the child's conceptual development will be inhibited (Parsons, n.d.).

It was generally asserted that inadequate language meant the absence of accepted school language and the first step toward learning required the acquisition of school English. To be sure, their view is less strongly held today, mainly because the advent of the study of social dialects has weakened it considerably. The whole foundation of compensatory education might have been attacked on grounds other than language, but there can be little doubt about the effectiveness of the criticisms raised by linguists. Perhaps most effective have been the writings of Labov (1969), Baratz (1970) and Cazden (1971) on this matter. The claims of early childhood education specialists that standard English is logical and nonstandards are illogical has been attacked by linguists who have shown that logical propositions may be adequately stated in vernacular as effectively as in standard English. The latter, in fact, may well help obfuscate logical expression.

Since most programs for preschool or early childhood rely heavily on language, considerable attention has been drawn to the use of vernacular in these settings. There is recognition now that such programs must encourage the child to be free to use his language regardless of the status generally accorded it in the adult world. There are very few ways for the child to communicate with the teacher other than in his habitual dialect and this fact is slowly but gradually being recognized. This is not to say that such programs always accept the legitimacy of vernacular dialect, or that they refrain from trying to wipe it out as soon as possible, or that they understand the relationship between rejecting a child's language and rejecting the total child. But some small progress seems apparent.

Beyond the preschool level, even less progress seems to have been made in dealing with the many legitimate varieties of the English language. The first reactions of school people were to eradicate such varieties. When it was suggested (Feigenbaum, 1971) that the schools try to develop a kind of bidialectism, counterarguments were presented, stressing that bidialectism was racist and that what was really needed was to change the attitudes of the majority to accept linguistic and cultural pluralism (Sledd, 1969, 1972). Programs for the schools have been developed for eradication—assimilation theory—and for the bidialectal approach (Feigenbaum, 1971), but nothing, as yet, for the third approach.

Perhaps the most troublesome aspects of the social dialect/oral language controversy have been the stances of those who have been involved. Little or no attempt is ever made to understand an opposing or different point of view. It did not seem reasonable to the bidialectalists, for example, that advocates of the eradication position might be acting sincerely toward the solution of a problem. Nor did it occur to eradicationists that bidialectalists might be acting with honesty and integrity. Most recently, the third position, one which defied a neat label but which may be symbolized as the "teach whites to improve their attitude" position, has characterized bidialectalists as ill-motivated opportunists.

In general, it has never been very clear what the schools can or should do about the speech of the students and it is not at all clear what direct good the study of social dialects has provided thus far. One serious question concerns whether or not children can even be taught to add to their speech repertoires or to wipe out their vernacular speech. (This does not mean that they cannot learn it; only that they cannot be taught it.) Indirectly, however, it seems that the schools are benefiting from the issue. Social dialect has provided a physical observable focus for an issue which might otherwise be too abstract to be observed. It has been difficult, for example, to identify aspects of black culture which are agreed upon by authorities and are clearly distinguishable from nonblack culture (Abrahams, 1972). Since vernacular black English has both qualitative and quantitative differences from other varieties, it provides a more physical focus. With such a focus, many questions of group identity, cultural pluralism, and style can be clearly addressed in the classroom. The subject of social dialect is at least known to the general public and although methodologies, materials, and philosophical underpinnings are far from settled, the question of language variation is clearly on the agenda for eventual consideration.

The teaching of reading.   If the relationship between the study of vernacular black English and the teaching of oral language has proved controversial, the relationship to the teaching of reading has been even more so. Again, the area of assumed evil motivation has been a central issue. At the moment, at least five approaches have been proposed for reducing the mismatch between the vernacular black English used by some first grade children and the middle-class language in which their initial reading materials are written (Shuy, 1972).

1. First teach children to speak standard English. Then teach them to read it.

2. Teach teachers about social dialect so that they will not confuse its use with reading problems.
3. Develop beginning materials in the targeted social dialect in order to reduce the mismatch of oral language use to the printed page.
4. Develop beginning reading materials which systematically avoid the mismatch of the spoken social dialect to standard English written materials.
5. Make use of the Language Experience Approach (which argues that the teachers write down exactly what the child says, then have him read it).

To date, there has been little reason to support any one of these approaches individually or in combination. Research has been hampered by inordinate negative public reaction to any attempts to implement number 3. Number 1, the traditional, historical approach, has never been proved to be supportable. Some progress is being made on number 2 but the road has been, and will continue to be, tortuous and rocky. Number 4 has been implemented in only the most indirect fashion to date. Number 5 has been restricted by the average teacher's difficulty in writing down exactly what a child says rather than what she *thinks* he says or what she might *wish* he had said.

Regardless of the apparent inconclusiveness of the above approaches, the study of social dialects has contributed certain benefits to the field of reading. The call of linguists for more realistic and believable language in beginning reading materials has helped remove some of the stilted language from primers. The focus on syntax by those who study social dialects, linked to stress on the importance of processing whole language units rather than mere letter-sound correspondences, has helped modify somewhat current reading instruction. The linguist's contention that surface-structure oral reading does not necessarily reflect deep-structure comprehension is helping teachers to deal with supposed misreadings such as *She go* for *She goes* by speakers of vernacular black English. Some progress is being made in helping teachers understand that learning to read and learning to speak standard English are not the same thing and that an attempt to teach and evaluate both at the same time is a confusion of tasks for the teacher and child alike.

The teaching of composition. Several years ago a large midwestern university instituted a special "relaxed admission" program especially geared to inner-city black students. Paradoxically, the students were flunked out of the program in one year by the freshman English program. An examination of the papers of a sample of these students revealed that 42 percent of the "errors" marked by the instructors were directly attributable to interference of vernacular black English phonology on the students' spelling or vernacular black English grammar on their sentence structure. To be sure, these students also had the more typical freshman composition problems (failure of pronoun to agree with antecedent, run-on sentences, sentence fragments, etc.) but they had the additional handicap of all the features which are often used to describe their home dialect. To this day, no commercially published materials exist which address the question of the special kind of interference noted above. One commercial publisher rejected a proposal to produce such materials on the grounds that the potential buying public would be too small. Another rejected the idea because it did not want to risk negative public reaction from the black or white general public. Under the sponsorship of the National Institute of Education, such materials are currently under development at the Central Midwest Regional Educational Laboratory in St. Louis (Long, forthcoming). This project grew out of the past research on vernacular black English, and, barring negative public reaction of the sort that has plagued the development of reading materials, it promises to add significantly to the teaching of composition in the classroom.

The development of teacher training programs.   As one might predict, the more institutionalized the setting, the slower desired changes can be brought about. Drastic changes in teacher preparation (such as placing language at the core of the education of elementary teachers rather than at the periphery) suggest drastic staffing problems. Should the professor of history of education be let go in favor of an educational linguist? The problem is not unlike the potential difficulty facing speech departments as they gradually change their programs by educating future speech teachers to distinguish between pathological and social variation in the speech of their students. If they suddenly require all speech teachers to take a course in social dialects, who will teach these courses? Not only are few speech professors trained in this area but also very few linguists. The education major (and often the speech major) frequently receives no instruction in phonetics and linguistics, despite the fact that the only communication system the child has when he enters school is his oral language. How do we incorporate this language training (general linguistics, language acquisition, and language variation should provide the bare minimum) without disturbing existing staff balance and reordering certification requirements? And how do we deal with the fact that it is ultimately the teacher who gets blamed for all the failures in her training and in her bureaucracy simply because there is no one else to blame except the children themselves? Change from within the system may be a great deal more difficult than even the most optimistic observer might suggest and will involve subtlety far beyond anything linguists have suggested to date.

Perhaps the influence of the study of social dialect has not yet made significant inroads in the preparation of teachers but there are many indications that some sort of change is in the offing. The International Reading Association recently formed a special Commission on Teacher Education which includes two members who represented the interests of linguistic and cultural pluralism. The American Speech and Hearing Association also has such a commission which focuses on the differences between speech pathologies and socially induced language difference. An early advocate of linguistic pluralism has been The National Council of Teachers of English, which has supported numerous publications in this area.

Procedures of evaluation. The study of social dialect is also at least partially responsible for the recent flurry of concern about fairness in the practice of standardized testing in this country. To be sure, the situation was brought to a head by the current search for educational accountability. Examination of extant standardized tests in English and reading has clearly demonstrated cultural and linguistic biasing toward the middle-class student. However, it is unlikely that exact pinpointing of mismatch between child language and test language would have been called to our attention without the flurry of research on social dialect, especially vernacular black English, of the past decade. The broader implication of this research, however, is that it has led to a number of other insights into the nature of language in standardized testing. As linguists examined such tests for potential mismatches they also observed areas of general weakness which went beyond the specific concerns of vernacular black English. It was discovered, for example, that by changing *mongrel* to *cur* in one question in one reading test, the scores of West Virginia white children could be increased by as much as three months on the scale of reading age (Connolly, 1969). Areas of general linguistic and contextual ability not related to vernacular black English were pointed out by Whiteman (1971) and Sullivan (1971) in their studies of The California English Test and the Iowa Test of Basic Skills, respectively. To be sure, specialists in reading tests have been questioning the misuses of such instruments by the schools, but it cannot be denied that the study of social dialect has also played a role in the current reexamination of excesses in this field.

Thus, despite the criticisms by people who represent those who no longer wish to be researched, by those who feel that researchers have exacerbated racial tensions by calling attention to an uncomfortable situation, by social dialect researchers who disagree with each other's research findings or approaches, or by those who see still other faults in what has gone on in the past decade of the study of social dialect, such study has resulted in certain advances. The general tendency in the schools was either to ignore the dialect situation or to attribute dialect differences to genetic inferiority, individual ignorance, or willful stupidity. In general, schools today are more enlightened. The door is beginning to open and we are beginning to move toward the solution of a number of broader educational problems which have to do with linguistic and cultural variability in a much larger context than that suggested by minority social dialects. The discovery that blacks have a wide repertoire of language styles is finally beginning to be seen for what it is—as much a linguistic advantage as it is a disadvantage. If we ignore for a moment the politics of education, which might argue for eradicating or modifying one or more styles or for building new ones, we can see that the existence of such a range of styles is beginning to look like a good and useful thing. The binary, right-wrong classroom paradigm is subject to question. People *do* use language in a number of contexts, for a number of purposes, to a number of different people. Variation in language can be seen to be the fantastically complex tool with which degrees of subtlety can be effected, tone can be manipulated, and poetry can be produced. At one time, we seemed to have wanted everyone to talk and write alike. Today, even the most pessimistic observer will have to admit that such attitudes are changing.

The Mission to Other Fields

Although the mission of social dialect study to linguistics and to education is, perhaps, its clearest and hitherto most dominant mission, other goals are also beginning to develop. To those who work with language, it has long been perplexing why other disciplines do not perceive more clearly how important language is to the successful understanding of their tasks. For example, linguists wonder why sociologists have not used language data to study social stratification, especially since language is apparently so unobserved by its users. It seems that a medium which is used unconsciously would provide a better index of stratification than the more conscious indices frequently used by social scientists. The answer, of course, is that the same unconsciousness exists for the sociologist as it does for the average speaker. Opening up such consciousness is one of the missions of social dialect study to sociology. In a very rudimentary way, correlations of the frequency of occurrence of a particular language feature characterized the early work in this area. In Detroit, for example, a study of the frequency of occurrence of multiple negatives before indefinites, such as *I don't want none*, yielded the sort of stratification noted earlier in figure 1. Further developments in the study of social dialects may help us understand other aspects of social organization as it is revealed through language (for example, openings, closings, interruptions, clarification, hedging), competence as personal ability (not merely grammatical knowledge, systematic potential, or superorganic property of the community), community boundaries as defined by shared ways of speaking (Hymes, 1972), and many other concepts.

While it may not be appropriate to catalog all of the current or potential uses of the study of social dialect to other disciplines, one example, from the field of medicine, may be used to illustrate some of the potential of this kind of research. Preliminary research on the problems of communication between doctor and patient reveals a continuum roughly as follows (Shuy, 1973):

Doctor speaking Doctor talk	Doctor speaking Doctor talk but also understanding Patient talk	Doctor speaking and understanding both Doctor and Patient talk	Patient speaking and understanding both Patient and Doctor talk	Patient speaking Patient talk but also understanding Doctor talk	Patient speaking Patient talk

By far the largest part of the medical history, from the data available so far, indicates a doctor dominance in language and perspective in the standard medical interview. That is, the patient is expected to make most of the linguistic adjustments. It appears that in medicine, as in the schools, the expert requires the client to understand the specialized language forms and functions. In the above continuum, when breakdown in communication occurs, it occurs more often and more seriously at the polar extremes. Some patients cannot or will not speak doctor language. The obvious area of communication lies in the central portion of the continuum, where a kind of bilingualism obtains. What is lacking, of course, is a realization by many physicians that language variation may be hindering them from the successful completion of their task. A great deal needs to be known about whether or not the specialist should (or could) learn to speak client language. But there is little question about the specialist's need to learn receptive competence of the various social dialects which he expects to meet. It is patently absurd for physicians to run the risk of getting inaccurate information in the medical interview simply because a patient does not want to admit his own ignorance of the question or because the question was indelicately asked.

It would be presumptuous to claim that the study of social dialects has permeated a number of fields or disciplines. But it would be foolish to overlook some of the expanded vision for social dialect research that has been developing in recent years. Those who were active in the field in the 1960s may well remember the general sense of inferiority attributed to social dialects of all sorts at that time.

Conclusion

The study of social dialects in this country has received increasing attention since about the middle of the 1960s. This increased emphasis has been particularly strong within the field of linguistics itself where an almost total reversal seems to be taking place from the former preoccupation with univerals rather than variability. Papers on some aspects of the study of language variation have increased both in number and in quality at meetings of linguists such as those of The Linguistic Society of America during the past decade. One outgrowth of this interest has been the creation of the Lectological Association, founded in 1972 at the first conference on New Ways of Analyzing Variation in English (also referred to as NWAVE or New Wave). This loosely conceived organization exists solely for the purpose of convening scholars of like interests annually and for keeping them abreast of new developments through its publication *The Lectological Newsletter*. Since its inception, the scope of interest of the organization has been expanded beyond the study of variation of English to other languages as well (see Bailey and Shuy, 1973; Shuy and Bailey, 1974; Shuy and Fasold, forthcoming).

The increased concern for the study of social dialects in linguistics has not overshadowed the development of such an interest in education. The National Council of Teachers of English, for example, has shown continued interest in such matters. One of the first publications on social dialects in the sixties, in fact, was *Social Dialects and Language Learning* (Shuy, 1965), a NCTE publication. Other publications on the interrelationship of social dialect to education include Aaron's special anthology issue of the *FL Reporter* (1969), publications by the International Reading Association (Laffey and Shuy, 1973), The Center for Applied Linguistics' entire Urban Language Series, many publications by Georgetown University Press, and several commercial press publications (Cazden, John, and Hymes, 1972; DeStefano, 1972; Shores, 1972). Considerable recent concern has been expressed over the effects of social dialects on educational testing, as witnessed by the International Reading Association's conference on testing held at Georgetown University in August, 1973. On the other hand, little or no progress seems to have been made in conveying the major tenets of social dialectology into teacher education preservice programs (Shuy, 1973).

Historians who in some future generation decide to determine what linguists were excited about in the 1960s and 1970s will undoubtedly see social dialect study as a recurring theme. Nor has the field come close to exhausting its natural resources. What began as a focus on minority variation in language has gradually begun to be understood as equally crucial for mainstream speakers of English. It is likely that future research will be done on the variation exhibited in the speech of those such as lawyers and business executives. We will need to find out what constitutes the substance and strategies of "good-guy" speech (strategies for humanizing one's status or position), service encounters (Merrit, 1973), and many other kinds of language encounters. The study of social dialects in literature has always been a fruitful area of investigation, but the newer developments in analytical procedures have reopened that door to further investigation. Descriptive studies are still lacking for many speech communities in America and it appears that the potential for further investigation will ensure a continuance of interest in social dialectology for many years to come.

REFERENCES

Aarons, A., Gordon, B. Y., and Stewart, W. A. *Linguistic-cultural differences and American education.* (Special anthology issue of *The Florida FL Reporter*.) North Miami Beach: Florida FL Reporter, Inc., 1969.

Abrahams, R. A true and exact survey of talking black. In R. Bauman and R. Abrahams, eds., *An ethnography of speaking.* London: Cambridge University Press, in press.

Allen, H. B. *The linguistic atlas of the Upper Midwest.* Vols. 1 and 2. Minneapolis: University of Minnesota Press, n.d.

Atwood, E. B. *The regional vocabulary of Texas.* Austin: University of Texas Press, 1962.

Bailey, C-J. N. *Variation and language theory.* Arlington, Va.: Center for Applied Linguistics, 1974.

Bailey, C-J. N., and Shuy, R. W. *New ways of analyzing variation in English.* Washington, D.C.: Georgetown University Press, 1973.

Baratz, J. Teaching reading in an urban Negro school. In F. Williams, ed., *Language and poverty*. Chicago: Markham, 1970.

Bauman, R. An ethnographic framework for the investigation of communicative behaviors. In R. Abrahams and R. Troike, eds., *Language and cultural diversity in American education*. Englewood Cliffs, N.J.: Prentice-Hall, 1973.

Bickerton, D. The structure of polylectal grammars. In R. Shuy, ed., *Sociolinguistics: Current trends and prospects*. Washington, D.C.: Georgetown University Press, 1972.

Cazden, C. Approaches to dialects in early childhood education. In R. Shuy (compiler), *Social dialects and interdisciplinary perspectives*. Washington, D.C.: Center for Applied Linguistics, 1971.

Cazden, C., John, V. P., and Hymes, D., eds. *Functions of language in the classroom*. New York: Teachers College Press, 1972.

Cedergren, H., and Sankoff, D. Variable rules: Performance as a statistical reflection of competence. *Language*, 1974, *50*, 333-55.

Chomsky, N., and Halle, M. *The sound pattern of English*. New York: Harper and Row, 1971.

Connolly, J. The Iowa Test of Basic Skills in a rural West Virginia community. Paper presented at A.E.R.A., Los Angeles, Ca., 1969.

DeCamp, D. Toward a generative analysis of a post-creole speech continuum. In D. Hymes, ed., *Pidginization and creolization of languages*. London: Cambridge University Press, 1971.

De Stefano, J. *Language, society, and education: A profile of black English*. Worthington, Oh.: Jones Publishing Company, 1972.

Fasold, R. W. *Tense marking in black English: A linguistic and social analysis*. Washington, D.C.: Center for Applied Linguistics, 1972.

Fasold, R. W., and Wolfram, W. Some linguistic features of Negro dialect. In R. Fasold and R. Shuy eds., *Teaching standard English in the inner city*. Washington, D.C.: Center for Applied Linguistics, 1970.

Feigenbaum, I. *English now*. New York: New Century, 1971.

Golden, R. Instructional record for changing regional speech patterns. *Folkways/Scholastic*, no. 9323, 1965.

Hollingshead, A. *Social class and mental illness*. New York: John Wiley and Sons, Inc., 1958.

Hymes, D. Models of the interaction of language and social setting. *Journal of Social Issues*, 1966, *23*, 8-28.

———. The scope of sociolinguistics. In R. Shuy, ed., *Sociolinguistics: Current trends and prospects*. Washington, D.C.: Georgetown University Press, 1972.

Jakobson, R. *Child language, aphasia and phonological universals*. The Hague: Mouton, 1968.

Kurath, H. *A word geography of the Eastern United States*. Ann Arbor: University of Michigan Press, 1949.

Labov, W. Contraction, deletion and inherent variability of the English copula. *Language*, 1969, *45*, 715-62.

———. *The social stratification of English in New York City*. Washington, D.C.: Center for Applied Linguistics, 1966.

———. The logic of non-standard English. In J. Alatis, ed., *Georgetown Round*

Table Monograph Series, no. 22. Washington, D.C.: Georgetown University Press, 1969b.

————. *Language in the inner city*. Philadelphia: University of Pennsylvania Press, 1972.

Labov, W., Cohen, P., Robbins, C., and Lewis, K. C. A study of the nonstandard English of Negro and Puerto Rican speakers in New York City. U.S. Office of Education Cooperative Research Project, no. 3288, 1965.

Laffey, J., and Shuy, R. W. *Language differences: Do they interfere?* Newark, Delaware: International Reading Association, 1973.

Legum, S. et al. The speech of young black children in Los Angeles. Southwest Regional Laboratory Technical Report, no. 3. Inglewood, Ca.: Southwest Regional Laboratory, 1971.

Long, B. *Teaching writing to speakers of non-standard English*, forthcoming.

McDavid, R. I. Needed research in Southern dialect. In E. T. Thompson, ed., *Perspectives on the South: Agenda for research*. Durham: Duke University Press, n.d.

Marckwardt, A. H. Principal and subsidiary dialect areas in the Northern-Central States. *Publication of the American Dialect Society*, 1957, *27*, 3-15.

Merrit, M. On service encounters. *Anthropological Linguistics*, in press.

Parsons, T. W. *Teaching young children*. Stanford: Professional Development Systems, n.d.

Pickford, G. R. American linguistic geography: A sociological appraisal. *Word*, 1956, *12*, 211-33.

Reed, C. E. The pronunciation of English in the Pacific Northwest. *Language*, 1961, *37*, 559-64.

Reed, D. W. Eastern dialect words in California. *Publication of the American Dialect Society*, 1954, *21*, 3-15.

Shores, D. *Contemporary English*. Philadelphia: J. B. Lippincott Company, 1972.

Shuy, R. W. *Social dialects and language learning*. Champaign: National Council of Teachers of English, 1965.

————. Speech differences and teaching strategies: How different is enough? In R. Hodges and E. Rudorf, eds., *Language and learning to read: What teachers should know about language*. Boston: Houghton Mifflin, 1972.

————. The study of vernacular black English as a factor in educational change. *Research in English*, 1973a (spring).

————. Problems of communication in the cross-cultural medical interview. *Sociolinguistic Working Papers*, University of Texas, no. 19, 1973b.

————. What is the study of variation used for? In R. Shuy and R. Fasold, eds., *New ways of analyzing variation II*. Washington, D.C.: Georgetown University Press, in press.

Shuy, R. W., and Bailey, C-J. N. *Toward tomorrow's linguistics*. Washington, D.C.: Georgetown University Press, 1974.

Shuy, R. W., and Fasold, R. W. *New ways of analyzing variation II*. Washington, D.C.: Georgetown University Press, forthcoming.

Shuy, R. W., Wolfram, W., and Riley, W. Linguistic correlates of social stratification in Detroit speech. U.S. Office of Education Cooperative Research Project, no. 6-1347, 1967.

————. *Field techniques in an urban language study*. Washington, D.C.: Center for Applied Linguistics, 1968.

Sledd, J. Bidialectism: The linguistics of white supremacy. *English Journal*, 1969, *58*, 1307-15.

————. Doublespeak: Dialectology in the service of Big Brother. *College English*, 1972, *33*, 435-56.

Sullivan, J. A sociolinguistic review of the Iowa Test of Basic Skills. In D. Smith and W. Riley, eds., *Georgetown University Working Papers in Linguistics*, no. 5 (Sociolinguistics). Washington, D.C.: Georgetown University Press, 1971, 61-75.

Warner, L. *Social class in America*. New York: Harper and Row, 1962.

Whiteman, M. Dialect differences in testing the language of children: A review of the California Language Tests. In D. Smith and W. Riley, eds., *Georgetown University Working Papers in Linguistics*, no. 5 (Sociolinguistics). Washington, D.C.: Georgetown University Press, 1971, 48-60.

Wolfram, W. Black/white speech differences revisited. In W. Wolfram and N. Clarke, eds., *Black-white speech differences*. Washington, D.C.: Center for Applied Linguistics, 1972.

————. The relationship of white southern speech to vernacular black English in the deep South. *Language*, 1974, *50*, 498-527.

X

Language and Society

Robin Lakoff

While doing linguistics is often both an enjoyable and scholarly activity, it is sometimes also distressingly ivory-towerish. Many theoretical linguists have assumed that their work has no direct relevance to the outside, or real, world, and often seem rather proud of that fact that anything "applied" is of necessity soiled by its very usefulness. They console themselves by thinking that if indeed their work is not able to be a force for good, at least it cannot be a force for evil. But there is a sense of despair at the thought of working *in vacuo*, of training students to teach linguistics to students who will teach linguistics to students, etc. It is heartening, therefore, to see linguists now taking the first tottering steps toward relevance.

Language interacts with other aspects of human social behavior: there is no science of linguistics that stands alone. Rather, all areas of linguistic research must be concerned with what makes people act the way they do and what makes people human. Linguistics, therefore, must be considered an interdependent component of a much larger field. This chapter will attempt to show why this interaction must exist, what linguists must bring to their study of language from extralinguistic knowledge, and how the incorporation of such knowledge into linguistic theory will enable linguistic phenomena to be described in a deeper and more satisfying way.

It is useful to remember that linguistics did not isolate itself in its ivory tower through sheer perversity. Rather, at an earlier stage in the life of generative grammar, such detachment was necessary for self-preservation. Generative-transformational grammar was originally a most elegantly simple theory, and it retained its svelte form precisely because it was able to reject the temptations that were offered it for expansion and diversification. Generative-transformational grammarians needed to feel that they were working within a finite theory, and would be likely to devise a complete grammar of English in the not-too-far-distant future.

But in order to maintain this youthful optimism, transformationalists had to put a damper on their creativity: a great many interesting questions they might have asked had to be summarily declared out of bounds—not part of linguistics proper. For if these limitations were broached, there would be too many unknowns, too many complexities, too many uncertainties for theorists to handle at this stage in the development of transformational theory. And, of course, had scholars become sidetracked at that point in time, linguists would not have the strong foundations they do today.

Social Aspects of Language Use

What were the aspects of language that were ignored in those early days because they were considered to be outside the domain of linguistic interest? A prime example was the social aspect of language use—the intention of an utterance, the way it was apt to be interpreted, its politeness, and its relationship to social role. The linguist must make a decision as to how to deal with a sentence like example 1, that is, at what point any analysis should *stop*:

1. It's cold in here.

A classical transformational grammarian might do a purely syntactic analysis, such as deciding whether or not *it* arose in deep structure. Some linguists have claimed that underlying sentence 1 is some structure as in sentence 2:

2. *In the room is cold in the room.

Such an analysis, created in desperation, serves as an example of the dangers of doing syntax by itself and for its own sake. The deep structure in sentence 2, underlying the surface structure in sentence 1, is attractive in providing a reason for the presence of the "empty" *it*. *It* is indeed a substitution for something, and since that something occurs elsewhere in the sentence, *it* is recoverable under deletion and is pronominalized. A pure syntactician might point out that the pronominalization is rather unusual in cases such as this. It is never the rightmost occurrence of the repeated phrase that is pronominalized, that is, a sentence such as example 3 is never found:

3. *In the room is cold it.

While backward pronominalization does, of course, exist, it does not exist under these syntactic conditions, and where it is found, it is generally optional, with forward pronominalization found as well.

The semantically alert syntactician is likewise suspicious of this analysis because he feels intuitively that sentence 1 does not have the same meaning as sentence 2; *it* in sentence 1 does not feel like a pronominalization of a prepositional phrase. There is no justification, moreover, in assuming such a redundancy in the underlying structure as is entailed by using the same phrase twice. While of course redundancies occur all over grammar, it is very strange to think of them occurring to this extent, and with such little communicative purpose. So once we allow semantic considerations to sway us in our syntactic analysis, a deep structure shown in sentence 2 becomes increasingly indefensible. While we are thereby robbed of an easy way out of a complicated analysis, it does tend to keep us closer to the straight and narrow path of good common sense, and away from implausible analyses that are adopted only because they represent the shortest path to the desired sentence structure.

There are other questions to ask, which, until recently, linguists did not consider theirs to ask, or even worth asking. The basic question is that of the intention of the speech act. Why does the speaker speak at all? And why does he phrase his utterance as he does? These are not obvious questions. The latter, particularly, resists an easy answer. We can assume that, being rational human beings, when there is a message to communicate, we will naturally pick the shortest route between expression and understanding, and say what is to be said directly. But a short examination of sentence 1 should disabuse us of this notion. Grice (1963), in fact, starts from this basic premise in constructing his rules of conversational logic. He assumes implicitly an ideal speech situation of the type hypothesized above. The speaker has something that needs to be said to the addressee, and he says it to him in the clearest possible way.

Such speech situations can indeed be found in the real world, although as conversational utterances in the normal sense of "conversation," they are relatively rare. In lectures, in formal instructions, between participants in a discourse who do not know each other well and are not seeking to become better acquainted but merely to transmit necessary information about the outside world, we may find a fairly strict adherence to Grice's maxims. But more usually we find them violated. However, its seems correct to say that a conversational maxim is not infringed unless something more important than mere logic will be imperiled by its enforcement.

Grice's conversational maxims have been much discussed in recent linguistic literature (see Gordon and Lakoff, 1971; R. Lakoff, in press), and therefore will be only summarized here. They consist of four major rules:

1. Quantity: Say only as much as is necessary for understanding the communication.
2. Quality: Say only what is true.
3. Relevance: Say only what is relevant.
4. Manner: Be clear.

These are related, perhaps rather tenuously, to the rules of communicative competence proposed a few years ago (R. Lakoff, 1972). The rules of conversational logic, it will be recognized, are in their explicit form applicable only to declarative utterances which are attempts to transmit information.

The rules of communicative competence attempted to provide guidelines for successful speech acts of all three basic types: declaratives, imperatives, and interrogatives. The first two rules essentially recapitulate Grice's maxims of quality and quantity. The latter three qualify them as follows:

> Rule III. In the case of statements, the speaker assumes that the hearer will believe what he says.
> Rule IV. With questions, the speaker assumes that he will get a reply.
> Rule V. With orders, he assumes the command will be obeyed.
> (R. Lakoff, 1972, p. 916)

So there are certain things demanded of a hearer, normally, in the speech situation, depending on the speech-act type, belief, response, or compliance. These correlate with what the addressee can reasonably expect of the speaker, if the speech act is to be considered successful. For a declarative utterance, the speaker should have the authority necessary to compel belief; for a question, he should have a need to know; for an order, sufficient authority to command obedience. It will be noted that the requisites are not completely equivalent or parallel to one another. To have a need to know puts one in rather a different position vis-à-vis a potential addressee from having the authority to compel obedience. This is a rather important corollary to these ideas as we shall see shortly when we attempt further analysis of sentence 1.

One thing that neither Grice nor I did—an oversight now being rectified (R. Lakoff, in press)—is to clarify the relation between the rules of conversation and speech-act types other than declaratives. Can one extend the notions of *truth* and of *sufficiency* so that the resultant extension covers nondeclarative utterances? And how does our intuitive notion of the relevancy of questions and orders relate to our idea of the relevancy of a directly informative speech act? Finally, what do we mean by a clear, unambiguous, or succinct order or question, as opposed to a declarative utterance having these properties?

If the notion of "truth" for declarative utterances may be thought to be paraphrasable as "reasonableness for compelling belief " (the necessary condition on the addressee in a declarative), then we may look for analogous conditions on the other speech-act types, and perhaps attempt a preliminary definition as follows:

> For *imperatives* the necessary condition for obedience to a command is that the speaker have *power* over the hearer. A question, to require a response, must be reasonable—that is, the questioner must have a *need* to know the answer.

These are, of course, essentially the conditions listed above, now further defined as parallel to the condition on a declarative speech act that is represented by Grice's maxim of quality.

Further, all speech-act types may be qualified or hedged. Qualification or hedging is apt to occur in either of two circumstances: when quality, in our broader definition, is in question, or if the *assumption* of adherence to quality would be construed, or might be construed, as an invasion of the addressee's rights. In the first instance, the speaker of the sentence feels that there really are real-world conditions that interfere with the "truth" in our extended sense of his utterance: in the latter, he is merely afraid lest his addressee interpret his utterance as a violation of quality. The difficulty to the participants in such a conversation is, very simply, that the reason for qualification may be misinterpreted, with confusion resulting.

It will help to give a couple of examples of the workings of this fragment of a system being outlined. Suppose *A* wants *B* to close the window. We must first ascertain *A*'s status vis-à-vis *B*'s. If *A* clearly outranks *B*, *A* has the *power* to utter a simple imperative:

4. Close the window.

Under these conditions *A* can be fairly sure that *B* will obey, as *B* has no choice. *A* will not thereby ingratiate himself with *B*, however, and sometimes ingratiation is more desirable than the pure exercise of raw muscle. It may also be the case that *A* does not actually outrank *B*—they are equals, or *A* may even be *B*'s inferior. In either event *A* is likely to hedge his speech act so as not to create difficulties: in the first case, *A* hedges because he wants to be polite and not to seem to be encroaching on *B*'s preserves; in the second, *A* hedges because quite literally *A* does not have the power to do otherwise. *A* might then say any of the following:

5. Please close the window.
6. Can you close the window.
7. I wonder if you'd close the window.

Returning to sentence 1, it may be said that, under the right conditions the sentence may function as a member of the set partially exhausted by examples 4 through 7. Yet in form it is altogether different from any of them. It is, superficially, a declarative rather than an imperative utterance, and the traditional syntactician would surely interpret it as a declarative and leave it at that.

But were the syntactician to do so, there might be a question about the correctness of his assignment, for instance, by taking note of the addressee's behavior in response to sentence 1 by comparing and contrasting it with his typical response to sentences 4 through 7 on the one hand (superficially quite different in form from 1), and, on the other, to utterances such as sentence 8 (superficially declaratives and thereby, again superficially, more similar to sentence 1 than to any of sentences 4 through 7).

8. It's cold here in Ann Arbor.

If we considered the probable effect of a speech act on its addressee, in part determined by the range of reasonable responses to that speech act, as part of its meaning in an extended sense of the term, we would have to assume that sentence 1 shared aspects of meaning with sentences 4 through 7 which it did not share with sentence 8—that under some conditions a declarative was more closely related to an imperative than to another declarative. For in response to sentences 4 through 7 the addressee might reasonably be expected to do any of the following: get up and shut the window; explain that the window was stuck and could not be closed; or say that he was quite comfortable as it was, so why not leave the window open? In short, he must either get up and close the window as directed, or give some plausible reason why he is not going to do so. But in response to sentence 8 the speaker feels no need to do either: clearly he cannot do anything to stop the cold, and since he cannot, he does not have to make excuses for not doing something about it. (If he does start excusing himself, we are apt to assume that his response is rather aberrant; overly defensive, perhaps even slightly paranoid; whereas such a response to imperatives goes unremarked unless it is carried to an extreme.)

So we might attempt a first generalization: an imperative utterance demands either compliance or an explanation for noncompliance from its addressee. A declarative demands neither. But we have in sentence 1 an apparent counterexample—under some conditions at least, either to get up and close the window, or explain why the window cannot or should not be closed will count as a normal response. And the speaker of sentence 1 will be satisfied with this response, rather than puzzled as he would if it were given as a reply to sentence 8. So both in its intention and in its effect, sentence 1 is sometimes analyzable as parallel to sentences 4 through 7 rather than to 8.

Two questions arise out of the consideration of these facts: (1) Why use a declarative as an imperative, when we have at our disposal perfectly good imperatives, whose communicative intent is clearer than declaratives so used and which, therefore, should be preferable to declaratives in this function? (2) Why are declaratives interpretable as imperatives only under certain conditions? What are these conditions?

Let us recall a point made earlier: the rules of conversational logic are violable only for the sake of maintaining politeness. Politeness is viewed as the only conversational goal of higher priority than clarity. The less likely an imperative is to be seen by the addressee as encroaching on his preserves, the more polite it is apt to be. And since sentence 1, at least in theory, gives the addressee even more choices than any of sentences 5 through 7, it is in theory more polite than any of them: it need not even be taken as an injunction.

The above also serves as a means of beginning an answer to the second question. In the first place, sentence 1 will only be used as a substitute for sentence 4 when the communicative framework involves politeness: that is, either the speaker wants to seem polite or when he wants to use the notion that sentence 1 is a polite utterance in order to be sarcastic. When the context in which sentence 4 would be uttered is one in which politeness does not play a part, where status disparities between speaker and addressee are acknowledged as explicit, sentence 1 is unlikely to be used, except in sarcasm.

Secondly, it is obvious that a sentence like sentence 1 will be used as an equivalent to sentence 4 only when the context of the utterance is such that an imperative with the sense of sentence 4 would itself be appropriate, that is, when the speaker has reason to expect that the addressee would be able to carry out the injunction. Therefore, presumably, sentence 8 is difficult to interpret as an indirect imperative since there is not much the addressee could do about the situation; but the addressee might be in a position to do any of several things in response to sentence 1, so that it can fairly easily be interpreted as a command.

There is one more interesting fact about the use of sentences like sentence 1 as commands. They seem usable only in case it is, in some sense, fairly evident that a command is in order and is intended. That is, they are usable most easily under contextual conditions that tend to disambiguate them, or otherwise, such sentences would be more confusing to interpret than they are already. And this is why, although hypothetically polite, utterances such as sentence 1 rather paradoxically often have the opposite effect—they are interpreted either as brusque or as sarcastic.

The brusque interpretation comes about because these sentences carry with them a hidden assumption. For example, the reason this apparent declarative is interpretable as an imperative in this conversation is that A would not talk to B *except* to issue an injunction—B is of no deeper interest to A, and A outranks B. And the sarcastic interpretation seems to arise by this sort of chain of thoughts: This utterance *appears* to be polite in that it gives B the option of not interpreting it as an order. But in fact there is no need for A to be polite to B, rather the reverse, B had better respect A and obey, and B knows it. So just as other forms of sarcasm reverse the explicit content of an utterance, sarcasm in this case is occasioned by a reversal of assumptions underlying the utterance.

Parallels are found in declarative and interrogative speech acts. For example compare the following sentences:

  9. John is a Communist.
  10. I guess John is a Communist.
  11. John is sort of a Communist.
  12. John is a Communist, isn't he?

In each of the examples 9 through 12, the declarative statement *John is a Communist* is qualified, either because the speaker thinks he does not have enough real-world information at hand to compel the addressee's belief, or because he feels that expecting the addressee to believe him—as would be implied by a simple declarative as in sentence 9—is impolite in reducing the addressee's options.

Hence, in such cases, the speaker is faced with a choice between communicative clarity, or directness, on the one hand, and politeness, or tact, on the other. Other things being equal, the latter typically takes precedence over the former.

Other things, of course, are not always equal, so that exceptions to our rule arise. Consideration must be taken of the personality of the speaker, the impression the speaker wishes to make on the addressee, and the real-world situation in which the speaker is operating. All three compose the determinants of communicative style. For what is being discussed here is, essentially, stylistics. From the issue of whether or not one should use a tag question in stating a belief, to the question of how to tell, offhand, whether we are reading Henry James or Thomas Pynchon is but a small step: if one can be talked about with any assurance, then something substantial could be said about the other. It may well be, too, that research in stylistics from the point of view of linguistic theory has been misdirected, in that it has adopted the subject matter, methodology, and interests of the literary critic. There is nothing wrong ipso facto with literary criticism and stylistic work done on that basis, but perhaps if linguists started from their own personal speech styles, they might frame more interesting questions and get more interesting answers, and ultimately come to understand both traditional and conversational stylistics more fully.

Appropriateness of a Conversational Contribution

Determining the appropriateness of a conversational contribution could be approached from the point of view of the novelist striving for verisimilitude. How does the novelist decide whether a character shall be given sentence 9 to say or one of its variations? Of course, the good novelist has an intuitive feeling which enables him to make the choice. (The novelist is a creator in the sense that he devises speech styles for others than himself, while the individual speaker has only his own situation and psyche to deal with, but both are doing essentially the same thing.)

The novelist will first have to determine what a character is like and where he or she is. He might make up a checklist like the following:

A. The speaker's social role (both in isolation and with respect to the addressee's)
   1. male or female?
   2. age: child, young adult, middle-aged, old?
   3. economic, social, and educational status?
   4. feeling of solidarity with addressee?

B. The conversational situation

    1. length of acquaintance of speaker and addressee
    2. number of participants in the discourse
    3. type of discourse
        a. social small talk
        b. information sharing

C. Speaker's psychological context

    1. speaker's confidence in what he is saying
    2. the impression the speaker wants to make
    3. the assumptions speaker has about himself; addressee; type of conversation; and appropriateness of style

So suppose we have a twenty-five-year-old male character who is going to be uttering the sentence. The author has established him as middle-class and college-educated, and that he has known the addressee for some time and feels comfortable with him. The addressee is a thirty-year-old male, of working-class status and high school educated. The speaker and addressee are holding a two-party conversation, possibly at a political meeting where John has just been nominated for office. The speaker is reasonably confident of his statement (he has read and heard plenty of evidence that tends to support his conclusion). He wants to impress the addressee more with his political savvy than with his savoir-faire.

In such a case, we can see that almost everything militates in favor of an utterance like sentence 9: the speaker outclasses the addressee on several bases, and in the rest is his equal; the situation presupposes some familiarity between the participants; forthrightness is more apt to make the desired impression than hesitancy; the conversation is primarily involving the exchange of information, and is less social than business.

Suppose we change the speaker, however, to a twenty-year-old woman, middle-class and college-educated, speaking to a man about five years her senior and of similar social and educational status. Let us keep the nature and conditions of the discourse the same, and say that now the speaker is not only anxious to communicate the information, but also eager to make a good impression on her addressee. That is, she wants him to like her, to believe in what she is saying, but really only secondarily. Now we are really engaged in a social, rather than business, situation, because that is the way the speaker defines her role. In such a case, the perspicacious novelist would be quite apt to put sentences 10, 11, or 12—most likely either the first or the last—into our character's mouth. What she seems to be doing, in both cases, is expressing uncertainty about her declaration, suggesting that, although a normal declarative speech act demands or expects the addressee's belief, hers leaves it up to her addressee as to whether he will believe what she says or not. She is at the same time commenting on her application of the rule of quality: "This may not be true." Yet, of course, she believes it is true, or she would not say it.

Now we would like to say that the knowing violation of the rule of quality constitutes a lie, or at best, misinformation. But here we are not only dealing with a lie, but if it later should turn out that the statement was in fact incorrect, our original speaker can then say, "Well, I only said I *guessed*," or "I was only asking." (But of course sentence 12 is not a bona fide question in that it does not leave the answer up to the addressee: he is being directed toward an affirmative reply, and will disconcert the speaker of sentence 12 should he reply, "No.")

But it seems as though the hedging of the speech act (as in both sentences 10 and 12) constitutes an evasion of the maxim of quality. If the speaker makes it clear to the addressee that what he is saying is to be taken with some caution, and that therefore the final decision is up to the addressee as to whether to believe the utterance, then the contribution is considered legitimate even if quality is indeed later shown to have been violated.

But we have also said that, purely in terms of the speaker's psychological frame of reference, the situation in this example is parallel to our earlier case in that both speakers are assumed to have good grounds for their belief. Hence it would seem that hedging on the grounds that quality might later be found to be infringed was pointless. That should only occur when there is legitimate reason for the speaker to fear that his contribution will later be discredited. But the novelist knows that sentences 10 and 12 are likely options for this speaker, where sentence 9 was more probable for the earlier one. Why does this speaker choose to express her conviction so unconvincingly?

To answer this question, it is again necessary to invoke politeness. Sometimes a speaker will mute the assertive force of his utterance in order not to cause offense, rather than in order to indicate uncertainty on his part about the veracity of the offered information. The speaker still is releasing the addressee from the need to believe the assertion, in this case, because her status, relative to his (as she perceives it), does not give her the right to demand or expect belief. Of course, it may not always be unambiguously clear to the addressee whether it is indeed a discrepancy in status or true uncertainty that is causing the speaker to give him options, and misunderstanding may easily ensue. Additionally, of course—as this case makes clear—the status distinctions implicit in giving someone else options are not always real. Often they are merely conventional, and recognized as such by all participants in a discourse. In this case, the addressee knows that he does not really have the "out" the speaker appears to have offered him: he is expected to treat the utterance as though it were a genuine declarative (or question, or command, in those cases), rather than withholding what he is apparently being invited to withhold. In other words, a speaker may, for reasons of conventional politeness, hedge such a question as sentence 13:

13. I'd like to ask how much you paid for that dress?

But the addressee still knows that he cannot respond to sentence 13 as though he had a right not to answer, nor even as though it were the hedge itself that were answerable; both sentence 14 and sentence 15 are inappropriate as answers to sentence 13:

14. No.
15. I bet you would.

The only legitimate way out, should the addressee be reluctant to answer, is to sidestep the issue:

16. Well, gosh, I . . . gee, I forget . . . .
17. Yeah, it's a pretty cool dress, isn't it?
18. Well, you know what clothes cost these days . . . .

Nevertheless, although everyone involved in such a discourse knows that a game is being played, it is almost universally true that everyone would rather play the game of conventional politeness than to waive the rules.

In the case with which we are dealing now, there is an additional complicating factor, that of sex role. It is probably not the case in present-day American society that a woman will use deferentially polite forms because she really feels her status is lower than a man's. But a woman certainly is more prone to use such forms, both to men and to other women. I have referred to the differences in levels of expected politeness in men's and women's speech, and suggested reasons for the discrepancy. Again a sort of conventionality is involved, specifically tied to woman's role in our culture, in her real status as nonparticipant in serious matters, and in her role as a decoration for her man. One who plays such a role is thereby made an outsider, and an outsider must be more polite than someone who is an active coparticipant.

Of the three alternatives for sentence 9, sentence 11 has not yet been discussed. To whom would the novelist assign this utterance? It is not an example of the use of deferential language based purely on social role. Rather, it is a form of hedging in order to mitigate the speaker's discomfort about the conversation itself: he has to say something potentially embarrassing, and seeks to avoid embarrassment through the use of a hedge. G. Lakoff, in the paper already cited (1972), has discussed hedges like "sorta" in their function as modifiers of something present in the superficial sentence. Often it is not easy to tell whether, indeed, a hedge of this kind is playing this role, or that of deferential politeness. For example, consider sentence 19:

19. John is sorta short.

Lakoff's formulation predicts that such a sentence would be used in case the speaker were in doubt as to how to judge John's height: he is, let us say, 5 feet 6 inches tall—fairly short but not markedly so. But there is another use. In this culture, tallness is a desirable trait in men, and it is therefore considered preferable for a man to be taller than any woman he accompanies. Now consider two situations:

a. Mary is 5 feet 11 inches; John is 5 feet 11 inches.
b. Mary is 5 feet 3 inches; John is 5 feet 6 inches.

In the first of these instances, John is not really short; but, being the same height as Mary, he is short relative to Mary. (If Bill is also 5 feet 11 inches, however, John is not short with respect to Bill.) Sentence 19 will be interpreted in this context as implying that while John is not *really* short, he is short with respect to Mary and the cultural norms. He is short with qualifications. This is akin to Lakoff's true hedges.

In the second case, however, John is no longer short with respect to Mary; he is, on the other hand, unqualifiedly short according to our culture's determination of average height. Therefore, strictly speaking, to hedge the assertion in this case would be inappropriate. Yet one might still use sentence 19, meaning, "John is short, but I want to soften the brusqueness of this (damaging) assertion."

A sentence like sentence 11 is of interest in that it apparently cannot function as a literal hedge. If one wanted to say "John adheres to some but not all of the tenets of Communism," rather than saying sentence 11, we would probably employ a sentence such as sentence 20:

20. John is a Communist of sorts.

Sentence 11, however, has only the polite, or defensive, reading, the one that qualifies the declarative performative verb itself rather than the assertion of the sentence. This form of hedging seems particularly characteristic of the young, in whose grammar it is a member of the same lexical class as *like, y'know, I mean*. Maligned by English teachers and rhetoricians, such forms cling tenaciously to the language, presumably because they serve an essential function. For we should always bear in mind that, if a speech form needs to be inveighed against, it is because it is of wide currency, and this in turn is because there is a deeply felt need for it. It is then pointless to try to eradicate the speech form; at best, an equally noxious substitute will insinuate itself in the place of the ousted form. But usually even this is too much to hope for. Rather, one should try to understand why a particular banality is of such widespread use; and perhaps take steps to cure the psychological or social malaise that underlies the linguistic disease. Linguistic inarticulateness very likely always goes along with feelings of social discomfort. If we want to banish *like* from the lexicon, we will first have to banish defensiveness from the human psyche and power imbalances from real-world interpersonal relationships.

Elsewhere in the grammar as well we find discourse commenting upon itself and its own sufficiency or intelligibility. For instance, it has been shown in James (1972, 1973), and R. Lakoff (1973) that interjections, another aspect of language use scorned as "performance" by some, as sloppy by others, and as meaningless by virtually everyone until recently, are actually none of the above. Thus, *well* and *why* comment on an aberration in either the speaker's own contribution, or the prior utterance of the addressee. Consider in this regard a discourse represented by the question of sentence 21, answered by one of the three variants of 22:

21. Where were you last night?
22. a. At the movies.
    b. Well, at the movies.
    c. Why, at the movies.

Now as far as pure denotative information, the three utterances of response 22 function equivalently. But in terms of the speaker's view of his response, and the assumptions he is making about the addressee's anticipations, they are quite distinct. The first, if uttered without special intonation, merely answers the question with the requisite information, treating neither question nor response as remarkable. As far as we can tell from this fragment, response 22a tells the addressee nothing *beyond* the denotative content he sought to discover.

If the speaker chooses option 22b, typically he will be warning the addressee, by his use of *well*, that the contribution that follows is deficient in some sense. Frequently a further contribution will follow immediately to rectify that deficiency. It is as if by the use of the utterance 22b the speaker were saying, "Here is the appropriate response to the question you posed. But in actuality your question was inappropriate, for by answering it appropriately I am constrained to give an insufficient answer. I shall therefore follow the rules by answering your question as given first, but marking my response as somehow unsatisfactory, and will then (or perhaps upon further and more appropriate questioning by you) amplify my response so that it provides you more precisely with the data you are really in need of." This is a lot to ask of one word, especially a random and meaningless interjection, but this does seem to approximate the force of *well* in response 22b.

In response 22c, on the other hand, the speaker of sentence 21 is being taken to task for the inadequacy of *his* contribution. The respondent of answer 22c is saying, in effect, "Your question was inappropriate in that I cannot see why you had a need for this information. I will, however, answer you, but indicate that I feel it to be unnecessary."

It should be noted that it is violations of the Gricean maxims of conversational logic that the speaker is commenting on in these cases: in response 22b, he warns that he is about to violate quantity by giving insufficient information; and in response 22c, that the questioner has previously violated quantity, in the manner suggested earlier in this chapter. Since causing someone else to violate a maxim itself constitutes a violation of that maxim, the speaker of sentence 21 violates quantity by forcing his addressee to do likewise in making an appropriate reply.

It thus becomes evident that *well* makes a much greater contribution to a discourse than merely acting as a place-holder while the speaker fishes for something to say. The same has been shown by James to be true of the interjections *ah*, *oh*, and *uh*, which James has differentiated from one another in terms of their range of applicability and has shown that their use is dependent upon syntactic criteria, that is, that since they participate in syntactic rules, they cannot be dismissed as "mere performance phenomena." Indeed, as G. Lakoff (1973) has shown, recent work such as James's as well as developments in variation grammar such as exemplified in the work of J. R. Ross, makes the postulation of a dichotomy such as that proposed by Chomsky distinguishing performance and competence both undesirable and in fact largely untenable.

To summarize: work done over the last five or six years has tended to obscure the line between language structure and language use. The intention behind an utterance is shown to be as important as the denotative informational content it seeks to communicate. Similarly the psychological stance of the speaker—how he feels about the strength and believability of his contribution, and how he feels he is socially related to his addressee— will have great significance in the determination of whether a sentence is to be uttered at all, as well as the form it is to take when uttered.

New Directions in Linguistics

Theoretical research has, of late, taken several new directions; and it is a reasonable prediction that as a result linguists will start to view themselves, and other people will start to view linguists as having other interests and capacities than had previously been thought. Linguistics is heading in the direction of practicality. There will be in the ensuing years an ever-greater emphasis on application of theoretical discoveries; and application will be considered as valuable in its own right as pure theoretical contributions to knowledge have been. In fact, it will be increasingly recognized that theory severed from application is suspect, that data generated in the rocking chair, tested at the blackboard, and described in learned jargon are probably ridden with errors and inaccuracies.

This change in emphasis will arise—indeed, it is at this very moment arising—for two principal reasons. First, because the kinds of questions that must now be asked are questions that are answerable only in terms of how language is really used. The hypothetical member of an ideal speech community, who speaks perfectly error-free "normal" language all the time, envisioned by the early transformational grammarians as their model, is not at present terribly relevant. We want to know more about the edges of acceptability—the interface between normality and eccentricity in language use. What about the speaker whose habitual mode is ironic? How are we to write rules governing sarcasm? Can we delimit the acceptable social contexts for punning? What is the correct social environment for the use of implicature? Can we say with any precision when we shall leave a thing unsaid?

More practically, interest in real-world application of linguistic theory is arising at present because of a precipitous decline in the employability of the pure theorist. His job possibilities are almost totally restricted to academia, where his function is to do pure research and teach other students to do likewise. Now that this market is essentially closed, the new Ph. D. will have to look for other ways to earn a living. Until now he has been unable or unwilling to look for work outside of the university: unable because he is untrained in anything but pure theory; unwilling because there is a stigma attached to not being in academia. Both of these conditions must change; indeed, they are changing rapidly, at least in the experience of many linguists. Almost invariably students feel rather embarrassed at having amassed only theoretical knowledge; they want to acquire expertise in second-language teaching, or language pathology, or sign language. This is a healthy trend, and given real-world conditions, it will certainly prevail. Linguists will continue to be conversant with theoretical discoveries, but will view theory more as a means to an end than a desirable aim in itself. They will seek to make themselves useful in the world.

A few promising areas in which advances in theoretical knowledge are occurring are also worthy of mention.

Language teaching and translation. As discussed in R. Lakoff (1974), contextual information must be incorporated into what is taught in second language courses. Native-speaker fluency will never even be approximated unless the learner becomes able to use interjections, hedges, and the like idiomatically, and this sort of idiomatic usage cannot be taught unless the conditions governing the use of such forms are incorporated into what is taught. A participant in one culture must be fully acclimated into an adopted culture if he is to speak that culture's language with ease. Very often lack of knowledge of pragmatic linguistic devices specific to one language or cultural group will be interpreted by speakers as character defects, and therefore unforgivable, rather than linguistic ignorance, which is forgivable.

The same is true of translatability. Much that eludes the translator of a work of art is classifiable as precisely this sort of social or psychological context coded into the language. And, of course, it follows that the more "personal" and emotive the type of literature that is to undergo translation, the more likely it is that what makes it memorable will be lost. Just as interjections, hedges, and the like are characteristic of nontechnical and personally revealing discourse rather than lecturing style, so in writing these are traits found in poetry and artistic prose, less so in journalistic or technical writing. It is at least partly for this reason that the computer has had some success in translating the latter type of prose, but invariably fails laughably when asked to translate "good" writing. Advances within linguistic theory in understanding these nondenotative uses, however, will still not enable us to use the computer to translate literature adequately; it will probably always be the case that a sensitive human mind must mediate.

Aesthetic theory.   As the remarks above on translatability suggest, the sort of work that has been done is germane to an understanding of how and why literary style affects the reader as it does. It is a question that combines psychology, sociology, and pedagogy, as indeed does all that has been discussed. Psychology is involved because we know that individuals react differently to a prose style; reader *A* may love Hemingway and hate Faulkner; reader *B* may feel just the reverse; and reader *C* may be lukewarm to both and like nothing better than Jacqueline Susann. So we cannot really discuss style *in vacuo*; what we must think about is style in relation to human sensitivity, that is, how the reader interprets a prose style; how the idiosyncratic traits of a given writer differently affect different individuals.

Forensics.   Forensics provides a richly promising place in which linguistic knowledge can bring much insight. Legal language is specifically designed to be free of ambiguity, though often at the cost of clarity. What lawyers have developed over the years is an intuitive technique for making presuppositions and entailments explicit, or, where possible, eliminating lexical items that embody them. The kind of work described here, incorporating as it does the relationship between superficial forms and unconscious mental attitudes on the part of the actors in a conversation, would seem to provide the beginnings of a principled way to develop a clear and unambiguous legal language, and to better understand why legalese works the way it does.

"New" psycholinguistics.   Hitherto psycholinguistics has been almost totally developmental and cognitive. Child first language learning has received the lion's share of theorists' attention, partly because Chomsky's interests lie there, partly because children are more fun to work with than, say, nonnative speakers of English, or aphasics, or schizophrenics. The field should be extended to cover all aspects of human communication that shed light on the operation of the human mind, including forays into clinical and abnormal psychology.

Nobody really knows exactly how language is used most effectively in psychotherapy. The sensitive therapist listens for verbal (as well as watching for paralinguistic) cues from his patient, and from them figures out what is bothering the patient, as well as how to respond so as to help him learn to cope with his environment. But since there are so many styles of psychotherapy, each requiring different types of verbal activity on the part of the therapist, and each training the patient differently in the use of verbal expression, is it possible to ask which is the most effective? What sort of verbal interplay best accomplishes the desired goals? We all sense that therapeutic discourse differs in several of its most salient features from normal discourse (see Falk, 1974). But specifically what are these features, and why are they employed in this aberrant way? Do the well-known therapeutic ploys serve, as Haley (1969) suggests, merely to enforce the therapist's power over the patient? Or is there really a justifiable reason for them? The work of such writers as Ruesch (1961) and Watzlawick, Beavin, and Jackson (1967) provides many examples of how an intuitive feeling for linguistic processes enhances a therapist's effectiveness. Perhaps, with theoretical knowledge derived from linguistic research buttressing that intuition, psychotherapy could be rendered still more valuable and more likely to produce the results that are sought. The combination of linguistic insight with paralinguistic examples are discussed sensitively by writers such as Goffman (1967, 1971).

Since psychoanalytical work depends almost wholly for its results on the use and interpretation of language by analysand and analyst, one might offhand expect to find in the voluminous psychoanalytic literature a treasure trove of sophisticated analyses of examples of such specialized language use, perhaps relating an analysand's language use to his unconscious thought processes, or describing the effects of the analyst's verbal choices on the course of an analysis. However, no such body of literature appears to exist. There seems to be nothing at all in the psychoanalytic literature making use of any advances in linguistic theory achieved in the last twenty years. Surely, then, linguists and psychoanalysts working together can in the future make contributions to both fields at once.

Beyond this notion of special uses of language to achieve insight into the workings of the conscious and unconscious mind lies the understanding of what language use can tell us about thought disorders, and how a sensitive use of language may help the victim of such disorders become able to function satisfactorily. In particular, schizophrenia has been categorized (see Arieti, 1955) as both an impairment of logical (thought) processes, and difficulties with interpersonal communication (see also in this regard Bateson, 1972; and Watzlawick, Beavin, and Jackson, 1967). The schizophrenic uses deviations from standard, or Aristotelian logic; it is not clear whether because he cannot tell the difference, or because he feels he can get away with it. (Small children appear to function in rather the same way.) These deviations may be reflected in the choice of lexical items schizophrenics use: what sorts of presuppositions may be expressed, what assumptions are considered normal, what sorts of speech acts need to be hedged. Similarly the schizophrenic does not utilize the same set of social interaction rules as does the normal person, or at least uses rules in different situations than might be deemed appropriate. Hence it is to be expected that socially based linguistic features such as hedges and interjections, as well as rule-of-conversation-related uses, will not appear in schizophrenic speech as they appear in the standard language. We may further hypothesize that since linguistic usage is tied to mental state, we should be able to pinpoint linguistic cues that can be used for diagnostic purposes much more precisely than can now be done on a purely intuitive basis. The diagnosis of schizophrenia may thus be able to be made with more assurance; and judgment as to improvement or deterioration in a patient's condition may be able to be made with greater confidence. As with less drastic forms of psychotherapy, therapeutic techniques used with schizophrenics generally rely heavily on verbal interaction; it may be possible to suggest improvements in therapeutic technique based on work such as has been discussed in this chapter. Through language we may reach an understanding of both the conscious and the unconscious processes of the human mind. And through effective use of language, we may have an effect on these processes in ourselves and others.

More within the tradition of orthodox psycholinguistic research, we might envision extending the type of work done within developmental psycholinguistics to include studies of the acquisition of the types of phenomena discussed here. In particular, we may ask when children acquire the rules of politeness and conversation. What sorts of mistakes are made by children in these areas, at what ages, and how are the correct forms learned? Just as syntactic dialects are hypothesized from different children generalizing differently on the basis of incomplete data, so we may assume that adult speakers of English use the rules of politeness in various ways, based on the fact that they have had to extrapolate from incomplete data. Psycholinguistic research on these topics would appear to be particularly fruitful since the learning of these kinds of rules seems to go on until a far later age than does the learning of syntactic rules. For all practical purposes, a child has the syntax of his first language well under control by the time he is four or five. But as anyone who knows children of that age will attest, their speech is rife with violations of both the conversational maxims and the rules of politeness. Is this because they have not learned the rules, or have learned them imperfectly? Or because they are sufficiently egocentric that, though they know the rules perfectly well, they do not always care to apply them?

Recent (unpublished) work by Ervin-Tripp on the acquisition by children of the rules of politeness, and by Gordon on the acquisition of other pragmatic phenomena, is of great potential significance for the various fields involved, and should be the basis for a great deal of important research over the next several years.

REFERENCES

Arieti, S. *The interpretation of schizophrenia.* New York: Robert Brunner, 1955.
Bateson, G. *Steps to an ecology of mind.* New York: Ballantine, 1972.
Falk, J. Toward a semantics of personal style. Unpublished paper, Linguistics Department, University of California, Berkeley, 1974.
Goffman, E. *Interaction ritual.* New York: Doubleday and Co., 1967.
———. *Relations in public.* New York: Harper-Colophon, 1971.
Gordon, D., and Lakoff, G. Conversational postulates. In D. Adams et al., eds., *Papers from the Seventh Regional Meeting of the Chicago Linguistic Society.* Chicago: Chicago Linguistic Society, 1971.
Grice, H. P. Logic and conversation. Unpublished paper, Philosophy Department, University of California, Berkeley, 1967.
Haley, J. *The power tactics of Jesus Christ.* New York: Avon, 1969.
James, D. Some aspects of the syntax and semantics of interjections. In P. Peranteau et al., eds., *Papers from the Eighth Regional Meeting of the Chicago Linguistic Society.* Chicago: Chicago Linguistic Society, 1972.
———. The syntax and semantics of interjections in English. Ph.D. dissertation, University of Michigan, Ann Arbor, 1973.
Lakoff, G. Hedges: A study in meaning criteria and the logic of fuzzy concepts. In P. Peranteau et al., eds., *Papers from the Eighth Regional Meeting of the Chicago Linguistic Society.* Chicago: Chicago Linguistic Society, 1972.
———. Fuzzy grammar and the performance-competence terminology game. In C. Corum et al., eds., *Papers from the Ninth Regional Meeting of the Chicago Linguistic Society.* Chicago: Chicago Linguistic Society, 1973.
Lakoff, R. Language in context. *Language,* 1972, *48.4,* 907-27.
———. Language and woman's place. *Language in Society,* 1973a, *2.1,* 45-80.
———. Questionable answers and answerable questions. In B. Kachru, et al., eds., *Papers in Linguistics in Honor of Henry and Renee Kahane.* Urbana, Ill.: The University of Illinois Press, 1973b.

————. *Language and woman's place*. New York: Harper and Row, 1975.

————. Politeness, performatives and pragmatics. In A. Rogers, ed., *Proceedings of the (1972) Austin, Texas, Conference on Performatives*. Washington, D.C.: Center for Applied Linguistics, in press.

Ruesch, J. *Therapeutic communication*. New York: Norton, 1961.

Watzlawick, P., Beavin, J. H., and Jackson, D. D. *Pragmatics of human communication*. New York: Norton, 1967.

XI

Literature

Donald C. Freeman

No attempt at an exhaustive review of all of the recent work in what has come to be called, rather loosely, *stylistics* will be made in this chapter. Any such attempt necessarily would fail to do justice to the many different approaches which linguists and critics have found useful in coming to grips with the language of literature. Rather, the intellectual backgrounds and assumptions of the most promising lines of research over the last fifteen years in this still rather amorphous, but rapidly growing, field of scholarship will be sketched. Work in English published in North America and Great Britain since the publication of Sebeok's *Style in Language* (1960) will be the focal point. A fuller account of developments in Europe can be found in Enkvist's monograph (1973).

Interest in linguistic approaches to literature has grown rapidly over the last fifteen years. Three new scholarly journals devoted entirely to this field—*Poetics, Language and Style,* and *Style*—have been founded; several collections of important papers (among them Chatman, 1971, 1973; Chatman and Levin, 1967; Fowler, 1966; Freeman, 1970; Kachru and Stahlke, 1972; Love and Payne, 1970) have appeared; two book-length bibliographies (Bailey and Burton, 1968; Milic, 1967a) have been published; and a growing number of papers in the field have been published in both linguistic and literary journals. Summarizing this flood of activity is necessarily something of an exercise in the construction of a procrustean bed. Nevertheless, it is possible to perceive two major directions in the emphases and methodologies of work in stylistics since *Style in Language*. These are (to adopt the terminology of Todorov, 1973, p. 162) the *endogenous* approach, on the one hand—the search for explanatory formal structures in poetic language (the term *poetic* used here to include all

229

literature), in each individual work, or in the work of a particular author, and on the other, the *exogenous* approach is the search for adequate descriptions of poetic language as contrasted with ordinary language, of the language of particular authors as contrasted with that of other authors, or of particular works with other works by the same author. This rough bifurcation corresponds approximately to the classic distinction between style as choice and style as deviation. The critical ancestor of the first approach is Samuel Taylor Coleridge and his notion of organic form; its linguistics is primarily the generative-transformational grammar of Chomsky and Halle and their students. The critical ancestor of the second approach is *explication de texte*; its linguistics is primarily (but not always) structural, with strong affinities for Prague School linguistics.

Exogenous Stylistics

Three main concerns are to be found in exogenous stylistics. These are the isolation, by means of contrastive analysis, of the language of literature (as one of a number of "uses" of language, see Quirk, 1962) as compared with the language of everyday life, the description of the language of one author or period by comparison with others, and characterization of particular "violations" in poetic language of the rules of ordinary language.

The most carefully worked out theoretical basis of this work was that of the Prague School. An important collection of Prague School papers was translated into English by Garvin (1964). Prague School stylistics depended upon what Mukařovský characterized as (in Garvin's translation) "foregrounding," "the violation of the scheme," the design of aspects of language which ask to be seen *as language*. "The violation of the norm of the standard," he wrote, "its systematic violation, is what makes possible the poetic utilization of language; without this possibility there would be no poetry" (Garvin, 1964, p. 18). Poetic language depends upon violation of the laws of ordinary language; poetic design must be seen against a background of the linguistic norm. For a useful review of Prague School stylistics, particularly more recent work, see Doložel and Kraus (1972).

Closely related to Prague School stylistics is the stylistics of the neo-Firthian or London School of linguistics, which views the language of literature in terms of its "context of situation." Language cannot be considered *in vacuo*. The word *head*, for example, can have many different meanings depending upon its context. A complete absence of anaphora would be strongly foregrounded in scholarly prose, but not at all in the language of a legal brief. The imperative, obnoxiously intrusive in ordinary conversation, is closer to the norm in the language of advertising.

This theory of the uses of language is most fully elaborated in Crystal and Davy (1969), where a complex grid of "dimensions of situational constraint" is laid out according to which stylistic features of a text or utterance may be analyzed. The grid includes such items as medium (the language of television advertisements, for example, differs markedly from that of advertisements for the same products in magazines, see Leech, 1966b), status (the language of personal conversation differs from that of the university lecture), and province (the vocabulary and lexical collocations of theoretical linguistics differ from those of astronomy). An earlier version of this theory of language in context was first applied to literature, together with a syntactic analysis based on scale-and-category grammar, in a study of Yeats's "Leda and the Swan" (Halliday, 1964). Halliday contrasts the Yeats poem with a similarly sized portion of Tennyson's "Morte D' Arthur" with respect to "verbality." He finds that Yeats uses the most powerful verbs in the "least verbal" structural positions, while the Tennyson passage displays five times the number of independent finite verbs. Halliday's fundamental principle of stylistic analysis is that "the creative writer finds and exploits the *irregularity* that the patterns allow, and in doing so superimposes a further *regularity*" (Halliday, 1964, p. 305). The necessary implication of contrastive analysis is clear. Later, Halliday (1971) describes and contrasts two "languages" used as narrative voices in Golding's *The Inheritors*.

In Leech (1965), Dylan Thomas's patterns of lexical choice in "This Bread I Break" are shown to center on natural growth to a greater extent than we expect in ordinary language, with the result that this pattern of choice is foregrounded. Again, the emphasis is on comparison: "To bring to light what is of most significance in the language of a poem, we have to deal with choices which would not be expected or tolerated in a normal language situation" (Leech, 1965, p. 68). In a later paper, Leech (1966a) offers a classification of rhetorical figures based upon syntagmatic and paradigmatic foregrounding, both types of deviance from the norm. Syntagmatic foregrounding is based upon patterning in chain relationships (the alliteration of Coleridge's "the furrow followed free," for example); paradigmatic foregrounding arises from patterns in choice relationships (Bacon's "Some books are to be tasted . . . ," where strictly speaking *taste* is not a member of the paradigm of verbs that can have *book* as their underlying object). See also Spencer and Gregory (1964); for a full elaboration of Leech's work in stylistics embedded in an admirably sensitive textbook, see Leech (1969).

Fowler (1971) has published a collection of his major papers containing the particularly valuable exchange between him and F. W. Bateson in *Essays in Criticism* on the possible contributions of linguistics to the study of literature. He effectively demolishes Bateson's implied claim that the alleged "scientism" of modern linguistics disqualifies it from effectiveness in literary study, and attacks the strawman arguments (for example, that linguists working on literature claim a more objective and scientific, hence superior, basis for their findings) so often advanced (for example, Fish, 1973) against the uses of linguistics in criticism. The other papers range in topic from the *Sermo Lupi* to e. e. cummings, but their theoretical stance can be summarized in one sentence from the most valuable paper in the book, "The Structure of Criticism and the Languages of Poetry": "in the experience of readers, poems are unequivocally in a language which exists independently outside the poems, and this fact guarantees 'reference out,' connection with the outside world" (Fowler, 1971, p. 90). In other words, poetry—and by extension, the language of literature—is a use of language, analyzable by comparison and contrast with other "uses" of language.

A different line of inquiry, using generative-transformational grammar, has been concerned more directly with deviance as it is related to the notion of grammaticalness. Thorne (1965) suggests treating deviant lines in poetry within a generative-transformational framework not by attempting to complicate the grammar of natural language to include them, but by writing a grammar for such poetry as if it were a different language. He writes a grammar for cummings's "anyone lived in a pretty how town" and compares its rules with those of ordinary language. In a later study (1970), Thorne shows that these rules must "meet one of the conditions for a counter-grammar" (Thorne, 1970, p. 195), they must be directly related to the rules of the standard language. In his pioneering transformationally based monograph, *Linguistic Structures in Poetry*, Levin (1962) proposed that poetry can be characterized as displaying a greater density of particular equivalences, positional and semantic, and, when these kinds of equivalences converge, there exists what he called a "coupling," the hallmark of poetic language.

A final group of studies in exogenous stylistics are the directly comparative analyses. These have in the main used statistics to buttress analyses of particular linguistic structures peculiar to individual authors or styles (for a sensible review of what has been called "stylostatistics," see Bailey, 1969). The best example of this approach is Gibson (1967), in which a "style machine" based upon frequency of such items as monosyllables, first- and second-person pronouns, passive voice, noun adjuncts, length and number of subordinate clauses, and subjectless or verbless sentences is constructed. This style machine then is used to isolate the linguistic properties of the "tough" syntax of such writers as Hemingway and Bellow, the "sweet" talk of advertising language, and the "stuffy" talk of bureaucracy. Two statistical studies employing generative-transformational grammar in their analyses are Hayes (1966, 1968), which trace the transformational history of passages from the eighteenth-century English historian Edward Gibbon. Hayes compares these data in turn to similar analyses of the prose of Hemingway and Samuel Johnson with respect to such features as number of transformations and embedded structures per sentence. Milic (1967b), in a study of Swift's prose style, conducts an intensive, computer-aided analysis of word classes (according to a modified version of the framework set forth in Fries, 1952) with comparisons both to many of Swift's contemporaries and to modern prose writers.

Endogenous Stylistics

The working hypothesis of what is here termed endogenous stylistics follows from a chain of postulates. Literature consists of linguistic objects designed with an artistic end. Linguistic objects are formal objects. A formal account of a linguistic object designed with an artistic end approximates a formal account of that artistic design.

This hypothesis may be expressed along a different dimension (following Ohmann, 1962, 1968a). A writer exhibits, probably without realizing it, certain systematic preferences for particular syntactic patterns. What do these tell us about the way he perceives the world? To what extent (following Freeman, 1975, forthcoming; Keyser, 1976) do they cohere with other formal aspects of design—meter, imagery, or theme—so as to be the constitutive principle of a writer's poetics and of a particular poem's (or novel's or short story's) deep form? Chaucer's iambic pentameter can be characterized (Halle and Keyser, 1966) with a small number of rules which account for all but a tiny handful of the lines in Chaucer's corpus. The same rules characterize all iambic pentameter written in English until the present time. These rules, based on the phonological primes and rules postulated for English as a whole (Chomsky and Halle, 1968; Halle and Keyser, 1971a) can be said to describe the "knowledge" of iambic pentameter form possessed by all poets in the mainstream of English verse. To what extent do these rules and principles constitute part of a writer's "poetic competence," an intrinsic and perhaps unconscious knowledge of his own poetic language comparable to his knowledge of his native language? (See the discussion of Ohmann, 1968a, below.) These are the sorts of questions being asked by workers in this area of stylistics. The major works fall into four categories, those concerned with general theory, prose style, metrics, and the grammar of poetry.

Endogenous stylistics: theory.   An indispensable theoretical treatise seeking to set a theory of poetics in the context of the general theory of generative-transformational grammar is Bierwisch (1965). Bierwisch proposes, as an adjunct to a generative-transformational grammar, a set of rules (or, as he calls it, a "poetic system") which would decide on the "poeticality" of particular structural descriptions generated by the grammar. A second set of rules would assign to these structural descriptions a "scale of poeticality." Bierwisch does not specify the form of the phrase-structure rules, but he would mark motivated deviances, that is, those which display regularity, and relationships such as synonymy, antonymy, and departures from the norm. It is worth pointing out how Bierwisch combines Prague School notions of markedness and foregrounding with the transformationally oriented notion of ungrammaticality.

Ohmann (1968a) directly relates the study of literature to the most fundamental concerns of modern linguistics: "literary criticism," he argues, "is the study of mental structures" (Ohmann, 1968a, p. 210). In a contrastive analysis of the prose styles of Gibbon, Bellow, and James, Ohmann shows that Gibbon's use of the passive (an early transformational rule) is heavily masked by later transformational rules which have the effect of partially concealing this important stylistic variant, leading to the "impersonality" always held to be a hallmark of his style. Bellow, on the other hand, exhibits a preference for a later rule, that of deletion of relative followed by tensed *be* (from "the man, who was walking toward the corner" to "the man, walking toward the corner"). This preference, Ohmann argues, leads to Bellow's free admission of the less structured, chaotic flow of existence. James's persistent deletion of human agents in passives yields the "double vision" of subject and narrator so typical of his style. Ohmann argues that the writer's intentions lead him to these choices (and to reject other choices) in a way analogous to the linguistic competence which leads a native speaker of English to reject as ungrammatical **Golf plays John* and correctly stress *prestidigitator*. In an analysis of poems by Yeats, Keats, and Wilbur, Ohmann shows how a reader's knowledge of his own language contributes to his understanding of poetic imagery.

The concern with poetry as pattern is central to Prague School stylistics, according to Jakobson (1968) and Jakobson and Jones (1970). Following his famous statement (Sebeok, 1960, p. 358) that "the poetic function projects the principle of equivalence from the axis of selection into the axis of combination," Jakobson emphasizes grammatical parallelism or reiteration as the central facet of poetry in an analysis of a fifteenth-century Czech song whose structural properties he compares to painting (see also his analysis of Blake in Jakobson, 1970). "There is," Jakobson concludes, "a remarkable analogy between the role of grammar in poetry and the painter's composition based on a latent or patent geometrical order or on a revulsion against geometrical arrangements" (Jakobson, 1968, p. 605).

A recent major theoretical study, Kiparsky (1973) is firmly in the Jakobsonian tradition. In an exceptionally rich paper written for a general audience, Kiparsky outlines how the central assumptions and concerns of modern generative-transformational grammar can and should be central to a theory of literature. He argues that since the forms of Western verbal art are remarkably stable and consistent (for example, no stanzaic form ever required that the last word in each line contain the same number of sounds), the central questions for a theory of poetry are, very simply, (1) what patterns are relevant in poetry? and (2) what linguistic sames are relevant in poetry? Kiparsky hypothesizes that "the linguistic sames which are relevant in poetry are just those which are potentially relevant in grammar" (p. 235). In syntax, two elements count as "sames" in a particular derivation "if they are labeled alike in the tree for that stage" (p. 236). Hence Dylan Thomas displays "strict" parallelism by patterning most of the constituents at the lowest points of the syntactic tree ("The force that through the green fuse drives the flower drives my green age. . . . The force that drives the water through the rocks drives my red blood. . . ."). In phonology, sounds participate in rhyme and alliteration in just the way they do in such types of linguistic change as reduplication; in some poetries, alliteration depends upon phonological representations earlier in the derivation (Kiparsky, 1968, 1972; Lasnik, in press). Kiparsky concludes that "[S]ome constants of poetic form are dependent on the structure of language itself" (p. 243).

Endogenous stylistics: prose style. The major contributor to the study of prose style for the period surveyed has been Ohmann, whose 1962 book on Shaw can be fairly said to have started, together with Sebeok (1960), modern stylistics. Style, Ohmann holds (an earlier study, 1959, provides most of the theoretical underpinning for the work under discussion), is epistemic choice: "stylistic preferences reflect cognitive preferences" (p. 22). Using a structural framework, Ohmann shows the linguistic bases for such characteristics of Shaw's style as his "drive for similarity order" (p. 39), preference for discontinuity, and what Ohmann calls his habitual "posture of opposition."

Ohmann also published the first major studies on prose style using a generative-transformational framework (1964, 1966). He argues that transformational alternatives of a particular kernel sentence are "different expressions of the same content" (1964, p. 431). In a comparative "analysis by detransformation" of selections from Faulkner, Hemingway, James, and Lawrence, Ohmann proposes a definition of style as "in part a characteristic way of deploying the transformational apparatus of a language" (ibid.). In a later study (1966), Ohmann shows how transformational analysis can reveal that a passage overtly about the narrator (of Conrad's *The Secret Sharer*) is, in its underlying syntactic structure, about Leggatt, the "sharer" of the tale's title, who is the subject of all of the sentence structures underlying a surface form whose superficial subject is the narrator. He concludes from an analysis of part of Dylan Thomas's poem "A Winter's Tale" that "the elusive intuition we have of *form* and *content* may turn out to be anchored in a distinction between the surface structures and the deep structures of sentences" (1966, p. 267). Ohmann's comparative study (1968b) of the prose styles of Arnold, Mill, Carlyle, and Newman builds on these principles and analytical techniques. Arnold, he shows, builds a strategy of definition on use of the copula *be* and on such transformations from deep structures of this form as *be*-deletion and relative-deletion, yielding a style marked by great syntactic depth. Mill transformationally deletes and shifts human nominals, prefers verbs in the general present, and omits time- and place-determiners, seeking in these choices to establish "irrefutable and commonly agreed-upon truth." Carlyle emphasizes concreteness by foregrounding human nouns in both deep and surface structure. Newman emphasizes judgment by using, in underlying structure, verbs requiring human subjects which emphasize acts of the mind (for example, *insist*, *advocate*, *praise*). Jacobs (1972) analyzes the prose of Baldwin and Updike in a similar manner.

In an important new departure, likely to produce the same kind of revolution in the study of prose style as did his book on Shaw and articles on transformational stylistics, Ohmann has proposed connections between prose style and the work of Austin (1962) and Searle (1969) on speech acts (Ohmann, 1971a, 1971b, 1972a, 1972b, 1973). When, to use Ohmann's example (1972b, p. 138), Yeats writes "That is no country for old men," the reader begins his attempt to make that utterance a felicitous speech act by postulating a speaker whose experience makes him an appropriate person to render such a judgment. Ohmann gives an extensive outline of categories of verbs establishing illocutionary force and their syntactic and semantic consequences. In a related paper, Ohmann (1971b) traces the systematic violations of the rules governing speech acts in Beckett's *Watt*. Ohmann bases an important approach to a definition of literature upon the peculiar character of illocutionary acts in works of verbal art: "Literary works are discourses with the usual illocutionary rules suspended, acts without consequences of the usual sort" (1973, p. 97). In experiencing a work of literature, a reader "builds on his tacit knowledge of the conventions—past and present, actual and possible—for illocutionary acts, and what he builds is an image of the world implied by the acts that constitute the work" (ibid., p. 99). This approach, with its concern for the nature of the speaker in a literary work, is distinctly in the tradition of the New Criticism of the 1940s (for example, the analysis of Donne's *Canonization* in Brooks, 1947, p. 11).

The first book-length study of a single figure's prose style using a generative-transformational framework is Chatman (1972), a study of the style of Henry James's late works. Chatman presents a very careful analysis of the "intangibility" of James's late style: his use of abstract subjects, cleft sentences, extrapositions with *it*, and nominalizations of psychological verbs. This last strategy in particular leads to what Chatman calls "[t]he conversion of mental acts into entities" (p. 233) and are part of a stylistic pattern leading to an elimination of overt *actors* from the surface structure of James's syntax in favor of a postulation of his characters' inner lives as initiators of action.

A linguistic approach to literature only now beginning to appear with significant frequency in scholarly journals in the United States is the application of discourse analysis to the study of literature. This approach seeks to describe "linguistic features that differentiate a coherent (connected) sequence of sentences (a text) from an agglomerate of sentences" (Hendricks, 1972, p. 83, a helpful survey of the field). For surveys emphasizing work in Europe, see Ihwe (1973) and van Dijk (1972). This rise in interest in what is variously called text grammar, text linguistics, or discourse analysis has proceeded together with increased interest in narrative structure—the "primes" of narrative and the rules of their combination into fictive entities, building on (in some cases) the theoretical structure of Propp (1958). (See Chatman, 1969, and Hendricks, 1973, especially chapter 6.)

Endogenous stylistics: metrics. Perhaps the most influential and far-reaching work in the application of modern linguistic theory to the study of literature has been in the field of metrics. The structural metrics of Epstein and Hawkes (1959), based upon the Smith-Trager theory of stress, pitch, and juncture, attributed metrical style to the degree of difference between the abstract metrical pattern, which had only two kinds of syllable—stressed and unstressed—and the four levels of stress postulated for English suprasegmental phonology. In an iambic metrical foot actualized by secondary-primary stress, for example, a greater degree of metrical tension was said to exist than in a foot actualized by tertiary-primary stress (see also Chatman, 1960). Thompson's excellent study (1961) of sixteenth-century English poetic meter is based upon structural metrics. The most fully elaborated study within this framework is Chatman's (1965). Although it is based upon Bolinger's theory of pitch accent, its conclusions are similar to those of Epstein and Hawkes. Chatman distinguishes between "meter-fixing" feet, which establish a poem's "metrical set," and "meter-fixed" feet. He isolates four categories of syllable which, in combination, create thirty-two possible feet, and concludes with an analysis of eleven recitations of Shakespeare's Sonnet 18. For a more extended discussion of traditional and structural metrics, see Freeman (1972).

The most successful work by linguists on poetic meter has been the generative-phonology-based approach pioneered by Halle and Keyser. This work began with their study of Chaucer's meter (Halle and Keyser, 1966), and was then extended in Keyser's work on Old English (1968) and a more embracing theory for post-Chaucerian iambic pentameter (1969), Halle's more theoretical treatise (1970), their book (Halle and Keyser, 1971a) in which the metrical theory was embedded in a general study of the nature and history of English stress, and a defense against criticisms that were raised (Halle and Keyser, 1971b).

Halle and Keyser made explicit a concept about English meter which is only hinted at in the work of the structural metrists, and which also is central to modern generative-transformational grammar. That concept is that meter is best characterized as having surface and underlying form, and the study of poetic meter is properly that of the rules which relate those two levels of organization. In giving an account of the underlying form of the iambic pentameter and of the correspondence rules which relate that form to actual line instances, Halle and Keyser account organically for all of the so-called permissible licenses (spondaic substitution, headless lines, etc.) which previously had been entirely unrelated.

In Halle and Keyser (1971a), a unified account is given of Old English and modern prosody which depends on a set of rules assigning stressed (and, for modern syllabotonic verse, unstressed) syllables to a pattern of abstract metrical entities. For the thirty-five postulated possible line types of the Old English of *Beowulf*, they propose an abstract metrical pattern. For the first half line, $(X)^*X$, where X realized alone is more complex; for the second half line, $X(W)^*$, where again X realized alone is more complex. W indicates an unalliterating primary stressed syllable; S indicates an alliterating primary stressed syllable. Each X corresponds to a single S *or* (in a more complex actualization) one X per half line may correspond to S and W in either order. The first eleven lines of *Beowulf* (the edition used here is Wrenn, 1953) may be scanned as follows according to the Halle-Keyser theory:

Hwæt wē Gār-Dena
       S

in gear-dagum
    S

þeod-cyninga
S

þrym gefrūnon,
  S   W

hū ða æþelingas
     S

ellen fremedon.
S   W

    Oft Scyld Scēfing
         S

sceaþena þrēatum,
  S   W

monegum mǣgþum
S   S

meodo-setla oftēah;   5
  S   W

egsode Eorle,
S   S

syððan ǣrest wearð
      S   W

fēasceaft funden;
S   S

hē þæs frōfre gebād;
        S   W

wēox under wolcnum
S   S

weorð-myndum þāh,
S   W

oðþæt him ǣghwylc
       S

þāra ymb-sittendra
       S

ofer hron-rāde
   S

hȳran scolde,   10
S   W

gomban gyldan:
S   S

þæt wæs gōd cyning!
      S   W

The initial half lines of these eleven verses sort into two types: line 2a, for example, consists of only one S since the stress of *cyninga* is reduced by virtue of its being in a compound, and does not alliterate; line 5a, on the other hand, consists of two S entities—that is, two syllables with primary stress which alliterate (and any number of unstressed syllables). The second half lines are likewise of two types: 1b, for example, is similar to 2a in that the stress of *dagum* is reduced under the compound rule, so that the half line consists of only one S; 2b, however, consists of S and W; a syllable with primary stress which alliterates with a syllable or syllables in 2a (*þrym*, alliterating with *þeod*) and a syllable which has primary stress but does not alliterate (*frū*).

With respect to Old English, the Halle-Keyser theory takes no account of the oral-formulaic nature of most Old English verse; their analysis also occasionally divides lines into half lines at different points from those

which are yielded by oral-formulaic analysis. Their complexity measure—
that half lines actualizing one S only or an extra SW or WS are more
complex—produces the right kind of result: lines, which under their
analysis are more complex, in general occur less frequently (and the most
complex theoretically possible actualizations do not appear at all).

Halle and Keyser carry forward this method of analysis to the iambic
pentameter. They abandon the notion of the foot, which had been adapted
from classical meters, in the process of establishing the *line* as the basic unit
of English meter, while characterizing the so-called permissible
licenses—exceptions from strict iambic pentameter—in terms of a unified
theory together with a complexity measure which provides an elegant and
intuitively correct account of the main stream of English verse. An iambic
pentameter line consists of these abstract entities:

$$(W)^*SWSWSWSWS \ (X) \ (X)$$

Again, a line which does not actualize initial W is more complex than one
that does; the X's at the end of the line may be occupied by unstressed
syllables only. With this abstract pattern is paired the following set of
correspondence rules (Halle and Keyser, 1971a, p. 169):

(i) A position (S, W, or X) corresponds to a single syllable
OR
   to a sonorant sequence incorporating at most two vowels (immediately adjoining or separated by a sonorant consonant)

Definition: When a fully stressed syllable occurs between two unstressed syllables in the same syntactic constituent within a line of
verse, this syllable is called a "stress maximum."

(ii) Fully stressed syllables occur in S positions only and in all S
   positions
OR
   Fully stressed syllables occur in S positions only but not in all S
   positions
OR
   Stress maxima occur in S positions only but not in all S positions.

As with the correspondence rules for Old English, the alternatives to (i) and
(ii) are increasingly complex actualizations of the meter. If a line violates
the third alternative of (ii), it is unmetrical, *viz.*:

How mány bárds gíld the lápses of tíme (Keats)
W   S W S   W   S W S W S

This line is actualized by the first alternative of (i), but, in respect to (ii), one S position does not contain a fully stressed syllable (violating the first alternative). Two W positions contain fully stressed syllables (violating the second alternative), and a stress maximum occurs in a W position (violating the third alternative and making the line unmetrical).

This theory accounts for the otherwise random "permissible licenses" in iambic pentameter: headless lines, extra slack syllables line-internally, and pyrrhic, spondaic, and trochaic substitutions. The headless line is accounted for in the parenthesized line initial W. Extra syllables are accounted for by the second alternative of (i), and the substitutes are subsumed in the concept of the stress maximum. In effect this principle assumes that the rules of English meter are proscriptive rather than prescriptive (what makes a line unmetrical is a stress maximum in a W position). It is consistent with the fact that in virtually none of the iambic pentameter lines that have been examined in English verse from Chaucer to the present, do two successive trochaic "substitutions" appear. In a later study (1971b), Halle and Keyser defended the theory against criticism which arose (Magnuson and Ryder, 1970; Wimsatt, 1970), and a separate account of it (Halle and Keyser, 1973) appears in Wimsatt's (1973) valuable collection of essays on versification.

Halle and Keyser (1966) led to efforts to characterize metrical style in terms of what would become, in the later book, parts of their theory of line complexity. Beaver (1968) showed that placement of stress maxima in particular line positions is a stylistic determinant distinguishing the metrical style of Donne from that of Shakespeare. Freeman (1968) sought to characterize the "sea-change" in English metrical style between Gascoigne and Marlowe in terms of a change in the number of stress maxima typically actualized in a line, and to show that later stylistic changes in the history of English meter depended upon different kinds of evidence elicited by the 1966 version of the Halle-Keyser theory. Beaver (1971), Freeman (1969), and Hascall (1969) proposed extensions of the theory, some of which were adopted by Halle and Keyser (1971a). Within the Halle-Keyser theoretical framework, studies were made of the meter of John Lydgate (Hascall, 1970), Gerard Manley Hopkins (Scott, 1974), and Emily Dickinson (a preliminary study was Freeman, 1972, which included a general review of recent work in metrics; for a more detailed study see Hascall and M. Freeman, forthcoming). Hascall (1971) made a separate study of trochaic meter. There can be little doubt that the Halle-Keyser theory of meter was the major contribution of linguistics to the study of literature during the period of this survey.

Endogenous stylistics: poetic syntax.   The fourth and final area of what is here termed endogenous stylistics is poetic syntax, or the grammar of poetry. The basic thesis of this work can be loosely summarized as follows. If syntax is, in a sense, the most abstract aspect of linguistic organization, deep form in poetry—that aspect of poetic form at once most fundamental and least available to introspection and explicit statement—must be found in the syntax of poetry. Several recent studies depend upon a characteristic of poetic language first noticed in Thorne (1969): the differences between poetic language and standard language are chiefly in deep structure. This work argues, in effect, that the essential features of poetic design are in deep structure, and in transformational strategies by which these structures are deformed into surface structures.

The earliest sustained treatments of poetic grammar in a transformational framework were by Levin (1962, 1963, 1965) and were centered primarily on deviance from grammaticality. Chatman (1968), who wrote the first study of syntax in poetry seeking to relate transformational strategies to keep poetic form, traces the history of participle usage in English poetry. He shows how in his later poetry Milton's practice changes from heavy use of the present participle (a reduced form of an underlying sentence in which the functionally shifted verb modifies its subject—*the creating God* from underlying *God creates*) to emphasis on the past participle (where the functionally shifted verb, if it is transitive, modifies its direct object—*the created world* from underlying *X created the world*). In *Paradise Lost*, Chatman points out, the "implicit" subject of the past participle is God, who is thus made omnipresent in the poem's syntax as well as in its theme.

Fairley (1973) carries this method forward to analysis of "the function of syntactic deviation as a device of structural cohesion" (p. 216) in several poems by e. e. cummings. In "a like a," maximal compression, using the transformational processes of relative clause reduction, deletion of main-verb *be* and nominalization, creates a motif of stasis central to the poem and to cummings's imagist poetics. In "when god lets my body be," a pattern of topicalization and subject-verb inversion interacts with the poem's stanzaic form (quatrains, themselves "sprung" by the poem's typography), and an alternation of "shall" (natural) and "will" (human), creating an emblem of the sea, source and end of the cycle of life.

Keyser (1976) shows how content is exactly mirrored in syntactic form in four poems by Wallace Stevens, "Death of a Soldier," "Poetry is a Destructive Force," "Anecdote of the Jar," and "The Snow Man." In "Death of a Soldier," Stevens deletes from the poem's surface structure all agents, and persistently uses the "timeless" present tense (instead of the present progressive used to express present in English), with the result that its statements about the inevitability and finality of death are lawlike rather than transitory (p. 583). In "The Snow Man," Keyser shows that the syntax of the poem's single sentence requires the reader to reanalyze it as the poem proceeds, deepening the syntactic embedding at each reanalysis. The reader's experience of the poem thus mirrors its theme: the need to change outward perspective in order to understand reality, figured in the changing syntactic perspectives required to experience the poem.

Freeman (1975, forthcoming) argues that the syntactic strategies of a poem are central to its design. In three of Dylan Thomas's poems, "Light Break Where No Sun Shines," "The Force that through the Green Fuse Drives the Flower," "A Refusal to Mourn the Death, by Fire, of a Child in London," the poet follows, in his manipulation of syntactic transformations, strategies of fusion. In "Light Breaks" he fuses natural process and human history by a strategy of contradiction between adverbial and main clauses. In "The Force" he fuses natural energy and human sexuality, aging, and death through tightly organized, maximally condensed relative clauses. In "A Refusal" he fuses the girl's death with the entire history of the created world by leftward shifting at several syntactic levels, with the result that the poem's grammar forces the reader to experience an account of both the Creation and the Last Judgment before he can know of the central event of the girl's death. Freeman (forthcoming) shows that in three of his odes Keats designed his syntax so that the reader is forced, in experiencing the poem, to reenact the poetic process which is its subject. Keats dislocates the relationship between transitive verbs and their implicit or explicit subjects, and defines affirmatively by negation, creating in the poems' syntax as well as in their imagery what the critic Kenneth Burke (1945, p. 449) called the "mystic oxymoron," the "eternal present" made permanent through the poetic process which is the heart of his poetics.

Conclusion

Endogenous stylistics—namely, the search for organic form in literature through examination of writers' strategic manipulation of syntax and meter—appears to be the most promising approach in current work. Modern linguistics has undergone a theoretical revolution in the last twenty years; now two major areas of that revolution have made material contributions to explanations of literary form. The work of the last several years on poetic meter depends crucially upon the insights of generative phonology. The research discussed in the previous section on the grammar of poetry proceeds directly from the assumptions and methodology of transformational syntax. Ohmann's work on speech acts in literature has its intellectual roots in the semantics of Searle, Fillmore, Austin, and Zwicky, among others. Some of the work in text grammar barely alluded to in the present survey makes use of the generative semantics of Lakoff, Ross, and McCawley. Precisely because it seeks a formal account of the nature of the knowledge we have when we say we "know" a language, modern linguistics now gives promise of making major contributions to the central task of the literary critic: characterizing the source of our response to literary art.

We respond first in literature to form, but, initially at least, we may be entirely unable to perceive that form explicitly. Part of the process of understanding a work of literature is making its implicit form explicit. The first cause of that form resides in its language, the stuff of which it is made, and the interactions of that form with the words of creator and experiencer in which it must exist. In poetry, at least, as we interpret the designed syntax of a poem we reenact the life of that design. A formal account of the language of a work of literature, and of its design, whether that account be conscious or unconscious, knowing or unknowing, is central to the task and the joy of the literary experience.

> Words, after speech, reach
> Into the silence. Only by the form, the pattern,
> Can words or music reach
> The stillness, as a Chinese jar still
> Moves perpetually in its stillness.
>
> —T. S. Eliot, *Four Quartets*.*

REFERENCES

Austin, J. L. *How to do things with words*. Cambridge, Mass.: Harvard University Press, 1962.

Bailey, R. W. Statistics and style: A historical survey. In L. Doložel and R. W. Bailey, eds., *Statistics and style*. New York: American Elsevier Publishing Co., 1969.

Bailey, R. W., and Burton, D. M., S. N. D. *English stylistics: A bibliography*. Cambridge, Mass.: M.I.T. Press, 1968.

Beaver, J. C. A grammar of prosody. *College English*, 1968, *29*, 310-21.

———. The rules of stress in English verse. *Language*, 1971, 47, 586-614.

Bierwisch, M. Poetik und Linguistik. In H. Kreuzer and R. Gunzenhäuser, eds., *Mathematik und Dichtung*. Munich: Nymphenburger Verlag, 1965. (English translation in Freeman, 1970).

Brooks, C. *The well wrought urn: Studies in the structure of poetry*. New York: Harcourt, Brace and World, 1947.

Burke, K. *A grammar of motives*. Englewood Cliffs: Prentice-Hall, Inc., 1945.

Chatman, S. Comparing metrical styles. In T. A. Sebeok, ed., *Style in language*. Cambridge, Mass.: M.I.T. Press, 1960, pp. 149-72.

———. *A theory of meter*. The Hague: Mouton, 1965.

———. Milton's participial style. *PMLA*, 1968, *83*, 1386-99.

———. New ways of analyzing narrative. *Language and Style*, 1969, *2*, 3-36.

———, ed. *Literary style: A symposium*. New York and London: Oxford University Press, 1971.

———. *The later style of Henry James*. Oxford: Blackwells, 1972.

———, ed. *Approaches to poetics*. New York: Columbia University Press, 1973.

Chatman, S., and Levin, S., eds. *Essays on the language of literature*. Boston: Houghton Mifflin, 1967.

Chomsky, N., and Halle, M. *The sound pattern of English*. New York: Harper and Row, 1968.

Crystal, D., and Davy, D. *Investigating English style*. London: Longmans, 1969.

Doložel, L., and Kraus, J. Prague School stylistics. In B. B. Kachru and H. Stahlke, eds., *Current trends in stylistics*. Champaign and Edmonton: Linguistic Research, Inc., 1972, pp. 37-48.

Enkvist, N. E. *Linguistic stylistics*. The Hague and Paris: Mouton, 1973.

Epstein, E. L., and Hawkes, T. *Linguistics and English prosody. Studies in linguistics*, Occasional Papers, 7, 1959.

Fairley, I. R. Syntactic deviation and cohesion. *Language and Style*, 1973, *6*, 216-29.

Fish, S. E. What is stylistics and why are they saying such terrible things about it? In S. Chatman, *Approaches to poetics: Selected papers from the English Institute*. New York: Columbia University Press, 1973, pp. 109-52.

Fowler, R., ed. *Essays on style and language*. London: Routledge and Kegan Paul, 1966.

———. *The languages of literature*. London: Routledge and Kegan Paul, 1971.

Freeman, D. C. On the primes of metrical style. *Language and Style*, 1968, *1*, 63-101.

————. Metrical position constituency and generative metrics. *Language and Style*, 1969, 2, 195-206.

————, ed. *Linguistics and literary style*. New York: Holt, Rinehart and Winston, 1970.

————. Current trends in metrics. In B. B. Kachru and H. Stahlke, eds., *Current trends in stylistics*. Champaign and Edmonton: Linguistic Research, Inc., 1972, pp. 67-81.

————. The strategy of fusion: Dylan Thomas's syntax. In R. Fowler, ed., *Style and structure in literature*. Oxford and Ithaca: Blackwells and Cornell University Press, 1975.

————. Syntax and poetics in three odes of John Keats, forthcoming.

Fries, C. C. *The structure of English*. New York: Harcourt, Brace and World, 1952.

Garvin, P., ed. and trans. *A Prague School reader on esthetics, literary structure, and style*. Washington: Georgetown University Press, 1964.

Gibson, W. *Tough, sweet, and stuffy*. Bloomington: Indiana University Press, 1967.

Halle, M. On meter and prosody. In M. Bierwisch and K. R. Heidolph, eds., *Progress in linguistics*. The Hague and Paris: Mouton, 1970.

Halle, M., and Keyser, S. J. Chaucer and the study of prosody. *College English*, 1966, 28, 187-219.

————. *English stress: Its form, its growth, and its role in verse*. New York: Harper and Row, 1971a.

————. Illustration and defense of a theory of the iambic pentameter. *College English*, 1971b, 33, 154-76.

————. The iambic pentameter. In W. K. Wimsatt, ed., *Versification: Major language types*. New York: New York University Press, 1973.

Halliday, M. A. K. The linguistic study of literary texts. In H. G. Lunt, ed., *Proceedings of the ninth international congress of linguists*. The Hague: Mouton, 1964.

————. Linguistic function and literary style: An inquiry into the language of William Golding's The inheritors. In S. Chatman, ed., *Literary style: A symposium*. New York and London: Oxford University Press, 1971.

Hascall, D. Some contributions to the Halle-Keyser theory of prosody. *College English*, 1969, 30, 357-65.

————. The prosody of John Lydgate. *Language and Style*, 1970, 3, 122-46.

————. Trochaic meter. *College English*, 1971, 33, 217-26.

Hascall, D., and Freeman, M. H. Meter in Emily Dickinson's poetry. Forthcoming.

Hayes, C. W. A study in prose styles: Edward Gibbon and Ernest Hemingway. *Texas Studies in Literature and Language*, 1966, 7, 371-86.

————. A transformational-generative approach to style: Samuel Johnson and Edward Gibbon. *Language and Style*, 1968, 1, 39-48.

Hendricks, W. O. Current trends in discourse analysis. In B. B. Kachru and H. Stahlke, eds., *Current trends in stylistics*. Champaign and Edmonton: Linguistic Research, Inc., 1972, pp. 83-95.

————. *Essays on semiolinguistics and verbal art*. The Hague and Paris: Mouton, 1973.

Ihwe, J. On the validation of text-grammars in the "study of literature." In J. S. Petöfi and M. Rieser, eds., *Studies in text grammar*. Dordrecht: D. Reidel, 1973.

Jacobs, R. A. Transformational analysis and the study of style. In R. A. Jacobs, ed., *Studies in language*. Lexington, Mass.: Xerox College Publishing, 1972.

Jakobson, R. Poetry of grammar and grammar of poetry. *Lingua*, 1968, *21*, 597-609.

———. On the verbal art of William Blake and other poet-painters. *Linguistic Inquiry*, 1970, *1*, 3-23.

Jakobson, R., and Jones, L. G. *Shakespeare's verbal art in th'expence of spirit*. The Hague and Paris: Mouton, 1970.

Kachru, B. B., and Stahlke, H. F. W., eds. *Current trends in stylistics*. Champaign and Edmonton: Linguistic Research, Inc., 1972.

Keyser, S. J. Old English prosody. *College English*, 1968, *30*, 331-56.

———. The linguistic basis of English prosody. In D. Reibel and S. A. Schane, eds., *Modern studies in English*. Englewood Cliffs: Prentice-Hall, Inc., 1969.

———. Wallace Stevens: Form and meaning in four poems. *College English*, 1976, *37*, 578-98.

Kiparsky, P. Metrics and morphophonemics in the Kelevala. In *Studies presented to Professor Roman Jakobson by his students*. Cambridge, Mass.: Slavica Publishers, 1968.

———. Metrics and morphophonemics in the Rigveda. In M. K. Brame, ed., *Contributions to generative phonology*. Austin: University of Texas Press, 1972.

———. The role of linguistics in a theory of poetry. *Daedalus*, 1973, *102*, 231-44.

Lasnik, H. Metrics and morphophonemics in early English verse. Unpublished.

Leech, G. N. "This bread I break"—language and interpretation. A *Review of English Literature*, 1965, *6*, 66-75.

———. Linguistics and the figures of rhetoric. In R. Fowler, ed., *Essays on style and language*. London: Routledge and Kegan Paul, 1966a.

———. *English in advertising: A linguistic study of advertising in Great Britain*. London: Longman, 1966b.

———. *A linguistic guide to English poetry*. London: Longmans, 1969.

Levin, S. R. *Linguistic structures in poetry*. The Hague: Mouton, 1962.

———. Deviation—statistical and determinate—in poetic language. *Lingua*, 1963, *12*, 276-90.

———. Internal and external deviation in poetry. *Word*, 1965, *21*, 225-37.

Love, G. A., and Payne, M., eds. *Contemporary essays on style: Rhetoric, linguistics, and criticism*. Glenview, Ill.: Scott, Foresman, 1970.

Magnuson, K., and Ryder, F. G. The study of English prosody: An alternative proposal. *College English*, 1970, *31*, 789-820.

Milic, L. T. *Style and stylistics: An analytical bibliography*. New York: The Free Press, 1967a.

———. *A quantitative approach to the style of Jonathan Swift*. The Hague: Mouton, 1967b.

Ohmann, R. Prolegomena to the analysis of prose style. In H. C. Martin, ed., *Style in prose fiction*. New York: Columbia University Press, 1959.

———. *Shaw: The style and the man*. Middletown: Wesleyan University Press,

1962.

————. Generative grammars and the concept of literary style. *Word*, 1964, *20*, 423-39.

————. Literature as sentences. *College English*, 1966, *27*, 261-67.

————. Mentalism in the study of literary language. In E. M. Zale, ed., *Proceedings of the conference on language and language behavior*. New York: Appleton-Century-Crofts, 1968a.

————. A linguistic appraisal of Victorian style. In G. Levine and W. Madden, eds., *The art of Victorian prose*. New York and London: Oxford University Press, 1968b.

————. Speech acts and the definition of literature. *Philosophy and Rhetoric*, 1971, *4*, 1-19, a.

————. Speech, action, and style. In S. Chatman, ed., *Literary style: A symposium*. New York and London: Oxford University Press, 1971, pp. 241-59, b.

————. Speech, literature, and the space between. *New Literary History*, 1972, *4*, 47-64, a.

————. Instrumental style: Notes on the theory of speech as action. In B. B. Kachru and H. Stahlke, eds., *Current trends in stylistics*. Champaign and Edmonton: Linguistic Research, Inc., 1972, pp. 115-41, b.

————. Literature as act. In S. Chatman, *Approaches to poetics: Selected papers from the English Institute*. New York: Columbia University Press, 1973, pp. 81-107.

Propp, V. *Morphology of the folktale*, tr. Laurence Scott. *IJAL*: Publication X of the Research Center in Anthropology, Folklore, and Linguistics, 1958.

Quirk, R. *The use of English*. London: St. Martin's Press, 1962.

Scott, C. T. Towards a formal poetics: Metrical patterning in "The Windhover." *Language and Style*, 1974, *7*, 91-107.

Searle, J. *Speech acts*. London: Cambridge University Press, 1969.

Sebeok, T. A., ed. *Style in language*. Cambridge, Mass.: M.I.T. Press, 1960.

Spencer, J., and Gregory, M. J. An approach to the study of style. In N. E. Enkvist, J. Spencer, and M. J. Gregory, eds., *Linguistics and style*. London: Oxford University Press, 1964.

Thompson, J. *The founding of English metre*. New York: Columbia University Press, 1961.

Thorne, J. P. Stylistics and generative grammars. *Journal of Linguistics*, 1965, *1*, 49-59.

————. Poetry, stylistics, and imaginary grammars. *Journal of Linguistics*, 1969, *5*, 147-50.

————. Generative grammar and stylistic analysis. In J. Lyons, ed., *New horizons in linguistics*. Harmondsworth: Penguin, 1970.

Todorov, T. Structuralism and literature. In S. Chatman, *Approaches to poetics: Selected papers from the English Institute*. New York: Columbia University Press, 1973, pp. 153-68.

van Dijk, T. A. *Some aspects of text grammars*. The Hague and Paris: Mouton, 1972.

Wimsatt, W. K. The rule and the norm: Halle and Keyser on Chaucer's meter. *College English*, 1970, *31*, 774-88.

————, ed. *Versification: Major language types*. New York: New York University Press, 1973.

Wrenn, C. L., ed. *Beowulf, with the Finnesburgh fragment*. Boston and London: D. C. Heath and George Harrap, 1953.

XII

Language Disorders

Haiganoosh Whitaker and Harry Whitaker

The subject matter of neurolinguistics is the relationship between language and the central nervous system. Therefore, one focus of research in neurolinguistics is on linguistic performance, or more specifically, on the mental (performative) grammar which underlies the use of language (Watt, 1974). The second focus is on the nervous system, specifically the structures of the brain which are responsible for language and the functions that these structures have in linguistic communication. Quite understandably much of the research in neurolinguistics has been based upon the impaired language abilities of patients who have sustained damage to the central nervous system. This chapter will deal mainly with research on the varieties of aphasia and on the linguistic aspects of aphasic language.

Other research paradigms are also possible (see Dingwall and Whitaker, 1974). The dichotic listening paradigm consists of presenting two auditory stimuli simultaneously, one in each ear; the subject is asked to report what is heard as accurately as possible. In the typical case when other variables are controlled, linguistically encoded stimuli heard in the right ear are perceived better than such stimuli heard in the left ear. The right ear advantage for linguistic stimuli is considered evidence for the processing of language by the left hemisphere; the asymmetry of the ears is matched by the reversed asymmetry of the cerebral hemispheres. The dichotic effect has been used to study a number of aspects of language processing: distinctive features, prosodic features, and syntactic structure.

Neurosurgical operations on the brain may impinge upon or may affect the normal functioning of the language areas of the brain. One of the techniques for relief from severe epileptic seizures is to divide the corpus callosum in two, in effect to separate the left from the right hemisphere and create what is known as the "split brain." Since it is possible to transmit visual information selectively to either hemisphere, it is therefore possible to test the linguistic capacities of either hemisphere in the split-brain patient by means of visual stimuli. The findings of such studies corroborate the research on aphasia: the left hemisphere is specialized for language in most people and the right hemisphere has limited though detectable language functions.

Neurons, the primary functional units of the brain, produce a measurable amount of electrical activity which varies according to location in the brain and the nature of the behavioral task. The electrical potentials which precede, accompany, or follow language processing are quite direct indicators of the correlated brain states. This electroencephalographic (EEG) research has revealed differences between the two hemispheres, differences within the left hemisphere and differences in the same hemispheric locus, for various articulatory, phonetic, and semantic aspects of language. Because the brain state and the language function are correlated in real time, EEG research holds great promise for delineating aspects of a performance model.

Aphasic Language

The use of aphasic language data as a basis for hypothesizing aspects of a performative grammar naturally raises questions about aphasia itself. One might reasonably inquire whether or not there is one or a limited number of general factors which account for the deficit in aphasia, without recourse to linguistic components of a mental performative grammar. Some factors which have been suggested in the past are word frequency, the abstract-concrete dimension, temporal order, a simple-complex dimension, and a generalized thought disorder. What has been claimed by proponents of a limited-factor view of aphasia is that one (or a small number) of these factors explains the language deficits observed in aphasic patients. In fairness it must be noted that, on certain tests and performance measures with certain types of aphasic patients, each of these factors can be shown to play a role in the explanation of a language deficit. Nonetheless, careful analysis of other tests with the same or different types of patients has shown that each of these factors is insufficient in accounting for all aspects of aphasia. For example, while word frequency (and the interrelated variables of segmental length and complexity) may account for the severity of phonological distortions in one group of patients, syntactic category and derivational complexity account for similar distortions in another group.

One might also consider the fact that in some patients transitive and intransitive imperatives and *wh-* questions are easier to process than either the future tense or a noun phrase containing two adjectives; it is difficult to imagine how any notion of simple versus complex linguistic structures could be meaningfully applied in such cases. Again, some patients find nouns so much easier to process that they attempt to convert verbs and adjectives into their derived nominal forms; other patients find verbs facilitated and attempt the reverse. For some patients the major phonological error is one of sequencing: the majority of errors are either anticipatory or perseveratory and are easily predictable from the surrounding phonological context. In other patients, the phonological errors are predominantly those of feature specification of individual segments: there may be mistakes in voicing, nasality, tenseness, and the like, in spite of a normal neuro-muscular-articulatory competence. Those patients with sequencing errors may produce jargonlike utterances and those patients with segmental feature errors may produce foreign-accented utterances. On the whole aphasia is more marked by its linguistic diversity than by uniform, extra-linguistic factors.

The use of aphasic language data as a basis for hypothesizing aspects of brain function raises still another set of issues. First of all, the clinical terminology used to describe the varieties of aphasia is neither uniform nor consistent. This situation has existed virtually from the beginning of clinical aphasia studies in the latter half of the nineteenth century. For example, the following terms have been used to describe patients whose language impairments are primarily phonological errors and dysfluency of verbal expression: *aphemia, Broca's aphasia, motor aphasia, expressive aphasia, verbal aphasia, verbal dyspraxia, apraxia of speech, efferent motor aphasia, aphasic phonological impairment*, etc. The reasons for the multiplicity of terms are that some researchers are in different disciplines, some have been committed to different philosophical and psychological theories, and some have based their classification schemes on neuroanatomy and others on behavioral or linguistic function.

In addition to the biases of researchers, the other contribution to this problem is the variability of the clinical data. It is an indisputable fact that a patient's linguistic performance, and the type and locus of the lesion in the brain, rarely conform precisely with classification schemata. The question of localization is itself still a matter of active debate. A simplistic localization theory is clearly inadequate and would not be defended by anyone today. To use an example of Luria's (1964), there is no such thing as a "writing center" because different brain mechanisms contribute to writing in different ways; the model that Luria uses is that of a system or network of component functions which participate in the general function of writing.

While most researchers would reject a naive localization theory, they would at the same time reject a holistic theory. The problem of localization is determining precisely what functions different parts of the brain have, not in ascertaining that there are different parts of the brain. As knowledge of the psychological, neurological and linguistic aspects of language increases, more sophisticated modeling is clearly required. What seems to be the intrinsic advantage of taking a localizationist position (actually, a physicalist position, since there is much more to language representation in the brain than mere topography) has as much to do with heuristics as it does with philosophy: as the position is challenged in its details but retained in principle, the investigator is led to a richer and empirically more disconfirmable theory of human language capacity.

The Major Varieties of Aphasia

The following discussion of the major syndromes of aphasia agrees in outline with that of the Boston School (Green, 1970; Goodglass and Kaplan, 1972), to which have been added some observations of a more linguistic nature. The advantages of this characterization are easily recognized: it provides a basis for elaboration and refinement of the neuroanatomical mechanisms of language, and the relative involvement of the four modalities of language use provides a rationale for neurological as well as linguistic assessment. The disadvantages are that this classification does not easily lend itself to describing mixed or intermediate types of aphasia, and it does not do justice to the intricacy and specificity of the linguistic impairments in aphasia. Figure 1 is a schematic drawing of the left hemisphere. It should be noted that Heschl's gyrus, the primary auditory cortex, is actually in the depths of the Fissure of Sylvius and not exposed on the surface of the left hemisphere.

Syndrome of Broca's aphasia. The locus of the lesion that produces Broca's aphasia is in the posterior, inferior region of the frontal lobe though not necessarily restricted precisely to the region of Broca's area. Both grey matter (nerve cells) and white matter (axonal connections) are usually damaged, but the effects of lesions in each on speech and language are different (Hecaen and Consoli, 1973). The spontaneity of both speaking and writing is usually quite severely impaired; speech being hesitant and dysfluent with frequent pauses and mild to severely deficient intonation contours. Both speech and writing are marked by segmental (or letter) substitutions, perseverations, and anticipations, although the segments (or

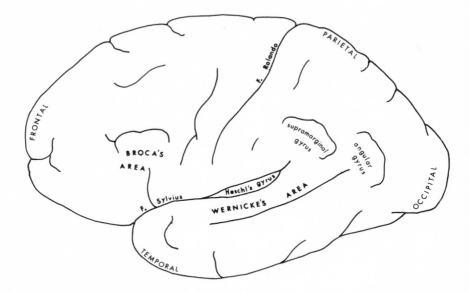

Fig. 1. Schematic drawing of left hemisphere.

letters) themselves are typically well formed. In other words, the deficit is
not neuromuscular in character. The phonological component of this syndrome is underscored by the fact that patients whose native language is
Japanese typically find Kata-kana and Hira-kana (the phonetic-syllabic
writing systems) impaired significantly more than Kanji (the ideographic
writing system).

Syntactically, both speech and writing frequently exhibit agrammatism, a "telegraphic style" that results from the omission or incorrect use
of grammatical formatives (for example, plural and possessive morphemes),
determiners, and those prepositions which carry a low semantic load.
Surface word order is generally correct, adequately conveys meaning, and
indicates that there is a fairly normal degree of semantic processing. Lexical
formatives (for example, nouns and verbs) are generally preserved although they may be phonologically distorted. The ability to repeat may be
mildly impaired, although model utterances spoken by an examiner often
assist the patient's production. Comprehension, both in the visual and
auditory modalities, is relatively normal although careful examination may
reveal problems with grammatical formatives parallel to the expressive
agrammatism (Zurif, Caramazza, and Myerson, 1972). Self-monitoring is
typically well enough preserved that these patients are aware of, and
become quite upset with, their expressive impairments.

It is obvious from the above description that several aspects of speech production are involved. Therefore, some researchers have made a further division of the expressive disorders, using both clinical and pathological criteria. For example, Luria (1970) distinguishes afferent motor aphasia from efferent motor aphasia. Afferent motor aphasia is a disorder of the articulatory target (vocal tract shape): the accuracy and the selection of segments are impaired. Although afferent motor aphasia is not neuromuscular (that is, is not dysarthric) in character, it is sometimes difficult to distinguish precisely between it and dysarthria because in addition to substitutions of segments there may be substitutions of allophonic variants of segments. Certain types of dysarthria may also lead to incorrect choices of allophones; consequently, the distinction between dysarthria and afferent motor aphasia may occasionally be made only in terms of the consistency with which specific muscle groups are involved (Whitaker, in press). If specific muscle groups are consistently affected, the impairment is dysarthria and a subcortical pathology may be assumed; variable patterns of muscle deficits indicate a cortical lesion, implying a diagnosis of afferent motor aphasia. Luria observes that there are letter substitutions in writing that are analogous to spoken errors and that reading may be mildly affected in this syndrome.

The syndrome of efferent motor aphasia, according to Luria, is comparable to the other aspects of Broca's aphasia: expression is agrammatic and dysfluent, and stress, pitch, and juncture are impaired (dysprosodic). Segment errors are typically described as serial order, sequencing, or transition problems with consonants more disrupted than vowels. It is argued that difficulty in proceeding from one articulatory gesture to the next (likewise, from one word to the next, etc.) accounts for the perserverative tendencies seen in many patients; a previously uttered response is produced again and again as the patient seemingly gropes for the correct response. Luria has also argued that there is a tendency in many patients to retain only the nominative forms of lexical items, a phenomenon that has been observed in other types of aphasia as well (Marshall, Newcombe, and Marshall, 1971; Whitaker, 1972).

Syndrome of Wernicke's aphasia. A lesion in the posterior temporal lobe, in the superior regions nearer the Sylvan fissure, produces an aphasia that predominantly affects language comprehension but which may compromise expression in a variety of ways. Because of the importance of Wernicke's area and the surrounding cortex to the semantic and syntactic aspects of language as well as to language-mediated cognitive behaviors, patients with lesions in this region exhibit a wide range of impairments. In fact the range is so wide that it is not easy to maintain the notion of a single syndrome entity. In contrast to the Broca's aphasic, the Wernicke's aphasic usually retains fluent verbal expression with relatively normal intonation contours. However, what the patient actually says may be semantically vacuous or content-less utterances of indefinite noun phrases and cliches, or may be a meaningless concatenation of actual words, or may be an uninterpretable jargon of neologistic utterances that appear to be based on orthodox phonetic segments, junctures, and intonation. In some Wernicke's aphasics there is a semblance of normal syntax, for example, some researchers have identified normal derivational affixes attached to neologisms. In other such patients, certain basic syntactic structures have been identified (Buckingham and Kertesz, 1974).

The comprehension of language, particularly through the auditory modality, is generally impaired and the severity of the auditory-comprehension deficit is usually taken to be the measure of the severity of the aphasia itself. Wernicke's aphasics can often distinguish speech from nonspeech (or at least give the impression of being able to), can distinguish their native language from a foreign one, and occasionally can distinguish a question from a command (Boller and Green, 1972). A frequent and striking clinical observation of patients with severe comprehension deficits is that they respond readily and accurately to certain requests such as *Please take off your glasses* or *Please stand up*. Not surprisingly, the ability to read is affected to the same degree as auditory comprehension, although cases demonstrating a dissociation of these tasks (modalities) are on record. Also, as would be presumed, the ability to repeat is comparably impaired.

If one disregards the comprehension/understanding problem and merely examines speech output, it is evident that normally the patient retains both lexical and grammatical formatives. However, usually the lexical formatives are contextually erroneous; the substitution of one word for another (paraphasia) may follow semantic criteria, that is, may be within the same semantic field (Rinnert and Whitaker, 1973) or may appear to be random. There is usually little effort on the part of these patients to correct themselves, apparently due to the deficit in auditory comprehension. Perseveration is commonly observed in Wernicke's aphasics, but it seems quite different from that observed in patients with lesions nearer to Broca's area (more anteriorly located). The Broca-type perseveration may be described as a difficulty in switching from one task to another; the Wernicke-type perseveration is more like the random but frequent repetition of some sound or some word. The Wernicke's aphasic may retain his natural handwriting from the standpoint of letter formation and inter-letter connections, but in all other respects it is usually unintelligible. In the less severe cases, writing is similar to spoken language. Clearly, there is a wide variation in the impairments following from lesions to Wernicke's area; in part due to this fact and in part due to theoretical biases of researchers, a number of different names have been proposed for this syndrome: *receptive aphasia, sensory aphasia, verbal amnesia, semantic aphasia, syntactic aphasia, acoustic aphasia, fluent aphasia, impressive aphasia*, and so on.

Syndrome of anomic (amnestic) aphasia. Anomia, the difficulty in finding words, particularly for the names of things, is a rather pervasive problem in all varieties of aphasia, although it can occur in relative isolation from other symptom complexes. The presence of dyslexia (reading deficit) or dysgraphia (writing deficit) is not consistently related to this syndrome. Although word-finding difficulties may occur in different syndromes, they are not necessarily similar in each. Some patients simply block and cannot find the word that they want; some patients will substitute a word that is semantically associated with the target word; some patients may substitute a circumlocutory expression that describes the target word; some patients may substitute an indefinite word (*thing, stuff, some*, etc.) for the target word. The anomic phenomenon is frequently seen in Wernicke's aphasia and these two syndromes overlap to a considerable degree. Some research-ers have suggested that the lesion locus for anomia is in the middle posterior temporal region, below Wernicke's area, but it is generally recognized that damage to almost any part of the language area of the brain may result in word-finding problems. In addition, space-occupying lesions (for example, tumors) in remote parts of the brain can produce anomia due to the increased pressure within the skull; this factor contributes to the nonlocalizability of anomia. It should also be recognized that naming deficit may not be uniform in the same patient: a patient whose ability to name objects on confrontation is preserved to some degree may not easily be able to find the identical names of objects when he is speaking spontaneously, or vice versa. Thus, the anomia may be more severe in one modality or in one linguistic task than another: a patient may verbally block on a word but then be able to retrieve it by writing it down with pencil and paper. The circumlocutions observed in some anomic aphasics follow syntactic patterns: Konorski (1967) noted that there are groups of patients whose speech is characterized by a preponderance of verb forms and a corresponding lack of nouns.

Syndrome of conduction aphasia. The hallmark of the conduction aphasic is a severely impaired ability to repeat, contrasted with a relatively intact and fluent spontaneous expression and a relatively intact auditory comprehension. It is one of the classic "disconnection" syndromes (Geschwind, 1965), attributed to a lesion of the arcuate fascicle. The arcuate fascicle is the tract which joins Wernicke's area with Broca's area. The supramarginal gyrus, also lying between Wernicke's and Broca's area, has also been implicated in conduction aphasia. Challenging the classical position, Luria (1970) stresses the fact that repetition impairments are features of both expressive and receptive disorders; specifically, he says that they can be found as components of efferent motor aphasia, afferent motor aphasia, and Wernicke's aphasia. However, in these cases the repetition deficit is only one component of the overall disorder; documented cases have been published in which the repetition deficit exists unaccompanied by problems in articulation, auditory comprehension, or short-term auditory memory (Kinsbourne, 1972).

The repetition deficit is usually phonological in nature: errors in the sequencing and selection of segments, analogous to those of the Broca's aphasic, are the typical manifestation. The main difference is that these phonological errors do not appear as often in spontaneous speech. The conduction aphasic is generally aware of his erroneous production (repetition) in both speaking and copy writing, a fact which is consistent with the claimed lesion locus. Continued repetition of the target word by the examiner does not help this patient produce the target; this is unlike the Broca's aphasic who is often aided by hearing the correct target. Goodglass and Kaplan (1972) note that word type may be a factor in the repetition deficit: some conduction aphasics are able to repeat numbers much more successfully than other types of words. The length and the frequency of occurrence of words and phrases affect the conduction aphasic's ability to repeat: shorter and more common utterances are repeated more successfully on the whole.

Isolation syndrome. This somewhat rare syndrome (also called mixed transcortical aphasia) occurs when the so-called primary language zone (Wernicke's area, the arcuate fascicle, Broca's area) is cut off or disconnected from the remainder of the brain including the other language areas. Its rarity is primarily due to the fact that only certain kinds of disease processes can cause a border zone lesion in the association cortices of the three major lobes—frontal, temporal, and parietal. Two known causes, based on autopsied material, are carbon monoxide poisoning and the diffuse degeneration associated with a variety of Pick's disease (presenile dementia). Although there are few published cases, two of them have been exhaustively studied anatomically and clinically (Geschwind, Quadfasel, and Segarra, 1968; Avakian-Whitaker, in press).

The isolation aphasic retains a striking ability to repeat what is said, coupled with an almost total lack of spontaneous speaking, writing, and auditory or visual comprehension. The repetition response is in fact echoic, that is, it appears as though the patient is unable to control the echoing as well as unable to comprehend the stimulus. Detailed studies have revealed some very remarkable linguistic features to this echolalia. One patient was shown to have learned the words and tune of a song heard on the radio. Another patient was shown to have phonological and syntactic (involuntary) control over the echo repetition: when a purposely erroneous stimulus was given (for example, errors in segments, stress, or "low-level" syntactic rules) the patient's echo response changed the stimulus to its correct surface form. The conclusion is that at certain levels of phonology and syntax, a nonvolitional grammatical filtering mechanism is operating in these cases. There does not appear to be any selection for certain categories of lexical formative and both lexical and grammatical formatives are echoed equally frequently. Fluency, with respect to the echoed response, is relatively normal; there is no spontaneous expression.

Syndrome of transcortical motor aphasia. Lesions in the frontal lobe anterior to Broca's area (and superior to it, as well) may produce the syndrome of transcortical motor aphasia, also called frontal dynamic aphasia. It is debatable whether or not this is really a language disorder since the principal impairment is in the spontaneous initiation of speech and writing. Auditory and visual comprehension are relatively intact; repetition is also generally intact and does not show the phonological impairments of the typical expressive aphasias. There are no salient linguistic deficits with respect to lexical or grammatical formatives; naming objects may be impaired, although this may be more due to the problem in initiating speech than to an actual anomia; writing ability is quite unpredictable, although the nearer the lesion is to Broca's area, the more likely that writing will be aphasic. There are cases on record of lesions to the inner surface of the frontal lobe (the region interfacing the opposite hemisphere) producing transcortical motor aphasia. It is possible that a lesion in the frontal association cortex may interfere with the function of the frontal language areas to produce this syndrome.

Syndrome of alexia and agraphia. One of the major areas of the brain subserving visual linguistic symbols is the angular gyrus. This region is at the intersection of the inferior parietal lobe, the posterior temporal lobe, and the anterior occipital lobe. Thus, it has been proposed as an association area of association areas. Lesions in the angular gyrus invariably produce disturbances in both reading and writing (alexia and agraphia, respectively). In the classic case, auditory comprehension and verbal expression may be normal while reading and writing are virtually impossible. The reading and writing impairments may take a variety of forms: one common one is that recognition of individual letters is preserved but the ability to read words is not. A rarer but documented form is the converse: whole word recognition is better than individual letter recognition. Productively, the impairment may selectively affect written spelling or oral spelling (Kinsbourne and Rosenfield, 1974). Patients with alexia and agraphia may have a fairly well-preserved auditory-verbal comprehension and expression as noted; however, closer examination may reveal deficits in these modalities too. A patient with apparently only alexia and agraphia was unable to recognize or produce rhymes in speech. From the standpoint of linguistic structure, the alexic-agraphic patient is similar to a Wernicke's aphasic: there is often differential impairment of nouns as opposed to verbs or adjectives, and of grammatical as opposed to lexical formatives, and so on (Whitaker, 1971).

Syndrome of word deafness.   An interesting and well-documented disconnection syndrome is "pure" word deafness, also called auditory agnosia for speech (Goldstein, 1974). There have been some differences of opinion as to the locus of the responsible lesion, some researchers maintaining that a subcortical involvement of the temporal lobe is the basis and others maintaining that the basis is a cortical lesion which separates Heschl's gyrus from Wernicke's area. It is clear that the functional basis is the inability to process linguistically encoded auditory input from either ear; the word-deaf patient has normal or near-normal hearing (pure tones, environmental sounds, etc.) within the acoustic range of speech, he has normal understanding and intellectual functioning (when tested visually), and his reading, speaking, and writing are completely normal. The word-deaf patient cannot understand spoken language. There are no documented examples of differential impairment within one class of linguistic items as opposed to another, nor is there any evidence that common expressions or cliches (*Good morning*, etc.) are heard and understood any better than any other spoken language.

The preceding discussion of the various syndromes of aphasia cannot convey an accurate picture of the actual complexity of each clinical case; it misleadingly conveys a sense of discreteness to each clinical entity. Any summary would be equally guilty in these respects. It must be observed that: (*a*) the descriptions represent an average or typical constellation of impairments from which an actual patient may deviate; (*b*) the descriptions in part represent a linguistic interpretation of the language behavior of patients who fall within these broad classifications; and (*c*) the descriptions in part represent judgments reached by a consensus of researchers in the field. With respect to the lesion locus (and, indirectly the issue of localization) it is worth recalling the summary remarks made by Freud (1891) following his critical review of theories of aphasia and the discrete localization of language centers which were prevalent in the late nineteenth century:

> We set out with the intention of examining whether the principle of localization could really offer as much for the explanation of the aphasias as has been claimed, and whether one is justified in differentiating between centre and pathways of speech and between the respective types of speech disorders . . . . Our concept of the structure of the speech apparatus was based on the observation that the so-called speech centres border externally (peripherally) on parts of the cortex which are important for the speech function, while interiorly (centrally) they enclose a region not covered by localization which probably also belongs to the speech area. The following factors have proved to be decisive for the effect of lesions on the speech apparatus so organized: the degree of destructiveness of the lesion, and its situation relative to the interior and the periphery of the speech region. If situated on its periphery, i.e., in one of the so-called speech centres, its symptoms are related to its localization; depending on whether it causes complete or incomplete destruction it either results in a loss of only one of the elements of speech associations, or it alters the functional state of this element in a way described as Bastian's modifications. If the lesion is situated centrally in the speech region the whole apparatus of speech suffers functional disturbances such as arise from its character as an instrument of association, and which we have attempted to enumerate (pp. 101-4).

Linguistic Studies of Aphasia

Linguistic studies of aphasia not only characterize the language deficits that result from brain damage, but they also delineate features of performative grammars. Different levels of the grammar may be impaired in aphasia and the effects of an impairment at one level may be observed. Some common methods of studying aphasic patients include in-depth analyses of single case histories (for example, to examine correlations between behavior and anatomy), analyses of patient populations grouped according to the locus of the lesion or according to the clinical variety of aphasia (for example, to characterize the essential features of such populations), and analyses of mixed populations of patients (for example, to study some specific aspect of language).

The theoretical linguistic frameworks of aphasia studies have mirrored the various linguistic theories current in North America, Europe, and elsewhere; in practice, many of the studies are best described as informal structuralist approaches although some have been frankly tagmemic, statificational, or transformational in orientation. Since the relationship between abstract linguistic theories and mental or performative grammars is not yet fully and precisely defined (Watt, 1974), it is unrealistic to assume that aphasic language data could provide evidence supporting or disconfirming one or more of the current theories in linguistics. In fact, it may even be questioned whether such data could help choose between competing models within one theoretical framework, although such proposals have been offered (Whitaker, 1972). A more conservative view would be to group these studies into those which focus on the lexicon and semantic features, those which focus on syntax, and those which focus on phonology.

Blumenstein (1973) analyzed the patterns of phonological errors made by patients with Broca's aphasia, Wernicke's aphasia, and conduction aphasia. She employed the distinctive-feature framework of generative-transformational grammar and found that errors more frequently involved one feature than several and a marked segment than an unmarked one. Her study is exhaustively reviewed by Lecours and Caplan (1975). A unique and important study by Schnitzer (1972) provides evidence for the performative reality of the underlying lexical (systematic phonemic) level of the generative-phonology model. His evidence is that simple errors in the feature presentation at the systematic-phonemic level can account for widespread and seemingly random phonetic-level errors. Certain aspects of Schnitzer's (1972) study and a study by Kehoe and Whitaker (1973) of the same patient relate to problems of the lexicon and will be discussed in more detail below. There are, of course, many other studies of phonological aspects of aphasia: Avakian-Whitaker (in press); Brown (1972); Goodglass and Kaplan (1972); Johns and Darley (1970); Johns and LaPointe (in press); Lecours and Caplan (1975); Luria (1970); and Whitaker (1971).

Zurif, Caramazza, and Myerson (1972) solicited judgments of syntactic relatedness of words in sentences from a group of Broca's (agrammatic) aphasics, and compared these judgments to those made by a group of control subjects. What they discovered was that the agrammatic aphasic patients did not strongly associate the determiners *a* and *the* with their following nouns, but the control subjects did. When the results are graphed, the judgments of the control subjects resemble a surface-structure tree diagram while the judgments of the aphasic patients resemble a deep-structure tree diagram. Such evidence indicates that the encoding of determiners in the performative grammar is a process distinct from the encoding of the deep phrase structure since this process can be separately impaired in both production and comprehension. Goodglass, Gleason, Bernholtz, and Hyde (1972) also studied syntax in the agrammatic Broca's aphasic. They found that different syntactic structures are differentially impaired, as shown in the following:

(EASIEST)	Imperatives
	Adj + Noun
	WH-questions
	Declaratives
	Comparatives
	Passives
	Yes-No Questions
	Direct Object + Indirect Object
	Embedded Sentences
(MOST	Adj + Adj + Noun
DIFFICULT)	Future Tense

Brown (1972); Dingwall and Whitaker (1974); Goodglass (in press); Green (1970); Luria (1970); Whitaker (1971); and Zurif and Caramazza (in press) contain further references and discussion.

A great deal of the interest in studying lexical structure in aphasia is due to the fact that many of the clinically distinguishable varieties of aphasia can be characterized in part by selective lexical deficits. The agrammatic patient experiences most difficulty with grammatical formatives (function words) while the anomic patient experiences most difficulty with lexical formatives (content words). Some Wernicke's aphasics find nouns easier to process than verbs or adjectives while other Wernicke's aphasics have more difficulty with nouns than any other category. Some Broca's aphasics produce more phonological errors when attempting content words than when attempting function words. There is no doubt that the mental lexicon is structured and differentiated in a variety of ways; research on lexical structure in aphasia has provided some insights into lexical organization in the performative grammar.

Marshall, Newcombe, and Marshall (1971) studied a patient with a residual long-term dyslexia that was relatively specific for certain semantic and syntactic features. There was a facilitation of nouns such that for a noun target another noun was produced (*liberty* read as *freedom*) but for a verb or adjective target a nominal was produced (*beg* read as *beggar*). Their patient had twice as much difficulty with verbs as with nouns; and adjectives were in between nouns and verbs in difficulty. They noted a tendency for nonstative verbs to be easier than statives and certain nouns marked for [+human, +role] such as *uncle*, *priest*, and *poet* were more difficult than [-human, +animate] nouns such as *horse*, *lion*, and *insect*. The patient demonstrated a tendency to preserve the markedness of adjectives of quantity: *large* was read as *long*, *little* was read as *short*, and so on.

The subject studied by Schnitzer (1972), and Kehoe and Whitaker (1973) showed specific impairments of syntactic and phonological features. A mild nearly undetectable aphasia was manifest only when complexly derived words such as those of Latin origin were singled out for testing. For this type of word, the patient typically would misplace stress assignment, substitute vowels and consonants, and occasionally delete syllables. She was thoroughly tested in all aspects of verbal and performance intelligence measures and with aphasia test batteries; her deficit was shown to be limited to these particular lexical items. The following data are illustrative of the errors she usually made in reading aloud, in repeating, in writing to dictation, and occasionally in spontaneous speech.

1. VERB   NOUN   (substitution)

   analyze   əˈnæləsis

   confiscate   kanfisˈkejʃən

   demonstrate   dɛmənˈstɹejʃən

   compensate   kamɛnˈsejʃən

2. VERB   NOUN   (stress shift)

   consent   ˈkansɛnt

consist   ˈkansist

lament   ˈlæmɛnt

3. ADJ   NOUN

investigative   invɛstəˈgejʃən

pathological   pæθalədzij # ikəl

anticipatory   æntəpəˈtejʃən # oɹij

bandaged   ˈbændədz # əd

bacteriological bæktiɹijˈalədzij # ikəl

4. NOUN   ADJ

logic   ˈladzikəl

5. NOUN   VERB BASE FORM

clarification   ˈklɛɹəfaj # ˈkejʃən

determinancy   dijˈtəɹmən

explanation   ɛksˈplejn

6. NOUN   BASE FORM BLEND

logician   ˈladzəkən

variety   ˈvɛɹətij

succession	sək^ˈsijʃən
documentation	dak^yuw^ˈmɛnʃən
domesticity	dow^ˈmɛstəktij
plurality	^ˈplʊɹəltij

7. VERB   BASE FORM BLEND

tabulate	^ˈtejb^yuwlejt
catholicize	^ˈkæθəlajz

8. ADJ   BASE FORM BLEND

ethereal	^ˈijθijəl
tabular	^ˈtejb^yuwləɹ
reputable	ɹij^ˈp^yuwtəbəl
courageous	^ˈkəɹədzəs

It is clear from these data, and from the lack of any other aphasic errors, that the semantic features of the lexicon are intact. Some of the errors involved whole-word substitutions in which the substituted word had the correct phonetic shape (categories 1 and 5) but was in a different syntactic category. The examples in category 5 also indicate that the base form is processed separately from its derivational affix. The examples in category 2 suggest that the patient is erroneously assigning these verbs to that class of verbs which change stress placement only in the derived nominal form (*ˈprogress* vs. *pro ˈgress*). Apparently these forms were thought to be nouns, misassigned to the derivational class, and then produced with the appropriate phonetic shape. Note that the patient adjusted the vowel quality correctly, given the misanalysis (see Schnitzer, 1972, for a full discussion).

Inappropriate phonetic sequences are avoided as seen in the changing of the final /d/ in *succeed* when adding *-ion* or changing the final /t/ in *document* before the same suffix (category 6). When inappropriate sequences would not result from the misanalysis, the base form is more resistant to alteration: thus, one finds the (incorrect in terms of the target) sequence /kʃ/ in the response for *relaxation*; this phonetic sequence is found in other English words such as *action*. There is also a /kt/ sequence in the response to *domesticity*, a sequence which is admissible in English at least at morpheme boundaries as in *buckteeth*.

Clearly the source of this patient's difficulty is in the derivational morphology of English, probably at the level of the dictionary entry itself. She knows the semantic representation and the basic phonetic shape; the errors appear to be caused by the derivational affixal changes in phonetic shape and stress which are to some degree idiosyncratic for these words. If this is the case, then it should follow that she should be able to produce nonsense words which pattern like the phonology of English but which have neither base forms nor derivational extensions. This did turn out to be the case: in a manner consistent with a normal subject's pronunciation, she said without difficulty nonsense words such as *slisnicious, nimmigathy, hofbratter, disantropic, maygradation, romerculous*, and others. It should also follow that she should be able to produce long complex words which do not have derivational forms but which do occur, though infrequently, in the English lexicon; again, this turned out to be so, for she had no trouble with *Popocatepetl, Mesopotamia, yestermorn, Mississippi, Canandaigua, Rochester*, and others.

One thing suggested by these studies is that base forms and affixes are functionally separate in the mental lexicon, as has been observed in other studies. Lecours and Caplan (1975) noted that some patients with inferior parietal lesions (the same lesion locus in the patient studied by Schnitzer, 1972, and Kehoe and Whitaker, 1973) produced word substitutions which they called neo-syntagms: an incorrect affix-stem combination resulting in a nonexistent word. Frequently, the affix was one which actually occurred in French, but the stem was either the wrong one or an invented one. Another type of error noted by Lecours and Caplan actually resulted in filling in a "lexical gap" in French. Caplan, Kellar, and Locke (1972) also studied the inflection of neologisms, nonexisting forms which are phonologically acceptable (that is, which conform to the phonological rules of the patient's native language). Some of their examples given below (as they wrote them) illustrate how such forms are inflected comparably to nouns and verbs:

> . . . yes, I know what the persite is . . . .
> . . . things that devorodation have had.

. . . they will have to presite me . . . .
. . . many things I didn't have years agoth and I persets abowth abrow.
. . . yes, because I'm just persessing to one.

Taken together, these studies clearly demonstrate the divisibility of base forms and affixes and the combinatory rules for joining them, at least for English and French. Of course, one should not conclude that all complex words are so organized in the mental lexicon; it is quite reasonable to assume that some frequently used words might be stored or represented as whole units in their surface phonetic form. But the fact that some words are stored in separable parts provides a mental-neurological basis for the well-known productivity of certain classes of derivational affixes, that is, an account, in part, of our capacity to create new words.

Some semantic aspects of lexical organization were considered by Rinnert and Whitaker (1973). This survey analyzed data from published literature sources taken from a variety of aphasic syndromes in different languages as well as personally studied case histories. The question raised was the semantic relationship between what a patient said or wrote (regardless of test format) and what the correct target word should have been. These data were then compared to published studies of word associations by normal subjects. It was found that aphasic semantic confusions could be compared in terms of features that the response and the target both shared and differed in. The shared features tended to represent major semantic categories, thus reinforcing intuitive notions of semantic fields, and the contrasting features tended to represent minor and/or highly specific functional distinctions.

9. SEMANTIC
   CONFUSION

a. pen   → pencil
b. pipe   → cigar
c. shovel → spoon

COMMON
FEATURES

IMPLEMENTS
a. writing
b. smoking
c. scooping

DIFFERENT
FEATURES

a. medium and mechanism
b. shape, manner of smoking
c. size, material used with

10. SEMANTIC CONFUSION	glasses	→	eyes

COMMON FEATURES	VISION

DIFFERENT FEATURES	mechanical aid
	natural receptor

In example 9, the errors *pencil*, *cigar*, and *spoon* are related to their targets in that they are classes of implements for writing, smoking, and scooping; they differ as to mechanism, size, or shape, or the material used in conjunction with each implement. A similar analysis accounts for the substitution of *eyes* for *glasses* in example 10. When this and other similar data were compared with word association norms, it was found that the two sets of data were remarkably alike; if anything, the semantic confusions of aphasic patients are slightly more specific in terms of semantic features than the data obtained by the word-association technique used on normal subjects. Rinnert and Whitaker supported the hypothesis that the word-association paradigm operates on the same lexical structure which is impaired in many types of aphasia and suggested that either data source will provide insights into the lexicon of the mental grammar.

Early observers of the expressive language capacity of brain-damaged patients frequently noted a deficit in naming when patients were confronted with an object. Although this deficit is usually found in conjunction with other aphasic impairments, in the classical literature it is identified as a separate syndrome and called anomia, verbal amnesia, amnestic aphasia, or nominal aphasia (Brown, 1972; Geschwind, 1967; Goldstein, 1948; Head, 1926). Classically, this syndrome may be described as the impaired use or loss of nouns in both spontaneous conversation and in metalinguistic tasks such as naming pictures, naming objects, and repetition. It is interesting to note that while the anomic patient has an impaired use of nouns compared to other syntactic categories, other patients show a remarkable facilitation for nouns. Whitaker (1972) studied three patients who showed this in a rather dramatic form. Not only were verbs read as nouns (*remember* was read aloud as *memory*) they were often repeated that way (given the word *receive*, a patient asked, "Did you say *reception*?")

While such data clearly indicate that the syntactic category noun can be separately affected in brain damage, and therefore is functionally distinct in the lexicon of the mental grammar, it is not possible to conclude that noun is hierarchically more important or significant than other categories. Other patients exhibit clearly opposite tendencies. Konorski (1967) reported on a patient with a severe auditory comprehension deficit accompanied by an anomia for objects. However, this patient had virtually no difficulty in naming an action demonstrated by the examiner: he could easily identify the actions of getting up, sitting down, putting one's hands in one's pocket, walking, raising one's hands, and the like, with an appropriate sentence and the correct participial verb form. Konorski noted that his patient's speech was almost exclusively filled with verb forms and notably lacked noun forms. While the patient could not name objects, he could and did describe them in functional terms (circumlocution); in the examples, the target object is to the left in parentheses and the patient's response follows:

11. (knife)   this is for cutting
    (pencil)   this is for writing
    (cigarette)   this is for smoking

The aphasic patient who blocks on a particular word may or may not recognize that word if cued by the examiner; that is, some patients just simply do not appear to have any recognition or understanding of the lexical item that they cannot retrieve. The more usual case, however, is that the patient will overtly demonstrate some knowledge of the word he is trying to retrieve, either by giving a circumlocution that indicates the function, by producing a word in a similar semantic field, by providing a partial description of the word or object he is attempting to name, or by producing an approximate attempt that bears a strong phonetic resemblance to the target word. A patient reported in Whitaker's study (1971), best characterized as a fluent anomic, was attempting to read the printed sentence *He eats his breakfast*, which was part of a children's story. His attempts to read this sentence are given in example 12; he clearly indicated by pointing that the word *breakfast* was the main problem he had in reading the sentence aloud:

12. To have, something to eat. He's having food which is /tʃ əɹ/, to eat in the morning and it's the first thing you eat for, for morning. . . he's eating, right here, your /ɛf/.

His best approximations to *breakfast* were *chur* and *ef* but it is clear that he understood the word and when he was asked if he was trying to say the word breakfast he *immediately* assented. Interestingly enough, he usually could not repeat aloud the words he had difficulty in reading, no matter how carefully he was cued by the examiners.

Another aspect of the word-finding problem, which illustrates one of the strategies employed by patients whose productive language is impaired in this manner, is the so-called empty speech of the receptive aphasic. In this case there is a continual reliance on indefinite nouns and pronouns, without overt specification of what they refer to. A sample of an interview with such a patient, who had sustained a temporo-parietal lesion, is shown in example 13:

13. Examiner: How long have you been sick?

  Patient: Well, I think it started, it began first, that was the first one, the first one that had before any of it, I don't know if it was but somebody did once.

In this case, direct cueing of individual words did not help the patient retrieve the content words, although a lengthy description helped; that is, if the examiner asked the patient directly if he was talking about his head injury, the patient did not understand the question. If, however, the examiner asked the same question using several descriptive phrases, such as *Are you talking about the blow on your head that you received when you fell down the cliff, when you hit your head on the rocks, and were knocked unconscious?* then the patient would frequently indicate assent or disagreement. Needless to say, the examiner was often wrong about what the patient was trying to discuss, and some exchanges would continue for ten or fifteen minutes before the topic of the conversation could be ascertained. Leaving aside the strategy of employing indefinite nouns or pronouns, though, another aspect of lexical organization can be seen in such responses: indefinite words are not randomly accessed in the mental grammar, but are associated with large semantic classes with appropriate syntactic links. Words like *it, one, stuff, way, thing, business, someone,* and the like, may retain their feature representations in terms of (animate/inanimate), (singular/plural) or (human/nonhuman) such that speech output is syntactically quite normal albeit semantically vague or even vacuous.

Experience with different kinds of lexical impairments in different aphasic syndromes leads us to conclude that there are three principal points at which the process of lexical retrieval or use can be affected: (*a*) the initial access itself may be affected in which case there is a simple block (in these cases, cueing will not help); (*b*) the output may be blocked, although internally access may have taken place in a relatively accurate manner (in these cases, cueing does help and recognition of the cue is rapid and accurate); and (c) access and retrieval take place, but the process is impaired at some point so that the final output is in error (in these cases the errors may be phonological, syntactic, or semantic in nature). The third situation is the one which produces data that can provide insights into the organization of the mental lexicon. Evidently, each of these components or levels has a separate functional status because they may be separately impaired: the semantic representation of a word including its featural components, the syntactic categorization of a word, and the phonological structure of a word including separate representation of segments and their sequential order.

Conclusion

Clearly, linguistic theory has already outlined all of these details of lexical structure as well as others not mentioned; however, this fact can easily obscure the more important datum—linguistic theory is neutral as to whether the brain actually makes use of these sundry distinctions, and as to whether there is psychological reality to theoretical entities. What the aphasic data indicate by virtue of dissociated impairments are the functional mental status of these theoretical entities.

It is unlikely that aphasic patients are restructuring their deficient language systems into new, simpler, or different grammars. Rather, it seems as though genuine aspects of the mental grammar are impaired, occasionally in relative isolation, although it is important to take account of other factors of performance as well, for example, word frequency, stress or salience, motivation, position in the utterance, and the obvious factors of intelligence and education.

Some linguistic deficits cut across topography; a common linguistic pattern can be found in the impaired language of patients who have clinically distinct syndromes. Localization is not the issue here, the structure of the mental grammar is (see Blumstein, 1973; Gardner, 1973; Poeck, Orgass, Kerschensteiner, and Hartje, 1974). The errors seen in aphasia, like the errors seen in normal slips of the tongue, and probably like the errors seen in schizophrenia, reveal aspects of the linguistic structure of the mental grammar. The aphasia data have the additional advantage in that insights into which parts of the brain underlie components of the mental grammar can sometimes be obtained.

REFERENCES

Avakian-Whitaker, H. A case of the isolation of the language function. In H. Avakian-Whitaker and H. Whitaker, eds., *Studies in neurolinguistics*. New York: Academic Press, in press.

Avakian-Whitaker, H., and Whitaker, H., eds. *Studies in neurolinguistics*. Vols. 1 and 2. New York: Academic Press, in press.

Blumstein, S. *A phonological investigation of aphasic speech*. The Hague: Mouton, 1973.

Boller, F., and Green, E. Comprehension in severe aphasics. *Cortex*, 1972, *8*, 382-94.

Brown, J. *Aphasia, apraxia and agnosia*. Springfield: C. C. Thomas, 1972.

Buckingham, H. W., and Kertesz, A. A linguistic analysis of fluent aphasia. *Brain and Language*, 1974, *1*, 43-61.

Caplan, D., Kellar, L., and Locke, S. Inflection of neologisms in aphasia. *Brain*, 1972, *95*, 169-72.

Dingwall, W. O., and Whitaker, H. A. Neurolinguistics. In *Annual review of anthropology*. Palo Alto: Annual Review, 1974, pp. 323-56.

Freud, S. *On aphasia*, 1891. (English translation, London: Imago, 1953.)

Gardner, H. The contribution of operativity to naming capacity in aphasic patients. *Neuropsychologia*, 1973, *11*, 213-20.

Geschwind, N. On disconnexion syndromes in animals and man. *Brain*, 1965, *88*, 237-94 and 585-645.

———. The varieties of naming errors. *Cortex*, 1967, *3*, 97-112.

Geschwind, N., Quadfasel, F. A., and Segarra, J. M. Isolation of the speech area. *Neuropsychologia*, 1968, *6*, 327-40.

Goldstein, K. *Language and language disturbances*. New York: Grune and Stratton, 1948.

Goldstein, M. N. Auditory agnosia for speech (pure word deafness). *Brain and Language*, 1974, *1*, 195-204.

Goodglass, H. Agrammatism. In H. Avakian-Whitaker and H. Whitaker, eds., *Studies in neurolinguistics*. New York: Academic Press, in press.

Goodglass, H., Gleason, J., Bernholtz, N., and Hyde, M. Some linguistic structures in the speech of a Broca's aphasic. *Cortex*, 1972, *8*, 191-212.

Goodglass, H., and Kaplan, E. *The assessment of aphasia and related disorders*. Philadelphia: Lea and Febiger, 1972.

Green, E. On the contribution of studies in aphasia to psycholinguistics. *Cortex*, 1970, *6*, 216-35.

Head, H. *Aphasia and kindred disorders of speech*. New York: Hafner, 1926. (Republished, 1963.)

Hacaen, H., and Consoli, S. Analyse des troubles du langage au cours des lesions de l'aire de Broca. *Neuropsychologia*, 1973, *11*, 377-88.

Johns, D. F., and Darley, F. L. Phonemic variability in apraxia of speech. *JSHR*, 1970, *13*, 556-83.

Johns, D. F., and LaPointe, L. Neurogenic disorders of output processing: Apraxia of speech. In H. Avakian-Whitaker and H. Whitaker, eds., *Studies in neurolinguistics*. New York: Academic Press, in press.

Kehoe, W., and Whitaker, H. A. Lexical structure disruption in aphasia: A case study. In H. Goodglass and S. Blumstein, eds., *Psycholinguistics and aphasia.* Baltimore: Johns Hopkins, 1973.

Kinsbourne, M. Behavioral analysis of the repetition deficit in conduction aphasia. *Neurology,* 1972, *22,* 1126-32.

Kinsbourne, M., and Rosenfield, D. B. Agraphia selective for written spelling: An experimental case study. *Brain and Language,* 1974, *1,* 215-26.

Konorski, J. *Integrative activity of the brain.* Chicago: University of Chicago, 1967.

Lecours, A. R., and Caplan, D. Review of S. Blumenstein, A phonological investigation of aphasic speech. *Brain and Language,* 1975, *2,* 237-54.

Luria, A. R. Neuropsychology in the local diagnosis of brain damage. *Cortex,* 1964, *1,* 3-18.

––––––. *Traumatic aphasia.* The Hague: Mouton, 1970.

Marshall, M., Newcombe, F., and Marshall, J. The microstructure of word-finding difficulties in a dysphasia subject. In G. B. Flores d'Arcais and W. Levelt, eds., *Advances in psycholinguistics.* Amsterdam: North-Holland, 1971, pp. 416-26.

Poeck, K., Orgass, B., Kerchensteiner, M., and Hartje, W. A qualitative study on token test performance in aphasic and non-aphasic brain damanged patients. *Neuropsychologia,* 1974, *12,* 49-54.

Rinnert, C., and Whitaker, H. A. Semantic confusions by aphasic patients. *Cortex,* 1973, *9,* 56-81.

Schnitzer, M. L. *Generative phonology: Evidence from aphasia.* University Park: Pennsylvania State University Press, 1972.

Watt, W. C. Mentalism in linguistics II. *Glossa,* 1974, *8,* 1-38.

Whitaker, H. A. *On the representation of language in the human brain.* Edmonton: Linguistic Research, 1971.

––––––. Unsolicited nominalizations by aphasics: The plausibility of the lexicalist hypothesis. *Linguistics,* 1972, *78,* 62-71.

––––––. Disorders of speech production mechanisms. In E. C. Carterette and M. Friedman, eds., *Handbook of perception.* Vol. 7, chapter 17. New York: Academic Press, in press.

Zurif, E. B., Caramazza, A., and Myerson, R. Grammatical judgments of agrammatic aphasics. *Neuropsychologia,* 1972, *10,* 405-17.

Zurif, E. B., and Caramazza, A. Psycholinguistic structures in aphasia: Studies in syntax and semantics. In H. Avakian-Whitaker and H. Whitaker, eds., *Studies in neurolinguistics.* New York: Academic Press, in press.

XIII

Language Testing

John W. Oller, Jr.

Ever since Carroll's paper on fundamental considerations in language testing first appeared (1961), the controversy over the *discrete-point* versus the *integrative* approach to language testing has continued to build. This very controversy marked clear lines of division among an international group of researchers at the 1974 Language Testing Symposium held in Washington, D.C., sponsored by several agencies of the federal government and the Testing Commission of the International Association of Applied Linguistics. Differences in viewpoint ranged from the advocacy of discrete-point tests instead of integrative tests, to a mixture of the two, to advocacy of integrative tests. The significance of the controversy was highlighted by Spolsky, one of the organizers of the symposium, in his concluding remarks when he suggested that the conflict was likely to be a major theme of research for years to come.

Historically, the discrete-point approach articulated by Lado in *Language Testing* (1961) antedates the integrative approach. The methodology which Lado developed has largely dominated professional practices ever since. Carroll's paper took Lado's book into account and noted the fundamental differences between what Carroll labeled the *discrete-point* approach, typified by the methodology Lado preferred, and the *integrative* approach, which Carroll himself preferred. Although three other major books on language testing (Clark, 1972; Harris, 1969; Valette, 1967) have appeared since Lado's, not to mention a great many articles (Gradman, 1973), the discrete-point approach is still the basis for most extant published tests.

The discrete-point approach to language testing requires the isolation of skills (such as listening, speaking, reading, and writing), aspects of skills (such as recognition versus production, or auditory versus visual processing), components of skills (such as phonology, morphology, syntax, and lexicon), and finally, discrete elements (such as phonemes, morphemes, phrase structures, etc.). In general, the discrete-point approach requires different subtests for each skill, aspect, and component. Each subtest in its turn must consist of separate items which sample the distinctive elements within that particular skill, aspect, and component.

The integrative approach to language testing, on the other hand, tries to measure global proficiency and pays little attention to particular skills, aspects, components, or specific elements of skills. It is worth noting that integrative testing procedures have scarcely been defined except in opposition to discrete-point procedures. Whereas the discrete-point method analyzes, the integrative method synthesizes. While the one tries to measure language proficiency point by point, in clearly demarcated bits and pieces, the other tries to get at what Spolsky et al. (1968) called *overall proficiency*. The items of a discrete test purport to be like a series of well-aimed rifle shots intended for a matching series of particular well-defined targets (namely, discrete elements of grammatical knowledge); an integrative test, on the other hand, is more like a grenade thrown in the general vicinity of a not very well-defined target (namely, the internalized grammar of the learner).

As Upshur (1969) noted, trends in language testing have tended to follow trends in language teaching, and the latter have tended to follow trends in linguistics. The truth of Upshur's observation is apparent in Lado's appeal to contrastive analysis as a basis for the construction of test items. According to Lado, "contrastive analysis" was the scientific basis of language teaching; consequently language teaching in his view was based on the "linguistic analysis of language." Because of the direction of the influence, from linguistics to language teaching to language testing, there have been significant (though perhaps necessary) lags from the time an insight is developed in linguistic theory to the time of its application in language testing. Until recently there has been hardly any influence in the opposite direction, from language-testing research to linguistic theory (however, see Carroll, 1972).

The linguistic theory from which many of the concepts of contrastive analysis were derived was decidedly *not* the linguistic theory of the late 1950s contemporaneous with Lado's writings on language teaching and language testing. His work on language teaching was based primarily on the linguistic theory of Bloomfield (1933). By the early 1960s, however, about the time that the book *Language Testing* appeared, Chomsky's views on linguistics had already risen to prominence. Nevertheless, Bloomfieldian-based contrastive studies were still preeminent in language teaching texts, and those texts in their turn provided the chief basis for the discrete-point approach to language testing.

The time lag between the development of a new paradigm in linguistics and its application in language teaching is illustrated in the fact that what is probably the best known contrastive study ever completed (Stockwell, Bowen, and Martin, 1965), appeared in the same year as Chomsky's *Aspects of the Theory of Syntax*. By that time, the discrete-point approach to language testing had already been crystallized in the first form of the *Test of English as a Foreign Language (TOEFL)* which had been produced in 1963. The *TOEFL*, which is easily the world's most used foreign language test, has remained in roughly the same format for the last twelve years (Kaplan, 1969; Oller and Spolsky, in press; and Slocum, 1969). Although the *TOEFL* planners rejected contrastive analysis as a basis for constructing items, they did so for practical reasons. Examinees to be tested ranged the world over and came from far too many different language backgrounds for contrastively based items to be practical. However, the *TOEFL* planners retained almost in toto the rest of the discrete-point approach advocated by Lado.

The first section of the discussion that follows focuses attention on the theoretical underpinnings and the practical methods of the discrete-point approach. The second section considers proposals for an eclectic synthesis of discrete-point and integrative approaches. The third and final section presents an alternative definition of integrative testing and argues that integrative tests can be placed on a firmer footing in terms of a pragmatic theory of expectancy grammar. Each of the three sections roughly characterizes competing trends in language-testing methods and research. Each trend will also be shown to have theoretical ties to linguistics, connections to language teaching, and relations to language-testing research.

Development of the Discrete-Point Approach to Language Testing

The term discrete-point approach (Carroll, 1961), clearly encapsulates the method Lado (1961) advocated. Lado implicitly and explicitly rejected what Carroll (1961) called the integrative approach, though Carroll never really defined integrative testing except by example and as the antithesis of discrete-point testing. Rand (1972, 1973, 1974) continued to define integrative testing by opposing it to discrete-point testing.

Roots of discrete-point philosophy. As a basis for the discrete-point approach, Lado (1961) referred back to the distinction that Bloomfield (1933) made between the "situation" and "the elements of language" (pp. 26-29), offering the following paraphrase of Bloomfield's argument:

> The situations in which language is the medium of communication are potentially almost infinite. . . . It is easy to find situations in which a person who speaks and understands a language natively fails to understand what is said because the subject matter is not within his experience.
>
> At the same time it is easy to think of situations in which one would understand what a speaker means even without understanding the language. . . (p. 26).
>
> . . . even if we could pick only valid situations and even if we could be sure that understanding these situations occurred through the language used, we would still have the problem of the great variety of situations which must be sampled.
>
> The elements of the language on the other hand are limited, and it is more profitable to sample these elements than to sample the great variety of situations in which language can be used (p. 27).

The discrete-point philosophy of language testing was capsulized in Lado's conclusion that ". . . we need to test the elements and the skills separately" (p. 28). For Lado the term *elements* sometimes meant phonemes, morphemes, phrases, clauses, and sentences (p. 25); sometimes it meant the skills themselves: "speaking, listening, reading, and writing" (p. 26); and yet at other times he clearly had in mind some subpartitioning of "skills" and "units." For instance, he claimed that because the list of "linguistic problems" to be tested (as determined by "a contrastive analysis") "will differ somewhat for production and for recognition, different lists are necessary to test the student's pronunciation in speaking and in listening" (p. 45).

Even when he used the term integrated test Lado meant no more than a collection of discrete-point items to test "the linguistic problems. . . with the accuracy that linguistic analysis [i.e., contrastive analysis] makes possible" (p. 29). For instance, with reference to the "integrated skill" of "auditory comprehension" he says:

> The test . . . will have to choose a few sounds and a few structures at random hoping to give a fair indication of the general achievement of the student (p. 28).

Thus, when he says that the language tester sometimes has a choice between a test of "elements" and a test of "skills" he apparently means that some discrete-point tests are appropriate for assessing knowledge of "separate elements" and others are appropriate for assessing "integrated skills" (p. 27).

In other words, Lado consistently argued in favor of discrète-point tests and never in favor of integrative tests (at least not in Carroll's sense of the term *integrative*). The division that Lado proposed of elements of language into units of structure like phonemes, morphemes, and so forth, as well as his concern for the differentiation of elements of language in the sense of the sound system versus the morphological system or in the sense of recognition versus production was related to a certain view of language structure.

The two dimensional matrix of skills (see figure 1) proposed by Harris (1969, p. 11) is reminiscent both of Lado and Bloomfieldian linguistics. Cooper (1972) suggested a similar but more elaborate three dimensional matrix. He included language variety as the third dimension. Whereas Harris's matrix suggests the possibility of sixteen different subtests, Cooper's matrix multiplied the figure to thirty-two cells.

Components	Language Skills			
	Listening	Speaking	Reading	Writing
Phonology/ Orthography				
Structure				
Vocabulary				
Rate and general fluency				

Fig. 1. A componential breakdown of test types (from Harris, 1969).

For reasons of economy, the call for so many different subtests was never fully adhered to in practice. Nevertheless, the widely used *TOEFL* to this day still embodies key points of discrete-point philosophy. It contains subsections for the measurement of listening comprehension, reading comprehension, and writing ability. This fact reflects the claim of discrete-point philosophy that different skills should be tested separately. Also, the subtests for English structure and vocabulary are evidence of the attempt to separate elements in the sense of components of grammar as well as the discrete points of structure or vocabulary contained in the items of those subtests.

Discrete-point-test philosophy was a natural outcome of an emphasis in structural linguistics on such principles as segmentation and classification. For example, having separate items for specific phonemes (or phonemic contrasts as Lado advocated) is a fairly obvious extension of what Chomsky (1964) called "taxonomic phonemics." Similarly, the insistence on separate subtests for components of phonology, morphology, etc., or aspects such as productive versus receptive in the various skills can also be traced to structural linguistics.

In addition to connections with structural linguistics, discrete-point philosophy has important ties with the prevailing psychometric methods of the 1950s. Lado relied heavily on notions gleaned from *The Mental Measurements Yearbook* series edited by Buros which summarized much of the serious psychometric thinking during the 1950s. Elsewhere Lado stressed the desirability of objective (that is, multiple choice) tests (p. 28). Spolsky (in press) suggests that this emphasis was a result of trends in educational measurements, and Stevenson (1974) documents the argument.

Connections to language teaching/learning.   Although many authors in recent years have challenged Lado's claim that tests should be based on a contrastive comparison of the target language against the native language, the influence of contrastive analysis is still felt in attempts to interpret test data diagnostically (Clark, 1972; Harris, 1969; and Ingram, 1968). Clark, for example, acknowledges shortcomings of language tests based on point-by-point comparisons of the target and native language (Upshur, 1962), but unflinchingly recommends items that test one point of structure at a time.

The joint influence of contrastive analysis and audio-lingual pattern drills can be seen in discrete-point-test philosophy. The concentration on the elements of language at the expense of the situation was perhaps carried to its greatest extreme in the language-learning theories of Morton (1960) and Brooks (1960). Both advocated that students should learn to "manipulate" the patterns before they attempted to "use them for communication." The issue was not so much what a particular sequence meant but how it was structurally similar to other sequences in the language. Thus, discrete-point proponents suggested the teaching and testing of such unlikely minimal pairs as *ship* and *sheep*. It is a rare context indeed where both could occur. They stressed the need for pattern drills to automatize grammatical inflections, and the conversion of statements to questions, affirmatives to negatives, actives to passives, all for the sake of illustrating or testing certain grammatical patterns. Disconnected and unlikely sentences such as *Are you tall?*, *Are you hungry?*, *I can come*, *I can wait*, *I can't come*, *I can't wait*, prevailed both in pattern drills and in the disjointed items of discrete-point tests.

Research. Very little research was conducted on the basis of discrete-point-test philosophy until the late 1960s and early 1970s. Naturally, research designs and the interpretation of results were influenced greatly by the prevailing theory. Typical studies in the 1960s, for instance, employed the traditional psychometrics of item analysis and occasionally looked at the correlations of part scores within the test being examined. Item analyses usually included measures of item difficulty and discrimination (that is, the tendency of a given item to divide proficient and nonproficient examinees in accord with total test scores, or possibly subtest scores). Correlations of part scores, as on the *TOEFL* for example, were expected to be low as discrete-point theory would predict.

Lado (1961) wrote, for instance:

> The problems in speaking are not necessarily the same as the problems in listening. For example, the question, "Does he speak?" is often a problem in speaking for some foreign students because they add an "s" ending to *speak* and say, "Does he speaks?" In listening, this is not a problem because the correct ending is given by the native speaker and it does not confuse the student (p. 24).

Thus, when intercorrelations of the several parts of *TOEFL* ranging from .49 to .80 were computed in a typical study (College Entrance Examination Board and Educational Testing Service, 1967), they were interpreted as indicating that the various subtests of the *TOEFL* were in fact measuring different skills as is required by discrete-point philosophy. However, no one has yet succeeded in identifying unique portions of test variance which can be attributed to well-defined and clearly distinct factors such as ability to read as opposed to ability to listen with comprehension. Until this is done, the research base of discrete-point philosophy remains weak. Studies such as the one by Rand (1972) notably failed to turn up unique portions of variance attributable to specific skills, aspects, components, or elements. Stevenson (1974) also failed to show higher correlations of the listening comprehension section of the *TOEFL* with an oral cloze test than with a written one.

Discrete-point philosophy has influenced some of the recent research which has purported to investigate or even advocate integrative testing procedures. This is especially true for the widely publicized cloze procedure in which every *n*th word of a text is deleted and the examinee must attempt to fill in the resulting "blanks." Some researchers have inadvertently focused attention on certain grammatical structures or, more obviously still, have deliberately salted a passage with particular patterns or have deleted only certain morphological endings or the like (see Bondaruk, Child and Tetrault, 1974; Davies, 1974; Gould and Spencer, 1974). In each of these cases, the experiment with an integrative technique is in part aborted by the surreptitious presupposition that discrete-point philosophy was actually right all along. Similarly, attempts to do what has been called criterion-referenced testing have resulted in discrete-point tests of specific points of knowledge (witness the tests recently constructed by the Defense Language Institute, Peterson and Cartier, 1974).

The Eclectic Synthesis of Discrete-Point Philosophy and Integrative Testing

The merging of discrete-point and integrative testing was proposed first by Rivers (1967, 1968) and later by Clark (1972); however, it was hinted at in Carroll (1961):

> The work of Lado and other language testing specialists has correctly pointed to the desirability of testing for very specific items of language knowledge and skill judiciously sampled from the usually enormous pool of possible items. This makes for highly reliable and valid testing. It is the type of approach which is needed and recommended . . . where knowledge of structure and lexicon, auditory discrimination and oral production of sounds, and reading and writing of individual symbols and words are to be tested (p. 34).

However, Carroll indicated preference for another type of test altogether:

> If we limit ourselves to testing only one point at a time, more time is ordinarily allowed for reflection than would occur in a normal com-

munication situation, no matter how rapidly the discrete items are presented. For this reason I recommend tests in which there is less attention paid to specific structure points or lexicon than to the total communicative effect of an utterance (p. 34).

His further arguments in favor of integrative testing included the following points: (1) it improves the sampling procedure; (2) it is generally applicable to language testing problems which are independent of any particular curriculum; (3) anticipation and interpretation of test results are more straightforward; and (4) it does away with contrastive analysis for item construction (p. 34).

No doubt Carroll's remarks influenced Rivers (1968), who, like Clark (1972), advocated an eclectic synthesis of discrete-point and integrative testing:

Just as the teacher needs to identify the specific skill he wishes to test, so he must distinguish carefully the various aspects of that skill and test these one by one, as well as finally testing them as part of an all-round performance (p. 296).

In spite of their eclecticism, however, Rivers and Clark both insisted on a clear distinction between discrete-point tests and integrative tests— Clark labeled the former "diagnostic achievement tests" and referred to the latter as "general achievement tests" (Clark, 1972, p. 26). The former he identified with "linguistic proficiency *per se*" and the latter he associated with "the ability to communicate readily and effectively in real-life situations." He argued that the two "have tenuous correlation" (p. 119) and that this was the reason for keeping them clearly separate. With reference to the Oral Interview technique used by the Foreign Service Institute, for example, he said:

The mixing of communicative and linguistic criteria in a single testing system or rating scheme serves only to obscure the distinction between the two types of measurement and decrease the validity of the test as a direct measure of communicative proficiency (p. 126).

Relation to linguistic theory. It is not difficult to see the connection between Clark's argument for keeping the two testing techniques separate and the Chomskyan distinction between linguistic competence and linguistic performance. Early Chomskyan linguistics made a clearcut distinction between the capacity of the native speaker to use his language and actual instances of use in real-life situations. However, it had become apparent to many linguists in the early 1960s that the attempt to capture and express the native speaker's intuitions concerning his language in a grammar that had no semantic component was strangely anomalous (see the review of Chomsky, 1957, by Reichling, 1961). Hymes (1962) insisted that communicative competence was just as creative as the linguistic competence defined in Chomsky's early writings. Hymes argued that language teachers and practically minded theorists ought to be concerned with communicative competence rather than any purely autonomous syntactic knowledge of language, or linguistic competence.

Actually the controversy was manifested (perhaps unknowingly) in the two types of tests advocated by Clark and Rivers: on the one hand discrete-point tests concentrated on structural aspects of language (something that might be identified with linguistic competence), while on the other integrative tests concentrated on the communicative use of language in tasks parallel to real-life situations (something that might be identified with communicative competence).

Eclecticism in language teaching/learning.   The roots of the eclectic philosophy advocated by Clark and Rivers can be found in language teaching. Clark says that Rivers (1967) drew

> a distinction between two hypothetical levels of progress in learning to understand a spoken foreign language. The first or "recognition" level is considered to include the development of an ability to discriminate the phonemes of the target language and to perceive the distinctive elements of pitch and intonation. Also included in the first level of accomplishment is the perception of structural interrelationships among the various component elements of spoken utterances. Most aspects of "spoken grammar" would be included under this rubric, including the recognition of tense cues, person, number, "actor" and "acted-upon," and other syntactically or morphologically determined features of sentence structure (pp. 42-43).

Clark adds:

> According to Rivers, second-level ability cannot be effectively acquired unless the first-level perception of grammatical cues and other formal interrelationships among spoken utterances has become so thoroughly learned and so automatic that the student is able to turn most of his listening attention to "those elements which seem to him to contain the gist of the message" (p. 43).

It is a short step from seeing certain elements of structure as first-level skills to seeing discrete-point-testing procedures as appropriate to first-stage testing. Clark claimed that discrete-point items are best for testing "sound discriminations, basic patterns of spoken grammar, items of functional vocabulary and so forth" (p. 43), and he related integrative tests to a more advanced stage of learning:

> As the instructional emphasis changes from formal work on discrete aspects to more extensive and less closely controlled listening practice, the utility (and also the possibility) of diagnostic testing is reduced in favor of evaluative procedures which test primarily the student's comprehension of the "general message" rather than the apprehension of certain specific sounds or sound patterns (p. 43).

Discrete-point tests are for the first stage and integrative tests are for the second and never shall they meet. The gap between the two methods is mirrored in what Bowen and Stockwell (1968) identified as "the most difficult transition in learning a language," namely, the problem of "going from mechanical skill in reproducing patterns acquired by repetition to the construction of novel but appropriate sentences in natural social contexts" (p. vii). Bowen and Stockwell hint at the same two stages of language learning advocated by Brooks, Morton, Rivers, and Clark: "language teachers meet with beginning classes with confidence; they not infrequently fumble and despair in later courses, however, when confronted with the challenge of leading students comfortably over this hurdle" (p. vii).

Research into the eclectic position.   If the eclectic position is basically correct, there should be research to demonstrate Clark's claim that discrete-point tests are more obviously correlated with each other than they are with integrative tests. For example, discrete-point tests of reading comprehension should be more highly correlated with each other than with tests of listening comprehension. Furthermore, we should find higher correlations between alternate forms of subtests of grammatical knowledge, for example, than between a grammar subtest and vocabulary subtest. A subtest of vocabulary ought to correlate better with another vocabulary test than with a reading comprehension subtest, or an oral interview, etc. In general, subtests within skills, components, aspects, and elements of skills ought to intercorrelate better than the same subtests across skills, components, etc.

As noted already there is a general failure of discrete-point-test research to demonstrate clearly separable components of skills with unique variances. What research has tended to reveal is the opposite: a tendency for all of the subcomponents of a test like the *TOEFL*, or the *UCLA English as a Second Language Placement Examination* (*UCLA ESLPE*) or the *Michigan Test of English Language Proficiency* or just about any battery of language tests to load on one major factor which can be identified only with global language proficiency. Also, if one looks at individual correlations of part scores, certain facts arise that are anomalous within the discrete-point theoretical framework. Pike (1973) found that the listening comprehension section of the *TOEFL* correlated as well with scores on an essay writing task as did scores on the writing ability section of the *TOEFL*. Similar results are reported by Stubbs and Tucker (1974), using the *English Entrance Exam* at the American University of Beirut (*AUB EEE*); Irvine, Atai, and Oller (1974), using the *TOEFL*; and by Rand (1972) using the *UCLA ESLPE*.

Integrative Testing as Pragmatic Testing

A pragmatic theory of expectancy grammar incorporating an element of real time provides a theoretical basis for integrative tests. Arguments for contextualizing materials to be learned in a foreign or second language setting provide the connection with language teaching/learning theory, and a good deal of research exists in support of the proposed framework.

Pragmatics and expectancy grammar. Until recently no grammatical theory existed which was equipped to explain the findings of language-testing research. Clearly, a theory of the sort advocated by Chomsky (1957), which did not attempt to explain the instrumental use of language, could only be used to support some version of discrete-point testing, or at best a version of integrative testing that would stop short of full communication. When Chomsky (1965) modified his position to incorporate the thinking of Katz and Fodor (1963) and Katz and Postal (1964), the grammar was still a mechanism which associated structural descriptions with sentences in isolation. There was no attempt to relate sentences to the contexts of communication.

More recently, however, theorists have begun to turn attention to pragmatics in addition to phonology, syntax, and semantics. In the 1960s linguists began to discuss theories which attempted to incorporate a semantic component and in the 1970s discussions of pragmatic questions have become socially acceptable. Fraser, the Lakoffs, Fillmore, and other leading transformationalists, not to mention philosophers and logicians like Searle and Montague, mathematical linguists like Woods, and sociolin-

guists like Gumperz and Hymes are bringing a formidable array of expertise to bear on the difficult problems of speech acts—as distinct from
sentences in the abstract. A crucial question in all these pragmatic investigations is: under what conditions can a sentence (or any other unit) be used
in order to achieve a particular communicative effect?

As Watzlawick, Beavin, and Jackson (1967) have emphasized, it is
important to distinguish between *content level* and *relationship level* communication. Fraser (1974) uses the terms *sentence meaning* and *sentence
force* with somewhat the same distinction in mind. If someone says *Strange
mountains loom in the fog*, he may be making a statement of fact, or issuing
a warning, or quoting the first line of a poem, or doing any number of other
things. In each case, the sentence meaning or content is relatively constant, but the sentence force or relationship, that is, the way the sentence is
to be taken, varies.

Often, in English at least, sentence meaning is determined by the
encoding of certain words, phrases, clauses, etc., whereas sentence force is
determined mainly by tone of voice, volume, rhythm, gesture, facial
expression, and the like. Also, sentence meaning is generally concerned
with objective facts and situations while sentence force is concerned with
attitudes and subjective valuations that are emotionally potent, particularly
in the realm of human relationships and self-concept. Linguists have often
preferred to leave the relationship level of communication to the
sociologists and the psychologists, but recent grammatical investigations
have forced some of these thorny problems to the forefront. To say whether
a speech act is one of promising, requesting, lying, asserting, persuading,
informing, demanding, insisting, or something else forces decisions about
issues that bristle with troublesome matters of attitudes and value systems.

Fillmore (1971) hinted at the need to grapple with value systems in his
discussion of a possible benefactive case. Fraser (1974) tried to limit attention to illocutionary acts rather than perlocutionary acts, but he admitted
doubts as to whether the two could be consistently distinguished. If illocutionary acts inform and perlocutionary acts persuade, the distinction
seems clear. However, it breaks down immediately if we admit that informing someone of something is causing them to believe something they did
not believe before. When perlocutionary acts that change belief systems
are introduced, the grammar gets tied into some sort of value system.

Regardless of how the many puzzles that perplex the theoreticians are
resolved, one of the clear results of pragmatic investigations thus far is that
speech acts are immensely more complicated than the theories of structural
and transformational grammars might have led us to believe. They have

properties and complexities to which the earlier linguistic theories were impervious. One of the factors which contributes to the uniqueness and complexity of speech events in real life is the element of time. Until very recently, most grammatical theories ignored this factor. Taxonomic structuralisms and transformational syntaxes alike operated without reference to real time.

Carroll (1961) indicated that he saw the element of time as a crucial factor in explaining the superiority of integrative tests over discrete-point tests. Whenever native-language users understand and utter sentences even in simple speech acts, they do so with amazing rapidity and ingenuity. The listener who is comprehending what is being said is always at least partly hypothesizing what the speaker will say next. Sometimes the speaker says something that was completely unexpected, and when this happens dramatic reversals in previous hypotheses may be made, or the listener may hypothesize that the speaker misspoke and maintain his former hypotheses. By the same token, the speaker is planning what to say some distance ahead of what is being articulated at any given moment and, as Chafe (1974) has demonstrated, he is anticipating to a great extent what the listener will infer from what is said.

The remarkable speed as well as the intricacy with which native-language users integrate their own grammar-based expectancies with the physical phonetic forms of speech acts requires explanation in linguistic theories. From the listener's point of view, grammar-based expectancies may be thought of as confirmed hypotheses about what the speaker has said and tentative ones about what he is apt to say next, and from the speaker's point of view they are plans concerning what to say next and hypotheses about what the listener has so far understood. From the reader's vantage point, grammar-based expectancies are confirmed hypotheses concerning the writer's intentions and tentative hypotheses about what is coming next in the context. From the writer's point of view, they are hypotheses about what the reader has so far understood and plans about where to go next.

Thus, the kind of grammar that would do the sorts of integrative tasks that language users perform in speech acts might be termed an *expectancy grammar*. A primitive model that characterizes how such a grammar might operate is suggested by the work of Woods (1970), and in Woods and Makhoul (1973). The *recursive transition network model* (Woods, 1970) is capable of interpreting sentences that are transformationally complex, and it provides insight into aspects of sentence interpretation that have been obscured by the more traditional transformational models. Woods's grammar interprets sentences by generating grammatical descriptions which incorporate semantic information.

We can extend the principles embodied in Woods's model to the case of a real expectancy grammar incorporating semantic and pragmatic information by illustrating how a sentence like *Strange mountains loom in the fog* might be interpreted. No claim to completeness for the proposed analysis is intended.

As soon as the lexical item *strange* is recognized, the grammar hypothesizes that it is encountering a noun phrase and it expects a head noun to follow the identified adjective. It expects moreover that the noun phrase it has encountered is the subject of a declarative sentence. The content-level meaning of *strange* as an adjective is retrieved and depending on the tone of voice with which it is uttered and the context of the speech act itself, an attitude is formed which constitutes a tentative hypothesis about what the speaker's attitude toward the meaning is. This hypothesis may help the listener (or in this speech act, the reader) to decide what sort of speech act he is interpreting. (In this case, because of its context the reader is likely to hypothesize confidently that the model sentence is an act of exemplifying or illustrating intended to inform and possibly also persuade the reader on the topic of expectancy grammar. The reader may be in doubt as to whether the example is to be taken seriously or lightly.)

When the grammar encounters *mountains* and recognizes it as a plural noun, it takes the noun phrase *strange mountains* as the expected subject and it continues processing expecting to encounter a predicate in the form of a verb phrase. The grammar associates the noun phrase with either strange mountains that are in fact visible, or it infers a situation in which strange mountains could be said to appear. This leads to subsequent expectations about the kinds of predicates or modifiers that might follow. The grammar specifies that there may be one or more adjectival phrases (like *with snowy peaks*) or clauses (such as *that I saw in my dreams*) but they fail to materialize and the plural verb *loom* appears. The lexicon has *loom* as a noun or a verb, but in this case it can only be a verb because the grammar has no way of interpreting the noun phrase *strange mountains loom* (of course, *strange mountain looms* would present a different problem—it too could be resolved, however, by the same methods), and besides, the grammar is expecting a verb and *loom* can be taken as a verb. If the grammar were not equipped to handle intonational cues, this could be the end of a sentence: *Strange mountains loom*. However, we are assuming the grammar is equipped to take advantage of the fact that intonation, even if the speaker pauses, would serve as a cue that there is more to come in this sentence. The grammar may note the fact that the stylistic tone of the adjective *strange* and the verb *loom* harmonize and this may confirm or disconfirm the hypothesis formed earlier concerning the speaker's attitude toward the meaning of the utterance. Because the grammar specifies a wealth of information about what sorts of objects may be referred to as *mountains* and what kinds of circumstances may be referred to as *strange*, and because the grammar specifies what it is for something to *loom*, certain expectations are formed concerning the nature of the state of affairs that is being referred to (whether metaphorically or actually, or both is irrelevant at this point). The syntactic limitations of the grammar specify that the sorts of things that may follow the verb *loom* are adverbs of time, such as *at five in the morning*, or *at dawn*; adverbs of manner such as *suddenly*, or *frighteningly*; or adverbs of location such as *in the fog, out of the night, on the horizon*; or some combination of the foregoing such as *out of the fog in the early morning*. When the grammar finds *in the fog* with a terminal intonation contour, the previous hypothesis concerning the interpretation of the preceding elements is sustained and the terminal intonation pattern indicates the completion of the sentence.

Of course, having said all of the foregoing about the interpretation of the exemplary sentence, we have not finished saying by any means what hypotheses the expectancy grammar is likely to continue to generate concerning subsequent parts of the hypothetical speech act (or the real one for that matter that is occurring as the writer and reader, at different times, work through this prose). If the speaker were to continue *The Captain shouts, "This ship's off course": He scans his log*, the listener might correctly infer that this was an act of quoting poetry—if he were a particularly well-read listener, he might even identify the poem as "Dead Reckoning" by Rail, a contemporary American poet.

The example illustrates some of the parameters embraced by a pragmatic theory of expectancy grammar. It suggests a basis for describing integrative or pragmatic tests as tests that invoke the expectancy grammar of the learner. One may complain that as the notion of expectancy grammar has just been described, there is no way to differentiate between a language test and a test of knowledge of the world. This is largely true. However, whether or not it is a criticism of the proposed framework for integrative language testing is an empirical question. The problem is whether or not real grammars incorporate such knowledge.

Within the proposed framework, it is possible to redefine the purpose of a language test as one of assessing the efficiency of the expectancy grammar of the learner. The problem of test validation is to show that a particular test or testing technique does in fact assess the efficiency of the learner's grammar. The research reported below concerns this definition of the test validation problem and examines the operational basis for defining the *efficiency of the internalized grammar*.

Concomitant with the move away from contrastive analysis and point-by-point structure drills there has been a resurgence of emphasis on the meaningful sequence of normal communicative events. Generally, you do not approach someone on the street and proceed to recite "The Night Before Christmas." Nor do you in normal circumstances utter the sort of nonsense that Samuel Foote immortalized about the "she bear that ambled up the street, popped her head in the shop and very imprudently married the barber. . . ." In the usual contexts of communication, saying a poem or uttering nonsense out of the clear blue is rarely encountered except in the writings of linguists who are fond of exemplifying abnormal speech acts. As Jespersen (1904) stressed, there is a certain connection between the utterances that occur in normal communication. Or, as Watzlawick and his collaborators put it more recently, *"in a communicational sequence, every exchange of messages narrows down the number of possible next moves"* (1967, p. 131).

Both the verbal and nonverbal contexts of communication have the effect of limiting what may follow in any given sequence of elements, and they also have the effect of specifying and differentiating linguistic elements that might otherwise be confused (Richards, 1970, 1971). It can be seen quite easily how the adjective *strange* in the example discussed above serves to limit subsequent grammatical possibilities, and it is equally obvious that knowledge of the nature of objects which may be referred to as *strange mountains* serves to restrict possible predicates. It would surely be unusual if not in fact abnormal to say *Strange mountains danced in the fog*, or *Strange mountains pondered his circumstances*. Similarly, the state of affairs depicted by the sentence *The Captain shouts: "This ship's off course"* is serious if we have just heard in somber tones about the strange mountains looming in the fog, but if they had been dancing, surely the Captain's shout would have been interpreted differently. (Perhaps he was imbibing Christmas cheer on the quarterdeck?) Different contexts serve to differentiate similar linguistic sequences.

Because of these facts, it has been argued (Oller, 1963-65) that maximum contextualization of materials to be learned in language classrooms will facilitate the differentiation of linguistic sequences that are similar structurally to each other (as in pattern drills) and will increase the inherent redundancy of the material to be learned (as in dialogs or narratives).

The approach to foreign or second language teaching described briefly in the preceding paragraph assumes that the fundamental task of language teaching is to instill in the learner the sorts of expectancies concerning the relations between verbal sequences in the language and nonverbal contexts that the native speaker utilizes. Further, it is to provide the learner with the necessary and sufficient information for the internalization of the grammar of the language which specifies those relations. In brief, a pragmatic approach to language teaching attends to communication episodes as the basis for organization and subordinates syntactic and structural matters to the facts, attitudes, and situational contexts which accompany normal language communication.

Although the discrete-point philosophy of testing was based on a structure-dominated approach to language teaching, even its own sympathizers and advocates acknowledged that manipulative skills based on pattern drills alone would not be enough. The student had to make a difficult transition to communication. Similarly, in the eclectic merging of discrete-point and integrative philosophies, the gap between manipulative and communicative skills still existed (Clark, 1972, p. 126). However, when we come to integrative-test philosophy based on pragmatic language teaching, the gap or hurdle between manipulative and communicative skills is dissolved because the focus (as Jespersen urged) is on communicative events (or speech acts) from the very first day of instruction.

Moreover, if the teaching theory is related to a pragmatic linguistic theory, it is clear that communicative events are the smallest elements that either language courses or tests can profitably deal with. There is increasing recognition of this important fact in the *TOEFL* which, in its new form (as of September, 1976), will give greater emphasis to tasks which require the comprehension of life-like episodes of communication.

Research with pragmatic tests.   Whereas discrete-point testing had to rely on the testimony of experts from the beginning, integrative testing had to overcome it. Many language teachers used integrative testing procedures like essay writing, drama reenacting, reading aloud, dictation, fill-in-the-blank, translation, oral interview, and other tasks, but such techniques were usually not favored by the experts.

A few isolated empirical studies appeared in the early 1960s but usually the conclusions they drew were cautiously weakened to avoid offending the prevailing discrete-point theory. Nevertheless, an occasional bold attempt appeared, such as the study by Valette (1964). She concluded that a dictation by itself worked about as well as a lengthier and *more difficult to prepare* traditional final examination (that is, a discrete-point test). Several years later, after considerable further experimentation, Johansson (1972, 1973) stated the case for dictation still more forcefully. In spite of what the discrete-point theorists said the research showed that unless the person giving the dictation made the error of reading the material at an unnaturally slow pace, a brief dictation requiring only a few minutes to administer provides an excellent global estimate of the examinee's ability to comprehend rapidly spoken sequences of the target language.

Furthermore, the research indicated that correlations between dictations and other pragmatic language tests fluctuated very little with variations in the level of difficulty of the passages (Oller, 1972). The average score for a given population varied with the difficulty level of the passage, but the test variance and its tendency to overlap with variances on other pragmatic tests tended to remain *relatively* constant. In short, the procedure proved to be exceedingly robust. Kirn (1972) has also shown that it resists a practice effect. This cannot be said of discrete-point tests which are apparently much too susceptible to practice effects (Upshur and Palmer, 1972).

Angelis (1972) showed that the kinds of errors that nonnative speakers make when taking dictation are similar in fundamental respects to the kinds of errors that they make in producing sequences in the target language. A similar conclusion may be drawn from research with cloze procedure (Bebout, 1974). Both studies contradict the maxim of discrete-point philosophy that the problem areas in one aspect of a skill will be different from those in another. They suggest that if a learner says *Does he speaks?*, to use Lado's example, he is also likely to hear *Does he speaks?*, when the question *Does he speak?* is uttered by a native speaker. A look at errors that nonnative speakers make in taking dictation (or even native speakers for that matter) will reveal immediately that the claim that reading and listening are passive skills where all the information is given is simply incorrect (see Johansson, 1973; and Wijnstra and Van Wageningen, in press). Another research report by Swain and Dumas (1974) drew similar conclusions on the basis of investigations of translation and imitation tasks. That is, a close look at the kinds of errors learners made in performing translation or imitation tasks revealed fundamental similarities between those errors and the kinds of errors the same learners made in spontaneous speech.

These results help to explain the remarkably high correlations that have recently been observed between tasks like listening comprehension (either taking dictation, or comprehending episodes of communication and answering questions about them as on the *TOEFL*) and cloze procedure. The former task utilizes an auditory input and the latter uses a visual one. Nevertheless, the observed correlations are extremely high—usually in the .7 to .9 range (Oller, 1972; Pike, 1973).

Another integrative technique that was proposed in the 1960s along with dictation and cloze procedure was Spolsky's noise test. The noise test reduces redundancy by using white noise to mask sentences recorded on tape. (White noise is simply a technical term for a broad spectrum of random noise sounding roughly like "shhhhhh.") Surprisingly, both procedures produce good estimates of global language skill and share the properties of robustness and resistance-to-practice effect described in connection with dictation above (Gradman and Spolsky, 1974).

The cloze procedure has repeatedly proven itself a reliable and valid measure of global language proficiency. Darnell (1968) may be credited with arguing the case for cloze procedure first, but his report was followed quickly by several independent studies (Anderson, 1969, 1971). Also, McLeod and Anderson (1966, 1970, 1972) have done extensive research with various aspects of cloze testing. An especially interesting study just completed by McLeod (in press) involved the construction and administration of cloze tests in five different languages (Czech, Polish, French, German, and English). McLeod's results generally confirm the earlier findings of Oller, Bowen, Dien, and Mason (1972), who investigated cloze tests in English, Thai, and Vietnamese. It is apparently the case that the procedure is not only applicable in widely different languages, but McLeod's study suggests ways of mathematically equating tests across languages in order to draw inferences about reading levels across linguistic and national boundaries.

Research with cloze procedure that falls more obviously within the purview of second language learning/teaching includes Oller (1972), using the *UCLA ESLPE* as a validating criterion; Pike (1973), using the *TOEFL* as criterion; and Stubbs and Tucker (1974), using the *AUB EEE*. In each case, the magnitude of the correlations between cloze procedure and other integrative tasks was surprisingly high. In all three studies the correlation between the exact-word-scoring method (counting as correct only the replacement of the word that was originally deleted) and either the contextually acceptable method (counting as correct any word that fit the total context of the passage) or the clozentropy method Darnell developed, was high enough (.94 to .97) to recommend the exact word scoring method for global proficiency testing purposes.

Item analyses of cloze tests generally indicate their superiority over discrete-point tests (Oller, 1972; Stubbs and Tucker, 1974). Moreover, in general, cloze tests and other integrative tests seem to correlate better with discrete-point tests than the latter intercorrelate with each other (Irvine, Atai, and Oller, 1974). This finding contradicts the prediction by Clark

(1972) and also Rand (1974) that there ought to be a tenuous correlation between what Clark called "diagnostic achievement tests" and "general proficiency tests." It seems that integrative tests are simply better windows through which to view language proficiency than are discrete-point tests. There is no research to indicate that the original insistence on the testing of one point and one skill at a time was correct, and there is much evidence to the contrary. It appears that it may not be just difficult to assess skills, aspects of skills, components of aspects, and atomlike elements separately; it may be quite impossible in principle. In any case, research indicates that attempts to do so have thus far been fruitless.

Research with integrative testing procedures has suggested a way to operationally define the *efficiency of the internalized expectancy grammar* of a particular learner. While discrete-point tests focused on the minute details revealed by the grammatical analyses that were prevalent in the 1950s, integrative tests seek an index of global proficiency. Such an index can be defined operationally by comparing nonnative performance against the criterion of native performance. For instance, if you want to know how well a foreign student reads in relation to college freshmen at some university, it is not difficult to test the performance of a representative sample of natives on an integrative reading task and test the foreign student on the same task and compare the results. It is assumed on the strength of linguistic theory that the native speaker's performance is the best criterion of grammatical skill against which to compare the performance of the nonnative.

The relative *efficiency* of the nonnative could also be defined in reference to a population of nonnatives, but this is a less desirable approach. If the test is normed against nonnatives rather than natives, there will probably be a tendency for its content and structure to gravitate toward classroom experience rather than to represent faithfully the normal expectancy grammars that native speakers have internalized. In other words, there may be a tendency for a language test to become a test of a kind of freak grammar that is internalized in the unusual and often artificial context of the classroom. One dramatic indication that this is possible came from a study by Angoff and Sharon (1971). Of sixty items on the writing ability section of the *TOEFL* (an error recognition task), thirteen items were easier for a large population of nonnatives than they were for a comparable group of native speakers. This result dramatically shows the possibility of test drift toward freak grammars due to the peculiar bias in the norming population. Such drift could be avoided if the test were referenced against native speaker performance.

The efficiency of any nonnative speaker's internalized grammar is to be judged operationally by comparing his score on the test with the score of the native speaker. Of course, it is possible to be more explicit in defining nonnative deficits in performance on a test in terms of specific errors. Contrary to some arguments, a comprehensive error analysis based on an integrative test (Clark, 1974; Davies, 1974) is apt to be more informative than a listing of the items missed on a discrete-point test. Integrative tests are apt to be far better instruments for diagnosing learner problems than discrete-point tests (see Angelis, 1972; Bebout, 1974; Dulay and Burt, 1974; Johansson, 1973; Richards, 1970; and Swain and Dumas, 1974). The explanation of an error on an integrative test is helped, not hindered, by the presence of a greater amount of context. On the other hand, to try to say why an examinee picked a particular alternative out of a set of alternatives on a discrete-point item is much more difficult.

REFERENCES

Anderson, J. Application of cloze procedure to English learned as a foreign language. Ph.D. dissertation, University of New England, Australia, 1969.
———. A technique for measuring reading comprehension and readability. *English Language Teaching*, 1971, 25, 178-82.
Angelis, Paul. Listening comprehension and error analysis. Paper presented at the Third International Congress of Applied Linguistics, Copenhagen, Denmark, 1972.
Angoff, W. H., and Sharon, A. T. A comparison of scores earned on the TOEFL by native American college students and foreign applicants to U.S. colleges. *TESOL Quarterly*, 1971, 5, 120-36.
Bebout, L. J. An error analysis: Comparing the ability of learners of English as a second language to extract information from written material. Ph.D. dissertation, Cornell University, 1974.
Bloomfield, L. *Language*. New York: Holt, Rinehart, and Winston, 1933.
Bondaruk, P., Child, R., and Tetrault, D. Language tests for the Department of Defense. Paper presented at the Language Testing Symposium, Washington, D.C., 1974.
Bowen, J. D., and Stockwell, R. Introduction to W. Rutherford, *Modern English: A textbook for foreign students*. New York: Harcourt, 1968.
Brooks, N. *Language and language learning: Theory and practice*. New York: McGraw Hill, 1960.
Carroll, J. B. Fundamental considerations in testing for English language proficiency of foreign students. *Testing*. Washington, D.C.: Center for Applied Linguistics, 1961. Reprinted in H. B. Allen and R. N. Campbell, eds., *Teaching English as a second language: A book of readings*, 2d ed. New York: McGraw Hill, 1972.

————. Defining language comprehension: Some speculations. In J. B. Carroll and Roy O. Freedle, eds., *Language comprehension and the acquisition of knowledge*. Washington, D.C.: Wiley, 1972.

Chafe, W. Language and consciousness. *Language*, 1974, *50*, 111-33.

Chomsky, N. *Syntactic structures*. The Hague: Mouton, 1957.

————. Current issues in linguistic theory. In J. Fodor and J. Katz, eds., *The structure of language: Readings in the philosophy of language*. Englewood Cliffs, N. J., Prentice Hall, 1964.

————. *Aspects of the theory of syntax*. Cambridge, Mass.: M.I.T. Press, 1965.

Clark, J. L. D. *Foreign language testing: Theory and practice*. Philadelphia: Center of Curriculum Development, 1972.

————. Theoretical and technical considerations in oral proficiency testing. Paper presented at the Language Testing Symposium, Georgetown University, Washington, D.C., 1974.

College Entrance Examination Board and Educational Testing Service. *TOEFL: Interpretive information*. Princeton: Authors, 1967.

Cooper, R. L. Testing. In H. B. Allen and R. N. Campbell, eds., *Teaching English as a second language: A book of readings*, 2d ed. New York: McGraw Hill, 1972.

Darnell, D. K. *The development of an English language proficiency test of foreign students using a clozentropy procedure: Final report*. Boulder: University of Colorado, US DHEW project no. 7-H-010, ERIC ED 024 039, 1968.

Davies, A. Two tests of speeded reading. Paper presented at the Language Testing Symposium, Georgetown University, Washington, D.C., 1974.

Dulay, H., and Burt, M. Natural sequences in second language acquisition. Paper presented at the Eighth Annual TESOL Convention, Denver, Colorado, 1974. In *Language Learning*, 1974, *24*, 37-53.

Fillmore, C. Some problems for case grammar. R. L. O. Brown, ed., *Twenty-second annual Georgetown monograph series on language and linguistics*. Washington, D.C.: Georgetown University Press, 1971.

Fraser, B. Review of J. Searle *Speech Acts*. *Foundations of Language*, 1974, *11*, 433-46.

Gould, J., and Spencer, J. Critical evaluation of the cloze procedure. Manuscript, American University, Cairo, Egypt, 1974.

Gradman, H. L. Fundamental considerations in the evaluation of foreign language proficiency. Paper presented at the International Seminar on Language Testing, San Juan, Puerto Rico, 1973.

Gradman, H. L., and Spolsky, B. Reduced redundancy testing: A progress report. Paper presented at the Language Testing Symposium, Georgetown University, Washington, D.C., 1974.

Harris, D. *Testing English as a second language*. New York: McGraw Hill, 1969.

Hymes, D. The ethnography of speaking. In T. Gladwin and W. C. Sturtevant, eds., *Anthropology and human behavior*. Washington, D.C.: Anthropological Society of America, 1962.

Ingram, E. Item analysis. In A. Davies, ed., *Language testing symposium*. London: Oxford University Press, 1968.

Irvine, P., Atai, P., and Oller, J., Jr. Cloze, dictation, and the Test of English as a

Foreign Language. *Language Learning*, 1974, *24*, 245-52.

Jesperson, O. *How to teach a foreign language*. London: Longmans, 1904.

Johansson, S. Controlled distortion as a language testing tool. Paper presented at the Third International Congress of Applied Linguistics, Copenhagen, Denmark, 1972.

———. Partial dictation as a test of foreign language proficiency. *Swedish English Contrastive Studies*, report no. 3, 1973.

Jones, Randall L., and Spolsky, B., eds. *Testing language proficiency*. Washington, D.C.: Center for Applied Linguistics, 1975. (Included in this book are the papers presented at the Language Testing Symposium, Washington, D.C., 1974.)

Kaplan, R. TOEFL in 1969—a reappraisal. *NAFSA Newsletter*, 1969, *21*, 7-9.

Katz, J., and Fodor, J. A. The structure of a semantic theory. *Language*, 1963, *39*, 170-210.

Katz, J., and Postal, P. M. *An integrated theory of linguistic descriptions*. Cambridge, Mass.: M.I.T. Press, 1964.

Kirn, H. The effect of practice on performance on dictations and cloze tests. *Workpapers in TESL*, 1972, *6*, 102.

Lado, R. *Language testing*. London: Longman, 1961.

McLeod, J. *Comparative assessment of reading comprehension: A five country study*. Saskatoon, Canada: Institute of Child Guidance and Development, in press.

McLeod, J., and Anderson, J. Readability assessment and word redundancy of printed English. *Psychological Reports*, 1966, *18*, 35-38.

———. An approach to assessment of reading ability through information transmission. *Journal of Reading Behavior*, 1970, *2*, 116-43.

———. Development of a standardized reading test designed to discriminate effectively at the adolescent level. *Journal of Reading Behavior*, 1972.

Morton, F. R. The language lab as a teaching machine: Notes on the mechanization of language learning. Manuscript, University of Michigan, Ann Arbor, 1960.

Oller, J. *El espanol por el mundo*. Chicago: Encyclopaedia Britannica Films, 1963-65, 4 vols.

Oller, J., Jr. Scoring methods and difficulty levels for cloze tests of ESL proficiency. *Modern Language Journal*, 1972, *56*, 151-58.

———. Cloze tests of second language proficiency and what they measure. *Language Learning*, 1973, *23*, 105-18.

Oller, J., Jr., Bowen, J. D., Dien, T. T., and Mason, V. Cloze tests in English, Thai, and Vietnamese: Native and nonnative performance. *Language Learning*, 1972, *22*, 1-15.

Oller, J., Jr., and Spolsky, B. The test of English as a foreign language. In B. Spolsky, ed., *Current trends in language testing*, in press.

Peterson, C., and Cartier, F. Research in language testing at DLI-SDA. Paper presented at the Language Testing Symposium, Washington, D.C., 1974.

Pike, L. W. An evaluation of present and alternative item formats for use in the Test of English as a Foreign Language. Manuscript, Educational Testing Service, Princeton, N. J., 1973.

Rand, E. Integrative and discrete point tests at UCLA. *Workpapers in TESL (UCLA)*, 1972, *6*, 87-92.

———. Comments on a reply. *Workpapers in TESL (UCLA)*, 1973, *7*, 95-100.

———. Some evidence for the predictive validity for the *ESLPE*. *Workpapers in TESL (UCLA)*, 1974, *8*, 51-62.

Reichling, A. Principles and methods of syntax: Cryptanalytical formalism. *Lingua*, 1961, *10*, 1-17.

Richards, J. C. A noncontrastive approach to error analysis. Paper presented at the TESOL Convention, San Francisco, 1970. *English Language Teaching*, 1971, *25*, 204-19.

———. Error analysis and second language strategies. *Language Sciences*, 1971, *17*, 12-22.

Rivers, W. Listening comprehension. In M. R. Donoghue, ed., *Foreign languages and the schools: A book of readings*. Dubuque, Iowa: Wm. C. Brown, 1967.

———. *Teaching foreign language skills*. Chicago: University of Chicago Press, 1968.

Slocum, J. B. *TOEFL* in 1969—an appraisal. *NAFSA Newsletter*, 1969, *22*, 6-7.

Spolsky, B. Linguists and language testers. *Current trends in language testing*, in press.

Spolsky, B., Sigurd, B., Sato, M., Walker, E., and Arterburn, C. Preliminary studies in the development of techniques for testing overall second language proficiency. In J. A. Upshur and J. Fata, eds., *Problems in foreign language testing. Language Learning*, 1968, special issue no. 3, 79-101.

Stevenson, D. K. Construct validity and the Test of English as a Foreign Language. Ph.D. dissertation, University of New Mexico, 1974.

Stockwell, R., Bowen, J. D., and Martin, J. *The grammatical structures of English and Spanish*. New York: McGraw Hill, 1965.

Stubbs, J. B., and Tucker, G. R. The cloze test as a measure of ESL proficiency for Arab students. *Modern Language Journal*, 1974, *58*, 239-42.

Swain, M., and Dumas, G. Translation as an elicitation device. Paper presented at the Research Seminar at the TESOL Convention, Denver, Colorado, 1974.

Tucker, G. R., and Scott, J. A. Error analysis and English language strategies of Arab students. Manuscript, American University, Beirut, Lebanon, 1974.

Upshur, J. A. Language proficiency testing and the contrastive analysis dilemma. *Language Learning*, 1962, *12*, 123-27.

———. Productive communication testing: Progress report. Paper read at the Second International Congress of Applied Linguistics, Cambridge, England, 1969. Reprinted in G. E. Perren and J. L. M. Trim, eds., *Applications of Linguistics*. London: Cambridge University Press, 1971.

Upshur, J. A., and Palmer, A. Measures of accuracy, communicativity and social judgments for two classes of foreign language speakers. Paper presented at the Third International Congress of Applied Linguistics, Copenhagen, Denmark, 1972.

Valette, R. The use of the dictée in the French language classroom. *Modern Language Journal*, 1964, *48*, 431-34.

————. *Modern language testing: A handbook.* New York: Harcourt, 1967.

Watzlawick, P., Beavin, J., and Jackson, K. *Pragmatics of human communication.* New York: Norton, 1967.

Wijnstra, J. M., and van Wageningen, N. The cloze procedure as a measure of first and second language proficiency. *Dutch Journal of Psychology,* in press.

Woods, W. A. Transition network grammars for natural language analysis. *Communications of the ACM,* 1970, *13,* 591-602.

Woods, W. A., and Makhoul, J. *Mechanical inference problems in continuous speech understanding.* BBN report no. 2565, 1973.

Contributors

Lois Bloom (Ph.D., Columbia University, 1968) is associate professor of psychology and speech pathology at the Teachers College, Columbia University. Formerly she was assistant chief of the Department of Speech and Hearing at New York University Institute of Rehabilitation Medicine. Dr. Bloom is on the editorial boards of *Child Development, Society for Research in Child Development Monographs*, and the *Journal of Speech and Hearing Research*. In addition, she is a consulting editor for the *Journal of Experimental Child Psychology, International Journal of Cognition, Psychological Bulletin, Psychological Review, Cognitive Psychology*, and *Developmental Psychology*. Among her many publications are *Language Development: Form and Function in Emerging Grammars, One Word at a Time: The Use of Single-Word Utterances before Syntax*, and *Language Development and Language Disorders* (with M. Lahey).

H. Douglas Brown (Ph.D., University of California at Los Angeles, 1970) is associate professor of linguistics and education. He was acting director of the English Language Institute at the University of Michigan from 1974 to 1976, and chairman of the Psycholinguistics Program in 1975-76. Dr. Brown is the editor of *Language Learning*, and serves on the executive committee of the Teachers of English to Speakers of Other Languages. He was the recipient of the University of Michigan Distinguished Service Award in 1973. His publications include "Children's Comprehension of Relativized English Sentences," "Cognitive Pruning and Second Language Acquisition," "The Psychological Reality of 'Grammar' in the ESL Classroom," and "Affective Factors in Second Language Acquisition."

Donald C. Freeman (Ph.D., University of Connecticut, 1965) is professor of linguistics and English at the University of Massachusetts, Amherst. Previously he was director of the Department of Linguistics and associate dean of the faculty of humanities and fine arts. He has served on the faculties of the University of California at Santa Barbara, McGill University, and the University of Lancaster in England. In 1974 he was codirector of the Golden Anniversary Linguistic Institute of the Linguistic Society of America, held at the University of Massachusetts, Amherst. His major publications include *Linguistics and Literary Style* (editor), "On the Primes of Metrical Style," "Current Trends in Metrics," and "The Strategy of Fusion: Dylan Thomas's Syntax."

301

ROBIN T. LAKOFF (Ph.D., Harvard University, 1967) is associate professor of linguistics at the University of California at Berkeley. Previously she was assistant professor of linguistics at the University of Michigan. Dr. Lakoff was chairman of the *Language* Review Committee for 1972-73 and currently serves on the executive and publications committees of the Linguistic Society of America. Some of her publications are "Transformational Grammar and Language Teaching," "Language in Context," "Pluralism in Linguistics," and *Language and Woman's Place*.

JEAN MALMSTROM (Ph.D., University of Minnesota, Minneapolis, 1958) is professor of English at Western Michigan University. Dr. Malmstrom is a recipient of the Western Michigan University Alumni Award for Teaching Excellence and the Michigan Council of Teachers of English Charles Carpenter Fries Award. She is active in the National Council of Teachers of English, and is a past president of the Michigan Council of Teachers of English. She has published the following books: *Dialects - U.S.A.*, *Language in Society*, *An Introduction to Modern English Grammar*, *Teaching English Linguistically: Principles and Practices for High School* (with Janice Lee), *Transgrammar: English Structure, Style, and Dialects* (with Constance Weaver), and *Language Alive: Linear A* and *Linear B* (with Barbara Bondar).

JOHN W. OLLER, JR. (Ph.D., University of Rochester, 1969) is chairman of the Department of Linguistics and associate professor of linguistics and educational foundations at the University of New Mexico. Previously he was associate professor of psycholinguistics at the University of California at Los Angeles. Dr. Oller served on the Examiners Committee for the Test of English as a Foreign Language produced by Educational Testing Service from 1971 to 1974, and is a member of the executive and research committees for the Teachers of English to Speakers of Other Languages. His major publications include *Coding Information in Natural Languages*, *Focus on the Learner: Pragmatic Perspectives for the Language Teacher* (edited with Jack Richards), "On the Relation Between Syntax, Semantics, and Pragmatics," "Discrete Point Tests and Tests of Integrative Skills," "Pragmatic Language Testing," and "Cloze Tests of Second Language Proficiency and What They Measure."

JACK C. RICHARDS (Ph.D., Laval University, 1972) is currently a consultant to Oxford University Press, South East Asian Branch, and editor of the *RELC Journal*. Previously he was a specialist in the psychology of second language learning at the Regional English Language Centre, Singapore. He has served on the faculties of Satja Wacana University, Sir George Williams University and Laval University. He has participated on several language research projects in Quebec, Ottawa, and Kuala Lumpur. Dr. Richards has distinguished himself as a scholar in second language acquisition with the following selected publications: *Focus on the Learner: Pragmatic Perspectives for the Language Teacher* (edited with John Oller, Jr.) and *Error Analysis: Perspec-*

tives on Second Language Acquisition (editor), "A Non-Contrastive Approach to Error Analysis," and "Error Analysis and Second Language Strategies."

WILLIAM E. RUTHERFORD (Ph.D., University of California at Los Angeles, 1973) is assistant professor at the American Language Institute, University of Southern California. Formerly he was assistant professor of English communications at that university. Since 1973, Dr. Rutherford has been the Regional College and University chairperson of the California Teachers of English to Speakers of Other Languages. He is the author of *Modern English: A Textbook for Foreign Students, Sentence Sense*, "Deep and Surface Structure and the Language Drill," and other articles in the *TESOL Quarterly* and *Language*. He is currently developing *The Rutherford English Series*.

ROGER W. SHUY (Ph.D., Western Reserve University, 1962) is professor of linguistics and director of the Sociolinguistics Program at Georgetown University. He is also associate director of the Center for Applied Linguistics. Dr. Shuy has served on the faculties of Michigan State University and Wheaton College. He is on editorial boards for *American Speech, Language in Society*, and *International Journal of the Sociology of Language* and he is a general editor for Newbury House Publishers. Dr. Shuy has chaired committees in the International Reading Association and the Linguistic Society of America. Outstanding in a long list of publications are *Linguistic Correlates of Social Stratification in Detroit Speech, Teaching Black Children to Read* (coeditor), "Teacher Training and Urban Language Problems," "The Sociolinguists and Urban Language Problems," "Speech Differences and Teaching Strategies: How Different is Enough?" and "Language Problems of Disadvantaged Children: A Sociolinguistic Perspective."

BERNARD SPOLSKY (Ph.D., Université de Montréal, 1966) is dean of the graduate school, professor of linguistics, elementary education, and anthropology and director of the Navajo Reading Study at the University of New Mexico. Previously he was chairman of the Program in Linguistics and Language Pedagogy and director of the English as a Foreign Language Program at Indiana University. He has also served on the faculties of McGill University and the Université de Montréal. He has served on the editorial boards of the *TESOL Quarterly, American Anthropologist, Linguistic Reporter*, and *International Journal for the Sociology of Language*, and chaired the committee of examiners for the Test of English as a Foreign Language from 1967 to 1970. Among a multitude of publications are *The Language Education of Minority Children: Selected Readings* (editor), "Attitudinal Aspects of Second Language Learning," and "Linguistics and Language Pedagogy—Applications or Implications?"

RICHARD L. VENEZKY (Ph.D., Stanford University, 1965) is professor of computer sciences and chairman of the Department of Computer Sciences at the

University of Wisconsin at Madison. He has served as a research fellow at Tel Aviv University and was a consultant on reading and spelling for Science Research Associates from 1966 to 1973. Dr. Venezky is a consultant on computing terminology for the *Oxford English Dictionary Supplement* and is an advisor for data processing for the *Dictionary of Old English* (University of Toronto and Lincoln College, Oxford). He is chairman of the subcommittee on computing for the Modern Language Association Old English Group and a panel member for the National Endowment for the Humanities. He also serves on the editorial boards of *Computers and the Humanities* and *Visible Language*. In addition to many articles, Dr. Venezky has published two books, *The Structure of English Orthography* and *Testing in Reading*.

ROSE-MARIE WEBER (Ph.D., Cornell University, 1965) is presently a visiting fellow at the Department of Modern Languages and Linguistics, Cornell University. She has held the posts of assistant and associate professor of linguistics at McGill University from 1968 to 1975 and previous to that has served as a research associate at the Center for Applied Linguistics and assistant professor of linguistics at Cornell University. Dr. Weber chairs the Linguistics and Reading Committee of the International Reading Association and serves on the education committee of the Interamerican Program on Linguistics and Language Teaching. Among her publications are "A Linguistic Analysis of First-Grade Reading Errors," "The Study of Oral Reading Errors: A Survey of the Literature," "Learning to Read: The Linguistic Dimension for Adults," "Adult Illiteracy in the United States," "Dialect Differences in Oral Reading: An Analysis of Errors," "First Graders' Use of Grammatical Context in Reading," and "Some Reservations on the Significance of Dialect in the Acquisition of Reading."

HAIGANOOSH WHITAKER (Ph.D., University of Rochester, 1971) is assistant professor of psychology and instructor in neurology at the University of Rochester. She is an elected member of the Academy of Aphasia. Dr. Whitaker is assistant editor for *Brain and Language* and is editor of the three volume set, *Studies in Neurolinguistics* (in press). Other publications include "Linguistic Theory and Speech Pathology" (with H. A. Whitaker), "An Introductory Glossary for Speech Pathologists" (with H. A. Whitaker), "The Spelling Errors of Children with Communicative Disorders" (with H. A. Whitaker), "Linguistic Structures in Stereotyped Aphasic Speech" (with H. W. Buckingham and H. A. Whitaker), and "Alliteration and Assonance in Neologistic Jargon Aphasia" (with H. W. Buckingham and H. A. Whitaker).

HARRY A. WHITAKER (Ph.D., University of California at Los Angeles, 1969) is associate professor of psychology and assistant professor of neurology at the University of Rochester. He served as a postdoctoral fellow at the Mayo Clinic in 1971 and 1972. Dr. Whitaker is editor of *Brain and Language* and *Perspectives in Neurolinguistics and Psycholinguists* (series). He is an elected member of the Academy of Aphasia, Society for Neuroscience, Psychonomic Society, and New York Academy of Sciences. He is currently on the program committee for the Linguistic Society of America. His publications include *A Model for Neurolinguistics, On the Representation of Language in the Human Brain, Studies in Neurolinguistics* (edited with H. Avakian-Whitaker), "Linguistic Competence: Evidence from Aphasia," "Unsolicited Nominalizations by Aphasics: The Plausibility of the Lexicalist Hypothesis," "Lexical Structure Disruption in Aphasia: A Case Study" (with W. J. Kehoe), and "Broca's Area: A Problem in Language-Brain Relationships" (with O. A. Selnes).

Index